NEURAL THEORIES OF MIND

Why the Mind–Brain Problem
May Never Be Solved

Books by William R. Uttal

Real Time Computers: Techniques and Applications in the Psychological Sciences

Generative Computer Assisted Instruction (with Miriam Rogers, Ramelle Hieronymus, and Timothy Pasich)

Sensory Coding: Selected Readings (Editor)

The Psychobiology of Sensory Coding

Cellular Neurophysiology and Integration: An Interpretive Introduction

An Autocorrelation Theory of Form Detection

The Psychobiology of Mind

A Taxonomy of Visual Processes

Visual Form Detection in 3-Dimensional Space

Foundations of Psychobiology (with Daniel N. Robinson)

The Detection of Nonplanar Surfaces in Visual Space

The Perception of Dotted Forms

On Seeing Forms

The Swimmer: An Integrated Computational Model of a Perceptual-Motor System (with Gary Bradshaw, Sriram Dayanand, Robb Lovell, Thomas Shepherd, Ramakrishna Kakarala, Kurt Skifsted, and Greg Tupper)

Toward a New Behaviorism: The Case Against Perceptual Reductionism

Computational Modeling of Vision: The Role of Combination (with Ramakrishna Kakarala, Sriram Dayanand, Thomas Shepherd, Jaggi Nalki, Charles Lunskis Jr., and Ning Liu)

The War Between Mentalism and Behaviorism: On the Assessibility of Mental Processes

The New Phrenology: On the Localization of Cognitive Processes in the Brain

A Behaviorist Looks at Form Recognition

Psychomythics: Sources of Artifacts and Misrepresentations in Scientific Psychology

Dualism: The Original Sin of Cognitivism

Neural Theories of Mind: Why the Mind–Brain Problem May Never Be Solved

NEURAL THEORIES OF MIND

Why the Mind–Brain Problem May Never Be Solved

William R. Uttal
Arizona State University

LEA
2005
LAWRENCE ERLBAUM ASSOCIATES, PUBLISHERS
Mahwah, New Jersey
London

Lawrence Erlbaum Associates, Inc., Publishers
10 Industrial Avenue
Mahwah, New Jersey 07430

Cover design by Kathryn Houghtaling Lacey

Library of Congress Cataloging-in-Publication Data

Uttal, William R.
Neural theories of mind : why the mind–brain problem may never be solved / William R. Uttal.
p. cm.
Includes bibliographical references and indexes.
ISBN 0-8058-5484-3 (cloth : alk. paper)
1. Cognitive neuroscience. 2. Mind–brain identity theory. 3. Dualism. I. Title.
QP360.5.U87 2005
153–dc22 2004061915
CIP

Books published by Lawrence Erlbaum Associates are printed on acid-free paper, and their bindings are chosen for strength and durability.

Printed in the United States of America
10 9 8 7 6 5 4 3 2 1

For Mit-chan

Contents

Preface

Theory! There is perhaps no more overused and misused word in all of cognitive neuroscience than this. Psychological and neurophysiological "theories" of all kinds abound from the far extremes of humanistic self-help, psychotherapy, and personal philosophy to the most hardnosed versions emerging from psychophysical and neuroscientific laboratories. Despite the popularity of some of the parascientific endeavors, it is only to the latter topics to which this book is addressed.

Modern cognitive neuroscience is primarily an empirical effort. Theories emerge, but, in general, those that do are microtheories seriously limited in their range and domain. Underneath the theories, however, there exist a foundation of axioms, assumptions, and hypotheses that guide and direct the experimental protocols. These more fundamental elements in neuroscientific thinking are, from one point of view, proto-theories; from another, they are just initial hypotheses or concluding statements. To understand the difference, it is necessary to develop a clear statement of what it is that is meant by the word *theory*.

Later in this book, I discuss the enormous range of ideas, concepts, and models that have been identified as cognitive neuroscientific theories. At the outset of this work, however, it is most important to appreciate that the word *theory* encompasses such an enormous variety of ideas that it may have lost much of its meaning for serious scientific purposes.

One purpose of this book is to bring some order back to the use of the word *theory* so that it can rise above the trivialities to which it is all-too-often attached by current researchers. To do so, it is necessary to consider the history of the idea of theory, to examine how it is has been and is being used in cognitive neuroscientific circles these days, and to suggest a consistent framework for its future use.

The main goal of this book, however, is to assert that, however large the multitude of biology-based theories of mind, none has succeeded. There has been a failure of substantial magnitude in all efforts to answer the question—How does the brain make mind? This continuing failure has not inhibited scholars and scientists from confidently, perhaps even dogmatically, expressing their views. Enormous amounts of energy and resources have been directed at generating a variety of explanations of the means by which brain substance gives rise to mental processes. The hope has been that with the rapidly accumulating knowledge about other aspects of the brain, we may be approaching some understanding. However, there is another possibility—that the failure so far is based on deep reasons, both principled and practical, that may make the problem intractable into the distant future and perhaps forever. In other words, it may be that the problem is inherently impossible to solve and no convergence on a final and complete explanation is possible.

To understand this profound difficulty, we must tread several different paths. It is important that we understand what is meant by a theory in general and a neuroscientific theory in particular. Even more important, however, this book presents a minitaxonomy of neuroreductive theories of the mind so we can understand what theories have been proposed and what are the difficulties and challenges that make the task of each so unlikely to be fulfilled.

There is no better place to start this discussion than to note that the pejorative use to which "theory" is all-too-often put (i.e., an ill-supported interpretation or extrapolation from the available data) is a feeble misuse of the term. The suggestion that a theory is just an unproven statement temporarily standing in for true knowledge yet to be substantiated by solid empirical facts reflects a widespread misunderstanding. As we see, this trivialization of the word expresses a profound ignorance of the fact that a *theory* is not just a preliminary explanation in waiting, but rather is the ultimate goal of all science. Data, facts, findings, and obtained experimental results of all kinds are useless until they are encompassed within a broad integrative framework. A theory is what gives meaning to measurements, just as measurements give substance to nature. In other words, a theory is not just something one expresses prior to adequate observation, but rather is the ultimate motivation and final culmination of the scientific enterprise. Theories are integrations of as much relevant data as can be made available and represent the maximum level of understanding to which a science can aspire at any point in time.

This idealization of a theory, of course, means that most so-called theories will, of necessity, be incomplete, premature, or, at worst, patently erroneous. Indeed, the purpose of this book is to show that the three[1] main types of brain–mind theory proposed so far are, at best, preliminary speculations and, at worst, misleading failures. They may represent interesting metaphors and provide useful heuristic extrapolations; nevertheless, the universally disappointing fact is that none has led to even a glimmering of how we might solve the great mind–brain conundrum. There is a surprising amount of agreement on this contentious assertion.

On the other hand, there are integrative theories in other fields of science that are supported by so much convincing evidence that they must be considered the best explanations of the past, by far the best unifying statement of our current condition, and by far the most likely predictors of things to come. It is not inappropriate to mention the two great theories that guide modern biology (including all aspects of psychology)—evolution and genetic coding. Despite some counterarguments based on nonscientific arguments, evolution—the explanation of the emergence of diverse species—and the macromolecular theory of the genetic code—the explanation of the transmission of organic traits and characteristics from generation to generation—dominate scientific thinking in our times. These two great unifying ideas have provided the framework for our understanding of biology. Neither can be considered to be an ill-supported extrapolation from inadequate data, instead, each is a unifying statement that incorporates ideas from many different fields. Although there may be future changes in the details of each of these two theories, each must be considered to be accurate in its broad theme. There is no acceptable contrary evidence that would support any alternative to either theory. In a certain sense, both of these ideas instantiate the ideal of what a theory is meant to be.

This does not mean that everything is understood or likely to be understood as a theory develops. Rather, a fertile theory is only a stepping-stone to the next fuller and more complete one. The best theories provide a framework for the accretion of new ideas. Furthermore, not all theories are of the same nature. Some theories peer into lower levels of analysis in an effort to "explain" how a particular underlying structure can give rise to an observable event. Others are prevented by epistemological barriers of one kind or another from such "reductionism" and must retreat to a descriptive role. Indeed, there is no a priori need for a theory to be reductionist. A highly satisfactory theory may only be capable of a precise description of what happened in the past history of some domain and prediction of what is likely to happen in the futures. Such a theory may quite plausibly remain neutral with regard to what mechanisms lay beneath the observational sur-

[1]In another work (Uttal, 2001) I dealt mainly with the problem of localization. It is possible to consider this as a fourth class of psychobiological theory of mind. I do so by linking this theoretical orientation with the other three in the summary chapter of this present book.

face. Mind–brain theories are not of this class, however, the ones discussed in this book are patently reductionist. They are not intended to be simply descriptive, but to bridge the anatomical and physiological domains to the psychological one. They also differ in other ways from more satisfying kinds of theory: They are much more complicated than the genetic and evolutionary ones. Obviously, the more complex the systems under study, the more difficult it may be to either reductively explain (because of multiple possible underlying mechanisms) or operationally describe its behavior (because of nonlinear complexity).

The point of this brief introductory comment is that we make facile, glib, and uncritical use of a word—theory—that is conceptually far more complicated than it may at first seem. I argue here that progress in science is dependent as much on a thorough understanding of capabilities and limits of the grand tool of theory and its underlying assumptions as it is on the findings of our laboratories. Nowhere in science is this need for understanding the logic of theory building greater than in the context of the mind–brain problem. Nowhere is the history of mistaken theories longer than in this context. Yet, many cognitive neuroscientists seem unwilling to look up from their laboratory benches to consider the issues raised in this book.

The expository effort to consider cognitive neuroscience *theory* at its most fundamental conceptual roots carried out in this book is in line with the rest of my work in the last few years. My goal has been to examine the foundation assumptions of a number of key topics in psychology and cognitive neuroscience. These issues (and the books in which I have developed my ideas) include:

- Reductionism—*Toward a New Behaviorism: The Case Against Perceptual Reductionism* (1998)
- Accessibility—*The War Between Mentalism and Behaviorism: On the Accessibility of Mental Processes* (2000)
- Localization—*The New Phrenology: The Limits of Localizing Cognitive Processes in the Brain* (2001)
- Perception—*A Behaviorist Looks at Form Recognition* (2002)
- Sources of Erroneous Thinking—*Psychomythics* (2003)
- Residual influences of cognitivism—*Dualism—The Original Sin of Cognitivism* (2004)
- Theoretical Explanation—(The present book)

Although all of the earlier books dealt peripherally with the theories relevant to each individual topic, in this book, I zero in on the assumptions that guide efforts to develop a neuroreductive theory of the mind itself. I deal with the limits and powers of biologically reductive theories of mind. Most of all, I seek to sharpen our views of what may well be the multiple meanings of cognitive neuroscience *theory*.

To make this work more salient and specific, another goal of this book is to survey three of the main theories that have been offered as explanations of the relationship between mental and neural activity. By examining and classifying these proposed explanations of the mind–brain relation, I am convinced it will be possible to sharpen our understanding of what they mean, to determine how the idea of a theory is now used in this very important field of modern science, and to clarify the limitations of each approach.

One can easily sustain the argument that there is no more important science or difficult intellectual challenge than the mind–brain problem. Cosmology and basic particle physics, evolution and genetic coding, however important they may be, do not come close to the grand task of cognitive neuroscience—to understand (to the extent that it is possible) the nature of our minds and their origins in neural activity. Unfortunately, our current level of accomplishment, I argue here, does not balance the importance of the task.

This book's discussion leads us to a number of surprising and remote areas of science. If my reader's have a deeper understanding of the use and misuse of the word *theory* in the special field of cognitive neuroscience, when I am done, my goals in writing it will have been achieved.

In many ways this book is a sequel to my earlier work *The Psychobiology of Mind* (Uttal, 1978). In that book, I suggested that the psychobiology of mind (the mind–brain problem actually consisted of three issues. These were localization, representation, and learning. One of my earlier books expanded on the localization issue (Uttal, 2001). This present book deals mainly with the problem of representation. To reiterate, the issue is: How does neural activity represent or become mental activity? My thesis is that answering this question is an unobtainable goal because of deep-seated flaws in *all* of the different approaches to theorizing or "explaining" in cognitive neuroscience.

In this present work I tease out the conceptual and logical problems of the cognitive neuroscience effort to explain how the brain makes the mind and omit the much greater mass of technical material that I emphasized in the earlier book (Uttal, 1978). In a few cases, I have included a few updated passages to make this book self-contained. In each case the material has been updated and either expanded to meet the needs of this work or shortened to remove extraneous material. Specific mention is always noted where such insertions have been made. Nevertheless, this is a new book in which the content, implications, and conclusions drawn are well beyond the suggestions of any of my earlier books.

It is also important to point out that the mind–body problem has been an issue for centuries before cognitive neuroscience emerged. Theologians and philosophers have attempted in the past (and continue to do so in the present) to unravel this great issue without recourse to the substantial body of modern neuroscientific knowledge. I do not deal in detail with the long history of discussion in these companion fields. The reason for this exclusion is that I believe the mind–body or mind–brain problem is a scientific question and not one that philosophers on any side of their continuing debate can resolve.

Finally, I have to acknowledge that this is a very critical examination of current cognitive neuroscience theory. I am sure there will be substantial disagreement with my conclusion that all current efforts fail to solve the problem and that there is a high likelihood that none of them can. My view certainly will be considered "pessimistic." However, I believe it is "realistic" and based on a careful consideration of the scientific limitations and weaknesses of each theoretical approach. Of course, no one can predict the future and surprises almost certainly lie ahead. However, there is a substantial scientific foundation for the realism I offer here as discussed in the rest of this book.

—William R. Uttal

ACKNOWLEDGMENTS

Writing a book like this one is of necessity a solitary task. Nevertheless, it could not have been done with out the support of colleagues, friends, and family. I am deeply grateful to ASU's Department of Industrial Engineering led by Gary Hogg for the continued support of my work since my retirement in 1999. Summers in the last two years have been spent on visiting appointments at the Department of Psychology at the University of Hawaii. Karl Minke, ever the good host and chair of the department, demonstrated the meaning of "Aloha" during my stays there.

I was also pleased to interact with colleagues in Honolulu—in particular, Professor David Crowell and Professor Abe Arkoff—in a way that added greatly to my thoughts as several key chapters were written.

Sondra Guideman and her staff continue to provide amazingly competent services during the editing and production work on the manuscript.

Most of all, however, Mit-chan remains the foundation of my personal and professional life. What a great time we are having!

CHAPTER

1

An Introduction to the Concept of Theory

1.1 QUESTIONS PERTAINING TO COGNITIVE NEUROSCIENTIFIC THEORIES

This is a book about epistemology–the part of philosophy that is concerned more with what we *can* know than with what we *do* know. It is about epistemology as it is applied in a very important modern field of scientific endeavor–cognitive neuroscience–the field asking: How does the brain make the mind? In particular, it is concerned with the nature of the theories that have emerged, mainly in the last half-century or so. During this period, this field of science has matured far beyond the most imaginative expectations of its speculative antecedents.

The outline of this book is clear-cut. After reviewing the meaning of theory in general, I seek the intellectual roots of this science as it has developed over its history. It is there that the fundamental assumptions that govern modern cognitive neuroscience are to be found. I then review a sampling of the theories that have been offered in this modern and exciting field of science. Finally, some concluding and summarizing judgments and opinions are expressed concerning the direction that cognitive neuroscience should most profitably take in the future.

Such a project is quite timely now, not only because of the importance of the research program undertaken by workers currently active in the field, but also because cognitive neuroscience has subsumed much of classic scientific psychology within itself, in particular cognitive psychology. Unfortunately, because of the intrinsic complexity of the subject matter, cognitive theory has left a trail of uncertainty, contentious debate, and confusion behind it.

The epitome of this confusion and uncertainty is found in the plethora of theoretical ideas that populate this field. Cognitive neuroscience, dealing as it does with some of the most important issues of human existence, has not developed a consensus concerning the relation of the mind and the brain beyond the monistic ontology that the former is a function of the latter. Herein is the thesis of this book; no satisfactory solution to the mind–brain yet exists. The first corollary of this thesis is more speculative and contentious. This corollary argues that such an explanation may be beyond the powers of even a future science. This future intractability is not because of any deep-seated mystery; rather, it arises out of knowledge and proofs with which we are already familiar.

Unfortunately, many denizens of psychological and neurophysiological laboratories currently active around the world are often so driven by the demanding requirements of their empirical search for new discoveries that they do not often deal with the underlying assumptions, constraints, and conceptual limits of their work. Perhaps, because so many exciting results are waiting to be uncovered, there has been little perceived need for reflection and epistemological inquiry.

In a certain sense this belies the antiquity of the field. Humans from their origins have always sought to answer some of the grand questions that still motivate cognitive neuroscience. Whether framed in terms of the supernatural continuity of the spirit, the mind–body problem, or the relationship between cognition and the brain, it is likely that humans have always asked questions about their self-awareness and its relation to their physical being. The recent emphasis on empirical research may actually have the negative effect of preventing or delaying consideration of profound epistemological concerns.

There are substantial reasons that an increased interest in theory should begin to capture the attention of modern cognitive neuroscience. It was only recently that the idea of formal computer and mathematical models were anathema to most biologists. In the last few years, however, enormous changes have been occurring in the theoretical sophistication of cognitive neuroscientists. New equipment, broader interdisciplinary training, and the increasingly predictive impact of those formal models that have appeared have accelerated a reinvigorated theoretical approach to the resolution of the mind–brain problem. Clearly, this is a wonderful and timely opportunity to reconsider how theory can and should develop in this all-important field of science.

A major premise of this work is that the development of comprehensive theory is the raison d'être of science, in general, and should be of cognitive neuroscience, in particular. I argue here that all our laboratory skills, resources, and energies should be aimed at the ultimate goal of determining a comprehensive understanding of our world and ourselves. The simple accumulation of empirical or factual knowledge, although forming the basis of such a comprehensive understanding, is not the ultimate goal of science. Rather, science aspires (or should aspire) to the integration of that empirical knowledge into inclusive theoretical understanding. In the words of the distinguished philosopher of science Abraham Kaplan (1964):

> Whether or not theory formation is the most important and distinctive scientific activity, in one sense of the term "theory", this activity might well be regarded as the most important and distinctive for human beings. In this sense it stands for the symbolic dimension of experience, as opposed to the apprehension of brute fact. (p. 294)

It is the purpose of this book to look at the current status as well as the epistemological limits of cognitive neuroscience theory. To begin progress toward this goal, it is useful to tabulate some of the questions that are implicitly, if not explicitly, asked by cognitive neuroscientists as they make the transition from observation, on the one hand, to explanation or description, on the other. The following queries preview topics discussed in this book.

Some Questions About Cognitive Neuroscience Theory

1. What is a theory?
2. What is an acceptable theory in cognitive neuroscience?
3. Is a unified theory of mind–brain relationships possible? (Will it always be a system of microtheories?)
4. What are the conditions of necessity and sufficiency that make a theory or law acceptable?
5. Are the methods of a science evolved from the needs of physical sciences appropriate for the development of theories of cognitive neuroscientific processes?
6. Is there a psychological or physiological "uncertainty principle" (which says that we cannot examine mental or neural processes without altering them) that will obstruct theory development in this field of science?
7. Why is description not the same as explanation?
8. Does it matter to cognitive neuroscience which particular ontological approach—monism or dualism ("mindless materialism or baseless spiritualism")—underlies theory?
9. Is there some kind of a biophysical reality that is the ultimate target of our theories?

10. Can the controversy between identity theory and other monisms, on the one hand, and dualisms on the other, be resolved?

11. What is the relation between mathematics and computer models to the processes they describe?

12. How can analogies mislead us into assuming that some processes are homologous rather than coincidental? In other words, how can functional isomorphisms mislead us into assuming that some processes are identical with regard to their origins when, in fact, they are examples of convergent evolution?

13. Can a semantic engine be successfully simulated by a syntactic one?

14. What are the crucial differences among the various schools of cognitive neuroscience theory?

15. What kind of a balance should be established between achievable pragmatic concerns and what may be an unachievable biopsychological theory? Should such a balance be sought?

16. What kinds of theories are useful for cognitive neuroscience?

17. Which so-called "theories" are only superficial restatements of intuitions, experimental results, or anecdotal observations?

18. Finally, for cognitive neuroscience the big question is: Are the data of cognitive neuroscience sufficiently objective, simple, robust, and comprehensive so that the great question can be resolved? In other words, are there intractable barriers to developing reductive theories that bridge between mental and neurophysiological constructs? Alternatively, can we look forward to theories that are as well structured and axiomatic as are those found, for example, in physics?

To answer questions such as these for cognitive neuroscience in particular, we must first look abroad to see what has been said about theories in general. That is the purpose of the rest of this chapter.

1.2 TRADITIONAL DEFINITIONS OF THEORY

In this section, I seek a broadly acceptable definition of theory. In doing so, I must warn my readers that the definition at which I finally arrive may differ from that used by others. A consensus definition is not likely to be achieved; one only has to examine the abundant literature that seeks to answer the question—What is a theory?—to appreciate how diverse are the views that seemed at first to be a simple matter of lexicographic definition. However, by comparing a number of points of view, perhaps some convergence on a useful definition, if not a consensus, can be achieved.

Definitions come in many guises. Some are highly technical, some metaphorical, and some are strings of words that sometimes strain credulity and clarity. It is not always clear which are the most useful. Some intentionally fuzzy definitions are intended to help us to "feel" a meaning more than to delineate an exhaustive list of properties and characteristics. For example, note Popper's (1959) metaphorical, almost poetic, statement to sense the grandeur of the term:

> Theories are nets cast to catch what we call 'the world': to rationalize, to explain, and to master it. We endeavour to make the mesh ever finer and finer. (p. 59)

Hooker (1987) also proposed a metaphor—the pyramid—for theory, but one that moves slightly further from Popper's somewhat romantic expression toward a more precise idea of what is meant by the term. Indeed, it has embedded within it some connotations that help us make the next step toward a definition of theory.

> At the bottom of the deductive pyramid lie the so-called observation sentences—those sentences whose truth can be checked experimentally—whilst at the apex of the pyramid lay the most general theoretical principles of the scheme. Just exactly where the twin elements of theory and observation permeate this structure is a matter of contemporary controversy. . . . (p. 109)

The metaphor of the pyramid introduces some important initial ideas into our quest for a definition of theory. First, it emphasizes the idea that a mass of observational findings must provide the underlying foundation for what is a reduced number of theoretical terms. Theory without a sustaining foundation of empirical observations would be meaningless. The end product of such a nonempirical theory would inevitably invoke supernatural concepts that should have no place in science.

A second contribution of Hooker's pyramid metaphor is the idea that theories are inclusive of a large mass of data (i.e., they are intended to be universal synoptic statements of particular observations). Thus, theories may be thought of as intellectual generalizations that condense the information content of a science by expressing a huge mass of specific observations in a much smaller number of comprehensive terms and concepts.

Nevertheless, as scientists, we wish to be a little less metaphorical and a little more precise in arriving at a definition of a theory than have been Popper or Hooker. One of the best places to seek understanding about any word is to trace its use in the past. Clearly, a diluted and imprecise, but still useful, kind of insight can come from checking the dictionary. However unsatisfactory the various interpretations may be, they do provide a preliminary framework and reminder of what some of the issues are likely to be in considering the real meaning of the word theory. My on-line dictionary defines theory as follows:

1: the analysis of a set of facts in their relation to one another

2: abstract thought: SPECULATION

3: the general or abstract principles of a body of fact, a science, or an art <music theory>

4a: a belief, policy, or procedure proposed or followed as the basis of action <her method is based on the theory that all children want to learn> b: an ideal or hypothetical set of facts, principles, or circumstances—often used in the phrase in theory <in theory, we have always advocated freedom for all>

5: a plausible or scientifically acceptable general principle or body of principles offered to explain phenomena <wave theory of light>

6a: a hypothesis assumed for the sake of argument or investigation b: an unproved assumption: CONJECTURE c: a body of theorems presenting a concise systematic view of a subject <theory of equations>

Synonyms see HYPOTHESIS

(*Merriam-Webster's Collegiate Dictionary*, 2000)

Although this set of definitions begins to suggest a meaning (actually several different meanings) of the word theory, there is a softness and ambiguity to several of the alternative meanings expressed here that make them inadequate in our quest to understand the scientific use of the word. For example: 1: and 5: are too general and, therefore could hardly provide a guide to the serious scientist seeking a satisfactory definition; 2: confuses theory with any kind of organized (or, for that matter, disorganized) thought. Indeed, 2: is almost an antonym of theory, simply because it does not relate theory to some real-world database, a sine qua non of a true scientific theory. Furthermore, it substitutes reverie for logic and mixes up science with free-floating contemplation.

Conversely, definitions 3:, 4:, and 6c: confuse the concept of organized, integrative theory with the observational details or data set upon which the theory must be based. In doing so these subdefinitions promote the idea that a simple aggregation of facts or principles represents a theory. Finally, 6a: and 6b: instantiate the popular misuse of theory as an unproven conjecture or yet to be proven supposition. Unfortunately, none of these definitions exclude the simple restatement of an empirical observation as a theory.

The appended synonym for theory—hypothesis—is especially misleading. A hypothesis, as it is used (or should be used) by most scientists, is a much more narrowly defined concept connoting a suggestion or a preliminary possibility raised in a much more limited context, usually at the outset of a scientific inquiry. On the other hand, a theory, we are beginning to appreciate, connotes something much more general, an intellectual structure that emerges as the end product of a systematic exploration of a broad domain of inquiry rather than from a single experiment.

This confusion of a comprehensive cumulative theory with an initial hypothesis has led some scholars to suggest that all empirical research is guided by a priori theories. I believe this to be a simple semantic error. Theory, in this sense of the quoted dictionary definition (6a:) or the appended synonym, is totally inconsistent with the broader meaning beginning to emerge in this chapter's discussion.

Of course, this does not mean that a theory may not feed back to produce a specific hypothesis in the preliminary stages of an investigation. All but the most initial explorations are (or should be) guided by some stimulating idea and context. On the other hand, science also moves ahead by atheoretical or nonhypothetical explorations. Such questions as—What is over there? What would happen, if I did this or that? Would this independent variable have any effect on this dependent variable?—are also important. However useful they may be, such justifications for preliminary explorations are not (or should not) be considered to be theories or even hypotheses in the sense of the words to be presented shortly.[1]

An exception to this generality is that some experiments are designed to test specific theories. In this case, of course, the theory has already been constructed from a preexisting body of empirical evidence and the new experiment is intended to sharpen, extend, or test some particular aspect of it. The hypothesis, in such a case, is still quite restricted. Unfortunately, theories in cognitive neuroscience, in particular, seem to be extremely elastic. It is, therefore, unlikely that any comprehensive theory in this field of science will ever be rejected on the basis of a single test of a hypothesis.

The confusion illustrated in the erroneous theory–hypothesis "synonym" is based on the substantial difference in intended breadth between a hypothesis and a theory, respectively. An initial hypothesis is intended to be much narrower than a cumulative theory. It may adequately serve the purpose of guiding a particular experiment. However, hypotheses do not meet the criteria for comprehensiveness that I believe are essential for a satisfactory definition of theory. For example, I am sure that Darwin did not have even the slimmest insight into what was to become his monumental theory of evolution when he embarked on the *Beagle*. Rather, observations were made (i.e., specimens collected) that supported what is now acknowledged as the already existing hypotheses that species evolved from other

---

[1]It is not always appreciated just how atheoretical some well established sciences can be. For example, as Valenstein (1998) discussed, the way in which psychoactive drugs are used in today's mental health therapeutic situations is largely ad hoc and practiced with little solid theoretical foundation. Assuredly, a given potion may work to assuage human despair, but for reasons and explanations for which our modern science has little to offer.

earlier forms. It took years of study, reflection, and integration of his observations before he was able to synthesize the great theory of natural selection and the explosive new law of nature—the survival of the fittest—on which it was based. Only then could Darwin's perspective be indisputatively categorized as an integrative and comprehensive theory summarizing an enormous variety of biological observations. There are, as noted in the Preface, few alternatives to this magnificent theory and none that can withstand rigorous scientific evaluation.

Darwin's theory of evolution, especially combined with today's macromolecular genetic theory, ties together an immense amount of biological data into a coherent, overall, and unified explanation of biological phenomena. It is, in the truest meaning of the word, a scientific theory, certainly not an unproven, speculative hypothesis. The only reason for denying its scientific merit today is the same as those of the past—the hypothesis that there is a supernatural world dominating the natural one.[2]

An argument can be made that boundary between observation and theory may not be as sharp as I make it here. In my career, I have met a number of people who believed that the demonstration of some observational fact was as far as it was necessary for an experimental scientist to go. The data were allowed, even encouraged, to "speak for themselves" in a sparse and terse concluding statement at the end of an empirical journal article reporting the results of some new experiment. Synthesis with other data into a theoretical explanation was actually discouraged by some of the main psychological journals of the 1960s and 1970s. Such a barefoot empirical philosophy about scientific research seems to me to miss the whole point of science. The mission of science, as expressed by Kaplan (see p. 3) and many others, is not just to collect data, but, in a much grander sense to synthesize a broad view of the domain under study from those data.

Guthrie (1946) had earlier warned against this hyperempiricism when he wrote:

> A flood of new publications is not automatically a flood of new facts. In addition, it may include many facts that do not contribute materially to the science of psychology. Collections of facts are not science. They are the material out of which science can grow, but they are only the raw material of science, and sometimes they are not even that. (p. 3)

By his use of the word science, I believe that Guthrie was specifically referring to what today we would call integrative theory. His comment highlights

[2]Of course, there are technical debates and differences of opinion concerning how the evolutionary process is effected. Is it continuous and gradual or punctuated and sudden? Such internal disagreements in no way diminish the global impact and certain truth of the great Darwinian theory.

the fact that much empirical research is useless in achieving the theoretical goal of broad understanding. Indeed, it is possible to go even further and assert that there are rarely any critical or essential experiments in cognitive neuroscience; there is always an alternative way to duplicate the impact of any given result; no particular observation is either necessary to or sufficient for the construction of a comprehensive theory.

A similar distinction may be made between a law and a theory. A law is an observed relation between two variables that robustly holds under many conditions and circumstances. However, a law is also the result of a set of observations; it can be argued that it does not represent a true theory. Laws, from this point of view, do not incorporate any of the necessary features of a theory. This point is likely to be quite contentious.

A theory can be distinguished from a law that is based on the outcome of an experiment or set of experiments. A law is much less comprehensive, "merely" describing the repeatedly demonstrated relationship between two or more observed variables. A law, in the sense I use it here, does not integrate many different kinds of observations; rather it codifies or quantifies repeated measurements of a particular kind of relation. Newton's famous proposition—**F = ma**—describes a very specific relation between force, mass, and acceleration, but contrary to some views, by itself it is not a comprehensive theory, it is only a specialized expression of an observed relationship. Collections of such laws, statements, and, most important, comprehensive generalizations from specific laws to more universal and global concepts more closely approximate the proper use of the word theory.

There are other ways of distinguishing between a finding or observation of a lawful relation, on the one hand, and a theory, on the other. For example, the fundamental criterion of control of the independent variables that permeates our experimental enterprise requires that each experiment be designed to measure a very narrow domain of activity. Today, more often than not, the critical design features of a proposed experiment are (a) the precision of control of single independent variable and (b) the precision of measurement of what is also usually a single dependent variable. From this perspective, it seems increasingly clear that the most fundamental touchstones of experimental design, highly constrained precision, on the one hand, and broad and inclusive theoretical formulation, on the other, are, to a certain degree, antagonistic to each other.

None of this mitigates the fact that even general theories can, even must, produce specific hypotheses or predictions that can and eventually should be tested; empirical testability of its specific predictions being the sine qua non of comprehensive scientific theory building. Any criterion for the truth of a theory that does not entail some notion of empirical testability pushes us from the realm of the natural into the supernatural.

Other proposed definitions of theory help us to converge further on a consensual definition. Kaplan's (1964) improved definition, for example, moves us forward in the precision of the language from poetic metaphors offered earlier by both Popper and Kaplan himself. He asserted that:

> Theory [is] the device for interpreting, criticizing, and unifying established laws, modifying them to fit data unanticipated in their formulation, and guiding the enterprise of discovering new and more powerful generalizations. To engage in theorizing means not just to learn by experience, but also to take thought about what there is to be learned. (p. 295)

And:

> A theory is a symbolic construction. (p. 296)

And:

> Theory is thus contrasted with both practice and with fact. (p. 296)

Defining what the word theory means for students newly exposed to science has always been a difficult task. For example, Kerlinger (1986) in a widely used introductory text defined theory as follows:

> A theory is a set of interrelated constructs (concepts), definitions, and propositions that present a systematic view of phenomena by specifying relations among variables, with the purpose of explaining and predicting the phenomena. (p. 9)

This definition is close, not only in construction, but also in meaning to one proposed by Rudner (1966) in his text on the philosophy of social science:

> A theory is a systematically related set of statements, including some lawlike generalizations, that is empirically testable. (p. 10)

Although some of the words used in these definitions may require further analysis in their own right, both Kerlinger and Rudner highlight several key aspects of the meaning of the word theory.

First, a theory is more than an empirical law in that (optimally) it involves several different kinds of relationships (i.e., a "set of interrelated constructs" or "a systematically related set of statements"). This is clearly a step beyond the idea of a simple, unidimensional, empirical law emerging from a series of observations. Both Rudner and Kerlinger argue strongly that a theory should have broad implications beyond that of a single kind of experiment, observation, or even a repeatedly confirmed law. On the other hand a law is only a statement of a repeatedly authenticated relationship, whose enunciation adds little to the causes and forces driving those situations in which it was observed.

Second, Kerlinger proposes that theories should be explanatory and permit prediction. As we see later when we consider such terms as *description*, *explanation*, *control*, and *prediction*, these terms are also loaded with superfluous and ambiguous meaning and their connotations vary considerably from theoretician to theoretician. However, it is clear that one of the prime requirements of a theory is that it allows us to interpolate or extrapolate beyond the immediately available observational data. It is this ability to expand our knowledge past the existing corpus of empirical data that is also a critical attribute of a theory.

Finally, Rudner (1966) made an important comment that must be repeatedly reiterated in any discussion of the meaning of the word theory. That is, a theory must be "empirically testable." Any generalization that involves entities that are not open to public observation or that are beyond the realm of generally acceptable measurement methodologies can hardly be considered to be a scientific theory. The word theory is, in those cases, entirely inappropriate and other terms such as belief, conviction, speculation, and even supernatural become operational.

Some psychologists have defined theory purely in terms of the deductive power of the involved mathematics. To, them, a theory is characterized by the ability to logically describe, by a process of formal deduction, the relations between a number of stimuli and responses. For example, Hull (1943) said:

> As understood in the present work, a theory is a systematic deductive derivation of the secondary principles of observable phenomena from a relatively small number of primary principles or postulates. (p. 2)

Hull's emphasis on mathematical deduction, however, is complicated by the fact that in order to relate the inputs and outputs of the behaving system, he (and all other psychologists) have had to infer the properties of internal mechanisms that could account for the transition from the former to the latter. In his mathematical system, these internal mechanisms became "intervening variables" (see MacCorquodale & Meehl, 1948, for an important distinction between intervening variables and hypothetical constructs). There is still, after more than a half century since his publications, considerable dispute whether Hull's interpretation of these intervening variables was that they were real physiological entities or just formal descriptions of the transformations implied by the fact that stimuli and responses were not always directly related.

This is an essential point concerned as it is with the accessibility of cognitive processes to an outside observer. It has always been obvious to any psychologist that there are some active processes at work between stimuli and responses that determines what we do. Whatever these processes were, their nature and effect had to be inferred from the relationships between the observed behavior and the input stimuli. According to Hull, these intervening variables then became "primary principles or postulates" that could be used as the fundamental axioms of other theorems to "explain" other kinds of behavior. His description of what they did, however, was not tantamount to defining what they were.

In the present context, however, the important issue is that Hull suggested a theory had to be expressed as a formal mathematical-deductive system. However, new problems arise. I have previously discussed (Uttal, 1998) the role of mathematics in theory building and noted that even this ubiquitous and powerful approach to science is clouded with debates and varying interpretations. To briefly repeat that argument, mathematics is a powerful means of describing systems of virtually any kind. However, mathematics itself is essentially neutral with regard to specific internal mechanisms and, at best, is able only to describe the behavior of a system. When additional assumptions (e.g., assertions concerning the neurophysiological instantiations of the mathematical components) are added to a mathematical model, it may take on the attributes of a reductive model. Nevertheless, it is not widely appreciated in cognitive neuroscience that these neurophysiological assumptions are distinct and separate from the mathematical ones with which they are represented. The mathematics of a theory may continue to work perfectly (i.e., describe and predict) even though the neurophysiological assumptions of the theory may be shown to be totally incorrect. An additional problem with a mathematical model is that it can sometimes impose its own properties (e.g., unrealistic or superfluous solutions) on the system being tested.

Now let's continue with our search for an adequate definition of the meaning of the word theory. A highly satisfactory and increasingly precise definition of theory has been attributed to Donald Darnell of the University of Colorado by his student John A. Cagle. I find it particularly insightful when Darnell says:

> A theory is a set of statements, including some lawlike (*sic*) generalizations, systematically and logically related such that the set implies something about reality. It is an argument that purports to provide a necessary and sufficient explanation for a range of phenomena. . . . At a minimum it is a strategy for handling data in research, [and] providing a conceptual system for describing and explaining. It must be capable of corrigibility—that is, it must be possible to disconfirm or jeopardize it by making observations. A theory is valuable to

> the extent that it reduces the uncertainty about the outcome of a specific set of conditions. (Attributed to Donald Darnell)[3]

Rose (1954) gets even more specific:

> A theory may be defined as an integrated body of definitions, assumptions, and general propositions covering a given subject matter from which a comprehensive and consistent set of specific and testable hypotheses can be deduced logically. The hypotheses must take the form "If a, then b, holding constant c, d, e . . ." or some equivalent of this form, and thus permit causal explanation and prediction. (p. 3)

Kuhn (1977) also helped us move toward a more complete definition of theory by tabulating the properties of a "good scientific theory." His five characteristics include:

1. Accuracy: A theory's predictions should agree with empirical observations.
2. Consistent: A theory should be both internally and externally consistent. That is, it should not contravene other well-established theories as well as not having any logical or substantive contradictions within its own structure.[4]
3. Broad in scope: A theory must have something to say about a domain of sufficient breadth and thus extend beyond particulars to generalizations.
4. Simple: A theory should bring order to a domain of interest by explaining many observations with the fewest possible statements.
5. Fruitful: A theory must help us to predict and understand other observations and extend the limits of our knowledge. (Abstracted and paraphrased from Kuhn, 1977, pp. 321–322)

Others (e.g., Popper, 1959, and Rose, 1954) have added supplementary criteria over the years, including:

6. Testable: A theory must be amenable to empirical examination. A corollary of "testable" proposed by Popper (1959) is that it must not only be testable, but refutable. (Here again, the link between empirical observability and

---

[3]Although I have encountered this quote by Darnell several times in different places, I have been unable to find the original source of this statement. Cagle (2003) quotes it in at least two Web sites. Indeed, Professor Darnell himself was not able to locate the source when I personally contacted him. Nevertheless, whenever he made this statement, it is especially perceptive and I use it here with his permission and approval.

[4]The property of internal consistency, of course, falls victim to the Gödel theorem, which denies the possibility of internal consistency for any theory. See page 112.

theory is reiterated.) It can be argued that testability is synonymous with accuracy (see 1. above).

7. Scientific: A theory must also be constructed in the language and methodology of a natural science. Any belief system that is not open to objective and repeatable scientific methods is not a theory in the context of the present discussion. Only natural terms are acceptable; supernatural, nonempirical, unobservable, theological entities can play no role in a truly scientific theory.[5]

8. Cumulative: A theory must be open-ended in the sense that new data must fit within its domain. Should it not be able to incorporate new knowledge, it would better be classified as an ex-theory. However, the theory must be sufficiently constrained that it is not totally open-ended. Such a property would permit it to expand without limit in spite of newly available contravening observations.

Such a tabulation of the properties of a theory may be more useful than seeking something as concise as a dictionary type definition. All of these efforts, however, do lead us to a more complete conceptualization of what we mean by a theory, in general, and a cognitive neuroscientific theory, in particular.

Of course, it must also be understood that this lexicographic exercise is, at best, an idealization of the characteristics of a scientific theory. In reality, theory building develops in a much more informal manner with ideas sometimes driven by metaphor and intuition as well as by purely empirical results. Similarly, as suggested earlier, the process is circular—theories beget specific experimental designs as well as the converse. Nevertheless, the ideal of a theory as a comprehensive statement of the overall meaning of a body of evidence has a powerful influence on scientific research. If nothing else these attributes of theory help us to distinguish between scientific theories and pseudotheories.

Given that theory development is held in such high esteem by the scientific community, it is also necessary to point out that theory can have a negative effect on research activities. Rose (1954), for example, suggested, "There are certain dangers in the use of theory in science" and then offered the following caveats concerning those dangers:

1. Theory channelizes research along certain lines.

---

[5]The biologist George Gaylord Simpson (1944) has been quoted as saying:

> The progress of knowledge rigidly requires that no nonphysical postulate ever be admitted in connection with the study of physical phenomena. We do not know what is and what is not explicable in physical terms, and the researcher who is seeking explanations must seek physical explanations only. (p. 76)

2. Theory tends to bias observations.
3. The concepts that are necessary in theory tend to get reified.
4. . . . [since] replications of a study seldom reach an identical conclusion . . . are we justified in formulating elaborate theories which assume consistency in findings?
5. Until a theory can be completely verified, which is practically never, it tends to lead to overgeneralization of its specific conclusions to areas of behavior outside their scope.
6. . . . rival theories of human behavior . . . seem[s] to encourage distortion of simple facts. (pp. 4–5)

These comments by Rose are extremely important, not so much in defining the nature of theories, but in reminding us of the powerful impact that a point of view, perspective, or theory may have on our choice of which experiments to carry out as well as on our interpretations of the resulting observations. It is extremely difficult to shake off the constraints of one's pet theory; there is no question that such constraints do affect our interpretations as well as our experimental designs and thus the findings themselves.

To a certain degree, a good measure of theoretical conservatism is necessary to avoid wild fluctuations in the current zeitgeist in any field of science. Indeed, it can be extremely dangerous to a young scientist's career to step outside the standard theoretical stance of one's contemporary scientific zeitgeist. Publication gets more difficult and ridicule more common. Unfortunately, such penalties and such conservatism can also sometimes inhibit the natural development of new points of view as new data and new ideas emerge.

Regardless of these "dangers," theory still represents the pinnacle of scientific thinking. It is now our responsibility to see if we can distil from these various general comments, a more complete conceptualization of what is meant by theory.

1.3 SOME STEPS TOWARD A MORE COMPLETE CONCEPTUALIZATION OF THEORY

We can now begin to see the nature of the properties that define a satisfactory scientific theory. The foremost criterion is that a theory should be characterized by breadth. It is not a statement at the level of a single fact, experimental result, finding, observation, or even law. Rather, it is comprehensive; it is primarily characterized by its ability to integrate across a multitude of experiments and observations—the more the better. Any so-called theory limited to the results of a single experiment is a serious misuse of the term; far more appropriate for such a situation would be terms such as *relationships* or, when the relationship is robust enough, *law*. Furthermore, scientific theories must be ultimately testable, if not already tested. In short, theory strives to extract universals while relationships and laws derived from one or a few empirical studies strive to describe particular interactions and relations. The idea of a theoretical explanation based on the results of a single experiment, from this perspective, is an absurdity!

Theoretical breadth and comprehensiveness is a realistic goal, but completeness is not. Theories are always dependent on current knowledge that is never complete. Although theories can extrapolate and predict to a certain limited degree, they do so at the risk of running amok in the dangerous fog of unexpected discontinuities. Furthermore, it is particularly unlikely that any biopsychological theory can ever be complete, however vigorously it strives to be broad enough to permit generalizations to other contexts. The reason for this particular limit is discussed later in this chapter.

In this same context, it has to be accepted that theories are, by virtue of their dependence on empirical observations, intrinsically temporary; history has repeatedly shown that theories come and go as new ideas, paradigms, and observations, become available. Today's theory is only the current and, momentarily, best available integrative statement of a set of findings and relationships within a scientific domain. The future is always certain to see such a current description of a limited universe supplanted by a newer, more up-to-date, and, hopefully, more accurate statement of the nature of reality. Perhaps the most damaging tendency in any kind of science is to persevere in one's support for a theory that has seen its time. Fortunately, there is no theory in cognitive neuroscience that has enjoyed such perpetuity and it is not likely that one will emerge in the future.

The languages used by a theoretician can come from many different sources. Although Hull (1943) and many others have stressed the importance of mathematics, this is not a sine qua non of theory, especially in the field of cognitive neuroscience—computation and logic being among the possible alternative theoretical languages. When sufficiently precise measurements are possible and systems are sufficiently stable and regular, however, mathematics can make an almost unique contribution to the clarity and precision of expression of a theory. More than anything else, the rules of mathematics and programming languages keep us from wandering too far astray from logical order; these rules constrain our thinking in a way that purely verbal language cannot.

The essence of the point made here is that, although highly esteemed and powerful in many contexts, a formal logical-deductive system such as mathematics is not a requirement for theory construction. It is also important to appreciate that, despite all of its wonderful power, mathematics is not omnipotent. Chapter 6 makes it clear that combinatorial or computational complexity as well as simple numerousness can make many classes of problems intractable and can quickly swamp the most powerful conceivable computer or mathematical algorithm.

So far in this section I have presented an ideal expression of what a theory should look like. However, philosophers of science and mathematicians have joined forces in recent years to argue that this ideal does not, and cannot, exist. I hope it is not too redundant to repeat the caveat that, in the real world, specific hypotheses derived from comprehensive theories do guide our experiments just as experiments cumulatively determine our theories. In no way, however, does this negate the view that theories are best considered as ex post facto synoptic summaries and only secondarily as a priori hypotheses generators.

Another important point is that many of the most basic attributes of a theory mentioned earlier have become points of contentious debates. For example, the notion of testability or verifiability of a theory has been attacked on several grounds. Total verification is not possible, according to scholars such as Gödel (1931), because of the intrinsic "incompleteness" of theories. Others, such as Popper (1959), have equally vigorously argued that theories cannot be verified, only falsified, at best. I consider these limits on the utility of theories in more detail in chapter 3.

1.4 TYPES OF THEORIES

Despite these general comments about the nature of theories, the fact is that they come in a bewildering variety of sensical and nonsensical forms. The word theory is still used willy-nilly in an enormous number of contexts far removed from the scientific role I have spelled out here. It is the purpose of this section to develop a tentative taxonomy of the wildly diverse gamut of theory types. As we now see, the use of the word theory can vary from the most inconsequential to the most formal.

1.4.1 Nontheoretical Theories

It is appropriate to begin this discussion by pointing out there are many instances in which the word theory has been used that do not come close to the meaning toward which the discussion in the previous section is converging. Most egregiously, the word has all-too-often been applied to ideas and concepts that have no identifiable empirical foundation that would stand up to even the most superficial scientific scrutiny. Regardless of the views of the many proponents of such pseudosciences as those exemplified in Table 1.1, the research basis for the "theories" they propose is at best highly controversial and more likely nonexistent. A brief sampling of

TABLE 1.1
A Sampling of Pseudosciences

1. Mesmerism
2. Astrology
3. Creationism
4. Phrenology
5. Orgone Boxes
6. Somatotypes
7. Psychosurgery
8. Psychic Surgery
9. Self-Help Psychology
10. Parapsychology including Telekinesis; ESP; Telepathy; Precognition
11. Suppressed and False Memories
12. Eyewitness Testimony
13. Dream Analysis
14. Medical Fads including Chiropractic; Faith Healing; Unsubstantiated Cures
15. Food Supplements
16. UFOs; Alien Abductions
17. Lie Detectors–Polygraphs; Voice Stress Analysis; Brain Scans; Body Heat Distribution
18. Jury Consultants
19. Criminologists
20. Profilers
21. Psychics; Channeling; Prophecy
22. Acupuncture
23. Graphology
24. Palmistry
25. Numerology
26. Psychosomatics (Mind over matter)
27. Psychotherapy

nonscientific, unempirical, and untestable theories gives a picture of how broadly misused the word has become.

Each of the items in Table 1.1 has been characterized by their founders and proponents as having the necessary "theoretical" orientation and "empirical" foundation for acceptance. However, they persist despite continuous challenges to virtually all of these pseudosciences, in some cases lasting for more than a century as well as continuing to this day. New pseudosciences seem to emerge almost daily with their own inadequate "empirical evidence" and "theories." Despite a continuing cascade of contrary evidence or the fact that their supposed supporting evidence does not exist, they are, as one wag put it, ". . . more difficult to eradicate than vampires." Nevertheless, for social and religious reasons that are beyond the scope of this book, many pseudosciences of this genre persist.

Where does all this stuff come from? Some of it is simply a matter of intentional deception carried out for monetary gain or notoriety. Some of it, however, is simply due to misinterpretations of an inadequate sample of data by even highly qualified scientists. For example, some of this pseudoscience emerges from the simple statistical fact that, given our criteria of significance, a certain proportion of all experiments will naturally lead to incorrect results.[6] Furthermore, sometimes even the most solid and replicable finding can be unintentionally misinterpreted. Another major source of the perpetuation of some of these fads is that existing communities of practitioners with strong vested interest continue to reinforce each other's erroneous work in spite of an abundance of contrary evidence.

The main reason for the acceptance of so much of this pseudoscientific junk, however, lies in the nature of the audience. Nearly everyone wants or needs answers to some extremely difficult questions affecting health and life at both a personal or corporate level. Unfortunately, the answers and cures to what are, at least, extremely complex or, at worst, intractable problems have often been found to be insoluble by normal science. Thus, many of these fads and fallacious "theories" continue to be foisted upon the community, when the needed answers are beyond the current accomplishments of standard science.

Readers who are interested in pursuing the impact that these false "theories" can have on our society would do well to read Sagan's (1995) book. Also of related interest are the continuing discussions in the journal *The Skeptical Inquirer* on the role of pseudoscience in general, Dawes' (1994) book directed specifically at psychotherapy, and my book (Uttal, 2003) on some of the sources of fallacious theories–in psychology in particular. Other important contributions include Loftus' (1996) discussion of eyewitness testimony, Loftus and Ketcham's (1994) study of repressed memory, and Lykken's (1998) book on polygraphic lie detection. In addition, there are more than a thousand other volumes that deal critically with pseudosciences and false theories of all kinds. The deeply distressing fact is how little effect this extensive critical and skeptical literature has had on currently popular thought.

1.4.2 Ideal Types; Typologies

Turning from the pre-, non-, and anti-theories that characterize the pseudosciences to the seriously scientific use of the term, we first encounter a set of theories that simply segregate topics into distinctive types or classes. That is, this approach to theoretical understanding postulates schemas that are based on the observed kinds of natural phenomena. It suggests a

---

[6]A particular example of such a situation can be found in the work of Valenstein (1986). He describes the empirical literature that gave rise to the ill-fated and dangerous psychosurgical technique for treating mental illness. This highly invasive therapy was based on the results of a two-chimpanzee experiment in which only one of the animals exhibited the effect that triggered that entire unfortunate enterprise.

nonhierarchical and causally unrelated (in terms of explanations) set of categories. Such theories are referred to as *typologies* and are characterized by the fact that there are no systematic or causal relationships developed between the various items in the scheme.

In psychology, typologies have had a long history in defining the different types of personalities. The classic Greek natural philosophers, Hippocrates, Empedocles, and Aristotle, among the most notable, argued that there were personality types associated with body types and that these body types and personalities were generated by different "humors." The prevalent idea of the time was of four humors derived from the hypothesis that the world was made up of four basic elements (fire, earth, air, and water).[7] These elements were transposed to a corresponding set of four bodily humors (blood, phlegm, yellow bile, and black bile, respectively). Each of these four humors was associated with one of the four personality types designated as active, apathetic, irritable, and brooding, again in the same order.

The history of personality types continued unabated in the following millennia and can be discerned in the thinking of the faculty psychologists as well as modern factor analysis scholars. The psychoanalytic psychologist Carl Jung and a host of followers of psychotherapeutic bent also championed descriptions of human behavior that are even more explicitly based on personality types. This literature on psychological typologies is far too extensive to be even abstracted here but, as a brief example, we may consider Jung's typology of human natures. He proposed a typology based on the four sets of opposing factors:

- Extroversion versus introversion
- Thinking versus feeling
- Sensing versus intuition
- Judging versus perceiving

Each of these eight terms could be combined with the others in various ways to produce a variety of personality types. For example, one type might be characterized as being introverted and intuitive whereas another could be extroverted and judging.

The enormous literature and the diversity of psychotherapeutic approaches, perhaps better than any other argument, suggest the nonempirical nature of this and other personality typologies. In general, the categories are arbitrary, the case histories that define the types idiosyncratic, and the nature of each individual therapist's diagnostic classification suggest

[7]The history and evolution of these early naturalist theories of the world is detailed in chapter 2.

that standards for a true theory developed earlier in this chapter have not been met by these personality typologies. In large part, they have been relegated to the fringes of psychotherapy these days.

Typologies based on physique played an important role in psychological theory for many years. The idea of associating body types and personality—somatotypology—was most recently championed by Kretschmer (1925) and other German psychologists in the first half of the 20th century. This typological tradition came to America and was supported here by William Sheldon in a series of books (Sheldon, Harth, & McDermott, 1949; Sheldon & Stevens, 1942; and Sheldon, Stevens, & Tucker, 1940). Somewhat surprisingly, Sheldon's now disparaged work was done in collaboration with one of the giants of American experimental psychology, S. S. Stevens. The three body categories suggested by Sheldon and Stevens were (a) Endomorphy (a fat physique), (b) Mesomorphy (a muscular physique), and (c) Ectomorphy (a thin physique). Each of these body types was associated in Sheldon and Stevens' somatotype theory with three personality types, respectively: (a) Viscerotonia (characterized by a relaxed, comfort-seeking personality); (b) Somatotonia (characterized as an energetic, risk taker); and (c) Cerebrotonia (characterized as an intense, apprehensive worrier)—Cerebrotonia being the type most likely to be involved in criminal activity, according to their typological theory.

Two influences led to a rejection of this kind of personality typology. First was the ultimate judgment that, despite some early suggestive evidence, there was little empirical evidence of any correlation between the three proposed body types and either normal or pathological personalities. Second, there was an emerging awareness that somatotypy represented a kind of prejudicial stereotyping based on physical appearance. In the dynamic equalitarian times of the second half of the 20th century in the United States, such a theory became politically objectionable.

Typologies, nevertheless, are still extensively used in criminology (e.g., Siegel, 2000), and other social sciences (e.g., Stinchcombe, 1987), as well as in business and economics as exemplified by Parnell (2002). The latter's business personality types included such "strategic types" as "prospectors," "defenders," "analyzers," and "reactors." Typologies also have been used in an effort to find a way of relating science and religion. Barbour (2000), for example, suggested four ways in which religion and science interact; conflict, independence, dialog, and integration. All of these simplistic typologies persist in the face of the emerging appreciation of the complexity of human behavior.

Typologies are obviously still with us despite their questionable empirical basis. From another disappointing point of view, it can be argued that they form the intellectual basis of modern psychological and psychiatric diagnostic manuals (e.g., the *Diagnostic and Statistical Manual of Mental Disor-*

ders [American Psychiatric Association, 1992]). This cornerstone of modern psychotherapy categorizes mental illnesses into the following types, each of which is broken down into more specific categories of mental illness:

- Adjustment disorders
- Anxiety disorders
- Childhood disorders
- Cognitive disorders
- Dissociative disorders
- Eating disorder
- Impulse Control disorders
- Mood Disorders
- Psychotic disorders
- Sexual and Gender Identity disorders
- Sleep disorders
- Somatoform disorders
- Substance-related disorders

A second broad category, distinguished from the items in this list, is then added, which includes:

- Mental retardation
- Personality disorder

It seems quite clear from such a list that the various categories of mental illness and disorder designated there are also highly arbitrary and represent, to a greater extent than clinical psychologists may wish to accept, an extensive typology rather than a comprehensive theory based on a solid foundation of empirical evidence. It is certainly the case that the categories are not exclusive, but rather that they extensively overlap.[8]

Typologies, in general, may be characterized by the fact that, for one reason or another, the possible relationships, causal or otherwise, between the various types are not elucidated. This may be true for excellent reasons; many systems in nature are extremely complicated and we simply do not have the scientific means to unravel complex and nonlinear systems. Intuition and arbitrary naming of observed types, therefore, tend to dominate the field and eventually lead to typological theory construction.

---

[8]I appreciate how strongly some of my psychotherapeutic colleagues may object to this characterization of clinical psychology, in general, and the *DSM–IV*, in particular. However, I am convinced that our lack of basic knowledge of the nature of the mind, its inaccessibility, and the obscure forces that drive our behavior justifies this conclusion.

What typologies do accomplish is to collect items into similar groups based on what are, at best, unexplained featural similarities with little or no attention to the intertype relationships. In other words, the relations between the various "types" are subordinate to the similarities of items within each type. One of the most serious problems of a pure typology, therefore, is that the ideas on which it is based, as well as its ultimate structure, do not encourage the investigator to determine any relationships between the types that might explain how they function or the causal forces or relationships that may exist between the types.

Typologies are invented within the domains of those activities for which there is little understanding of the complex interactions that actually energize the observed behavior. Typologies are, therefore, much more prevalent in the social sciences, areas of cognitive and personality psychology, and politics and business than in the "simpler" areas of human endeavor in which empirical experimentation is possible and for which some analysis of the interactions is available. Typologies, from this point of view, represent an early stage of the theoretical effort to organize phenomena in extremely complex fields in which neither the empirical qualifications have been met nor the necessary analytic steps required for a comprehensive theory have yet been made.

This critique does not mean that typologies are without value or influence today. Velleman and Wilkinson (1993), for example, criticized another very important typology that has had an enormous impact on modern psychological science—the one proposed by Stevens (1951) of the possible kinds of measurement scales.[9] This particular typology became one of the most influential and, yet, often criticized concepts in American psychology. Velleman and Wilkinson (1993) reviewed a substantial number of criticisms that have been directed at it.[10]

Stevens' proposed typology for measurement consisted of four types of scales—"Nominal," "Ordinal," "Interval," and "Ratio." Velleman and Wilkinson argued that Stevens' measurement typology does not represent a valid model of psychophysical reality. The misuse of these terms by other psychologists, they further contended, is based on the fact that Stevens' categories do not adequately describe "the attributes of real data." Furthermore, even if they did, Velleman and Wilkinson suggested there is no need to assume that such archetypical data types actually exist. Even if there

[9]It is interesting to speculate that Stevens' theoretical perspective—a typology of measurement scales—may have been influenced by his early relationship with Sheldon (see p. 21).

[10]Stevens' (1951) classic and influential paper on measurement scales has also been criticized on other grounds by Michell (1999). Michell argued that Stevens' suggestion that numbers could be assigned to psychological variables may have seriously misled psychology for more than a half century by assuming these variables were quantifiable when, in fact, they may not have been.

was such a need for these archetypes, they argued, typologies like Stevens' would not be effective in specifying the appropriate statistical method to evaluate each of the scale types.

The general suggestion that emerges from Velleman and Wilkinson's (1993) critique and the many other critical papers they cite is that there is a fundamental inadequacy in psychological typologies of all kinds, not just those used for measurement. The basic core of this weakness emerges from the lack of understanding of the interactions among the proposed types. For this reason alone, it is clear that there is no way to build a system of relationships of measurement in the way that Stevens proposed that would permit an investigator to designate the best method of analysis for each situation or, for that matter, to understand how the different scale types are related.

Once again, one must not be too critical. This negative analysis of types and typologies does not imply that typologies cannot play a useful, if preliminary, role in providing a foundation for true theory development. From a more optimistic point of view, typologies can be considered to be prototheories that can, at the very least, identify featural similarities among the items in a type. This may be an essential step in providing a foundation that ultimately leads to understanding the relational and causal interactions among the constituent types. For example, the work of the political scientist J. David Singer (1979, 1980) on the *Correlates of War* was essentially an empirical typology. Nevertheless, it was able to suggest some interactions and relationships that later became more truly theoretical concepts. Unfortunately, many other typologies, particularly in social science, psychology, business, and economics, reflect little more than personal prejudices or unformulated prototypes.

1.4.3 Taxonomies

In my freshman year at university, I took a biology course built around a wonderful book that I have kept in my collection for the last 56 years. It is now a tattered relic and I no longer can find the cover page so I do not know the details of its original publisher. Its third and newest edition, however, was published in 1978 by two entomologists–R. G. Bland and H. E. Jaques–and bears the title–*How to Know the Insects*. My original first edition was authored, I believe, by Jaques alone.

The reason I mention this piece of personal history is that I remember the Jaques version to have been a magnificent and exceptionally lucid example of a taxonomic theory, the second kind of theory now to be discussed. It represented an exemplar of a kind of theory that took a step beyond a simple typology by proposing strong relationships among the various insect classes. When a taxonomy is developed, important prototheoretical steps have already been taken beyond a simple typology. No longer must the scientist be satisfied with arbitrary and intuitively unrelated types; now there are systematic steps that lead from one "type" to another.

The steps that Jaques used to develop his taxonomy were simple queries that start off with a question such as—Does the insect have wings?—and required only a simple dichotomous answer: "yes" or "no." If "yes," the reader is directed to Section 19, the first step in a continuing series of ever more specific questions about insects with wings. If the answer was "no," the reader is directed to Section 2, where insects without wings were further classified. In each case, subsequent questions lead the reader to a specific family of insects.[11] Each step in the sequence of questions is based on the specific and observable properties of the insect being classified. Quantitative values such as the number of legs or body parts now replace the arbitrary attributes of a type.

My dictionary defines taxonomy as the "orderly classification of plants and animals according to their presumed natural relationships." The critical criterion with which taxonomies differ from the typologies described in the previous section is their "natural relationships." A taxonomy, therefore, expands upon the idea of a typology to a preliminary estimate of relationships; one in which the observed relationships direct the construction of the theory.

Taxonomy has a long and distinguished history in the biological sciences. For centuries, however, virtually all efforts to categorize animals or plants were arbitrary typologies and the names used to identify them were disorganized and idiosyncratic to each investigator. In the 18th century, Carolus Linnaeus (1707–1778) brought order to this chaotic situation by postulating two formidable ideas. The first was the introduction of the idea of a hierarchical system for organizing a taxonomy of plants and animals. His great taxonomy—*Systema Naturae*—was printed in many editions during his lifetime. The familiar levels of this hierarchy are now well known: kingdom, class, order, genus, and species. The Linnaean naming system assigned a name to each species for its genus and a name for its species. Thus, for example, a particular animal was defined as a member of the genus and the species by the designation *Homo sapiens*. Its membership in the family Hominidae (humans and the great apes of Africa) came later.

Linnaeus' second contribution was, perhaps, even more important in a scientific sense. He proposed that the types in his taxonomy not be as-

[11]It is not possible in any book to use such a system to identify a particular species. Even at the time the first edition of Jaques' wonderful manual was published, it was believed there were well over 625,000 different insect species. One current estimate (Erwin, 1997) is that there now exist an astonishing 50,000,000 insect species on the earth! There may be some computer systems that handle such huge numbers but it is far beyond a single volume's capacity. The simple question-and-answer strategy used by Jaques simply collapses in the face of such numbers.

signed willy-nilly, but should use the relationships among the properties of the observed plants and animals to fit them into the classification system. Based on this key idea, modern taxonomies are constrained by empirical observations and are, thus, forced (by nature) to organize the interrelationships. To the degree that these properties can be measured, the taxonomy becomes a true theory of the organization of the system it describes.

Over the years, as is usually the case in theoretical developments, Linnaeus' original system had to be modified and corrected and new attributes examined to determine how biological systems can better be classified and the taxonomy organized. There is still active change and controversy, especially in fields such as Paleoanthropology, where the observed material is scant and the origins of and relationships between members of the Hominidae still remain obscure. Nevertheless, the idea of a classification system based on the empirically observed relationships of the specimens to be classified represents one of the great intellectual developments in history.

The concept of a taxonomy has spread far beyond the plant and animal systems with which Linnaeus, the biologist, was originally concerned. For example, my book–*A Taxonomy of Visual Processes* (Uttal, 1981)–extended the idea to the phenomena of visual perception. Just a few other examples of the diverse use of the taxonomic idea can be found in the following list gleaned from a quick search of the Internet for the phrase *Taxonomy of*:

- Taxonomy of Viruses
- Taxonomy of Educational Objects
- Taxonomy of Internet Commerce
- Taxonomy of Tasks
- Taxonomy of Information Patterns
- Taxonomy of Socratic Questions
- Taxonomy of Data Types
- Taxonomy of Experiences
- Taxonomy of Violent Conflicts
- Taxonomy of Computer Systems and Different Topologies
- Taxonomy of Logical Fallacies

Many taxonomic systems were originally based on organizational criteria that we now know to be ambiguous and arbitrary. In recent years new techniques have been developed that more formally address the problems involved in establishing the taxonomic categories. A new science of classification called *Cladistics* has begun to attract the attention of scientists in many fields. Originally proposed and developed by Hennig (1966), the main advantage of this new approach to constructing taxonomies is its purported objectivity. Hennig was adamant in arguing that cladistics should be an objective and empirical method for building taxonomies. His method was designed to remove, to the greatest extent possible, any subjectivity in a proposed classification scheme by emphasizing the dominance of the data over the intuition of the taxonomist.

Cladistics is very closely related to evolutionary theory; it, too, is based on the idea that a taxonomic classification system must depend on common properties that a group of descendents receives from a common ancestor. Another evolutionary corollary assumption of cladistics is that there is a continuing change of the characteristics of the descendents over time. As the family evolves, according to Henning and other modern cladists, these new characteristics will exhibit similarities that can indicate the relationship among the descendent groups. The related groups or "clades" are typically plotted in the form of a branching tree or "cladogram" that provides a picture of how and when the various descendent clades diverged from the common evolutionary sequence.

A modern advantage of the cladistic approach is that although its logic may be complex and it may be difficult to program, it can be run on a computer. Thus, its objectivity is enhanced and human prejudices are removed even further from the construction of the taxonomy. Once the various characteristics and properties of a group of specimens have been determined by biologists, computer models such as PAUP 4.0 (Swofford, 2003) can be used to automatically determine the most "parsimonious" tree of clades. Programs such as PAUP 4.0 are able to calculate large numbers of alternative tree structures and pick out one that best fits the data. Of course, as the tree continues to branch and subdivide, cladistics will also fall victim to combinatorics and the connections will become noncomputable simply because of numerousness.

As usual, the assumptions built into computational procedures can determine the outcome from the computer analysis. Yang (1996), for example, has discussed the history of some recent controversies surrounding even the most objective computer procedures for applying cladistic ideas.

1.4.4 Models

The next type of theory to be considered is denoted by the term *model*. The use of this word has many different interpretations to theoreticians throughout the history of science. To many, a model is synonymous with a theory. However, I use the term here in a more restricted fashion than this putative synonym suggests. A model, from the point of view of this alternative meaning, comes closer to the connotation expressed by the word replica. That is, a model is a reconstruction of a system produced in order to simulate the structure and behavior of the system. The replica may be a mechanical one, a computational (as opposed to a mathematical) program, or a network of electrical components that behaves in much the same way as the real system being modeled. The key idea is that a representation of the system under study is built from the components of another kind of system. The alternative system, for one reason or another, may be easier to manipulate than the original one.

Another term that has a high degree of similarity to *model* (in the sense used here) is *analogy*. The programs established on analog computers, for example, may or may not fall in the category of a model. Some are explicit representations of differential equations; others, however, may represent estimates of the nature of the interactions between components without mathematical formulation. Essentially, an analog computer can be programmed as an electronic representation or on a mechanical or other kind of system.[12]

Models, in this sense of analogs or replicas, may be either preludes to or substitutes for formal theories. They are often required because certain classes of systems are so complex they exceed the possibility of any mathematical formulation, now or at any time in the future. Such systems may be complex not necessarily by virtue of component numerousness, but complex by virtue of the possible numbers of interactions among a relatively small number of parts. For example, there are problems that can be expressed within the confines of a checkerboard consisting of only 64 squares (e.g., optimizing the path of a traveling salesman) that can not be solved in any conceivable amount of time by any conceivable computer (Stockmeyer & Chandra, 1979).[13] Indeed, some processes that occur with phenomenal ease in nature (e.g., the unfolding of a protein molecule; Casti, 1996) are totally beyond the power of formal analysis, certainly currently and probably in the future. Sometimes by building a replica, even without the formality of a mathematical expression, and simply allowing the replica to run its course, system behavior can be observed that can provide deep insights into the natural process.

The question now arising is: If the computer cum mathematical model cannot solve a problem such as protein unfolding, how does nature do it? One answer is that the natural system enjoys the power of enormous intrinsic parallelicity. That is, even though it is not possible for a mathematical

---

[12]The earliest analog computers were, in point of historical fact, actually mechanical systems made up of gears, rods, and wheels rolling on metal discs. A gear ratio could simulate multiplication; a wheel on a disc could encode the process of integration; and so on.

[13]If any of my readers doubt the magnitude of the numbers that can occur in even small systems, please look up the definitions of combinations and factorials and carry out a few simple calculations. Also see page 232 in chapter 6.

analysis to solve the huge number of simultaneous equations that are required to represent such a complex system, the real system carries them out in parallel with all of the interactions being processed essentially simultaneously. From this viewpoint, the real system is a model of itself–indeed, the only full and complete model possible.

Although it is not possible to analytically predict the behavior of a multibody system, even one as simple as three interacting objects (e.g., planets or neurons influenced solely by their gravitational fields or synaptic interactions), it is possible to build a mechanical or electronic model of such a system that effectively carries out the simulated processes *in real time*! The trick, in this case of mathematical impossibility, but simulation possibility, is to build a model or replica of the system and let it run its course.

Furthermore, some models may have to run faster than real time; otherwise their "predictions" would be worthless. Happily, this can be done. For example, weather forecast models must project future events before they actually occur to be useful, and climate models commonly run programs over simulated time periods as long as 100–200 years to model climate records for the past and to predict the future. To accomplish this enormous data-processing task, models utilize "parameterization," a method by which complex processes are approximated by simple relationships. For example, the proportion of cloud cover at any moment might be represented by a function of temperature and humidity that does not incorporate all details of the involved physical processes, regional effects, aerosol interactions, or any other processes that can also affect local cloud formation. The success of such meteorological models is highly dependent on the success of such simple parameterizations to produce realistic results without trying to replicate all details of the system. It should be noted that, even with simple approximating parameterizations, atmospheric models often become so complex it is difficult to carry out the computations, much less to identify cause and effect relationships. In such cases, the complexity of identifying specific mechanisms in these models can be almost as difficult as the challenge faced when atmospheric physicists directly study the atmosphere itself.[14]

If one considers the example just given, another important point arises. It should be obvious from this discussion of atmospheric simulations that a model is almost always something less than the real system. A map, for example, is an eminently satisfactory replica of a geographical environment if one is concerned about finding one's way from one location to another. However, it is much less than the real environment and would not help at all if you were searching for a field of a particular kind of grain or a shovel

[14]I would like to acknowledge the advice and guidance given to me in the previous paragraph by Taneil Uttal who is both an atmospheric physicist at the National Oceanic and Atmospheric Administration (NOAA) at Boulder, Colorado and my daughter.

left behind a barn, or even the barn itself. On the other hand, a map is always something more than the real scene it represents; mapped roads may be colored red and towns represented by an abstract symbol (such as ◙), neither color nor symbol being associated with any real attribute of the road or town.

The point here is not to allow the properties of the model to become confused with the properties of the real system. Representation in a model is, at once, a reduction in the information content of the system being modeled but also the addition of spurious properties that can be conferred on the system if one is not careful.[15] In Alfred Korzybski's (1933/1995) words—"The map is not the territory."

Thus, to summarize, models are intended in the present context to mean replicas or analogs that can imitate natural systems without necessarily invoking explicit formal (i.e., mathematical or logical) representations. In this sense, they represent something less than a full theory, but something that can nevertheless produce an acceptable solution to the problem posed by an otherwise formally unanalyzable complex system.

1.4.5 Formal and Axiomatic Theories

By a formal theory, I refer to one that is expressed in the language of mathematics, either analytic or probabilistic, or that of logic. As we have seen, not all theories or models are formal mathematical or logical constructions. However, when applied, both mathematics and logic offer additional powerful tools for the development of an integrated and comprehensive statement of a variety of related observations. One of the most important tools is the constraint that such languages impose on the thought processes of the theoretician. It is remarkable how wildly off base or how ludicrous a theory can be when phrased only in the words of spoken or written language. The rules for verbal language usage are just not sufficiently precise or rigorous enough to convey the detailed logic and implications of many kinds of theory. What should be the outcome of formal implications or derivations are often replaced by non sequiturs in a theory expressed only in words. Leaps from preliminary assumptions to conclusions are all-too-often unfettered by any of the rule-based constraints that are inherent in the derivative techniques of formal languages. Transformations from one conceptual point to another during the expression of a verbal theory can occur in a manner that students of formal logic and mathematics would agree might better be considered transformational miracles!

[15]It is important to reiterate the caveat that the definition of a model presented here is not the usual one in which phrases such as "theoretical models" have proliferated.

Formal languages reduce the possibility of such looseness of derivation and definition. Rather, they require that whenever a system changes from one state to another or when an assumption or some datum leads to a conclusion, the transformations are governed by a precise set of rules—logical truth tables, in one case, or the rules of mathematical derivations in the other.

Another advantageous aspect of formal theories couched in the language of logic and mathematics is that they do not require the construction of a physical model or replica. In many cases, such a re-creation of the natural system would be impossible; in other cases, they would just be impractical. Mathematical equations can, to the contrary, represent a very complex or horrendously large system in an abstract and symbolic matter without physical instantiation. The physical properties of the solar system, for example, need not be replicated or even explicitly modeled to understand how our solar system works. Instead, the dynamics of such a system may be described by the rules and symbols of algebra, analytic geometry, and the calculus in a way that permits its behavior to be precisely described and even predicted. Mathematical experiments can be carried out in situations where "**m**" (symbolizing something as impossible to reproduce as a physical replica as the mass of the sun) can be represented by a symbol with infinitesimal mass.

Mathematics and logic are, thus, quite wonderful in their ability to deal with massive or distant systems as well as with ultramicroscopic ones. However, there are caveats even with this elegant type of theorizing that must not be overlooked. The most important limitation of a mathematical model is that, in achieving its symbolic status, it remains *neutral* with regard to underlying mechanisms. That is, *no matter how perfect a fit to the observed data and how successful a mathematical theory may be in predicting the future course of some system's behavior, it is, in basic principle, incapable of discriminating between the huge number of possible and plausible alternative mechanisms that could produce the predicted behavior.*

The problem is that a single mathematical expression can symbolically represent a true infinity of real systems that *could* exhibit the common behavior or processes described by the mathematics. For example, the second order differential equation that describes the behavior of a plumb bob on a spring also equally well describes the behavior of a population of fish subject to the oscillating pressures of the density of poisonous algae. Furthermore, it has been established that there are innumerable other natural and man-made systems that could also be represented by the same formulae. It is only when other definitions, axioms, assumptions, properties, and constraints are added to the purely mathematical ones, that the mathematical formalism can be uniquely attached to a specific system.

This caveat of mathematical neutrality holds in even the simplest situations. For example, suppose the numbers 2 and 3 were entered into a computer of unknown internal construction and the number 6 was returned. Although mathematically impeccable according to one arithmetic rule, there is no way that the internal logic or number system or anything else about the mechanisms that might be used internally by the computer to solve this problem can be determined from the input–output relationships alone. Nor, for that matter, can any plausible mechanism be excluded. The mathematics describing the system, no matter how accurate a process description relating the input to the output, is, therefore, indeterminate with regard to internal structure. It might as well be a binary circuit or a couple of monkeys as far as the external observer is concerned. Nothing in the mathematics of the input–output relations will permit determination of what is actually inside this miniature multiplier. As I have stated elsewhere (Uttal, 2002), there really can be no "Turing Test" (Turing, 1950) to distinguish whether a closed system encloses a computer or a human. Not only is the mathematics neutral but so, too, is the behavior of a closed system (including human behavior) with regard to its internal mechanisms.

This fundamental, in principle, neutrality of mathematics emerges from the fact that there are many, many instantiations that may be represented by a single mathematical formulation. Engineers refer to this as the black box problem, thus giving a name to the fact that the internal mechanisms of a closed box cannot be determined from the input and output properties of the system alone. The black box problem has been formalized by Moore (1956) in what should be a prime educational prerequisite for all aspiring cognitive neuroscientists. He put it this way:

> Given any [closed] machine S and any multiple experiment performed on S, there exist other machines [internal mechanisms] experimentally indistinguishable from S for which the original experiment would have had the same outcome. . . . This result means that it will never be possible to perform experiments on a completely unknown machine which will suffice to identify it from among the class of all sequential machines. (p. 140)

I believe this statement is extraordinarily germane to psychology, in particular, and by itself sets up an insurmountable counterargument to any mentalist school of thought including the currently popular cognitive approach. Indeed, this idea has been known, but apparently underappreciated, since the beginning of modern neuroreductive theorizing. In the seminal and pioneering article in neural network theory, McCulloch and Pitts (1943) also alluded to this problem when, referring to their implications of their theory, they said:

> It is shown that many particular choices among possible neurophysiological assumptions are equivalent, in the sense that for every net behaving under one assumption, there exists another net which behaves under the other and gives the same results, although perhaps not in the same time. (p. 115)

I return to this topic later in this chapter when I discuss mental accessibility.

Another important implication of the neutrality of mathematics is that any such formalization of a theory is always an abstraction of the real system it describes. Henkin (1967) described such formal systems (i.e., theories) in the following way:

> A formal system . . . is a device for explicating the notion of consequence. Although the system itself is formulated without reference to the meanings conveyed by the symbols and sentences of which it is constituted, the motive underlying its employment—and hence the criterion by which it must be judged—is the attempt to certify the truth of certain sentences based on the knowledge of truth of others. (Vol. 8, p. 62)

Henkin went on to specify the components of formal systems (i.e., theories) as (1) "a set of symbols"; (2) "formation rules for constructing sentences from those symbols"; (3) "logical axioms"; and (4) transformation rules (Vol. 8, p. 62), components (1) and (2) constituting the "grammar" and (3) and (4) the "deductive apparatus" of the formal language.

A further specialization of the idea of a formal theory is that of *axiomization*. Both mathematical and logical theories may be considered to be examples of this expansion of the meaning of a formal theory. An axiom is an initial proposition, premise, or assumption on which a theory is based. It is the starting point from which rules guide the development or derivation of theorems that may represent the behavior of the natural system under study. To the extent that the axioms of a theory are correct and that valid rules are followed, the theory may adequately describe the behavior of the system being studied.

In practical point of fact, almost all scientific activity is axiomatic in the sense that all research is based on certain assumptions or axioms, either implicit or explicit, that guide the research program. When explicit, we dignify the theory by characterizing it as an axiomatic theory; when implicit, scientists often go about their business without appreciating the foundation axioms that are guiding their day-to-day empirical activities.

Axioms, it should be noted, are not proven in the development of a formal theory, but are taken as givens. They are initial assumptions that may or may not be valid, but whose validity is not tested in the course of theory development. The axioms, when processed by the rules, lead to theorems or deductions. To the extent that these deductions are consistent with empirical observations, the originating axioms take on a certain implied validity.

Popper (1959) was very specific about the properties that a theory must have to be considered to be axiomatic:

> A theoretical system is "axiomized" if a set of statements, the axioms, has been formulated which satisfies the following four fundamental requirements. . . . (a) [The set] must be *free from contradiction* (whether self-contradiction or mutual contradiction). . . . (b) [The set] must be *independent*, i.e., it must not contain any axiom deducible from the remaining axioms. . . . (c) [The set must be] *sufficient* for the deduction of all statements belonging to the theory which is to be axiomized, and (d) [The set] must be *necessary* for the same purpose, which means that they should contain no superfluous assumptions. (pp. 71–72)

One interpretation of what Popper was saying in this quotation is that the number of axioms underlying a given theory must be constrained in two ways. First, there should be as many as needed to permit the rules to lead to conclusions (theorems). Second, the number should be as few as possible to avoid redundancy, wasted effort in applying the rules, and conceptual muddiness.

The archetype of axiomatic scientific theorizing has long been considered to be the Deductive-Nomological (DN) model,[16] typical of physics but only partially approached in the cognitive neurosciences, and only then with some stretching of the rules. A classic and precise description of the DN model was published by Hempel and Oppenheim (1948), although the idea of a deductive syllogism goes back to Aristotle at the very least. The basic deductive idea implicit in DN thinking is that if one starts from appropriate initial conditions and salient laws (and even relevant precursor theories) one can produce other statements (i.e., deductions, theorems, or conclusions) that satisfactorily describe observable phenomena. The DN model has the advantage that, barring some kind of a false law or an erroneous statement of the initial conditions, the premises will inevitably lead to a fixed conclusion.

The DN model is not a universal solution for all problems of science (statistical theories do not fall within this rubric), but it does represent what philosophers of science have long considered to be the ideal for any scientific theory-building endeavor. It is a form of theory generation so well structured that when it does fail it is often easy to find the sources of the failure. In examining these failures, one may find that a governing law is incorrectly stated or that one of the premises is invalid. This corrigibility is

[16]Please note that the word *model* is used quite differently here than the way I defined it on page 28.

an enormous advantage compared to some of the other means of developing theories.

For a theory to be a satisfactory explanation of some phenomena, Hempel and Oppenheim (1948) argued that it had to meet four "conditions of adequacy." Three of these (1, 2, and 4) characterize the logical structure of a sound DN theory. One (3) is concerned with its empirical nature. The following list presents their four conditions:

1. The phenomena explained (the explanandum) must be a logical consequence of the antecedent conditions and laws of the argument (the explanans).
2. The explanans must include at least one general law that is actually required to deduce the explanadum.
3. The explanans must be testable by experiment or observation.
4. The components of the explanans must be true. That is, a theory may be based on impeccable logic and yet be entirely false if the original conditions or the laws used in that logical process are incorrect. (Paraphrased from Hempel & Oppenheim, 1948, pp. 137–138)

Hempel and Oppenheim's formularization has had an enormous influence on modern thinking. It is the idealization of how a formal theory must be constructed. However, it is clear that not all scientific theories adhere to this formal structure. Many theories are not able to validate the laws that are used in the derivation and some theories simply do not have the logical or quantitative structure that make them amenable to this kind of analysis. Some, furthermore, may be dependent on random processes in such a way that they cannot be squeezed into this paradigm or represent processes that are so complex that the laws cannot lead from axioms to theorems. Thus, in some cases, prediction would become impossible since the outcome of say, a chaotic process, could not be fully deduced from the "laws" of causal relationship.

Hempel was not unaware of the fact that there were other models of science theory building. Following the Hempel and Oppenheim (1948) classic, he described other types of theorizing, especially in Hempel (1965). Salmon (2001) described the four types of theory emerging from Hempel's writing as:

1. Deductive-nomological explanations of particular facts by general laws. [As described previously in this section]
2. Deductive-nomological explanations of general regularities by universal laws.
3. Inductive-statistical explanations of particular facts by statistical laws.

4. Deductive-statistical explanations of statistical regularities by statistical laws. (p. 64)

Finally, however ideal Hempel and Oppenheim's theory of theories may be, science just doesn't work this way generally. DN theory does not incorporate the sudden insights and intuitions that lead to what seems to be an almost magical and sudden appreciation of a new theoretical explanation. Klee (1997) described the reality of scientific progress well when he said:

> Actual historical science is much messier psychologically, sociologically, and politically–than the pure and pristine reconstructions of the positivists [e.g., Hemple and Oppenheim] would otherwise suggest. The positivist model painted a picture of the workaday practitioner as a "little philosopher," maximally rational, logically astute, immune to irrelevant outside pressures, dedicated to the pursuit of knowledge above all else, and devoid of the foibles and quirks that beset other mortal beings. But a close look at the real life histories of scientists and their careers did not seem to bear out this happy picture of a community of learned minds practicing their craft with granite integrity. Rather, the historical record showed that scientists were often vain, conceited, willing to fudge data, willing to argue unfairly, willing to use larger power sources in society to further their own interests and beliefs, and that, in general, they were not little philosophers who are aware of all the epistemological, methodological, and ontological aspects of their chosen fields. (p. 130)

1.4.6 Some Dichotomous Taxonomies of Theories

The categories that I have suggested here–typologies, taxonomies, and formal axiomatic theories–do not exhaust the possible distinctions made by other students of the problem. Cummins (1983), for example proposed a dichotomy of theoretical types. First, he distinguished between transition and property theories. The former type is concerned with explaining the changes that occur in a system. In this case, explanation to Cummins meant that a transition theory would be able to tease out the causes that drive a system to go from one condition or state to another.

It is interesting to note that Cummins' concept of a transition theory was very similar to what is called perturbation analysis in engineering. His own explanation arose from the fact that something "disturbs" the system, thus destabilizing it. The actual response of the system, be it of the brain or an electrical circuit, is determined not so much by the force of the disturbance as by the properties of the system as it seeks to reacquire equilibrium. Nevertheless, to Cummins, a transition theory was only explanatory when the laws explaining the transition from one state to another were "causal" in nature. That is, it must be assumed (and the laws must be based on this assumption) that there are lawful cause–effect relationships operating on the system. Without such causal laws, transition theories are not possible.

Cummins (1983) suggested the following question as the archetype of the motivation behind a transition theory: "Why does system S change states from s-1 to s-2?" (p. 15).

The other extreme of Cummins' dichotomy designated the class of property theories. In this case, there is no effort to explain state changes by means of the causal laws, instead, the theoretician is concerned simply with determining the properties of a system. A property theory is, he argued, only directed at the identification of those properties and what it is about a system that accounts for them. For example, the idea that mental processes are accounted for by virtue of the interaction of a very large number of neurons is a property theory. The major effort in the property theoretical analysis of this system is to define the properties of the mind, not to carry out the reduction from the mental to the neural. (That would be a transition theory, but one that is unlikely to be realized.)

The hope, of course, is that someday such a property theory would become the grist for a specific transition theory that would actually explain how sequential, and presumably, different mental states sequence from one to another. According to Cummins (1983), property theories cannot succeed unless there is some hope such a reductionism is possible. That is, a property theory cannot be consummated if ". . . the properties [of a system] are not derivable from the properties of the elements of the analyzed system" (p. 26).

Cummins suggested the following question as the archetype of the motivation behind a property theory: "What is it for system S to have a property P?" (p. 15).

Kaplan (1964) proposed another dichotomous classification of theories. He distinguished between concatenated and hierarchical theories, the former including theories that were characterized as those whose ". . . component laws enter into a network of relations so as to constitute an identifiable configuration or pattern" (p. 298). He believed that a concatenated theory was exemplified by the theory of evolution. The latter category of theory—hierarchical—includes theories that are pyramidal in nature ". . . in which we rise to fewer and fewer more general laws as we move from conclusions to the premises which entail them" (p. 298). A hierarchical theory is exemplified by the theory of relativity according to Kaplan.

Kaplan (1964) also reminded us of the distinction between two kinds of theories made by Einstein (1934): "constructive or synthetic theories," on the one hand, and "principal or analytic theories" on the other. The former are synthetic in the sense that they start from a few simple ideas and "synthesize" descriptions of sometimes very complex phenomena. An example of a constructive theory is the kinetic theory of gases that starts from basic physical principles and synthesizes a theory of how molecules move about.

The second type—analytic theories—starts from observed empirical phenomena and attempts to develop a mathematical system to describe and analyze them to an ever-smaller number of more and more and more general laws. An example of an analytic theory is, according to Einstein, thermodynamic theory in which physical phenomena were examined to produce the conditions that such observations would have to satisfy.

Many of these efforts to divide theories into two types obviously have a close similarity to the classic dichotomy of induction and deduction, respectively. Inductive theories attempt to go from the very large set of observations to a few general principles. Deductive theories start with a relatively small number of principles and derive particular relations.

Clearly, there are many other ways of dividing up theoretical types, but these examples give some insight into the thinking of some of the greatest of present and past theoreticians about what they think they are doing when they develop a theory.

1.5 SOME BIG QUESTIONS

The introduction presented in this chapter to the enormously significant question of what is meant by a theory has presented a variety of views, problems, and limits. There is little question that the nature of a theory is an active field of discourse in philosophy of science circles. It would be presumptuous to assert there is anything close to a consensus. Instead, we now arrive at the same point we started this chapter—with a series of questions. The answers to some of these questions remain elusive despite their extreme importance. For example, philosophers have long argued about such questions as: What is causation? The physics and metaphysics of causation characterize a topic that goes far beyond the intended range of this book. It is all too easy to become bogged down in seeking an answer to this question, as easy as it is to seek a precise definition of mind.

There are, however, some "big" questions about theories and explanations that are specifically germane to the cognitive neurosciences that are within the intended scope of this book. The importance of these questions lies in the fact that their respective answers represent some key assumptions or axioms that are a basic, but usually unacknowledged, part of the "explanans" of cognitive neuroscientific theory. Depending in large part on the answers to these questions, the direction that cognitive neuroscientific theory should take in the future would be largely predetermined. This final section considers the most relevant of these critical questions, some of which have been alluded to earlier.

1.5.1 Explanation, Description, and Prediction

Over the years many scientists have raised two important and related questions about theories. First, are theories explanatory as opposed to descriptive? Second, are the goals of theoretical science simply prediction and control as opposed to explanation or description.

With regard to the first question, little progress can be made in resolving it unless we know what explanation and description mean. By explanation, I refer to a strategy in which efforts are made to interpret the process under investigation in terms of internal or lower level mechanisms. This approach to explanation, therefore, contains within it the implicit idea of some kind of reduction. The usual definition of *explain*—to make something understood—is totally inadequate; it makes no distinction between a good functional or behavioral description and a reductive explanation that teases out the specific manner in which such functions are instantiated.

Most theories in cognitive neuroscience or in any other kind of science, do not, in point of fact, *explain* in a reductive sense. Instead, most *describe* the course of the process that is being observed or correlations between measured events. By description I refer to any theory that uses a symbolic means (such as mathematics or words) to represent some measurable aspect of an action. Functional or molar descriptions of a process need not entail any analysis into components to show how the observed "behavior" of a system is produced by these components, but, rather, a descriptive theory represent the system as a whole.[17]

Furthermore, the distinction between explanation and description is not always as clear as we would like. Some efforts to define "explanation" do not distinguish between the descriptive and the explanative role played by the different axioms. For example, Hon (2001) suggested that:

> Explanation is obtained when the singular, isolated, particular phenomenon—the explanandum, is shown to partake in a general scheme—the explanans. (p. 7)

It seems to me, however, that this capsule definition does not discriminate between the two different kinds of axioms or postulates that can nearly always be discerned in any axiomatic theory nor the different ways in which the explanandum may "partake" in the scheme. Some axioms are purely formal or relational and simply describe the rules by which the logic of the

[17]It is not usually appreciated how the fictional components of a mathematical theory (e.g., a control systems model) may differ from the actual mechanisms of the system under investigation. Functional components such as "lag," although usually portrayed as a distinct "box" in such a system may actually be distributed throughout the entire system. Again, the point is that mathematical models of all kinds are neutral with regard to specific internal mechanisms.

theory is carried out. There is no allusion to the mechanics or underlying structure of the system. Another kind of axiom, on the other hand, includes the structural ones that link the systems to some kind of concrete underlying mechanism.

For example, in some classic theories of perception (e.g., metacontrast as originally discovered by Stigler [1910] and more recently analyzed by Weisstein [1972]), there are descriptive axioms and laws that represent and describe the action being observed. These nonreductive statements may be distinguished from the anatomical and physiological axioms that stipulate which structures and physiological events actually *cause* that course of action. Weisstein's theory of this paradoxical and interesting phenomenon presented a mathematical formula that closely approximated the behavior observed in the perception laboratory. Quite separately, in terms of the constituent axioms of the theory, it also proposed a simple network of neurons that could "explain the behavior" in terms of delayed transmission times.

The important point is that the descriptive formula of Weisstein's axiomatic model worked as well as any other of several alternative theories that were subsequently proposed to describe this phenomenon. Indeed, it turned out that all competing mathematical theories of metacontrast could be collapsed into each other. That is, they were all derivable from each other—"duals" in mathematical terminology. Thus, mathematical theories were not only equivalent in a formal sense, but equally capable of describing the metacontrast phenomenon.

The several alternative theories, all of which proposed equally good fitting mathematical descriptions of the process were, however, based on totally different neurophysiological postulates than the one proposed by Weisstein. It was only in this context of their respective physiological axioms that the theories could be distinguished from each. Nevertheless, since the mathematical descriptions were all the same for the different neurophysiological assumptions, the mathematics could not offer any help in suggesting which, if any, was correct. The end result is that no clear-cut neurophysiological model of this relatively simple perceptual phenomenon—metacontrast—has ever been forthcoming. Despite the precision of description and even of prediction, reduction to neural mechanisms remains elusive for this well-studied phenomenon.[18]

The point is that even the best description is not a reductive explanation. Barring some way of determining exactly what are the actual neurophysiological mechanisms, the mathematical laws and axioms can be as

---

[18]The soundness of this argument is not mitigated by the many neurophysiological studies that purport to show a neural correlate for metacontrast and many other illusions. What is often confused is some analogical neural activity and true identity. Isomorphism is not necessary; symbolic, semantic, or informationally significant means of representing perceptual events are plausible, possible, and likely alternative explanations.

precise as one could ask, and yet the physiological or "reductively explanatory" axioms of a theory remain indeterminate, if not invalid.

I hope these distinctions will help to convey modern definitions of these two key terms and answer the first of the two questions I posed at the outset of this section. That answer is that with the exceptions of those relatively simple open systems in which we can examine their inner workings, virtually all theories are descriptive rather than explanatory.

Any answer to the second question—What is the role of science: prediction and control or description and explanation?—is largely a matter of taste. Those who are pragmatically oriented seem content with the former, while those who seek some deep understanding would prefer the latter pair. What is clear, however, is that "explanation" in the sense of defining causal relationships among specific mechanisms is far more elusive than is generally thought in cognitive neurosciences.

1.5.2 Reduction

The next major question is more relevant to the field of cognitive neuroscience than the arcane matters of description and explanation just discussed. Indeed, this question lies at the heart of the entire enterprise in which an answer to the mind–brain question is sought. The specific form of the question at hand is: Can mental processes be reduced or explained by neural mechanisms? Of course, there are many corollaries of this question and many contexts in which it becomes salient. Sensory and motor relations can be contrasted with central mental processes; the microscopic action of neurons can be contrasted with the macroscopic action of regions of the brain; and the dynamics of behavioral change (i.e., learning) can be sought in the dynamics of synaptic changes or circulating impulses.

All of these forms of the reduction question depend on one's personal answer to another fundamental question: What is the essential level of psychoneural equivalence? That is, where, among all possible responses one could measure in the brain, should one look for the true processes that indisputatively account for mental activity? Probably the most current and generally accepted answer to this question is that mental processes emerge from the activity of the vast and complex set of interactions among the innumerable neurons of the brain. Mind, thus, is a correlate of organization and information, not of the "coincidental observations" such as the chemistry of neurons and neural transmission, slow waves, the behavior of single neurons, or chunks of brains examined by PET and fMRI techniques with such vigor these days.

This proposed answer—neuronal network interconnections are the psychoneural equivalent of all mental activity—means that no matter how much can be known of the details of their individual behavior and chemistry, nothing can be deduced about how the mind arises from the brain. In other words, our physiological and chemical knowledge of neurons is secondary simply because that knowledge is incidental to the actual information processes that are the true causal equivalents of mind.

If one accepts this network answer to this "level of analysis" question, what inescapably follows is a negative answer to the foundation question of the plausibility of neuroreduction itself. That is, it is not likely that we can reduce mental processes to specific neural networks. This negative answer is based on a number of considerations that are discussed extensively in Uttal (1998, 2000). They are briefly listed here to make this discussion reasonably self-contained; I refer my readers to the earlier works for more complete discussions and to chapter 6 where the details of neural network theory are presented.

1. The combinatorial complexity of cognitively relevant neural processes is so great that they are beyond computability or analysis. There is no mathematics that can solve nonlinear problems of a complexity comparable to those posed by the human brain.

2. Such complex systems are intractable challenges because their analysis would violate well-established physical principles such as the second law of thermodynamics. Mathematics and nature are one-way systems in which it is impossible to uniquely retrace the steps from initial conditions to final states. Entropy cannot be reversed to order in a closed system like the brain. The controlling metaphor is: "You cannot unscramble scrambled eggs."

3. The myriad initial condition information required for an analysis of complex systems such as the brain are no longer available when the brain matures according to new ideas from chaos theory. The controlling metaphor is: "When a butterfly in the Brazilian rainforest flaps its wings, it contributes to the fall of empires."

4. Closed systems cannot be uniquely reduced to their internal components by means of input–output relations. Furthermore, systems like the brain remain functionally closed even when surgically opened and the best conceivable neurophysiological measures are applied because of their complexity (see 1 and 2).

Constraints like these suggest that the attempt to find bridge laws that will reduce mental phenomena to neural mechanisms will be extremely difficult, if not impossible, to obtain. Indeed, at what I believe is the most likely level of psychoneural equivalence—that of the network of billions of neurons that is probably associated with even the simplest cognitive act—there has been absolutely no progress to date other than what is sometimes imaginative speculation. This kind of neuroreduction remains the Holy

Grail of cognitive neuroscience. Unfortunately, sound arguments, such as the ones just mentioned, assert that that a purely neural explanation of mental processes is no more likely to be found than the mythical grail. This does not mean that a very large number of consistent and inconsistent theories cannot be proposed. Rather, it means that most are *a priori* deeply flawed and correct only in a limited sense. As we review and critique the various kinds of theories of mind–brain in the latter chapters of this book, I hope this argument will become clear and sustainable.

1.5.3 Analysis

If the question of neuroreduction discussed in the previous section lies at the heart of the cognitive neuroscientific enterprise, then the question of analysis into mental components lies at the heart of cognitive psychology. The question is posed as: Can mental processes be reduced or explained by separating (i.e., analyzing) them into cognitive modules?

Once again, there is an enormous disconnect between the stated goals of the scientists involved in this field and what is actually achievable. I argue here that such an analytic search for the components or modules of mind cannot be achieved with any more likelihood than the quest for reduction described in the previous section. Countering the optimistic hope that such an analysis is possible is an increasing awareness that the task is dependent on the validity of certain assumptions about the nature of mind that cannot be justified.

The central assumption underlying cognitive psychology is that mind is modular in some fundamentally psychobiological manner and that these modules (e.g., judgment, learning, reasoning, perception, passion, anticipation) can be isolated and identified by some well-designed psychological experiments. Like the possibility of neuroreduction, the validity of this assumption has been debated for years without resolution. It is, however, generally, albeit uncritically, accepted by cognitive psychologists and other mentalists such as the faculty and factor analytic psychologists. The suggestion that modules exists and that they can be identified is, however, dependent on a simplistic point of view about the nature of mental processes.

The possibility of a cognitive analyzability is driven by antique traditions in science that served well for physics but may not be as applicable to mental activity. For example, one of the guiding principles of modern science has been the Cartesian Méthode, the traditional approach to studying compound systems. The dictate, most famously expressed by René Descartes (1649), was that, in order to study something, one must break it up into its parts and examine the effects of manipulating one part while holding the rest constant. The problem that the Méthode poses to the study of cognition is that it demands the experimenter assume that all of the component parts, including the one to be manipulated, will remain fixed and unchanged in their properties and actions regardless of the way the experiment is carried out. This advice is now known not to work for nonlinear systems far simpler than brain function, much less to be a valid description of the organization of the mind itself. A further problem is that mental modules may be fictions! The fragmentation of mental processes may be in accord with the Méthode but not with the true nature of the mind.

These arguments against analysis are mainly, as noted, based on the improbability of the required assumptions. Pachella (1974) has been the leader in clarifying the nature of these assumptions and the unreasonable demands they make on what can only be considered from this point of view to be an unrealistic kind of psychology—cognitive mentalism. These assumptions are simply listed here since they are discussed in detail in Uttal (1998, 2000).

1. *Modularity* in which it is assumed that cognitive processes are compounds of simpler component modules.
2. *Rigidity and Independence* in which it assumed that cognitive modules remain fixed in their properties regardless of the role they play in different tasks.
3. *Seriality* in which it is assumed that cognitive modules carry out their functions in serial order.
4. *Summation* in which it is assumed that the time taken process a cognitive module can be simply added to that of others to estimate the total time for a compound task to be executed.
5. *Pure Insertion* in which it is assumed that cognitive modules can be inserted into or removed from a compound process without either affecting the function of the other modules or itself.
6. *Precision* in which it is assumed that our psychophysical methodology is sufficiently discriminating to distinguish between alternative theories such as additivity or interaction.
7. *Replication* in which it is assumed that there is a sufficiently substantial body of replicated and confirmed data to justify particular theories.
8. *Methodological Constancy* in which it is assumed that our empirical techniques can overcome the adaptive variability of the human observer to produce unstable and non-replicated responses.
9. *Reification of Methodological Effects* in which it is assumed, incorrectly, that findings from cognitive psychological experiments are determined by some kind of psychobiological reality rather than by the utilized experimental methods and protocols, preexisting theories, or a priori hypothetical constructs.

10. *The Transparent Black Box* in which it is assumed that it is possible to determine the inner organization of a closed system by comparing its inputs and outputs (i.e., its behavior).
11. *Taxonomic and Lexicographic Adequacy* in which it is assumed that our definitions and classifications of cognitive processes are sufficiently precise to be quantitatively evaluated.

Unless these assumptions are accepted, one is hard pressed to understand how cognitive–mentalist psychology can proceed and how the aims of cognitive neuroscience, with its goal of localizing putative mental processes to neural modular components, can be fulfilled. The goal of analyzing cognitive processes into their parts demands that virtually all of these assumptions be true. Since all of these assumptions are, at the very least, still the topics of considerable controversy, it is difficult to accept the claims that a modular cognitive theory has the potential to adequately explain human mentation.

1.5.4 Accessibility

The final "big" question to be asked is not one immediately germane to the neuroscientific study of cognition with its neuroreductive goals. It is, however, enormously important for almost all other fields of cognitive research and, at least, of secondary importance to the neuroscientific quest. It would be terribly disappointing if we were searching for something (i.e., the mind) that was not, in fact, accessible to definition, description, or measurement.

This final one of the four questions posed in this section can be stated as: Can mental phenomena actually be accessed by introspective or experimental techniques in a way that permits quantification and scientific analysis? That is, can we really know by inference anything about mental processes beyond their behavioral outcomes? Alternatively–Are mental experiences intrapersonally private as opposed to interpersonally accessible? However it may be phrased, this question must be considered fundamental to any attempt to determine the nature of mental processes and then to reduce or analyze them. Despite the absolute dependence of so much of psychology (especially psychotherapy) on the assumption of mental accessibility, there are many arguments that suggest that, in fact, inaccessibility is actually the rule. Again, I merely list these arguments here and refer my readers to more complete discussion of the accessibility question in Uttal (1998, 2000).

1. Our mental processes are private and not available to public inspection. Therefore one of the prime requirements for scientific investigation–public comparability–is denied.

2. Because previous psychological events influence later ones, there is no possibility of true replication of a cognitive experiment. A kind of psychological uncertainty principle is operational—each intervention changes the state of the system under study.

3. There is no way to determine inner mechanisms from input–output relations. Behavior is thus neutral with regard to mental processes. (See, especially, the discussion on p. 32 of Moore's theorem.)

4. The data are cognitive processing is replete with inconsistencies and empirical reversals indicating a very fragile database on which to base accessibility.

5. A host of empirical findings suggest that subjects do not know why or how they do what they do.

6. Human observers can only report their thoughts after the fact. Thus, by attempting to report what they were thinking they are prone to modify what they were actually thinking. This is only one aspect of what has generally been called "cognitive penetration," a powerful force clouding all direct reports by observers.

7. In many cases we tend to reify observations by ascribing a tangible reality to what had merely been the behavioral outcome of a highly structured experimental protocol. Hypothetical constructs become explanations in a manner that tends to generate misconstrued psychobiological "realities" out of hypotheses. This kind of reification of hypotheses is endemic in psychological laboratories.

Obviously, the interrelated questions of reducibility, analyzability, and accessibility represent some of the most fundamental conundrums in cognitive neuroscience. Yet, they are rarely explicit in the thinking of theoreticians in this important field of human inquiry. In the remainder of this book, we leave behind the esoterica of the nature of theories and these profound questions to examine just what kinds of theories have been developed over the years concerning the relation between the mind and the brain. By examining these theories in the context of this essentially critical analysis of what constitutes a theory, we may be able to both distinguish between the valid and the invalid and achieve a better understanding of what the field of cognitive neuroscience is about.

1.5.5 What Is a Neural Theory of Mind?

We have finally arrived at a point at which it can be asked: What is a neural or psychobiological theory of mind? In its simplest form, a theory of mind is an expression of an idea in which a particular kind of objectively measurable neural activity is assumed to be related to some kind of mental or cognitive activity. This "mental" activity is often associated with some kind of sentience, consciousness, or awareness, perception, or feeling that is neither directly observable nor measurable. In postulating such a relationship, some behavioral or introspective reflection of what is going on in our minds is related to a specific form of neurophysiological activity. As has been shown in the discussion so far in this chapter, the construction of such a relationship is fraught with many conceptual and empirical difficulties, not the least of which is that these inner phenomena are not in any sense accessible, however real mind is.

As one digs deeper for a meaningful answer to the question of what is a theory of mind, however, it becomes clear that the answer is not as simple as we would like. Some philosophers and neuroscientists choose to particularize the problem to a more specific level. For example, Chalmers (2000), concerned with the problems of necessity and sufficiency, referred to a "Neural Correlate of Consciousness" (NCC) and defined it as:

> An NCC is a minimum neural system N such that there is a mapping from states of N to states of consciousness, where a given state of N is sufficient, under conditions C, for the corresponding state of consciousness. (p. 31)

The necessity–sufficiency issue was raised by Chalmers in the following context: Ideally we would wish that a particular N would be both necessary and sufficient to produce a particular mental state. However, Chalmers pointed out quite correctly that different Ns might be able to produce the same mental process. Thus, neither one is necessary and each is sufficient. However, he went on, sufficiency alone can be misleading since it permits other irrelevant aspects of the system to obscure the true correlate. What may be an ubiquitous concomitant may be nothing more than a metabolic background state. Therefore, Chalmers suggested that a further refinement of the concept of sufficiency to one of "minimal sufficiency" is appropriate to "capture what researchers in the field are after when looking for an NCC" (p. 24). By minimal sufficiency, he referred to a property of ". . . a minimal system is whose state is sufficient for the corresponding conscious state" (p. 25).

The very suggestion of a "correlate," however, raises certain problems that are not present in an assumption of identity. First, it is an opening into a kind of mind–brain theorizing suggesting that simple isomorphism, simultaneity, or functional similarity is acceptable as a theory of mind. As we see in later chapters this leads to some fanciful but useless hypothetical answers to this question.

Second, the concept of a *correlate* confuses the issue of causation, an issue I believe should be at the core of any explanation of mind–brain relationships that aspires to completeness.

Third, the idea of a correlate bears within it a dualistic connotation that does not express the intimate relationship of an identity of the neural activity and the mental process.

Fourth, it is possible that the meaning of correlate is not what is meant in a formal statistical sense, but the notion of a correlate or concomitant also inadvertently authenticates a kind of experimental design in which analogies may be misconstrued to be homologies.

Fifth, such a predisposition to correlation carries with it some serious conceptual baggage that may not be justified. One of the most serious is not acknowledging the wisdom of the admonition against spurious correlation by Yule (1926) that "Correlation is not causation."

Sixth, it assumes, without adequate consideration, that the "explanatory gap" (the possibility that there may be an unbridgeable conceptual chasm between the mental and physical domains; Levine, 1983; Beckermann, 2000) is real. This presumption provides succor to the idea that correlation is acceptable as theory and also opens the door to the insidious introduction of dualist ideas.

The following list summarizes what I believe should be the universal properties of any neuroscientific theory of mind, whatever its predilection and orientation.

1. The primary attribute of a neural theory of mind is the ontological assumption that the mind is a function of brain activity. Although it may be constrained and influenced by other aspects of the human body, or ameliorated by such equivocal terms as correlation, in the final analysis, no theory of mind (of the class considered in this book) can be constructed without being founded on this basic assumption. A neural theory of mental activity, should one ever be constructed, would, according to this attribute, be complete. No other entities or processes will be needed to "complete" the explanation. The endorsement of any nonnatural or nonmaterial relationship between the mind and the brain would run counter to the rest of science from the time of Thales to the present.

2. A corollary of 1. is that a true neuroscientific theory of mind must assume that some particular aspect of brain activity is the equivalent of mind; not just any correlated activity. Instead, the particular kind of neural activity that is invoked *IS* the psychoneural equivalent of whatever aspect of our mind is of interest. Deep within all of the neural theories of mind that are considered in later chapters of this book is the implicit assumption that what is observed neurophysiologically is just another way of measuring mental activity (including such hard-to-define concepts as qualia or consciousness). Although some neuroscientists may not agree with this point, without such an implicit assumption of potential completeness, theories can be inadvertently polluted with supernatural ideas and transcend the standards of science.

3. Another general attribute of a neuroscientific theory of mind is that of accepted complexity. With rare exceptions, all current cognitive neuroscientists working in this field accept the Neuron Doctrine—the idea that the nervous system is made up of contiguous, but not continuous, discrete neurons. Whatever measure of brain activity is used, the aggregate information-processing behavior of these abundant and interacting cells is the root equivalent of mental processing. Although there is considerable controversy concerning the means by which neuronal behavior is integrated, it is assumed (admittedly without much direct proof) that the information processing exhibited in the form of differential behavior is mediated by variable synaptic actions.

This, then, brings us to the end of this introductory chapter and introduces us to the topics discussed in the remainder of this book. It should become clear that there is a host of divergent views and theories. It should also be clear that there are solid reasons to argue that the quest for a complete neural explanatory theory of mind is going to be difficult if not impossible.

CHAPTER

2

Mind and Brain Before the Modern Cognitive Neuroscience Era

2.1 INTRODUCTION

In the context of cognitive neuroscience, the idea of a theory is currently embodied as a proposed answer to a very specific question: What is the relationship between mental or cognitive processes and the neural substrate on which mind is based? In other words, What is the neural equivalent of mind? Although we know a considerable amount about how sensory and motor signals are encoded for transmission to and from the brain, how the brain produces whatever it is that we call mind remains obscure.

The question of psychoneural equivalence is not an easy one to answer. Not only is the brain complex, but we still do not have a satisfactory definition of mind. In previous times the word *soul* served the role that mind does now; its seat and nature were the objects of questions comparable to those asked by current cognitive neuroscientists. I use soul here with the understanding that its theological overtones are to be ignored and that soul is, for all practical purposes, synonymous with what modern science now calls mind.

The extreme antiquity of the classic question, however it may have been formulated in terms of an uncertain bodily locus, is unquestioned as well as largely undocumented. Nevertheless, it is clear that humans have been concerned with this issue from the earliest glimmerings of consciousness experienced by our most distant ancestors. In one form or another, the question (and some ingenious as well as some profoundly important answers to it) must have arisen in at least an implicit form at the time the concept of death first loomed in human thought. The first answers to what was initially called the soul–body problem, then, the mind–body problem, and ultimately the mind–brain problem, were most likely that the mind and the body were not inexorably bound together. Rather, the terror of the concept of the transitory nature of one's personal consciousness (cognitive mortality), made so terribly obvious by the impermanence and corruption of the body, led early on to the suggestion of a separate kind of reality for the soul cum mind and the body cum brain.

From this initial hypothesis emerged virtually all ancient and modern religions as well as a substantial amount of contemporary philosophy and, just possibly, many mentalist psychological theories. My own version of this history is spelled out in an earlier work (Uttal, 2004) and does not bear repeating. However, it can be briefly argued that a profound fear of death was the original source of religion as people tried to provide an escape hatch from the terror of the extinction of their personal consciousness. The earliest theories of the relationship between mind and brain, therefore, were essentially dualisms expressing in one form or another the idea that mental processes and body processes represented two different levels of reality and existence. The persistent and central assumption of modern dualism is that the mind does not depend on the body's existence. It is currently assumed by a very large proportion of the world's population it can continue to exist long after the body is gone.

From these ancient questions concerning the relation between soul and body emerged modern physiological psychology, psychobiology, biopsychology, cognitive neuroscience, or whatever other name this science may have been endowed with over its history. In the case of modern science, the fundamental philosophy has been monist rather than dualist, expressing the axiomatic assumption that there is only one level of reality and that all mental processes are nothing more or less than manifestations or processes of the activities of the brain.

In these few words are the topics discussed in the later chapters of this book further specified. My purpose in writing this book is to review and criticize those theoretical answers that have been proposed describing the relationship between the mind and the brain. I consider the naturalist, materialist, monist, and (specifically) "scientific" alternatives to classical dualist theories that are characterized by neuroscientific postulates.

However, it is important to understand the historical forces that determined how we got to the theoretical positions now held by modern cognitive neuroscientists. To do so, it is necessary to explore the history of the problem. This chapter considers some ideas from antiquity that are clearly out of step with the modern view of the mind interpreted exclusively as a product of neural activity. This distant and remote history is an important part of the story and it would be incomplete not to note some of these predecessors of modern scientific mind–brain theories. We must consider the fact that many of the concepts that dominate our thinking today are influenced by ideas that emerged as long as several thousand years ago.

2.2 THE EARLIEST GREEK NATURAL SCIENCE

The most appropriate place to begin this discussion of mind–brain theory is with the classical Greek natural philosophers. It is to this small land that many of the most cherished ideas of Western civilization can be traced. In particular, it was there, it is now generally agreed, that the prevailing supernatural view of the world began to give way to a natural view. It is difficult to find any significant thought prior to this time that was not phrased in terms of the Gods and Goddesses and other supernatural entities.

Prior to the 7th century BCE supernatural forces of many kinds were universally thought to play a conscious and intentional role in influencing the lives of humans. Even the classical Egyptian medical documents, for example the longest and most detailed of them all—the Ebers papyrus (dated to 1534 BCE), which was remarkably insightful in terms of medical treatment, attributed wounds and illnesses to malevolent spirits. This document begins with incantations to defend against the supposed supernatural causes of disease and injury. Egyptian physicians were also priests and supernatural as well as natural "treatments" were simultaneously applied in the medical practices of this ancient civilization. Although the Greek scholars of whom we now speak also continued to honor their Olympian Gods, it is clear that it was there that some of the foundation nontheological ideas of modern scientific thought first emerged.

From what are now only partially understood beginnings, early Greek scholars broke with the theologies of the past to provide the attitudes, the methodology, and the substance of a new approach to the study of mental and physical objects and events. Indeed, we can trace the very idea of theoretical and scientific explanation back to those times. In preview, Table 2.1 lists a few of the most significant players in the development of early Greek natural science and, in particular, the development of our current ideas about the nature of the relationship between the mind and the brain.

2.2.1 Question: Who Was the First Theoretician? Answer: Thales of Miletus!

The histories of the earliest religions are replete with ideas and concepts purporting to explain the relation between the body and the soul. However, until the 7th century BCE virtually all theories were submerged in the mysteries of the supernatural. The current dominant scientific concept of a

TABLE 2.1
The Classical Greek Natural Philosophers—The Protoscientists
(All Dates BCE)

- 624–546 Thales
- 610–546 Anaximander
- 582–497 Pythagoras
- 570–500 Anaximenes
- 556–469 Heraclitus
- 500–428 Anaxagoras
- 492–432 Empedocles
- 469–399 Socrates
- 460–361 Hippocrates
- 460–370 Democritus
- 440–??? Leucippus
- 428–327 Plato
- 384–322 Aristotle

purely materialist, naturalist, or monist view of the world is quite distinct from those early dualist ideas.

Considering the fragmentary nature of evidence from the distant past, we should not have expected that the question of who was the first naturalist theoretician could be answered. Nevertheless, it is surprising to discover that modern historians believe that, in point of historical fact, this question actually has an answer. Increasingly, the Greek polymath—Thales of Miletus (634–546 BCE)[1]—is credited with the initiation if not the invention of a naturalist and materialist approach to theories of both the mental and physical world. It is, of course, possible that Thales was not an individual but a mythical personification of an emerging intellectual trend; nevertheless his historical existence seems to be more solid than some of the quasi-mythological characters that grace other times and other places.

We have no direct record of Thales' writing but he is frequently cited both by Plato and Aristotle, as well as their predecessors Diogenes and Hippias, as being the source of the insight—"The soul is the source of movement." This idea is an intellectual precursor of theories that have persisted to modern times. Specifically, it is a harbinger of work that emerged full blown in the 19th century with the emergence of Weber and Fechner's psychophysics as well as the modern fields of biomechanics. Even if the vo-

[1]The exact dates of the birth or death of any of the classic Greek natural philosophers discussed in this section are always shrouded in uncertainty. Even the best-documented dates are doubtful and some are only indirectly known through histories that were written centuries or more later. Please take any of the dates presented here with a large grain of salt. Often several dates have been provided for an individual by historians. I arbitrarily picked the ones from my research that seem the most often quoted or the most plausible, usually because of the sequence of ideas rather than any precision of historical record.

cabulary is a bit stilted, it says as well as we can today that the brain–mind controls behavior.

Because there are no extant copies of anything that Thales actually wrote (and there is some residual doubt that he actually wrote anything) there is a substantial amount of controversy in historical circles concerning his thoughts on the role of the supernatural. Philosophers who followed him suggested he had also proposed that "everything is full of the gods"; but modern historians suggest this phrase was more likely to have been added by his successors. In fact, such a statement would contradict much of what has otherwise been attributed to him, specifically his essentially modern materialism.[2] Indeed, since all of Thales' ideas have come down to us through second, third, and higher order quotations, it is often unclear what he said, much less what he actually meant.

It does not take long as one reads the literature on classical Greek philosophy to appreciate the uncertainties that plague this field. The problems that keep us from developing an unambiguous understanding of what was really meant by the ancient personages in this field are multiple. First, some of the most prominent left no direct statements of their thoughts. Second, those writings that were preserved are sometimes edited, translated, interpreted, and adapted to their own interests by the scholars and scribes who repeated and re-transcribed earlier works. Third, the exact meaning of the words and sentences that we do have are not always clear. Fourth, even some words familiar to us had different meanings attached to them by the ancients. Finally, early writings of these pioneering natural philosophers are not always internally consistent descriptions of the ideas, which themselves may have been muddy. In short, the fog between their expression and our reading remains thick and controversy is the usual state of affairs. My goal is in this chapter is to convey the generally accepted ideas and to point out historical controversy where it exists.

The salient fact about Thales was, as far as we know from his successors, that he was the first scholar in the western world[3] to suggest mainly natural explanations for a wide range of phenomena that were subsequently considered to be the targets of the sciences. He was a prototype of the mathemati-

[2]There is no question that there is a serious historical problem in teasing apart what may have been merely a pro forma acknowledgment of the contemporary religion from a serious commitment to the supernatural. Evidence for the independence of the natural ideas of these early Greeks from serious theological commitments remains a continuing problem in any study of the times. The discrepancy between a deep commitment and a "cursory tip of the hat" is most clearly evidenced later in this chapter when I discuss the famous Hippocratic oath.

[3]In this chapter, I emphasize the contributions of the Greek natural philosophers. Although it has long been assumed that the Eastern world (e.g., China) fell behind in this new development, the debate over how much was achieved there has recently been rekindled by Lloyd and Sivin (2002). Their treatise compares development in the sciences in the East and the West and attributes whatever differences did exist in scientific thinking to cultural differences. The main differ-

cian, geologist, astronomer, physicist, engineer, and philosopher as well as having expressed some of the earliest ideas that could be considered to be scientifically psychological. His enduring fame was based on the fact that, as far as we know, he was the individual who initiated a major reformation in human thought. In this new intellectual world, the Gods were set aside as mythical explanations of natural phenomena and natural causes were substituted as theories. Indeed, as we explore the writings and thoughts of the Greek philosophers in this chapter, there is a remarkable absence of any allusion to Zeus or any of his colleagues. Although there were vestigial dualistic overtones to the separation of the body and the mind, both of these domains of reality were considered by these pioneers as natural.

Thales, for example, was one of the first to answer the question—Of what is the world made?—in a natural, materialist sense. His answer was that the primary substance or principle was water. Of course, he was not correct in the details, but Thales' answer was likely to have been the first purely naturalist theory of nature. At the very least, for initiating purely materialist ideas, he is acknowledged to be the father of Greek science; at most, he was the first citizen of the world properly to be called a natural philosopher, or as we know it these days, a scientist.

Historians now believe that Thales was also the first to suggest a purely monistic solution to the mind–body problem. As Matthews (2000) puts it:

> The conclusion of the argument from Thales seems quite compatible with a soul's being, rather than a substance in its own right, merely an attribute, or a power, of certain bodies—a power of magnets, for example. (p. 133)

This monist conceptualization of the soul or mind as a function of the body (later to be particularized to the brain) is exceedingly modern. Although the idea was to be challenged by dualist philosophies throughout the rest of human history, this was still an intellectual breakthrough that represents the basic assumption of contemporary cognitive neuroscience.

Among Thales' other important developments were his theorems in geometry, and his role as a precursor of the great Pythagoras, who was known as the father of geometry. However, it is within this specific context that Thales begins to take on an almost mythological role. The few historical allusions to him suggest he had traveled to Egypt as a youth and perhaps brought back with him much of the practical geometrical lore that the Egyptians must certainly used in their massive construction projects.

Was there a real Thales? Or, was he only the personification in later writings of many of the intellectual developments of this budding period of clas-

---

entiating factor, in their analysis, was the patronage of science by the emperors of China in contrast to the relative freedom from political interference enjoyed by the Greeks. In any event, our scientific history was influenced mainly by the Greeks and it is their story that is told here.

sical Greek natural philosophy? So much is attributed to him that it is difficult to conceive of a single individual contributing so much. A real polymath or not, the first theoretician, or a mythical personification of the times, clearly Thales was a marker in the history of human thought. From his time on, a reformation, a renaissance, of human thinking occurred that was to become science as we know it today.

Unfortunately, it must be acknowledged that Thales and his naturalist and materialist followers have not won the battle between the natural and the supernatural, even to our times. Nevertheless, a seed was planted then of a scientific approach toward explanation and description of the world in which we live. Even though it still may be a minority view in a world still obsessed with the supernatural, the contributions Thales, his contemporaries, and his materialist successors, made set the world on a new way of thinking that has enriched human existence ever since.

For the reader interested in pursuing more details about the life and work of Thales, I recommend the recent book by O'Grady (2002).

2.2.2 Anaximander

The pre-Socratic Milesian school of philosophy was started by Thales but was also graced by a succession of his distinguished students and followers. Collectively they exerted a powerful influence on subsequent Greek thought. Although shrouded in uncertainty because of the limited historical records and almost always paraphrased (sometimes in questionable ways by later interpreters and copyists) Miletus was arguably the original home of modern science, as we know it.

We do know from later Greek writers that the immediate students and colleagues of Thales also made their mark in Greek science and philosophy. For example, Thales' astronomical ideas were further developed by his student Anaximander (610–546 BCE). The student particularized the master's general ideas, particularly in the field of cosmology. Anaximander proposed a surprisingly modern concept—a boundless universe—that was distinctly different from the bounded idea of the dome of the visible sky that was popular at his time. The idea of an unbounded universe can also be interpreted as an alternative to a personalized concept of a supernatural God narrowly confined to the interests of the known world. Unfortunately, the little we know of Anaximander's thoughts leave this issue of the role of an unbounded universe as an explicit alternative to supernatural ideas unclear at best. Inherent in it, however, are harbingers of indeterminacy and infinity that were to become major topics of scientific interest only millennia later.

Anaximander's work is directly known only by means of a single fragment of his writing and secondary sources. He was quoted by Aristotle

(384–322 BCE), later by Theophrastus (371–287 BCE) (Aristotle's student and successor as director of the Lyceum), and then much later by Simplicius (490–560 CE).[4] Even this fragment, as ambiguous and partial as it was, was enormously significant because it probably represented the first preserved piece of Greek scientific writing. It reads:

> The things that are perish into the things out of which they came to be, according to necessity, for they pay penalty and retribution to each other for their injustice in accordance with the ordering of time, *as he says in rather poetical language*. (Quoted from Simplicius by McKirahan, 1994, p. 43, italics added)

Unfortunately the authenticity of this fragment as a true quotation of Anaximander is challenged by the last seven words—seven words that strongly indicate the possibility of a paraphrasing of the original comment. The opacity of the ancient Greek language used here also raises questions about what Anaximander meant. At least one interpretation, however, raises the possibility that he had some insight into the cycles of nature ("things that are perish into the things out of which they came to be") as well as the increase in entropy ("they pay penalty . . .") with each successive generation. If he did appreciate these subtleties, Anaximander must have been a remarkable intellect, indeed.

Anaximander, like his mentor Thales, was also a man of many interests. In addition to his cosmological theories of the "boundless" universe, biological ideas were attributed to him that were especially notable in that they represented an early form of evolutionary theory. He proposed, again according to later writers, that life first emerged in the form of fish and humans evolved from this primitive state. Not exactly Darwinian in its breadth and magnificence; nevertheless, it still incorporated the basic idea of a progressive succession of forms—an advanced concept that is still not held by a majority of the world's population.

2.2.3 Anaximenes

The dates of another of the Milesian scientific philosophers—Anaximenes—are even more uncertain than those of his predecessors. Some partial evidence suggests he was born about 570 BCE and died about 500 BCE. All that

---

[4]It must not be forgotten that although the history discussed here occurred 2,500 years before our times, a couple of hundred years passed between the time of the contemporaries Thales and Anaximander (7th and 6th centuries BCE), and Aristotle and Theophrastus (4th and 3rd centuries BCE). This was a time in which written manuscripts were few and far between and those that did exist were frequently destroyed in the fires that swept some of the great classic libraries of the time. The obscurity of these most ancient times is, therefore, fully understandable. Even the great Aristotle's writing has survived by a series of almost unbelievable accidents, mainly in the Arabic world during the medieval years.

is known of his time was that he was younger than Anaximander, as some of his ideas seem to be derivative or successive. The written work of Anaximenes, however, fared better than that of his Milesian predecessors; it was more fully preserved and much more is known directly of his ideas.

For Anaximenes, the individual's soul was equivalent to air, which was also the primary substance of the world. The sun, moon, and, stars were, however, made of fire. Again it is Simplicius who conveys (through McKirahan, 1994) a quotation attributed to Anaximenes but which had been passed on by the earlier writing of Theophrastus:

> Anaximenes . . . like Anaximander, declares that the underlying nature is one and APERION, but not indeterminate as Anaximander held, but definite, saying that it is air. It differs in rarity and density according to the substance [it becomes]. Becoming finer it come to be fire; being condensed it comes to be wind, then cloud, and when still further condensed it becomes water, then earth, then stones, and the rest come to be out of these. (McKirahan, 1994, p. 48)

The theory that the basic stuff of nature is air is certainly not modern, but it still was founded on the assumption that natural, rather than supernatural, forces were responsible for the world in which we lived. What is generally important about the Milesian natural philosophers, therefore, is that collectively they initiated and developed a natural, material, and scientific theoretical approach to explaining the nature of the world that still provides the foundation of enlightened modern thought. This is as revolutionary an idea as one can find throughout the course of world history!

2.3 THE POST-MILESIAN DEVELOPMENT OF GREEK SCIENCE

2.3.1 Pythagoras

Pythagoras of Samos (582–497 BCE) was a contemporary of the Milesian natural philosophers and may have actually studied with them in Miletus or heard them lecture as they traveled about Greece. Whatever the source of his ideas, there is no question that the early mathematical and astronomical ideas that he had encountered at Miletus were extremely important in determining the course of Pythagoras' career. After many adventures, including becoming an Egyptian priest, he returned to Greece and started an academy in Croton that taught that mathematics explains reality better than any other language or method. Indeed, a prime tenet of the Pythagorean School was that the universe was a "number." This idea is reflected in modern physical thought in which it is argued by some physicists that successful mathematical theory is the final goal of their science. Although string theory and analytic geometry represent vastly different levels of mathematical sophistication, the modern foundation assumption of the primacy of mathematical representation is not too dissimilar from the Pythagorean ideal.

Although it only modestly diminished his role in scientific history, Pythagoras was heavily influenced by supernatural ideas and by the mystical nature of the numbers that were supposed to represent things. Pythagorism is closely linked to Orphism, a preexisting religious concept that invoked a Buddhist-like cycle of reincarnation and the immortality of the soul.

Despite this overtone of the supernatural and their religious fervor, Pythagoras and his school gave us some of the most basic and significant theorems of mathematics that have persisted to this day. Among these is his namesake—The Pythagorean Theorem—as well as many other ideas concerning the natural of geometrical forms. For example, such fundamentals as "the sum of the angles of a triangle is equal to two right angles (180°)" were first enunciated by the Pythagoreans. This is a basis of the Newtonian world that persisted until the dawn of the 20th century.

More than these specific theorems, however, was Pythagoras' assertion that the basic nature of the universe is mathematical and that mathematics can give us insights into its nature. Although his approach was contaminated to a degree by the concept that mathematics had mystical significance, his purely scientific contribution emerges as one of the great milestones of human thought.

2.3.2 Heraclitus

Heraclitus of Ephesus (556–469 BCE) also answered the question of what the world is made by invoking fire, water, and earth and the sequences in which they were intertransformed. This was the next step into what was to become the four-substance idea that was popular for many centuries to come. However, like the special role of water as proposed by Thales or of air as proposed by Anaximenes, fire was given priority; it was the basic substance by means of which the other substances of which the world was made interacted. The ephemeral nature of fire permitted it thus to be the "currency" or measure by which all other substances could be evaluated. Thus, fire was not unique but it was common to all other matter. In his words:

> This world-order, the same of all, no God nor man did create, but it ever was and is and will be: ever-living fire, kindling in measures and being quenched in measures. (Diels-Kranz, 1966/1967[5])

[5]Diels and Kranz (1966/1967) is a reprinting of a 19th-century collection of pre-Socratic writings by these two authors. It has been reprinted regularly and is now used as the standard source of these ancient writings. This quotation is from a secondary source.

And

> All things are an exchange for fire and fire for all things, as goods for gold and gold for goods (or, as money for gold and gold for money). (McKirahan, 1994)

The notion of the eternity of time inherent in the first of these quotations is a harbinger of questions to be asked in a more formal manner up to modern times. That is, how old is the universe? Heraclitus' answer is still an acceptable alternative today even in the context of modern cosmology's "big bang" theory. Incidentally, Heraclitus is often credited with the first use of the word cosmos (i.e., "world-order" in the usual translation).

Heraclitus was one of the first of the classic Greek natural philosophers to leave us particular writings about the nature of the soul. To him, the soul was another manifestation of fire. It seems clear now that the predominant idea about the soul, however it may have been instantiated among the Greeks as either a natural or supernatural process, was of something that survived after the death of the body. However, as befits their natural philosophy orientation, this duality was not expressed as a supernatural or religious property, but rather as another way in which the natural world expressed itself.

Whether these pre-Socratic philosophers believed in a personal afterlife or not is likely always to be controversial, their writings on this subject being both rare in number and ambiguous in style. (In fact, none of their writing has been directly preserved. All we have are fragments as quotations in later books such as those of Aristotle.) It is more likely that their theories of the mind were always mixed, to at least some degree, with then current prevalent religious ideas. The important conclusion is that the nature of the soul and the supernatural expressed by these natural philosophers was very different than the theologies of their contemporaries. Their emphasis throughout was on the natural processes that accounted for the soul/mind as an aspect of the natural and material world.

2.3.3 Empedocles

Empedocles of Acragas (492–432 BCE) is given credit for combining the four substances of natural existence into a single, comprehensive theory. For him, the existence of all matter was accounted for collectively by earth, fire, water, and air. These four different entities constituted what now must be considered to be the preliminary Greek version of the elements of nature. Empedocles suggested they could be combined in various ways and in various proportions to produce all of the different materials of the world—an interesting precursor to the molecular theory of matter that guides modern science.

Interestingly, Empedocles not only suggested these elements, but introduced a new idea, that of controlling forces ("Love" and "Strife") that could account for the ways in which their combinations could be attracted to or repelled by each other, respectively. The notion of basic units attracted or repelled by distinctive forces reflects ideas that were not to mature for another 2,500 years. Of course, the meaning of these words was probably very different to Empedocles than it is to moderns. However, it is not difficult to see these words as conceptual precursors of the modern ideas of magnetic or gravitational attraction and repulsion.

Like Heraclitus, Empedocles expressed a theory of the human mind in his proposition that the soul was specifically associated with fire—one of the basic roots of nature. In doing so both of these natural philosophers linked together the natural material world with the psychological world and set the stage for the reductionist theories of mind that were to come.

Empedocles also suggested a primitive version of how visual perception occurs. Along with such other philosophers as Democritus and Aristotle, he proposed that visual perception was accounted for by "effluences" from the viewed object. The effluences made their way to the eye where they were collected by receptive "pores." The interesting point about this hypothesis was that it was contrasted with the then much more popular idea that the eye emitted a stream of particles ("light" or "fire") that interacted with an object to account for its perception. This latter hypothesis of an "extramission" or "ray" theory was held by Alcmaeon, Plato, Euclid, and Galen among many others. We now know that Empedocles was more correct than not; nothing emanates from the eye but *particles* (*photons* as we now know them) move from the object to the eye where these photons are selectively absorbed by *pores* or *photoreceptors* in modern terminology. The modern "intromission" idea that the eye received particles was not definitively established until the time of the Arab scholars Al-Kindi (?–866) and Alhazen (965–1039). An elegant discussion of this controversy can be found in Lindberg (1976).

2.3.4 Anaxagoras

It should be clear by now that one of the great scientific questions for which an answer was being sought by these classical Greek natural philosophers concerned the material of which the world was constructed. What is unique in this emerging theoretical structure among the pre-Socratic philosophers was what distinguished it from their sometimes simultaneous theological views. It is uncertain if the natural philosophers discussed here were apostates from the prevailing polytheisms of the highly personal Greek Gods and Goddesses or free-thinkers of a kind rare in their times.

Into this melange of intellectual crosscurrents and controversy came another one of the giants of the classical Greek world—Anaxagoras of Clazomenae (500–428 BCE). Although Clazomenae, his birthplace, is in Asia Minor, an exceedingly important claim made of Anaxagoras' career was that he was the individual who brought pre-Platonic and pre-Aristotelean philosophy and science to Athens, the city to which so much of the magnificent subsequent product of Greek philosophy has been attributed.

It was also Anaxagoras who further developed the primitive idea of the world as a composite of various amounts of fire, water, air, and earth to what can be considered to be a prototype of the modern atomic theory of matter. His proposition was that the world was composed of an infinite number of infinitely small "seeds" of many kinds and varieties. Anaxagoras' version of an atomic theory, however, was unlike the modern version in that it suggested that each small seed contained all of the seeds that were found at higher levels and that lower level seeds were identical in all respects to those of the higher level. This extraordinary suggestion also has a modern intellectual descendent—fractal theory (Mandelbrot, 1983)—which invokes the idea of infinite regress of replication of the shapes of the components of complex figures.

Anaxagoras also made contributions to the early psychological theories. He was among the first to suggest that the source of bodily motion was mental. Specifically, it has been suggested that the word *mind* was first coined by him. If so, he set into action the queries and questions, problems and challenges, and advantages and disadvantages of the science that was to become psychology and ultimately cognitive neuroscience.

2.3.5 Hippocrates

It is not certain that Hippocrates of Cos (460–377 BCE) should be considered a "philosopher" in the same sense as others in this chapter. In fact, his writings were filled with attacks on what he considered to be untested current theories of his contemporaries. Nevertheless, Hippocrates brought an entirely new idea into medical science. Obviously responding to the earlier naturalistic teachings of his predecessors, who had mainly been interested in the physical world, he was the strongest ancient proponent of the idea that illness was not due to possession by demons or evil spirits; rather, to him, it was the response of a body to natural causes. Until his time, the prevailing view attributed illness or injury to the will of malevolent supernatural entities. I have already mentioned the Egyptian combination of medical and religious rituals in their ancient documents. Up until the time of Hippocrates, Greek medicine had been largely a function of priests such as the mythical Asclepius, himself perhaps originally a priestly healer or shaman, who was later to be deified as the God of Medicine.

Known as the "Father of Modern Medicine," Hippocrates made his student physicians take an oath that is still used as the central element of medical school graduation ceremonies. It is worthwhile reproducing it here as it illustrates a completely different approach to illness than the one that had dominated so much of history prior to his time. Although it begins with an obligatory nod to the Greek Gods, the content of the Hippocratic oath is materialist and practical in the Milesian tradition.

> I swear by Apollo Physician and Asclepius and Hygieia and Panaceia and all the gods and goddesses, making them my witnesses, that I will fulfil according to my ability and judgment this oath and this covenant:
>
> To hold him who has taught me this art as equal to my parents and to live my life in partnership with him, and if he is in need of money to give him a share of mine, and to regard his offspring as equal to my brothers in male lineage and to teach them this art—if they desire to learn it—without fee and covenant; to give a share of precepts and oral instruction and all the other learning to my sons and to the sons of him who has instructed me and to pupils who have signed the covenant and have taken an oath according to the medical law, but no one else.
>
> I will apply dietetic measures for the benefit of the sick according to my ability and judgment; I will keep them from harm and injustice.
>
> I will neither give a deadly drug to anybody who asked for it, nor will I make a suggestion to this effect. Similarly I will not give to a woman an abortive remedy. In purity and holiness I will guard my life and my art.
>
> I will not use the knife, not even on sufferers from stone, but will withdraw in favor of such men as are engaged in this work.
>
> Whatever houses I may visit, I will come for the benefit of the sick, remaining free of all intentional injustice, of all mischief and in particular of sexual relations with both female and male persons, be they free or slaves.
>
> What I may see or hear in the course of the treatment or even outside of the treatment in regard to the life of men, which on no account one must spread abroad, I will keep to myself, holding such things shameful to be spoken about.
>
> If I fulfil this oath and do not violate it, may it be granted to me to enjoy life and art, being honored with fame among all men for all time to come; if I transgress it and swear falsely, may the opposite of all this be my lot. (Quoted from Edelstein, 1943)

This is the classic version of the oath. Although adapted and modernized for today's medical school graduation ceremonies, the same natural science tone dating from the time of Hippocrates still persists. For those interested in the modern version, the version by Louis Lasagna most often used today can be found at the web site http://www.pbs.org/wgbh/nova/doctors/oath_modern.html

Hippocrates' magnificent contribution was not only to further naturalize what had been a form of medicine based on supernatural concepts but also to start, with the formation of his academy on the island of Cos, a long lasting tradition of specialized medical school training. His school produced many of the medical texts that influenced medicine for almost 2,000 years, not only in method but also in a natural theoretical approach to the science of medicine.

Although the Egyptians had a good idea of the relation between brain injuries and behavioral changes, Hippocrates was also one of the first of the Greeks to explicitly express the idea that the brain can control bodily functions. His diagnosis of epilepsy as a brain disease marked an important instance in which mental experiences (loss of consciousness) was specifically attributed to brain dysfunction. He also wrote about how the brain was responsible for sensory experience as well as cognitive processing. Hippocrates' famous and oft-quoted comments summarize his essentially modern point of view concerning the relation of the brain and the mind:

> Men ought to know that from the brain and from the brain only arise our pleasures, joys, laughter and jests, as well as our sorrows, pains, grieves and tears.

These ideas were harbingers of a theory of natural mind–brain relationships that were not to fully mature for many centuries. In the interim, the heart, and the ventricles of the brain, as well as a variety of other organs, bodily fluids, and vapors were suggested as the medium of the mind.

2.3.6 Democritus

Democritus of Abdera (460–370 BCE) is usually credited with the enunciation of the earliest atomic theory of nature. However, as I discuss in this chapter, the idea that reality was subdivided into different kinds of material had a long history prior to his time (e.g., see the discussion on Anaxagoras on p. 61). Indeed, Leucippus (who may or may not have lived some 50 or 100 years prior to Democritus) is sometimes credited for an earlier version of atomic theory. It seems possible, furthermore, according to some historians, that Leucippus' writing was simply inserted into that of Democritus either by Democritus himself or some of the scribes who worked in the centuries that followed.

Leucippus had another claim to fame. One prescient statement is attributed to him:

> Naught happens for nothing, but all things from a ground (logos) and of necessity.

This is certainly a harbinger of 17th-century (CE) Newtonian principles, specifically the first law:

> Every object in a state of uniform motion tends to remain in that state of motion unless an external force is applied to it.

Whatever contributory role Leucippus played in antedating Democritus' atomic ideas, it is the latter that history most completely remembers as the originator of this precursor to modern physical theories. Democritus' atomic theory was different than ours in detail but surprisingly modern in some of its general assumptions. He took exactly the opposite theoretical position to the universal stability of nature and the impossibility of empty space originally championed by another important Greek natural philosopher, Paramenides. He (Democritus) accepted the idea of empty space between his hypothetical atoms. In doing so he ascribed a material reality to the universe, not the illusory role that his predecessors, such as Paramenides, and his successors, such as Bishop George Berkeley (1685–1753), adopted.

Democritus' atoms were quite remarkably modern: They were eternal, indivisible, and existed in number of different kinds. They could combine to form new substances (molecules in our modern terminology) including the classic four substances—water, air, fire, and earth—of the traditional theory that held sway prior to his version of the atomic theory. The extraordinary thing is how close these "atoms" were to theoretical developments that did not mature until the 20th century. As one historian said, it was the "best guess of antiquity."

Democritus also expanded upon the initial version of the atomic theory to provide another early psychobiological theory of mind—or soul, as he referred to it. Building on the ideas of Heraclitus, he believed the soul was made up of atoms of fire. However, his location of the soul cum mind differed greatly from the usual practice of the time of assigning mental functions to the heart. Democritus was one of the first of the Greeks to locate the soul as a seat of cognitive processing in the brain[6] rather than the heart, referring to the brain as the "guardian of thoughts and intelligence."

---

[6]There is no question that Democritus was not the first to make the assertion that the soul/mind was in the brain. Clearly, much earlier expressions of such an idea had been suggested by the ancient Egyptian and Sumerian priest–physicians. However, the mainstream of theory at those earlier times placed it in the heart. Democritus' assertion that the brain was the seat of the mind had also been preceded by other Greeks, such as Alcmaeon, and followed by Plato, Erasistratus, and Herophilus and ultimately by the Roman school of physicians including Galen. The most notable exception to this idea was—surprisingly—the great Aristotle who placed the mind's source in the heart. On this issue, however, Aristotle was decidedly wrong. This "cardiac" theory of mind was a regression from the correct view of the brain as the seat of conscious activity that had achieved considerable acceptance by the time of Plato, his teacher. One wonders how this mistake was made and if it was not, in some way, a simple negative reaction to the teaching of his master that was made possible by the uncertainty at that time concerning this fundamental topic.

Leucippus (if he ever existed) and Democritus continued the Milesian tradition of a purely materialist explanation of the world. They moved far ahead of their predecessors in terms of the nature of the constituent components. However, they also maintained what was becoming the basic scientific idea that the events of the world were determined by physical forces and not by the machinations of supernatural beings. Furthermore, there was an implicit suggestion embedded in their point of view—the concept that there was no teleological raison d'être for the events of human life. Democritus proposed that the motion of his atoms was random, their combination equally so, and, therefore, so, too, was the fate of humanity. His model of a probabilistic universe, therefore, was a harbinger of another modern theory of matter—quantum mechanics.

2.3.7 Aristotle

It may seem surprising to some of my readers that after paying so much attention to the less well known early Greek philosophers, that I should pass so quickly two of the great names of Greek philosophy—Socrates (469–399 BCE) and Plato (428–347 BCE). There is a reason for this allocation of space and emphasis. The people and the ideas that have been discussed were part of what has been called the pre-Socratic period, just as the immediately following times were designated the Socratic epoch. The reason for this line of demarcation is that a major sea change occurred in the Greek philosophy following Democritus and Paramenides that lasted for about 100 years. For reasons that are still not completely understood, the early natural philosophers or protoscientists who preceded Socrates were largely replaced by a group of Athenians who were more concerned with ethics, logic, morality, politics, and other humanistic topics than with what we would now call science. Socrates was the most prominent and influential person in this change of dominant topics; because of his influence and prestige, he was largely responsible for what has to be considered by some historians to be a lacuna in scientific thought during this period. Socrates' philosophical transformation not only marked the transition from a primary concern with the natural physical and biological worlds to an emphasis on the social world of human intercourse for him personally, but also for the mass of Greek philosophers of the period and for many who followed.

Both Socrates and his student Plato had relatively little to do with the kind of scientific thinking that had been such a central part of their predecessors' activities. Plato, in particular, postulated a dualist explanation of the relation between the mind and the brain that was quite unlike the naturalist tradition initiated at Thales' Miletus. Thus, the contribution of these two giants to the history of neuroscientific theory is less than would otherwise have been expected. Indeed, however much they contributed to humanity in other contexts, it is difficult to identify any major development in *scientific* thought in the century during which Socrates and Plato were the most important philosophers of ancient Greece.

It fell to Plato's greatest student, Aristotle of Macedonia (384–322 BCE) to rejuvenate the kind of natural philosophy that truly can be called scientific. Aristotle lived an eventful life following his early studies with Plato in Athens. He was tutor to Alexander the Great for 5 years following 343 BCE and enjoyed continued support from him as Alexander went on to conquer much of the known world. A patron such as Alexander could do and did do much for this particular scholar's career!

It was Aristotle's tenure as leader of a new academy—the Lyceum—in Athens (to which he returned after an interval of 13 years following his departure from Plato's school) that anchored his fame throughout history. He became one of the most prolific authors of the ancient world, a world that has memorialized him as one of the great polymaths and most creative thinkers of human history. For several reasons (devoted students, later librarians, and the random events of history) his work was preserved much better than any other sage of the classical Greek period.

Despite the previous 300 years of speculative concern with natural philosophy, it was Aristotle's work that marked the beginning of experimental science as we know it. He not only collected and organized much of the factual knowledge of biology and physics that was to guide the world for the following millenium, but can be credited with some of the earliest developments of the empirical scientific method that lie at the foundation of the most modern sciences.

The works of Aristotle include an enormous range of topics. He wrote about logic, biology, physics, in addition to the humanistic topics stressed by his predecessors Socrates and Plato. Most germane to this present book, Aristotle may also be singled out as one of the first psychologists, although it is certain he never used the word. His great treatise on the human mind *De Anima* (see the Hicks translation, Aristotle, 1976) was his main contribution to this very important topic.

In *De Anima*, Aristotle asked the fundamental question that still guides modern physiological psychology cum modern cognitive neuroscience: Is the mind just a manifestation of body processes or is it something more and/or different? Given the ubiquitous dualism of his time and the prevailing idea of the mind or soul as representing a separate kind of reality, this is an extraordinary query, far in advance of conventional thinking at those times. Whatever his final conclusions, the very fact of asking the question was clearly a milestone in the naturalist tradition originated by Thales.

As van der Eijk (2000) pointed out, there is a great deal of ambiguity in the surviving writings of Aristotle concerning the relation between the *soul* and the *mind*. In some instances he seems perfectly content to define these mental processes as simple functions of the body, in others he suggests that the two interact in a way that is hardly different than the dualist ideas proposed by Descartes much later.

It is likely that Aristotle himself was not entirely clear on such issues and that the repeated translations may have further muddied the waters of intellectual history. Nevertheless, there is a novel theoretical bridge expressed in much of his writing that suggests his main emphasis was on the natural emergence of the intangible mind and soul from the body's tangible material. Certainly by the time he wrote *De Anima*, the mind or soul–body problem was being discussed in purely material terms.[7]

Aristotle distinguished between the *soul* (psyche) and the *mind* or *intellect* (nous), thus seemingly perpetuating some of the earlier Greek theological ideas concerning the soul. Aristotle's theology, however, was extremely abstract. God was for him an idea or a form, not anthropomorphic in any manner comparable to the way invoked by many of his contemporaries, but, rather, an idealization of the potential of humankind. Indeed, the word "nous" is used either to represent God as pure intellect (although in that context it was usually capitalized—Nous) or as an expression of human cognitive powers (nous).

Aristotle's theoretical suggestion was that the mind is a part or subcomponent of the soul and that mind's major role was to carry out the cognitive processes (e.g., reasoning and planning) that led to understanding. The soul for him, as just noted, was an idealization of the possible potential toward which humans might strive, through which humans might ultimately share in some kind of an abstract divinity.

The soul, according to another, but not exclusive, interpretation of Aristotle's idea, was that it was the "form of the body." This idea comes very close to the modern view that the mind and the brain are related in the same way as are mechanism and function; the form being an emergent property of the body's material—in particular, for Aristotle, the heart. The two ideas have much in common. Aristotle called this concept "hylomorphism" a word formed from the Greek roots of form—*morphe*—and matter—*hyle*. We call this idea "material monism."

Curiously, Aristotle believed that the soul was not only a human property but also associated with all living things—it was, from this perspective, a "general principle of life." His view was that certain parts or components of the soul were specific to each type of life (e.g., reason to humankind). Psychology, according to Aristotle, was the science of the soul rather than

[7]Van der Eijk (2000) believes that Aristotle's views were, quite simply, internally inconsistent and that both monist and dualist ideas were present in his theory of mind. Given the world in which even the great Aristotle lived was still in the grip of theologies and supernatural concepts, this is hardly a surprise.

of the mind as he respectively defined them. Thus, the word "psychology" was coined to define our science rather than what might have been more appropriately, if less elegantly, "Nousology."

The soul, as Aristotle imagined it, was a universal property that exemplified the highest state of development to which any species could aspire. Since the psyche was a general principle of all forms of life, his science of psychology also necessarily included the study of the soul of many living entities. In addition to his other contributions, Aristotle's natural philosophy thus formed the nucleus of the science we now call comparative psychology. His emphasis on the intimate interaction between the body and the soul also added impetus to what was ultimately to become physiological psychology.

Most important of all of his contributions, Aristotle was a natural philosopher—a scientist—in the truest sense of the term. In many ways his views instantiated one of the major criteria of a modern science—the fundamental assumption that it is essential to appreciate that little progress can be made on unraveling the mind–brain problem (Schopenhauer's "world knot") unless theological and other supernatural ideas are expelled completely. To Aristotle and the Greek natural philosophers who preceded him, we owe an enormous debt for breaking the bonds of the millennia of superstition and religion that had bound the hands of an incipient science until their time. What Thales had initiated, Aristotle brought to fruition and passed along to modern science.

However, it was not just this general naturalist and scientific orientation of Aristotle that was so important but also his compendium of empirical data and interpretations. For example, we can also attribute to Aristotle the fundamental idea that there are five special senses, the organizational theme still used by most modern texts of sensation and perception.[8] His ideas about the senses as the main gateway to knowledge lead us to think of him as the first of the empiricists, a point of view that was not to completely flourish until the British Empiricists made it popular more than a millennium and a half later. His fundamental empiricism was in sharp contrast to the Platonic ideas that reason and thought were the main mechanism of acquiring knowledge.[9]

Aristotle has been interpreted in various ways concerning his view of the possibility of some kind of an afterlife. Curiously, he is usually understood

---

[8]Two exceptions to this "typical" organization are to be found in Pieron (1952) and Uttal (1973). In those two works, the organizational theme is quantity, quality, time, and space. The commonalities of the senses are emphasized by this organization but obscured if one uses the classic Aristotelean scheme of the five senses of vision, audition, olfaction, gustation, and somatosensation.

[9]Plato's point of view has persisted to the present in the form of philosophical or Platonic rationalism.

to have written that the soul per se did not persist. Rather, only one important part of it—the mind—did. This kind of afterlife was described not as a survival of personal consciousness, the usual religious expression of an individual afterlife, but rather as the union of the ideas of the person with the ultimate nature of an abstract intellectual "God." This abstract version of an intellectual ideal played the same role as did a personified God in most religions. Clearly, however, it was a drastically different concept.[10]

The abstractness and elegance of this idea pays high honor to Aristotle whose ideas, though imperfect in detail from our modern perspective, still identify him as one of the greatest of human intellects. His influence has been so enormous that it is not difficult to discern his persisting effect on how current psychologists view their science. As one considers his views, it is surprising how Aristotelean are some of the most basic assumptions on which our science is based. The Milesian natural philosophy tradition, culminating in Aristotle, in particular, revolutionized human thinking about some of the most important questions ever asked by humans. The emphasis on the natural world and material explanations or theories of observable phenomena were drastically different than the way such issues were handled by their precursors in Sumeria, Egypt, the Indus Valley, and China, the other great centers from which civilization emerged. It was in Greece, during the 300-odd years from Thales' birth to the death of Aristotle, that the transition was made from a world of demons and shadows, Gods and Goddesses, and malevolent and benign forces to a world in which the beauty of scientific method and the power of natural theory flourished.

Aristotle was followed by some other extraordinary scholars. The engineer and mathematician Archimedes of Syracuse (287–212 BCE) and the astronomer and mathematician Hipparchus of Nicaea (190–120 BCE) both pursued the work of many other mathematicians, among whom the most prominent was Euclid of Alexandria (325–265 BCE).[11]

Greek natural philosophy did not end with Aristotle or Hipparchus but continued in a somewhat diminished and less influential form through the days of the Roman Empire. Mathematics, in particular, continued to be held in highest esteem[12] by the Romans and many of the "philosophers" of whom

[10]Of interest is the fact that some of the world's newest religions have returned to this idea of a union of the mind with an intangible, disembodied God. In particular, Sikhism and Baha'i both seem to follow the Aristotelean ideal of God as an abstraction rather than a personified entity. See Uttal (2004) for a discussion of their philosophies.

[11]The actual existence of Euclid is still debated. It has been suggested that "Euclid" was actually the name of a school of mathematicians whose members collectively wrote the great book *The Elements* rather than the work of a single individual.

[12]The Roman use of mathematics sometimes transcended its practical or theoretical use. Numbers became the mainstay of what were called the mystery religions in Roman times. Especially prominent were those built around the geometrical ideas of Pythagoras.

we know were actually mathematicians in the tradition of Pythagoras and Euclid. From this foundation, intellectual as well as material progress should have leapt ahead. For reasons that still are not fully understood, this actually did not happen for another 1,800 years. In the interim, other civilizations rose and fell and scientific theory waxed and waned during some very dark years. The most significant influence was the total domination of aggressively warlike cultures such as the Romans and the European "Barbarians" over the more intellectual Greeks.

2.4 NATURAL SCIENCE THEORY DURING THE ROMAN EPOCH

Greece prospered as an association of relatively independent city-states until the last two centuries BCE. However, in 146 BCE the rapidly growing Roman Empire conquered the Greek city Corinth and, soon after that, the entirety of what we now know as Greece along with much of the Greek-influenced world. Roman domination was not too onerous, however, and Greek influence in science, philosophy, and medicine remained strong throughout the Mediterranean for hundreds of years following the fall of Corinth. Hellenist[13] ideas were extremely important in such distant lands as ancient Judea around the time of Christ. Indeed, Greek ideas continued to be influential long after the adoption of Christianity by Constantine for the Roman Empire in 312 after the battle of Milvian Bridge.[14]

Proclus of Constantinople (411–485 CE), the Roman emperor Constantine's "new" city, is usually designated as the "last" of the classical Greek philosophers. Although born in Asia Minor, Proclus actually studied and taught at Plato's Academy which was still a significant educational organization 800 years after its founding. The longevity of the Academy, better than any other single fact, illustrates the continuing influence of Greek thought—an influence that lasted at least until the destruction of the Roman Empire by the invaders from northern Europe and central Asia.

Nevertheless, Roman armies, culture, and perspectives were politically and militarily dominant for more than 600 years following their conquest of Greece and it is to their science and philosophy to which our attention is now directed.

---

[13]The word *Hellenist* is generally used to refer to Greek culture and influence after the time of Alexander and Aristotle.

[14]The outcome of the battle between the two contending Roman emperors, Constantine and Maxientius, was attributed to the appearance of visions of Christian symbols in the sky. Based on his success there against a vastly superior force and these visions, Constantine made Christianity the official religion of a united Roman empire. This mythological explanation ignores the fact that it was very likely that regional politics played a decisive role in this important religio-cultural event.

In spite of the enormous contributions to natural scientific issues that have dominated our discussion so far, a disappointing development occurred at this point vis-à-vis the history of theoretical explanations of natural phenomena. No one can deny the enormous engineering and practical accomplishments of the Roman Empire. However, it must also be acknowledged that following the heady days of Aristotle and the other classical Greek natural philosophers, most of the Greek and Roman philosophers of the Roman era turned away from these protoscientific concerns and returned to the humanistic, ethical, social, and political issues that had dominated the thoughts of Plato and his times. Furthermore, there was a renewed interest in religion and other supernatural themes during the Roman hegemony; Roman theology typically reflected and preserved many of the more conservative theological tenets of Greek thought.[15] Unfortunately, the more abstract and theoretical natural sciences went into a state of decline for many years. How different the world might have been if Roman and Christian theology had not dominated the next two millennia is interesting to contemplate.

Roman philosophy was characterized during much of this period by such schools of thought as Stoicism, Skepticism, and various forms of Neoplatonism. These philosophies, like much of Roman philosophical thought, were traceable back to the 4th century BCE in Greece. Roman stoics regressed even further than just the Platonic concern with the politics and ethics to the belief that the world was made of fire, an idea that had been a part of Heraclitus' ancient cosmology. Democritus and Leucippus would have been terribly upset, should they have survived in one form or another, had they seen how their essentially modern atomic theory was rejected in terms of this antique idea.

The Stoics also preached that one should lead a dispassionate life and not allow the emotions to influence or detract from reasoned analysis. Thus, their name has become associated with a particular life orientation in which passionate responses are minimized. Of main interest to us, however, was the Stoics' introduction of the concept of the pneuma, an idea that was to become the centerpiece of Galen's mind–body theory (see p. 74).

The Skeptics argued that it was not possible to appreciate the real world because everything we know about it was transmitted and processed through our senses. Thus, we were not in direct contact with physical reality. The watchword of the Skeptics was "Nothing is; or if anything is, it cannot be known," a quotation originally attributed to Gorgias of Leontini

[15]Indeed, the Roman pantheon of Gods was virtually congruent with the Greek Gods. A full discussion of the relationship between the two theologies can also be found in Uttal (2004).

(483–378 BCE), a contemporary of Socrates and Plato.[16] With such a philosophy, one that at least accepted the possibility that "nothing is," obviously there would be little interest in that remote and inaccessible "unreal" real world. As a result, explanatory scientific theory fell, once again, into the scientific doldrums much as it had been in Plato's time. Roman antagonism against philosophy, in general, and Greek philosophy, in particular, reached a peak in the first century CE with the issuance of edicts against philosophical activity. This was followed by actual expulsions of philosophers from the Italian peninsula in 74 and 94 by the emperors Vespasian (9–79 CE) and Domitian (51–96 CE), respectively.

During these times, classical Greek philosophy was replaced by some new versions of older ideas. Neoplatonism, first introduced by Plotinus of Alexandria (205–270 CE), was much more a theology than a true descendent of Platonic philosophy. In Rome, Neoplatonism became a mystery religion combining Platonic philosophical ideas with mystical Pythagorean concepts about the supernatural significance of numbers. The combination was aimed at the development of the human spirit so that it could ultimately combine with the "One," the supreme God.

With such modest philosophical and resurgent theological foundations, theoretical science fell into disrepute at the same time that practical engineering reached its zenith in the Roman world. If we were to paint the relationship between classical Greece and Rome with the broadest brush, Greek natural philosophy cum science could have been seen as mainly theoretical and natural, but exhibiting relative weakness in civil engineering. Indeed, some said this was because the Greeks hated manual labor and, therefore, had turned to abstract issues to consume their time. The Romans, on the other hand, were the pragmatic engineers and warlike conquerors, concerned with building the wonderful monuments, roads, and aqueducts that still grace the remains of what was the great Roman Empire. As such, they eschewed pursuing the theoretical explanations that their predecessors, the Greeks had, considering that kind of abstract cogitation to be somewhat below their cultural "machismo."

Of course, such a broad-brush description minimizes the architectural and other accomplishments of the classic Greek period and some significant intellectual accomplishments of the Romans. The Parthenon in Athens, as well as the beautiful Greek remnants in Sicily and Asia Minor, make it clear that the Greeks were not totally neglecting the practical arts.

---

[16]A word in defense of my own position is appropriate here. Although modern behaviorism does champion a kind of inaccessibility that seems comparable to "it cannot be known," it certainly does not follow the admonition that "nothing is." Modern behaviorism accepts the physical reality of "everything" and the fact that much of our world "can be known" but eschews the specific idea that mental processes are accessible.

Two notable exceptions to the relative absence of natural science theory building during Roman times, are worth mentioning—Galen and Ptolemy.

2.4.1 Galen

The decline of Roman medicine is another example of the curious historical lacuna in scientific theory that has mystified historians of science for centuries. From about 200 to 100 BCE there is little evidence that anything resembling a physician was present in Rome. Medicine was something taken care of in the home or on the battlefield; surgery, to the extent it was practiced at all, was handled by ill-trained attendants who were, in large part, slaves. In general, the profession was held in relatively low repute by Romans of those times. This negative attitude hit its nadir at virtually the same time that important physicians were active on the Greek Peninsula. About 100 BCE, however, things began to change. For the next 200 years, Greek physicians were increasing imported and incorporated into Roman society, particularly into the homes of the wealthy who could afford their services.

By the beginning of the 2nd century CE, however, profound changes occurred in attitudes about medicine in Rome. Roman medical practice, still mainly following the Greek tradition, grew in popularity and the varieties of application. Despite the longstanding negative attitude toward medical theory, the Roman period fostered one of the greatest physicians of all time—a man whose ideas about diseases, anatomy, and physiology were so influential that his techniques dominated the western world for another 1,300 years. Galen's (129–203 CE) greatest contribution was to systematize the body of Greek medical lore and treatment and integrate it with the slowly evolving Roman practices and ideas. Most historians agree, however, that he went substantially beyond the work of his Greek and, to a lesser degree, his Roman predecessors, in theorizing about the sources and origins of diseases.

Although well known also as a systematizer, philosopher, and medical ethicist, Galen's real forte (and the basis of his long-lasting influence on western medicine) was as an anatomist and experimental physician. Based on his early experience as a physician to gladiators, he developed new surgical instruments and techniques, often, if not usually, based on Greek practices. He was also active as a dissector, but as was discovered later, mainly of animal, rather than human, bodies.

Based on an active program of dissection, Galen produced some long-lasting ideas (expressed in more than 100 still existing books) about the anatomy and physiology of the body. Perhaps his greatest anatomical contribution was his detailed knowledge of the nervous system including the brain and the peripheral nerves. It was, however, not until the 16th century that his work was critically reviewed and, to a certain degree, discredited by Andreas Vesalius. Vesalius' dissection research raised the possibility that most of Galen's drawings were actually based on dissections of animals rather than humans. It is now thought (Singer, 1957) that most of his work was based on the dissection of Barbary "apes" and Rhesus monkeys. In spite of this later historical interpretation, Galen's anatomical work was the unrepudiated standard for medical practice for more than a millennium.

The most complete of Galen's publications is believed to be the transcript of some lectures given in Rome around 177 CE. The treatise is entitled "On Anatomical Procedures" (177/1956) and has gone through numerous translations from the original Greek. It originally consisted of 15 books (really elongated chapters) but some of them were lost for centuries. In Singer's English translation (Galen, 1956) only the nine that were continuously known and which can be authenticated as the work of Galen are presented. Galen's ninth book in "On Anatomical Procedures" deals with the nervous system. It is, as promised, a highly technical description of his dissection procedures including discussions of the instruments used for teasing apart particular parts of the brain.

Galen's ideas about the mind, for all of their persistence, were largely continuations of Greek ideas from as far back as Empedocles. Specifically Galen was a proponent of the typology that the balance among four "humors" determined personality. Just as in the preserved but much more complete works of Aristotle, there will always be some residual ambiguity about the meaning of the words expressed in Galen's antique writings. Nevertheless, the dominant theme is that he was seeking natural explanations of mental processes. As we now see, his theories of the mind are mainly free of any allusion to supernatural forces. Though clearly erroneous in detail, they were at least materialist and scientific in general conception.

Galen thought of the soul[17] as the controlling entity in a complex of many different kinds of mental processes. It was responsible for the high levels of cognitive processing and bodily control (e.g., thought and voluntary motion). He distinguished these processes from those more or less passive functions that he believed were carried out by the senses without active cognitive mediation.

Galen's conception of the soul was closely related to other bodily functions and anatomy. Two essences, or pneuma, were central to Galen's theory of the mind—vital pneuma (the life force itself) and psychic pneuma (the stuff of the mind), both being derivatives of breath, one of the most obvious signs of life. Each pneuma was closely linked to a particularly bodily organ; specifically the left ventricle of the heart, according to Galen, was supposed to generate vital pneuma and the brain was assumed to secrete psychic pneuma.

---

[17]It seems to me that Galen's use of the word soul was not offered in a theological or dualist context. Rather, like many others from the time of Thales, his meaning was very close to that of the modern psychological terminology denoting mind or cognitive capacities.

It is problematical exactly what Galen meant by a pneuma. Was it a substance or a process or something even less tangible? von Staden (2000) believes that both kinds were "instruments to be used" rather than "substances" or "dwelling places" (p. 111). In some ways, this is not inconsistent with the modern idea that the mind is a process of the brain itself. Thus, it must again be emphasized that although the details of his model of the soul/mind have now been, in large part, replaced by modern ideas, the basic idea of nontheological, essentially materialist, explanations of mental and bodily processes held by Galen is essentially modern.

Indeed, in some ways Galen was remarkably prescient. For example, he was one of the first to distinguish between sensory and motor nerves and suspected they were the pathways through which sensory impressions and motor signals respectively passed, as well as being conduits for the mysterious pneuma. However the details may differ from modern views, Galen's work was another major step along the road initiated by Thales to a natural, as opposed to a supernatural, explanation of mental activity.

Galen was a prolific writer and in addition to his specific anatomical studies, often discussed general scientific method. He emphasized the empirical approach and argued that we should trust our sensory experiences to reveal the nature of the world. This later argument was, it is now thought, a deliberate and conscious effort to overcome the intellectually debilitating philosophy of the Roman Skeptics.

As noted at the outset of this discussion, Galen's ideas persisted for well over a millennium. As such, we have to acknowledge him as one of the greatest minds of all time. Not until the 14th and 16th centuries did anatomical knowledge, in particular, take further leaps forward under the direction of the next great anatomists—Mondino de Luzzi (1275–1326 CE) and Andreas Vesalius (1514–1564 CE)—respectively.

2.4.2 Ptolemy

Ptolemy of Alexandria (85–165 CE) was a Greek citizen of Rome who achieved a prominence and persistence of his ideas that were comparable to those of Galen, but in a completely different context. Although not directly related to the mind–body problem, his ideas concerning human cosmological thought were significant enough to deserve a few words here.

Ptolemy was most famous for his suggestion that the earth was the center of the solar system. Although lesser known to the general public, his mathematical description of the behavior of that system was also held in high regard by professionals. For his time, his geocentric model was the most advanced and remained so until Nicolaus Copernicus (1473–1543) proposed his revolutionary helioconcentric theory in 1530.

Ptolemy's influence on science was not limited to astronomy alone, however. He also was a strong believer in the Aristotelean empirical method of science and did much to preserve and extend the idea that the way to learn about nature—both biological and physical—was to measure and experiment in a well controlled and standardized manner.

Galen and Ptolemy stand out as the great bridging scientists from the Roman period to the Renaissance. Their influence in the medical and physical sciences, respectively, and the scientific method in general, was enormous, not being replaced for more than 1,000 years.

Between these two Roman-era giants and the 14th and 15th centuries, however, there occurred another of the great intellectual lacuna or dark ages that seems periodically to afflict the world. Except for distant and incomplete scientific activity in Asia and the Arabic world, natural philosophy came to be dominated by religious teaching and a thoughtless parroting of the works of Aristotle, Galen, Ptolemy, and a few others of their times. We are exceedingly lucky that their works, whatever their flaws, were preserved by the Arabs and the Irish (Cahill, 1996).

As noted earlier, Arabic medicine was instrumental in developing new ideas about the optics and visual functions of the eye (see p. 61). The Arab scientists who were active around the centuries near the turn of the first millennium were also responsible for the transition of chemistry and pharmacology from folk remedies to solid science. The most famous of the Arab medical scientists was, indisputatively, Avicenna (980–1037) whose book *Canon of Medicine* had a profound impact on the development of modern medicine, particularly with regard to pharmaceuticals used to cure a wide variety of diseases. Like so many of the other great geniuses to appear in this story, Avicenna was a man gifted with many skills. In addition to his medical contributions, he is still remembered in the Muslim world for his philosophy and poetry.

In spite of these bright spots in Ireland and the Middle East and a few other exceptions, for centuries science was clearly in the doldrums. Not only was empirical research largely ignored, but in addition, the development of theoretical science was retarded. With few notable exceptions, the lacuna lasted from approximately 200 CE to 1500 CE—from the time of Galen to the time of Leonardo da Vinci and Vesalius, and the great anatomists of Padua University—Falloppio and Eutascio. These men approached Galen's medical and anatomical teachings with an open mind just as the great Galileo looked anew at the work of Ptolemy and the Greek and Roman astronomers.

It is not easy to understand why this "dark age" happened, but, although longer than most others, it is clear that this 1,300-year hiatus in scientific thinking was not that unusual except in duration. Similar intervals of ignorance and the supernatural have permeated other times and other societies. It is, nevertheless, important to remain aware of this possibility so that we do not inadvertently allow it to happen and let superstition once again reign supreme.

Despite the prolonged period of anti- and nonintellectualism that followed, classical Greek and Roman times bequeathed to the world a view of the relationship between the soul cum mind and the body cum brain that had been unimagined by previous civilizations. There is no question that, by the end of the classic period, the brain was considered by these ancients to be the seat of the mind by all but a few exceptions. Of course the various theories differed greatly in detail because the technology necessary to even conceive of modern explanations and metaphors was simply not available. This allowed some wild ideas to percolate through those times. Plato's version of brain theory, for example, was not exceptional. He believed that the mind/soul was represented in three parts of the fluid-filled ventricles of the nervous system—intellectual functions at the top, the mortal portion in the upper part of the spinal cavity, and the appetitive functions in the lower part of the spinal cavity. The emphasis placed on the cavities or ventricles lasted for an almost unbelievable 2,000 years!

A general consensus emerged from these times; it assumed that the ventricles were the receptacles of a fluid or gaseous mind-stuff such as the mysterious pneuma mentioned earlier. Thus, the most widely accepted theory of the mind of the time was a hydraulic explanation. The idea of the ventricles as a receptacle for some kind of a fluid manifestation of the soul was supported not only by Galen, the great anatomist, but also by such theologians as St. Augustine, as well as by the Arab scientists who brought it forward to the Renaissance. There it was still championed, as discussed shortly, by such luminaries as Leonardo and Descartes.

The other great theme that was to develop into a dogma reverberating until modern times was a philosophical and scientific dualism—the idea that the soul or mind was of a separate kind of reality and need not follow the rules of the material world. It is not necessary to interpret this dualism as one that invokes supernatural forces as many kinds of religious dualism do. Rather, the prevailing dualism was of two kinds of natural reality—one mental, one material. Although frequently intertwined with matters of personal immortality, dualism is actually a separate issue. The important point about this pervasive dualism is that it influenced scientific thinking then and continues to do so today.

Our discussion has now progressed to the end of the Roman period and the beginnings of what have been referred to as the dark (intellectual) ages. Our discussion has mainly been aimed as the development of the scientific chain of thought that proposed answers to what started out as the soul–body question and evolved into the mind–brain problem. I now pick up the story of the roots of theoretical cognitive neuroscience from the 14th to the 17th century. It is here that the persistent questions of the field were formulated in what essentially was to be their modern form.

2.5 THE RENAISSANCE

The dark ages of natural science theory lasted from the collapse of Rome to the first stirrings of the Renaissance. It was not until the 14th century that there was the beginning of a resurgence of interest in posing questions and seeking explanations of natural phenomena. This revitalized interest in science, in general, included a variety of specific new efforts to explain the nature of the relationship between the mind and the brain.

Despite the fact that we know today that the mind–brain theories of the 14th and 15th centuries are largely incorrect, those ideas did stimulate the questions that still dominate modern thinking. Although the answers were wrong, in large part modern cognitive neuroscience and philosophy are still grappling with the questions asked in those exciting early years of the Renaissance. Several questions, in particular, had crystallized by the 14th century that were to guide thinking about mind and brain for the next half millennium:

1. Did the mind or soul and the brain represent one kind or two different kinds of reality? (The monism–dualism issue.)
2. Depending on which way one answered the monism–dualism question, there were two questions that followed logically. Assuming that the brain and the mind represented different expressions or measures of a single kind of reality, one must ask (a) How does the brain create mental activity?—The representation question; and (b) Where is the locus or seat of the mind (or its parts) in the brain?—The localization question.[18]
3. If, on the other hand, one accepted a dualist answer to the question, then one must ask: How do the two kinds of reality influence each other?

The quest for the knowledge to answer these questions set off in two different directions. The first direction was an upsurge in the accumulation of empirical knowledge about the structure of the nervous system by a new breed of Renaissance neuroanatomists. The second was the increasing amount of speculative debate among philosophers and the intellectual precursors of modern psychologists concerning the nature of the relationship between the mind and the body. Even though there was a growing separation between natural theories of the mind and theology, some philosophers still concerned themselves with the possibility of nontheological dualisms. Although often in direct conflict with natural science, such arguments still rage through some of the most sophisticated and modern schools of philos-

[18]The other great question was—How does behavior come to be modified as a result of experience? However, this issue did not become prominent until the rationalist–empiricist debates arose in the 17th century.

ophy. I have discussed these issues in an earlier book (Uttal, 2004). However, for a much more detailed discussion of the philosophical developments during the times from Thales to Descartes, I recommend Wright and Potter's (2000) excellent collection of papers on the topic.

The predominant conviction among most 21st-century cognitive scientists is that, although it is not yet known how the brain produces mental activity, it most certainly does so as a consequence of natural physical, chemical, and informational processes. The accumulating knowledge about the anatomy of the nervous system provided a fertile ground for continued development. Philosophers were stimulated to speculate about the significance of anatomical discoveries and, in turn, their often richly imaginative ideas sometimes stimulated anatomical explorations. It was a well-traveled two-way street. However subtle may have been the interactions between these two enterprises and how incorrect may have been some of the theories of the time, there is no question that the period from the 15th through the 17th century saw a reformulation of scientific and theoretical thought about the nature of the mind–body problem.

At the beginning of this period the consensus view of the nature and location of the mind was still the one prevailing since ancient Greek and Roman times. Namely, that the mind was a fluid of some sort that was accumulated in the ventricles, or as they were then referred to, the "cells" of the brain. Although there was some dispute about the number of cells and their respective roles, few other alternatives (specifically any alternative alluding to the role of the solid matter of the brain) were seriously considered at the time. As we now see, most of the great minds of the time adhered to the hydraulic–ventricle theory. Why this should have been the case is relatively obvious. One reason was that the then current technology was mechanics, especially the mechanics of fluids. Another was the emerging conviction that the ventricles and the enclosed fluids must play some role in the brain's function.

The 15th and 16th centuries were marked by the work of two additional giants of the history of cognitive neuroscience—Leonardo da Vinci (1452– 1519 CE) and Andreas Vesalius (1514–1564 CE). A number of lesser known but perhaps equally influential anatomists also studied and taught with Vesalius in what has long been considered to be the first European university[19]—

[19]There remains continual debate about which of two contestants rightfully can claim to be the first university. Both Bologna and Padua claim the title. Bologna was probably the first place that a faculty gathered, but after some political troubles in the year 1222, a group of professors and their students moved to Padua (Padova) and restarted the university. Is the first university where the faculty first resided? Alternatively, is it where the first faculty ultimately resided? The controversy goes on.

the campus at Padua, Italy—which became a world center of neuroanatomy in particular. The names of the Italian physician-scientists who gathered there still reverberate down into our current anatomical vocabulary—Bartolomeo Eustachio (1520–1574) and Gabriele Falloppio (1523–1562) being the most familiar, each having contributed the anatomical knowledge that led to naming of two important tubes of the body after them. Padua later also enjoyed, or perhaps I should say tolerated, the revolutionary lectures of Galileo Galilei (1564–1642)—a titan of science who was to revolutionize scientific thinking and yet to suffer such dire consequences because of his iconoclasm.[20] Clearly this must have been one of the most exciting places anywhere in the world during the latter years of the 16th century.

Although there is a common myth that the Renaissance Catholic Church prohibited the dissection of the human body,[21] this widely held belief is almost certainly incorrect. As early as 1302 (and possibly a century earlier) anatomists such as Mondino dei Lucci (1275–1327) had been dissecting corpses as part of the medical training program at the University of Bologna. This was almost certainly done with the approval of the pope as well as the local bishops. Nor was Mondino's book, *Anathomia*, censored at any time after its publication. Quite to the contrary, it was reprinted many times and was widely available at the time of Leonardo da Vinci's famous dissections of the human brain around 1500.

It seems more likely that the troubles that some of the anatomists had with the church concerned other issues such as their apostasy from what was considered to be classical medical teaching or religious ideology. Vesalius, for example, had been charged with atheism for reasons other than his widely celebrated dissections at the time. Rather, the church seems to have explicitly approved the educational use of human dissection, apparently without any problem during most of the Renaissance.

---

[20]Galileo's support of the Copernican theory of a solarcentric system in opposition to the Ptolomeic version of a geocentric system accepted by the Catholic Church led to his conviction and imprisonment on a charge of breaking an agreement with the Inquisition concerning teaching and publication. It was not the subject matter itself for which he was punished but his violation of a contract prohibiting its promulgation.

[21]The same argument has been made concerning Muslim teaching. However, once again, there is no specific prohibition against dissection of the human body in the Qur'an either (Rispler-Chaim, 1993). Modern Muslim tradition accepts postmortem dissection for scientific purposes in many countries. Orthodox Jewish tradition, however, does not permit postmortems or dissections according to Souder and Trojanowski (1992). In the more distant past, Alcmaeon had performed dissections as far back as 500 BCE. That he was able to do so then was a direct result of the change from purely religious to natural theories of human nature—the change that can also be initially attributed to Thales—and was continued by many of the natural philosophers of whom we have written.

2.5.1 Leonardo da Vinci

Leonardo da Vinci stands at the door into the 16th century scientific study of the brain with respect to the anatomical work he carried out during the latter part of the 15th century. It is almost a cliché to say that this remarkable man was best known as an artist, only to add that—"however he also was a great engineer and scientist." His paintings are considered to be some of the greatest of human treasures and his codices of engineering drawings represent marvels of imagination anticipating developments that did not become realities until centuries later. Almost submerged under all of these accomplishments, however, were his anatomical studies of the human body. His drawings of the shape and motion of the body, of course, contributed greatly to his art, but in some other less well-known cases his art contributed directly to an appreciation of the nervous system. Pevsner (2002), for example, pointed out, in an insightful discussion of Leonardo's contributions to the neurosciences, that one important reason that so little has been known of his neuroanatomical work was that most of his papers and drawings on these topics were not published until the 19th and 20th century. Nevertheless, it is now clear that he had made some important anatomical discoveries in the 1400s and 1500s even if they were only adequately communicated much later.

It is universally agreed that Leonardo was one of the great minds of all time. His reputation was enhanced for not slavishly following deeply ingrained dogma. Others who broke the intellectual bonds of Ptolomeic, Galenic, and Aristotelean dogma, of course, included Mondino, Vesalius, and Galileo. It was this revolution during the Renaissance against the accepted classical scientific doctrines that played a critical role in the development of modern science with its emphasis on direct observation and replication. Leonardo's accomplishments in the neurosciences, in particular, were largely built on his personal experimental observations rather than the blind acceptance of doctrine so characteristic of his time. His legacy to us was enhanced by his unparalleled artistic talents by means of which some of his discoveries were fortunately preserved.

There is no question that a new kind of intellectual freedom was abroad during those times that led so many to question prevailing dogma. Obviously, changes in the world's economy, its politics, and its social systems provided an enormous impetus to this rebirth of inquiry and the extraordinary overthrowing of traditions and ideas from the past. Whatever were the complex reasons for this explosion of critical thinking and artistic and scientific productivity, they will have to be left to other historians to determine. This is not a topic within the intended theme of this book. It would require a degree of insensitivity, however, not at least to ask—Whence came the scientific rebels like Leonardo da Vinci, Vesalius, and Galileo? An interesting corollary is—Could similar polymaths flourish in our extremely specialized times?

To return to the main theme of this short biography of Leonardo, it is important to recognize that he exemplified the theoretician as well as the experimentalist. The general anatomy of the ventricles—the great cavities of the living brain—had, as indicated previously, been known since Galen's time. However, the early dissectors had misunderstood the true significance of the watery fluids that escaped on dissection. A major change regarding the role of the ventricular fluids occurred about this time. Rather than being considered to be irrelevant accompaniments of dissection, the fluids now caught the attention of Renaissance scientists. What better place to locate the intangible mental processes that were now associated with the fluids, humors, or pneuma of one kind or another than these ready containers? Furthermore, the corollary question quickly arose—Could the fluid itself be the pneuma?

Pevsner (2002) described Leonardo's theory of the soul (i.e., the mind)—a version of the emerging hydraulic–ventricular theory—as follows:

> The brain was thought [by Leonardo] to contain an anterior ventricle, usually thought to house the *senso comune* [the common destination of sensory impressions], "phantasy" [*sic*] and imagination, a second ventricle that mediated cognition, and a posterior ventricle that served memory. (p. 218)

There are several important aspects of this expression of Leonardo's theory of the mind. As Pevsner also pointed out, it is another in a long series of purely material and natural theories of the mind. Whatever Leonardo's religious view may have been as he went on to serve his papal masters and paint his religious masterpieces, it seems clear that this theory of the mind did not involve any supernatural forces. Another aspect of Leonardo's beliefs is how very modern his vocabulary is; sensation, cognition, and memory are his terms of choice, just as they came to be hundreds of years later.

Another remarkable aspect of Leonardo's theory was how thoroughly he pursued his studies of the mechanisms of the mind. In 1489 and 1490, he drew some extraordinarily realistic pictures of the skull and the brain. He went on later in life (in 1504) to adapt a well-known casting technique—the lost wax procedure—to build three-dimensional models of what he believed were the all-important ventricles—the receptacles of the mind/soul. Injecting wax into the ventricles, he dissected away the brain tissue leaving the wax mold of these cavities. His drawings of these molds were among some of the greatest images in the history of neuroanatomy.[22]

---

[22]A more complete discussion of Leonardo's neuroanatomical ideas and copies of some of his famous drawings are available in the fine article by Pevsner (2002).

Leonardo's hydraulic–ventricular theory was typical of mind–brain theories of the time and an outgrowth of earlier theories that associated mind with fluids of one kind or another. Thus, as late as the end of the 15th century, the hydraulic theory still dominated thought. Like most other theories of the mind that were yet to come, it was stimulated by the scientific scene of the time.[23] The early Renaissance was a time of mechanical and hydraulic theories. Fluid mechanics was an important part of bridge, dam, and shipbuilding. (Leonardo's still existing drawings of the flow of water are considered to be among the greatest masterpieces of scientific art.) For these reasons, there was little serious opposition to the idea that the mental facilities were based on fluids located in the brain's ventricles.

Leonardo's attitude concerning the monism–dualism controversy is not clear. His studies of the human body were characterized by a kind of hydraulic–mechanical model as we have just discussed. Yet, he seems to have believed that an intangible force was necessary to activate this mechanism. His concept of a nervous center where the various senses converged (the "senso comune") and where mental activity became evident to the sentient human has a strongly materialist tone to it. His efforts to locate the mind or soul specifically as the insubstantial content of the ventricles, however, suggest that he did assume there were two different kinds of materials involved in the mind–body combination. At the time, theological dualism dominated thought and it seems likely that even this genius was not able to break those bonds completely. Indeed, as we see later, it took a long time for modern materialism to become widely accepted even in the most exalted and elevated scientific circles.

2.5.2 Andreas Vesalius

Andreas Vesalius, another notable scientist of the 16th century, was also a classic iconoclast. Strongly dissatisfied with the errors in Galen's millennium-old anatomy text as well as Mondino's incomplete work of the previous century, he carried out what were by the standards of his times an extraordinary series of dissections graced by his extraordinary graphic communication skills. His discoveries and the way they were presented to the world modified medical teaching and practice forever. Vesalius contributed to all aspects of human anatomy, not just to our current interest in the nervous system. His studies culminated in his epochal *De Humani Corporis*

[23]It must also be appreciated that whatever the most popular theory of the brain–mind is at any point in history, it is usually based on a metaphor derived from whatever contemporary technology dominates contemporary scientific thinking. The hydraulic theory has been replaced by models built on the steam engine, the telephone, the computer, and computer programs over the centuries. Currently, brain imaging technology rejuvenates theories based on the assumption that mental modules can be localized in specific regions of the brain.

Fabrica (*The Structure of the Human Body*) published in 1543. This milestone in anatomical studies is currently being translated by two groups, one by Richardson and Carman (Vesalius, 1543/1999) and the other by a team at Northwestern University. The latter can be viewed at: http://vesalius.northwestern.edu/.

The beauty of the original *Fabrica* lies both in the information it conveys and the splendid engravings of Vesalius' drawings, cut into wood blocks by an artist named Johannes Stephan van Kalkar. They are still considered to be classics in their own right as artistic expressions as well as modifying many of the erroneous concepts of the structure of the human body that Galen had perpetuated so many centuries previously.

The *Fabrica* was organized into seven books:

Book 1 The Skeleton
Book 2 Muscles
Book 3 Vascular System
Book 4 Nervous System
Book 5 Abdominal Viscera and Organs of Reproduction
Book 6 Thoracic Viscera
Book 7 The Brain

A shorter version of the Fabrica—*The Epitome of Andreas Vesalius*—was also published in 1543 and translated in 1949 (Vesalius, 1543/1949). The *Epitome* was organized somewhat differently than the *Fabrica,* collapsing the 4th and 7th books into a single 5th book on the brain and the nervous system, the version to which we now direct our attention.

It is in this 5th book of the *Epitome* that Vesalius expresses his theory of the mind–brain relationship:

> From the vital spirit adapted in this [arterial] plexus to the functions of the brain and from the air which we draw to the ventricles of the brain when we breathe in, the inborn force of the brain's substance creates the animal spirit, of which the brain makes use partly for the functions of the chief portion of the mind. Part of it the brain transmits by means of the nerves growing forth from itself to the organs which stand in need of the animal spirit. (These are chiefly the instruments of the sense and of voluntary movement.) A not inconsiderable part of the animal spirit spreads from the third ventricle under the testes of the brain into the ventricle common to the cerebellum and the dorsal medulla. This is subsequently distributed to all the nerves drawing their origin from the dorsal medulla. (From Lind's translation of Vesalius, 1543/1949, p. 69)

In this manner, Vesalius acknowledged the then current idea of the relation between the ventricles, animal spirits, and the nerves; namely that the mind was housed in the ventricles.[24] He also indicates his belief in the existence and role of animal spirits. However, according to O'Malley (1965), he was extremely skeptical about the role of the ventricles and suggested they were used only for accumulating the fluid remnants resulting from the process that actually created the animal sprits. It was this questioning of the dogma of ventricular spirits as the basis of mind that may have caused Vesalius to come into conflict with his contemporaries as much as anything else. In particular, Jacobus Sylvius (1478–1555), one of his teachers, attacked him in later life as a "madman" for disagreeing with Galenic teaching.

Vesalius expressed one of the earliest criticisms of the modular mind when he stated:

> I do not understand how the brain can perform the [separate] functions of imagination, judgment, cogitation, and memory, or subdivide the powers of the primary sensorium in whatever other manner you may desire according to your beliefs. (From O'Malley, p. 180)

In this context, of course, his ideas ran counter to a modern cognitive psychology that stresses mental modules. Quite to the contrary, he seems to have agreed with the assumptions of modern behavioral psychology that stresses mental holism.

Despite our current appreciation of his fine work, Vesalius came into conflict with the then current Galenic anatomical establishment. A trumped up charge of atheism was brought against him and, although avoiding the inquisition's death penalty, he was sent on a religious quest[25] to Jerusalem from which he never returned. Thus perished another of the great challengers of the status quo, victim to the dogmatic consensus that dominated scientific thinking at his time.

2.5.3 René Descartes

The 17th century's effort to unravel what was by then clearly a "mind–brain problem" was anchored in its early years by another luminous name of science. René Descartes (1596–1650) made so many contributions to philoso-

[24]An extraordinary collection of 15th and 16th century drawings of the ventricular system can be found in Magoun (1958). These figures and the adjoining text make it clear just how universally held was the ventricular hydraulic theory of mind during those years.

[25]There is some dispute in the literature about the motivation for Vesalius' ill-fated pilgrimage. Some historians report it as a penance for a disagreement with the inquisition, whereas others argue that it was the end-of-life decision of a deeply religious man. Another story was that he was being punished for inadvertently dissecting a living person. The full range of reasons that might have motivated his trip, none of which has been authenticated, can be found in Kingsley (1893).

phy and science that it is hard to characterize him solely as a mathematician, a philosopher, or as a natural scientist. Again the title of polymath leaps to mind to describe another of the most versatile and productive people in human history. His contributions were enormous; the invention of analytical geometry in 1637 and the Cartesian coordinate system changed mathematics forever and set the stage for the invention of the calculus by Isaac Newton (1643–1727) and Gottfried Wilhelm von Leibniz (1646–1716) in the 1660s and 1670s, respectively.

Descartes also changed the nature of experimental science in general by stressing the importance of Bacon's technique of studying things in parts—a technique Descartes referred to as the *méthode*. His philosophical contributions were equally profound; Cartesian interactive dualism is still taught in support, in contradiction, or as a point of view to be challenged and modified in modern philosophical studies of the mind–body problem.

It is, however, his views on what has come to be called in modern parlance—the neurosciences—that draws our present attention. Like Leonardo and Vesalius, Descartes grew up in an era of hydraulic theories, in which the ventricular fluids were still considered to be the essence of the soul/mind itself. It was to the metaphor of a hydraulically driven machine to which he, like his predecessors and contemporaries, turned to explain the operation of the minds and bodies of animals and men. Animals were, in his view, mere automatons that had no consciousness and responded strictly according to the impact of the stimuli that fell on them. The actions of the body in both animals and humans were accounted for by the flow of fluids through the nerves of the body to and from the brain. Descartes believed that sensory information, in general, fed into the pineal gland through the hollow hydraulic pathways of the nerves and, it was here that human sentience resided.

There was, therefore, one additional aspect that humans possessed that animals did not—the sentient soul or mind. For Descartes the "soul" was a "substance" of some sort, but one of a completely different nature than the substance making up the body. It was this unique soul–substance that was the basis of human mental activity. This mind-stuff was able to send out hydraulic signals through the nerves to control the volitional, as opposed to the reflexive, motions of the body. Descartes, of course, knew nothing of the electrical and chemical knowledge and theories that were yet to come, but he did have a more or less correct conception of the way in which the peripheral nervous system was laid out. His theory appreciated that the peripheral nerves provided pathways for both the senses and the motor activation of the body. To Descartes, however, the active, cognitive mind was much less tangible; he described it as "pure and incorporeal thought or intellect."

Central to Descartes' theory of the mind–body relationship was the assumption that the material of the human body and the essence of the mind were two distinctly different substances, not just substance and process. The problems then arising are where and how do these two different substances—the material body and the immaterial mind—interact? For reasons that still seem to be in doubt, but which obviously did depend on an excellent knowledge of the anatomy of the brain, Descartes identified the point of interaction between the mind and the brain as the pineal gland. Why he picked this particular organ remains a mystery to many historians. Perhaps it was because it was not a bilaterally symmetrical or paired structure as were most of the other parts of the brain and, thus, suggested to him a kind of unitary ideal. Perhaps it was that because of its close location to the optic nerves it looked like a place where the images for the two eyes could be combined into a single percept. Perhaps it was the continuing quest for the "senso comune" suggested by Leonardo and others that led him to seek out a common region where all of the sensory inputs could converge to produce the unified mind. Whatever the reason, it was here that Descartes suggested the two kinds of substance, the immaterial and the material, *interacted* to account for the control of human behavior by a sentient and insubstantial mind. His interactionism continues to play a central role in other dualist theories of the mind to this day.[26]

Descartes played an important role in subsequent philosophy as well as in the brain sciences. It was he who in large part clarified the questions and illuminated the trail upon which Thales set out so many years before for much of the remainder of the second millennium. We now know that most of his physiology was incorrect, but his dualistic philosophy still attracts enormous attention and his mathematical contributions remain the principal foundation of most of advanced mathematics.

2.6 THE BEGINNINGS OF MODERN NEUROSCIENCE

2.6.1 The Modern Anatomical Epoch

The 16th and 17th centuries saw the beginning of what we might call the modern era of neuroscience. There was an enormous outpouring of anatomical knowledge about the nervous system in particular. The macroanatomy of the brain was definitively explored and described by such neuroanatomists as Constanzo Varolio (1543–1575) who identified the pons in 1573; Thomas Willis (1622–1675) who studied the cranial nerves and named

[26] I have extensively discussed the various theories dealing with the tangle that the mind–body problem faces in modern philosophy in my earlier book (Uttal, 2004). I refer the reader there for a more complete discussion of the conflict between dualism and monism in particular.

many of the structures of the brain in the years around 1660; and Humphrey Ridley (1653–1708) in the publication of his important neuroanatomy text (Ridley, 1695). This important and timely book summarized much of the gross anatomy of the brain that was known at that time. In the next few years, Emanuel Swedenborg (1688–1722) made the key assumption that the cerebrum was the major player in mental activities and Francesco Gennari (1750–1795) discovered the layering of the cerebral cortex. In the 19th century, other anatomists explored the effect of injuries on the brain and proposed sometimes imaginative, sometimes incredible, theories of the organization of the brain and its role in sensation, cognition, and motor control.

The 1700s also opened up other conceptual doors to understanding the nature of the human brain. The development of the practical high magnification microscope[27] by Antony van Leeuwenhoek (1632–1723) was to have powerful implications for all of science. In 1683, he was the first to describe bacteria and in 1717 he made a major contribution to neuroscience by describing the cross-section of the optic nerve of a cow. The science of neural microanatomy was thus ushered in.

There was an exceedingly important development in the 18th century that eventually was to overshadow even these important anatomical discoveries—the emerging study of the *functional* roles by the then well known parts of the brain. Early discoveries by Jean Astruc (1684–1766) in 1736 led to his proposal of the idea of a *reflex*. In 1824, Francois Magendie (1783–1855) discovered that motor control was mediated in some way by the cerebellum. Both of these discoveries may be considered early examples of what was later to be called "functional information processing" by the central nervous system. Thus, arose the idea of central functional changes that transformed in some mysterious way sensory inputs into motor responses.

By the 19th century the functional exploration of the brain overshadowed the prerequisite anatomical studies. The Bell–Magendie law of the different properties of the dorsal and ventral spinal roots was elaborated, first by Charles Bell (1774–1842) in 1811 and then by Francois Magendie in 1821. In the latter parts of the 19th century such neuroscience luminaries as Paul Broca (1824–1880), John Hughlings Jackson (1835–1911), and Carl Wernicke (1848–1904) discovered the role of particular brain areas on speech. In 1870, Gustave Fritsch (1838–1927) and Eduard Hitzig (1838–1907) discovered the motor area of the cerebral cortex by electrically stimulating the exposed brains of wounded soldiers in the Franco Prussian war. Shortly thereafter, in 1881, Herman Munk (1839–1912) associated occipital lesions with visual dysfunction. David Ferrier (1843–1928) played a significant role in establish-

[27]Low-power microscopes were probably first designed by Zacharias Janssen as early as 1595 but their power was limited and it remained for Leeuwenhoek to develop a single-lens microscope that was powerful enough to see truly microscopic structures.

ing the principle of the cerebral localization of function with the publication of his book—*The Functions of the Brain* in 1876. The era of cerebral localization was well underway.[28]

There were, of course, some detours along the way. Franz Joseph Gall (1758–1828) proposed a theory of mind–brain localization in which the bumps on the skull were considered to reflect the shape of the underlying brain (Gall & Spurzheim, 1808). His work was vigorously promoted in later years by Johann Caspar Spurzheim (1776–1832) who was probably more responsible (Spurzheim, 1832) for what ultimately became its bad reputation than Gall himself. For some years their pseudoscientific theory had enormous popular appeal but was eventually discredited first by John P. Harrison (1796–1849) and then by a much more influential neuroanatomist, Pierre Flourens (1794–1867). Despite the unsavory reputation that phrenology has carried with it to the present, Gall otherwise had a distinguished career as a neuroanatomist and deserves some considerable responsibility for supporting the idea of cortical localization of higher cognitive processes. Spurzheim and some of the other proselytizers of the time do not come off as well historically.[29]

2.6.2 The Discovery of the Electrical Nature of the Nervous System

Another influential line of what was to be extremely relevant research was proceeding in parallel with these structural and functional theories of the brain. From ancient times it was known that rubbing certain materials together (e.g., amber [gr. Electron] and animal fur) could produce interesting little sparks and attract or repel other materials. By the early 18th century, the nature of electricity was beginning to be understood and there were even devices, such as Leyden jars, in which "it" (whatever it was) could be stored.

In 1780, however, the story of the development of knowledge about electricity joins our story of research discoveries in the neurosciences. It was that year that one of the great breakthroughs in this field happened by fortuitous accident. Luigi Galvani (1737–1798) and his students observed that

[28]The localization principle has guided and misguided cognitive brain science since Ferrier's time. My astute readers might have noticed that the localization topics discussed so far have dealt largely with sensory and motor processes. These functions are well anchored to physical parameters in the outside world. Few current neuroscientists disagree with these associations. The ascription of high-level cognitive processes to particular areas of the "association cortex," however, presents quite different problems. Despite the fact that this latter topic—the localization of higher cognitive functions—has become an industry unto itself, there are many reasons to suggest that the sensory and motor localization model may not hold for cognitive processes. This topic is considered in detail in an earlier book (Uttal, 2001).

[29]A much more compete story of the Phrenology episode is presented in Uttal (2001).

the muscles of a dissected frog's leg would twitch if a source of electricity were applied to it.[30] On the basis of this kind of experiment, Galvani (1791/1953) proposed that a kind of electricity existed that was special to animal tissue. Although he was wrong about the uniqueness of animal electricity,[31] Galvani's experiments established what was to become another axiom of the neurosciences, namely that the nervous system operates by electrical processes or by processes that can both be driven by electrical stimuli and produce electrical signals when activated. From this insight came the proliferation of electrophysiological studies that are a main theme of current research. An excellent history of the electrical activity of the brain is available (Brazier, 1961) that relates the work of such important figures as Emile Du Bois-Reymond (1818–1896) who first showed that electrical signals were present whenever neurons were activated and Richard Caton (1842–1926) who discovered the overall electrical activity of the brain.

2.6.3 The Establishment of the Neuron Doctrine

There is one other development worthy of special mention at this point in our discussion because it, too, has become a fundamental axiom of modern neuroscience. The development is known as the "Neuron Doctrine." For most of the 19th century, the microscopic structure of the nervous system was largely unknown. There was no staining technique that could be used to detail the fine structure of its otherwise transparent parts. The 19th century generally accepted notion (articulated by Joseph von Gerlach, 1820–1896) was that the nervous system consisted of a continuous "reticulum" or "syncytium" in which all of the constituent parts were protoplasmically interconnected. However, in 1873, Camillo Golgi (1843–1926) developed a staining technique based on silver that had the unique (for its time) property of selectively staining only a few of the many neurons present, but those that it did were stained completely.

The evidence that the Golgi Silver Stain produced under a microscope strongly argued that the nervous system was not a continuous reticulum but that it was composed of individual cells, each of which was completely surrounded by a membrane and, thus, protoplasmically separated from its neighbors, just as were the cells of any other organ system of the body. In 1891 Wilhelm Waldeyer (1836–1921) seems to have been the first to draw

[30]A wonderful anecdote is told by Sherrington (1940/1963, p. 197). He suggests that original discovery was not that of Luigi Galvani but, rather of his wife, Lucia, who told him that the frog's legs they were preparing for dinner seemed alive on the copper wire grill used in their kitchen.

[31]Galvani's theoretical error is less than understandable. Alessandro Volta (1745–1827) had already shown that electricity could also be produced by inorganic materials and that this kind of electricity seemed to be indistinguishable from the animal kind.

this conclusion and to propose what has come to be called the "Neuron Doctrine"—a discrete cellular theory of the nervous system. In addition, he also was the first to use the word *neuron* to refer to these nervous system cells. The Neuron Doctrine, contrary to the reticulum or syncytium theory, asserts that the nervous system is made up of aggregates of individual neurons that are not protoplasmically connected. Instead, they are separated from each other by cell membranes that continuously enclose individual neurons and, therefore, separate the contents of one from another.

The main thrust[32] of research using this new staining technique was carried out by Santiago Ramon y Cajal (1852–1934) who applied the Golgi process to many different parts of the nervous system. Regardless of what region of the nervous system he studied, Cajal observed many structures that confirmed Waldeyer's hypothesis of the Neuron Doctrine. It is surprising that, in spite of this early and very compelling evidence, there remained many supporters of the reticular hypothesis well into the 20th century. It is interesting to note that in this case even the demonstration of optical microscopic evidence did not deter the reticularists from their adherence to what clearly was an outmoded idea. Because of the small size of the microstructural components of neurons, the reticular idea could not be put to rest completely until the development of the electron microscope. This episode should serve as a warning to those of us who stick to outmoded ideas much too long.

Nevertheless, by 1900 Waldeyer's Neuron Doctrine had a substantial amount of support from a number of neuroanatomists on the basis of Cajal's extensive research. Cajal and Golgi jointly received the Nobel prize in 1906, the former for his histological studies of neurons and the latter for his development of the silver staining technique that Cajal had used to establish, beyond any reasonable doubt, the validity of the Neuron Doctrine.

In spite of this joint recognition, there was an extraordinary discrepancy between the theoretical conclusions to which these two microscopists respectively came. Cajal's support of the Neuron Doctrine was not seconded by Golgi who remained a "reticularist" until his death. It is illuminating to consider some of their words with regard to the Neuron Doctrine. First, let Cajal speak in the words of his 1906 Nobel address:

> From my researches as a whole there derives a general conception which comprise the following propositions:

[32]Although Cajal is often credited as being the sole contributor to this important development, Shepherd (1991) tells us that a much larger group of neuroscientists contributed to the establishment of the Neuron Doctrine. Such a simultaneous, if not integrated, effort would not be surprising; few scientists operate in isolation. Given the influence of the many media of communication that have always been available, multiple discoveries are the rule, not the exception.

> 1. The nerve cells are morphological entities, neurons to use the word brought into use by the authority of Professor Waldeyer. . . . [The] structures, whose form varies according to the nerve centers being studied, confirm that the nerve elements possess reciprocal relationships in contiguity not in continuity.
>
> These facts . . . imply three physiological postulates:
>
> (a) As nature, in order to assure and amplify these contacts, has created complicated systems of pericellular ramifications (systems which become incomprehensible within the hypothesis of continuity), it must be admitted that the nerve currents are transmitted from one element to another as a consequence of a sort of induction or influence from a distance.
>
> (b) It must also be supposed that the cell bodies and the dendrites are, in the same way as the axis cylinders, conductive devices, as they represent the intermediary links between afferent nerve fibers and the afore-mentioned axons.
>
> (c) The examination of movement of nervous impulses . . . proves not only that the protoplasmic expansions play a conducting role but even more that nervous movement in these prolongations is *toward the cell or axon*, while it is *away from the cell* in these axons. This formula [is] called the *dynamic polarization of neurons* . . .
>
> During twenty-five years of continued work on nearly all the organs of the nervous system and a large number of zoological species, I have never met a single observed fact contrary to these assertions. (pp. 220–221)

Although Golgi was largely responsible for the method that made this enormous breakthrough in understanding the organization of the nervous system possible, as noted, he stilled remained an ardent champion of the reticular idea. After a long discussion of what his impression of what the Neuron Doctrine meant (essentially in agreement with Cajal's statement), he argued in his 1906 Nobel address that:

> The conclusion of this account of the neuron question, which has to be rather an assembly of facts, brings me back to my starting point, namely that no arguments, on which Waldeyer supported the individuality and independence of the neuron, will stand examination.
>
> We have seen, in fact, how we lack embryological data and how anatomical arguments, either individually or as a whole, do not offer any basis firm enough to uphold this doctrine. In fact, all of the characteristics of nerve process, protoplasmic process and cell-body organization which we have examined seem to point in another direction. (p. 216)

What blinded Golgi and the other persistent reticularists to the Neuron Doctrine will always remain arguable. Nowadays, we are all firmly in Cajal's camp with regard to the separateness of the cells of the nervous system. The electrophysiological and electrochemical studies of individual neurons are among the crown jewels of the neurosciences. The synapse, the "contiguous," not "continuous," junctions (in the words of Cajal), from one neuron to the next have provided what is almost universally agreed is the basis of learning, perception, and all other kinds of mental information processing. If we had persevered in our adherence to the theory of a continuous reticulum of neurons, we would have been much delayed at arriving at the modern idea that permits us at least to speculate about the brain's creation of the mind. That idea is that it is the organization of the many neurons of the brain as mediated by the interactions (and their changes in conductivity) between neurons that accounts for all mental activity. The definitive historic account of the evolution of the Neuron Doctrine is presented in Shepherd (1991).

The final step in this discussion concerns the discovery and explication of the points of contiguous interaction between neurons. When the Neuron Doctrine was generally accepted, some explanation had to be provided concerning the transmission of information between these independent neurons. This functional, as opposed to structural, junction between neurons was named a "synapse" by Charles S. Sherrington (1852–1952). Sherrington (1906) went on to elaborate, solely on functional bases, the idea that the synapse was the basis of the "Integrative Action of the Nervous System." Although there was considerable support for an electrical mode of connection between neurons, the one-way transmission of activity and the electrophysiologically observed delay in conduction across the junction finally led to what is now an appreciation that most communication between neurons is carried out by chemical means.

However certain neuroscientists were that the chemical synapse existed, it was actually only a hypothesis constructed from electrophysiological studies until the invention of the electron microscope. The synapse was not visualized until 1954 by Palade and Palay (1954) and by de Robertis and Bennet (1954). The high magnification images produced by this powerful machine demonstrated an actual physical gap between neurons, presynaptic vesicles containing the yet to be chemically analyzed transmitter substances, and the postsynaptic receptor regions. Although the complete details of synaptic nervous action are yet to be known, from this point on the questions that had to be asked became apparent.

Shepherd (1991) has summarized the key principles of the Neuron Doctrine as follows:

1. Neurons, like all cells, are formed by common macromolecules and organelles, surrounded by a continuous surface membrane.
2. In most neurons, dendrites receive synaptic inputs and axons carry impulse outputs. [But there are exceptions.]

3. In most neurons, synaptic responses occur in dendrites and are graded in amplitude, whereas impulses occur in axons and have a voltage gated all-or-nothing character. [However there are exceptions.]
4. It follows from point 1–3 that any point in a neuron may function as a local processing unit . . .
5. The local subunits of varying properties mean that there is not a fixed correlation of structure and function within the different parts of the neuron. (Abstracted from Shepherd, 1991, p. 290)

Modifications have been proposed to the classic Neuron Doctrine in recent years in which the dynamics of neuronal masses integrate the action of individual neurons (see chap. 4); however, in any such theory, the neuron still plays a central role as the foundation element. Although the cumulative activity of large clusters of neurons is invoked in such theories, none of them denies the anatomical and functional separation between neurons implied by the original Neuron Doctrine. What they do propose are alternative functional units as the key representations of thought including clusters of neurons or, more extremely, the overall brain activity reflected in the EEG: alternatives that do not provide a satisfactory theory of the mind, as shown in chapter 4.

Shepherd (1991) finished his book by noting that the classic expression of the Neuron Doctrine was expressed by Waldeyer (1891) by four basic tenets:

> The nerve cell is the anatomical, physiological, metabolic, and genetic unit of the nervous system. (Shepherd, 1991, p. 4)

and these four must now be supplemented by:

> a major contribution of research in the future will be to add a fifth tenet: the neuron as a basic *information processing* unit in the nervous system. (Shepherd, 1991, p. 292)

It is this new role that has now begun to dominate cognitive neuroscience. A reasonably clear idea has developed about the neuron with regard to the first four tenets; the future will see an increasing emphasis on the informational aspects. It is this topic that is emphasized in this present book.

2.7 SUMMARY

The historical survey of older theories of the mind–body relationship is now complete; the discussion has now arrived at the dawn of modern cognitive neuroscience. The discoveries and developments of the 20th century represent a corpus of information that is so large that it defies any brief summary. There are extended timelines on the Internet that provide brief historical sequences. Two that I found useful are: http://faculty.washington.edu/chudler/hist.html and http://www.smithsrisca.demon.co.uk/neuro-timeline.html.

In this section, I summarize this chapter by pointing out the fundamental axioms and assumptions on which the modern field of cognitive neuroscience is based. These are the presumptions that guide modern theory and experimentation. However influential and important they may be, they are rarely made explicit in the sometimes arcane technical reports of cognitive neuroscientific discoveries published by the thousands every month. Nevertheless, these assumptions are what neuroscientists generally believe to be true today. Together, they represent a consensus that bubbles quietly along below the level of the more specialized controversies and disagreements that seem to consume so much time and effort these days. The previous portions of this chapter seek to explain how we got to this point in the development of our theories of the manner in which the mind emerges from brain. The following list tabulates the fundamental assumptions that I believe dominate cognitive neuroscience today.

1. *Philosophical Monism:* First and foremost is the basic philosophical stance without which cognitive neuroscience would be nonsensical. The materialist orientation to mind–brain theory originally postulated by Thales so long ago presupposes that there is only one kind of reality—that of the material world. The main corollary is that the mind is a process or product of complex, but real, processes occurring in the material brain. The salient metaphor is—The brain is the wheel; the mind is its rotation. The brain could exist without the mind but the mind could not exist without the brain (or some equivalent and equally complex information processing system). One is machinery; the other is the action of that machinery. There is no supernatural force or separateness of "substance" required to explain how the mind is produced by the brain.

2. *Complexity:* However difficult it may be to understand how the brain works, the complete or relative intractability of the problems faced by current cognitive neuroscience are fully explained by the complexity of the involved material mechanisms. The mysteries surrounding the mind–brain relationship may suggest something supernatural. However, whatever difficulties we face are due to natural forces and processes alone, albeit innumerable and intricately interacting ones.

3. *The Brain Is the Seat of the Mind:* There is no basis for any remaining question concerning the locus of the mind. It is only the brain to which we must turn for the answers to the "world knot." Any allusions to the idea that

the mind is distributed to other parts of the body or to the external environment are vestiges of the supernatural that are no longer tenable.

4. *The Solid Matter of the Brain Is Where the Action Is:* It is now certain that the physiological processes that generate mind are carried out within the solid portions of the brain, not the ventricles.

5. *The Solid Portions of the Brain Are Made Up of a Host of Anatomically Discrete Neurons:* The activity of the brain that is most salient for the production of the mind is to be found in the informational interactions of the myriad of microscopic neurons as specified in the Neuron Doctrine. The specific chemistry of these interactions is interesting in its own right and sets limits on the nature of these interactions. However, in principle, any other "technology" could do as well.

6. *Synapses Mediate the Interaction of the Discrete Neurons of the Brain:* The interaction among the membrane-isolated neurons of the brain is mediated by junctions called synapses. Most synaptic conductivity is explained in terms of chemical substances that physically move from the terminals of one neuron to those of another. The number of synapses on a single central neuron (which themselves are estimated to number as many as 10^{13}) may number in the thousands. This numerousness explains, in part, the enormous complexity of the brain and the difficulty it poses to a definitive reductive explanation.

7. *The Brain Is Highly Adaptive:* The adaptivity of the brain is accounted for by the synapses' ability to change their conductive efficiency as the joint effect of experience and maturation.

8. *Neural Activity Is Based on Electrochemistry:* The action of individual neurons can be measured by electrical instruments and integrated electrical signals can be detected in, on, and around the brain. Similarly, electrical signals can stimulate the brain. However, the electrical activity of the brain is mediated by ionic distributions rather than electronic mechanisms and, therefore, these neuronal signals occur with much longer time courses than electronic conduction.[33]

9. *The Fundamental Correlate of Mind Is Neural Interaction:* The bases of mental processes of all kinds are to be found in the complex interactions of very large numbers of discrete neurons. The ultimate task of all theoreticians interested in how the brain generates the mind is to understand these networks. The collective state of this network of individual neurons is the psychoneural equivalent of consciousness, mentation, and cognitive processes of all kinds. Although there is considerable attention being paid to the slow potentials recorded over the brain, it is likely that these signals, though correlated with mental activity, are epiphenomenal.

---

[33]Both magnetic responses of the brain and its sensitivity to magnetic forces are also now known.

10. *Localization Remains a Contentious Issue in Cognitive Neuroscience:* There is no question that specialized sensory and motor regions of the brain exist. However, whether specific high-level cognitive processes are located in particular regions of the brain is still controversial. Despite the general acceptance of the assumption of localization by many cognitive neuroscientists, this issue actually remains unresolved. It is more likely that as cognitive processes get more complicated, they recruit ever-larger regions of the brain. Although not equipotential or homogenous, the critical brain equivalents of cognition are probably far more distributed than many of our contemporaries believe.

Thus, there are continuous tensions between cellular and field theories, on the one hand, and distributed and localized theories, on the other. In many ways, these two debates collapse into one another.

There is one other general point that has to be made, remade, and then made once again. In a field of science investigating a topic as complex as the mind–brain relationship, there is a powerful tendency to ascribe meaning to our data that does not actually exist. As we see in chapter 1, theories go far beyond simply generating hypotheses to be tested in the laboratory or dictating the measurements to be made. Far more important is that they have an enormous influence on what we believe our findings signify. The perceptual power attributed to single cells in the period between 1970 and 1980 and the use of compound potentials such as the EEG to "explain" higher level cognitive powers are both cases in point. Only by appreciating the role of theory and the impact that an a priori assumption may have on our interpretations, are we likely to arrive at a truly objective resolution of the great problem—Can the mind–brain problem be solved? The main challenge to answering this question lies in Assumption 2—the enormous complexity of the brain. Many mathematical theorems suggest insurmountable obstacles may exist in our quest. Because of the uncertainty surrounding the exact nature of how brain activity generates the mind, theories of the brain–mind abound today. Some are toy theories; some are fanciful extrapolations from current technological developments; some may have the germ of an insight that may possibly be the breakthrough needed to solve the great problem. It is the purpose of the rest of this book to survey modern theories of how the brain produces the mind and to inspect their assumptions and arguments.

CHAPTER

3

The Limits of Cognitive Neuroscience Theory—An Epistemological Interlude

3.1 PRELUDE

The purpose of this book is to review the many theories of how the mind emerges from the action of the nervous system and its components, especially the brain. At the outset of this review, however, it is important to reiterate three fundamental propositions concerning the assumptions on which the discussions in this book are based:

Proposition 1: All of human mentation, including perceptions, all other cognitive processes, emotions, thoughts, and reveries of all kinds, in fact everything involved in our mental lives is the result of the activity of our nervous system. Perhaps the greatest question of human history is how these mental processes arise from brain activity.

Proposition 2: The most likely level of analysis at which a neural foundation of mental processes occurs is that of the innumerable interactions of a multitude of discrete neurons (i.e., the details of the interneuronal connections).

Proposition 3: At the present time, we have absolutely no answer to the fundamental question—How does the brain make the mind? Furthermore, there are ample reasons to believe that it never can be answered.

I am aware that Assumption 3, in particular, will not find happy acceptance among the many psychologists and cognitive neuroscientists who believe they are on the edge of understanding the bridge between neural activity and cognitive processes. Nevertheless, no one has yet produced an explanation of how the highly interconnected networks of vast numbers of neurons produce our mental life. It is at this level that the question must be answered. As Chalmers (1995) put it when he argued that studies from such diverse fields as quantum mechanics and neurophysiology leave the fundamental question of how mind and brain are related "entirely unanswered":

> It would be wonderful if reductive methods [e.g., neurophysiology, quantum physics, etc.] could explain experience, too; I had hoped for a long time that they might. Unfortunately there are systematic reasons why these methods must fail. Reductive methods are successful in most domains because what needs explaining in those domains and are structures and functions, and these are the kind of thing that a physical account can entail. When it comes to a problem over and above the explanation of structures and functions, [e.g., consciousness] these methods are impotent. (p. 208)

Other philosophers have made the same point in similar words. McGinn (1989), for example asserted:

> We have been trying for a long time to solve the mind–body problem. It has stubbornly resisted our best efforts. The mystery persists, I think the time has come to admit candidly that we cannot resolve the mystery. (p. 349)

Searle (1997) made the same point when he referred to the lack of progress on this most important conundrum of science as the "dirty secret of contemporary neuroscience" (p. 198).

Some scholars have referred to the intractability of the mind–brain problem as an "explanatory gap" (Block & Stalnaker, 1999; Levine, 1983). In almost all of these cases there is no rejection of the ontological statement expressed in Proposition 1, but there is a somewhat sad acceptance of the epistemological barrier that separates the vocabulary and concepts of psychology from those of neurophysiology expressed in Proposition 3.

Some of modern times' most distinguished neurophysiologists[1] have come to the same conclusion. Ragnar Granit (1977), arguing against neuroreductionism, suggested:

> A lower stratum in the hierarchy can never fully explain the raison d'être of the high stratum above it. It follows that the properties of conscious awareness cannot be explained by any of the numerous physiological process

[1]Horgan (1999) interviewed a number of even more current neuroscientists and philosophers. Throughout his book he alludes to the doubts that many of them had concerning the hope that the mind could be "explained" by even the most advanced future technology. These doubts come through his interviews not because these scholars view current knowledge as inadequate, but as the result of a deep conviction that the task is impossible for reasons of deep principle.

> within reach of our technical prowess, even though without them consciousness is bound to fade away. (p. 213)

Even philosophers totally committed to the "eliminativist" position that all "folk psychology" will ultimately be reduced to neurophysiological concepts at least agree with the current state of affairs. For example, Grush and Churchland (1995) stated:

> Consciousness is almost certainly a property of the physical brain. The major mystery, however, is how neurons achieve effects such as being aware of a toothache or the smell of cinnamon. Neuroscience has not reached the stage where we can satisfactorily answer these questions. (p. 10)[2]

Even those with different theoretical stances ultimately come to the same conclusion. Crick and Koch (2000), who argued for what I believe is an incorrect theory of a "small fraction" of neurons, share this conviction that the mind–brain problem is so far unanswered when they say:

> What remains is the sobering realization that our subjective world of qualia—what distinguishes us from zombies and fills our life with color, music, smells and other vivid sensations—is possibly caused by the activity of a small fraction of all of the neurons in the brain, locate strategically between the inner and outer worlds. How these act to produce the subjective world that is so dear to us is still a complete mystery. (p. 109)

Donald Kennedy (2004), a distinguished neuroscientist in his own right and editor of the highly empirical journal *Science*, apparently joined these skeptics when he said in a recent editorial ". . . it seems so unlikely to me that our knowledge of the brain will deepen enough to fuse it with the mind" (p. 373).

Furthermore, the very variety of the theories that are discussed in this book is itself supportive evidence that cognitive neuroscience is beset by some much more formidable barriers to understanding the mind–brain bridge than is usually appreciated. That so many conjectures can flourish at the present time suggests that none has yet come close to solving the greatest challenge of all—that which Arthur Schopenhauer (1788–1860) reputedly referred to as the "world knot."[3]

---

[2]Grush and Churchland (1995) did go on to express the idealistically optimistic view that "promising research programs do exist" (p. 10) but this is more a hope than any indication of real progress toward the goal.

[3]Although it is repeatedly asserted that Schopenhauer's "world knot" referred to the question of how matter became mind, it has been argued that what he was actually referring to was "the identity of the subject of willing with that of knowing" (Poole, 2000).

Proposition 3, as conservative as it is, must be evaluated in the bright light of the many other kinds of undeniable accomplishments of researchers in neuroscience. There are many examples of exciting and informative discoveries in this field of science. Studies of the putative localization of hypothetical cognitive processes in the brain, of the electrical activity of the brain, of the biochemistry of synaptic conduction, or of the interconnectedness of the larger nuclei of the brain, among many others, while fascinating and interesting in their own right, do not approach the mind–brain problem directly. The findings in those research programs have proven extremely exciting and frequently enlightening, but they do not speak to the problem at the "critical level of analysis."

Nevertheless, it is often the case that findings from these otherwise laudable activities become the grist of theories of mind–brain interaction of considerable irrelevance and fantastic construction. Indeed, a close analysis of the germane theoretical literature reveals that many, if not most, of the explanations that have been proposed to bridge this gap are either: (a) analogous simulations (which create functionally similar models based on operational principles that may be very different than those used in the brain) or (b) attacks on irrelevant, but solvable, problems at lesser levels of complexity than the one most likely to be involved in creating mentation. (This is what the ethologists used to call "displacement activity.")

Proposition 2 asserts that the most likely level of psychoneural equivalence is the informational interaction of a huge number of individual neurons. For reasons discussed later, this produces a level of complexity that is not amenable to scientific methodology as we know it and, despite some optimistic assertions to the contrary, to science as it can be known.

Is the possibility of a limit on answering the fundamental cognitive neuroscience question of concern to others who have studied the problem? Alternatively, is this nothing but the constrained and idiosyncratic expression of a limited personal view? These are fair questions that must be faced by anyone willing to challenge the optimistic milieu that currently characterizes this field of science. The answer is clear enough. A select group of scholars have considered this question and come to the strong conclusion that not all scientific questions can be answered for well defined and understood reasons. This book argues that the mind–brain relationship is likely to be among the most thoroughly intractable of all.

3.2 ON THE LIMITS OF THEORY BUILDING AND THEORY

As noted in chapter 1, there is a substantial amount of thought in scientific circles that theory building is arguably the noblest calling in science and, perhaps, in human history. The most persistent heroes in the scientific pantheon are the geniuses who put together related assemblages of empirical observations into the comprehensive statements we accept as theories. Nicolaus Copernicus (1473–1543), Isaac Newton (1692–1727), Carolus Linnaeus (1707–1778), Charles Darwin (1809–1882), Gregor Mendel (1822–1884), Dimitry Ivanovitch Mendeleyev (1834–1907), Albert Einstein (1879–1955), and others are remembered as a group for their syntheses to a degree that is not enjoyed by the much larger group of empirical observers or explorers.[4] In this regard it is interesting to note that the Nobel prizes and other important scientific awards are more often given to specialist experimentalists who discovered some important fact or who have generated some new methodology rather than to the generalist theoreticians who integrated a spectrum of observations into a synoptic interpretation.

There is much current controversy about the "limits of science." Some optimistic scientists and philosophers argue that there are no limits other than practical ones. We need only wait until a newer and faster computer comes along or for the development of some new mathematical theorem or measurement methodology to solve *all* of the problems that might be faced by humans now or in the future. We need only to continue exploring, collecting data, and developing new investigative technologies; then, at some future time, we will either be rewarded by explanations of everything or make substantial "progress" toward such a goal. Ultimately, this optimistic, but unrealistic, epistemology of science argues that totally complete explanations are, in principle, available for all of nature.

On the other side of the controversy, some equally convinced scholars emphatically argue that there are limits to scientific inquiry and explanation.[5] Their main point usually is that it can be shown (logically or mathematically) that some scientific problems are intractable for insurmountable practical reasons or because of some in principle barrier to their ultimate solution. No matter how hard we work, no matter how many data are collected, and no matter how much time is spent on the task, proponents of

---

[4]As usual, even this generalization has been challenged. Some scientists have argued that experimentation and theory are collapsing into each other. I don't think this is the case. What is really happening is that theory and experiment are more often than in the past being carried out by the same person. The sociology of modern science is such that more "theoreticians" are willing to get their hands dirty than in previous generations and that "bench grunts" are now more often generating their own theories. An additional factor is that theory is dictating ever-clearer hypotheses for experimentalists to evaluate.

[5]It is important to distinguish between those who believe there are structural limits on scientific accomplishment and those who feel that there is an end of science close at hand because all of the important problems have been solved. Scientific "completion" has always been a treacherous argument to make, particularly since the discovery of X-Rays by Wilhelm Roentgen (1845–1923) in 1895. This paradigm-shifting discovery came at a time when it was assumed by many that physical science had discovered everything that was to be discovered. The failed concept of a "complete" science and its history were described in detail by Badash (1972).

this point of view reflect the opinion that certain questions about the natural world can never be answered. Theoreticians of this ilk are represented by Bremermann (1977) who argued that:

> In summary, many mathematical, logical, and artificial intelligence problems probably cannot be solved because the computational cost of known algorithms (and in some cases all possible algorithms) exceeds the power of any existing computer. (p. 171)

This topic is discussed in greater detail in chapter 6. For the moment, the issue of the practical nature of complexity is raised as a reminder that it is an impenetrable obstacle to solving some much less complex problems than understanding how mind emerges from brain.

The view that there are intractable problems in science is held for a number of other reasons. Krausz (2000), for one, believed that science, especially social science, is limited because it can never achieve the necessary "objectivity." Rescher (1984), on the other hand, argued that there are some questions that are invalid, mainly because of the assumptions that they incorporate into their logic. His three categories of invalid questions were:

1. Improper Questions: Questions of this class are based on demonstrably false assumptions. For example, the question–How do you build a perpetual motion machine?–is improper because the assumption that such a machine can be built is known to be false.
2. Problematic Questions: Questions of this class are based on assumptions that themselves are indeterminate or unresolved. For example, the question–How do extraterrestrials communicate?–is problematic because the matter of their existence or nonexistence has not yet been resolved.
3. Ineffable Questions: Questions of this class are based on meaningless (i.e., "conceptually inaccessible") assumptions. For example, the question–What are the qualia of phenomenal redness?–is based on the assumption of the accessibility of intrapersonal perceptual dimensions, an assumption that itself may be unjustified. (Adapted from Rescher, 1984, pp. 8–9)

On the other hand, Rescher argued that there are no a priori "insolvable" problems. The invalid questions that he just tabulated are not the same, he contended, as valid questions that just have not been answered yet. Questions of this kind may not be answerable at the present time because we do not know how to carry out a specific measurement and we cannot predict the future. As Rescher (1984) summed it up:

> The cardinal fact is simply that no one is in a position to delineate here and now what the science of the future can and cannot achieve. No identifiable issue can be confidently placed outside the limits of science. (p. 127)

However, there is one fly in this soothing ointment. Rescher ignores the powerful force of mathematics to establish theorems that demonstrate the "insolvability" of certain propositions. Some theorems (e.g., the work of Hilgetag, O'Neill, & Young, 1996, 2000, as well as the just mentioned work of Bremermann, 1977) strongly argue that some questions of neural organization cannot be answered for solid reasons that can be precisely specified at the present time. Mathematics is also replete with constraints on the solution of certain easily defined tasks in a way that is not any different than the "insolvability" constraint.

The problem is that it is not always possible to distinguish between an "insolvable" question and an "improper" one. What at one time may well have seemed like a solvable, although difficult to resolve, question may metamorphose over time into an improper question as we learn more about the world.

3.3 AN ANALYSIS OF SOME CONTEMPORARY THOUGHT

Although the popular media regularly distorts the thoughts of contemporary cognitive neuroscientists, sometimes a useful service is performed by allowing them (the scientists) to speak in their own words in the public record. In November 2003, the *New York Times* published a series of articles on their Internet site (nytimes.com) dealing with the great questions of Science. One of these—How Does the Brain Work?—was summarized by Blakeslee (2003). Her summary was an interesting mix of interpretations of a series of comments provided by a group of eminent cognitive neuroscientists in the preceding day's issue (Anonymous, 2003). Blakeslee drew the following insightful conclusion after discussing some of the obvious progress in modern neuroanatomy and neurophysiology.

> Researchers do not know how the six-layered cortical sheet gives rise to the sense of self. They have not been able to disentangle the role of genes and experience in shaping brains. They do not know how the firing of billions of loosely coupled neurons give rise to coordinated goal-directed behavior.
>
> They can see trees but no forest. (Blakeslee, November 11, 2003, p. 1)[6]

---

[6]All page numbers listed in this discussion are from the two printouts I obtained from the Internet Websites and may not correspond to those obtained by other readers.

Blakeslee's summary was about as clear as this complex and confused field gets these days. She then went on to recite some of the progress that has been made in the brain sciences. She summarized her brief review by acknowledging that much that has been accomplished still doesn't begin to resolve the remaining great "mysteries."

To understand how Blakeslee arrived at these conclusions, it is useful to analyze material collected from the cognitive scientists who posed the answers to the question of how the brain works that were collectively presented in Anonymous (2003). It is important to point out that all scholars who were invited to respond to this great query are all currently active cognitive neuroscientists and are enthusiastic about what they see as the enormous progress being made in this field. Nevertheless, almost all of them alluded, either directly or indirectly, to the enormity of the challenges faced by brain–mind theories. In the following paragraphs, in the order in which their responses were presented, I abstract their comments and suggest some of the reasons their enthusiasm is well constrained. (All of the following comments are in Anonymous, 2003.)

Martha J. Farah, University of Pennsylvania: Farah summarizes several of the important developments in cognitive neuroscience but then argues that "Now[adays] you CAN'T study cognitive psychology without encountering neuroscience" (p. 1). From one point of view she is entirely correct, but a more germane question from a slightly different perspective is—Can you study cognitive psychology without neuroscience? Based on the enthusiasm of cognitive neuroscientists, the answer to this rhetorical question seems to be "no." However, given the limits on our ability to understand the critical level[7] of brain activity, a strong argument can be made that the answer to this rhetorical question should be—not only *can* there be, but there *must* be a future for scientific psychology outside of neuroscience. The reason for this is simple enough: Much of what we know about human mentation and behavior is likely to be beyond the realm of the most extreme neuroreductionist accounts.

Farah then went on to assert that ". . . we know almost nothing about the neural basis of individuality" (p. 2). It is here that she made a logical leap that I believe is incorrect. The indisputable progress that has been made in some of the anatomical and physiological sciences does not justify the ". . . hope we'll have some answers . . . 25 years from now" (p. 2). The problem is that the "basis of individuality" to which Farah alludes is the heart of the question, not an ancillary one. The rest is secondary anatomy, physiology,

---

[7]The debate over what is the "critical level" of neural activity that corresponds to mental activity is well evidenced by the variety of theories described in this book. As should be obvious by now, I believe that it would be incorrect to attribute mind to anything other than the information processing of large networks of discrete neurons. Others, obviously, feel quite differently.

technology, chemistry, and physics. Progress that demonstrates that a certain neuron's response correlates with some sensory input or that a place in the brain lights up when we think about something in particular, however interesting, simply does not speak to the fundamental question of how the brain makes the mind.

Michael Posner, University of Oregon: Posner's comments dealt in their entirety with networks of macroscopic brain regions. He stated, "It's all about networks of brain areas" (p. 2). From my perspective, however, looking to "widely scattered" brain areas (to account for cognitive processes) attributes those processes to the wrong level of brain activity and obscures the fine structure and the state of the network of individual neurons. Arguably, it is at this latter level that the brain operates to produce mind. It is, of course, "all about networks" but Posner was attending to the wrong kind of networks.

Mriganka Sur, Massachusetts Institute of Technology: Sur succinctly, and from my point of view correctly, reviewed the accomplishments made in cellular neurophysiology. However, he then went on acknowledge that "the ability to process information via networks, remains least understood today" (p. 4) and ". . . we are far from a compact description of how networks [of neurons] function" (p. 4).

P. Read Montague, Baylor College of Medicine: Montague correctly identified the main accomplishments made in neuroscience as "taking apart cells and synapses all the way down to the molecular level including the gene families involved"[8] (p. 4). He also pointed out the accomplishments of psychologists who study visual perception. He then joined the prevailing opinion in noting:

> What I think is missing lies in the "in between zone"—those levels of organization that connect the brain-a-collection-of biological-components to mental operations; in short, something like a software-level description. (p. 5)

It is, however, at this "in-between level" that the problems, obstacles, limits, and constraints operate most strongly to prevent such a description, much less a reductive explanation of how the brain makes mind. Montague proposed, instead, "Chronic electrophysiology experiments in behaving [animals]" (p. 5) as the paradigm of choice for future neuroscientific research. However, his proposed experiments were more or less traditional studies in sensory and motor function and do not attack the nut of the problem: How does the brain produce the mind? The proposed experiments are ex-

---

[8]I disagree with one point made by Montague. I do not believe it is appropriate to append "neuroimaging techniques for more molar measurements during cognitive function" to his list of accomplishments (see Uttal, 2001).

cellent suggestions for studying peripheral neural information transmission; however, they do not speak to any of the "ineffable" mental processes that are at the crux of the mind–brain problem.

Terry Sejnowski, Salk Institute: Sejnowski correctly identified one of the strong biases in brain–mind theory as the plethora of data from single neurons. He directed our attention to the "overall pattern of activity" (p. 7) but acknowledged that ". . . we don't yet have a theory that explains what we are seeing" (p. 7). He also, equally correctly, from my point of view, alluded to the fact that sleep remains a "huge embarrassment" for neuroscience (p. 7).

Antonio Damasio, University of Iowa: Damasio eschewed any discussion of consciousness ("which, as you [Blakeslee] say, is both irritatingly and insufficiently covered . . ." p. 8). He, thus, ignored what many philosophers, psychologists, and neuroscientists currently consider, to the contrary, to be one of the keys to the brain–mind problem. I believe he was correct, considering what already has been said in previous chapters, about the accessibility and the difficulty of defining mind or consciousness. Damasio then considered other issues, e.g., how the body may signal controls to the brain "which supports cognition" (p. 8). Without further comment, I would argue that his choice of the word *supports* to describe the relation between brain and mind is typically (if not intentionally) ambiguous and reflects the failure of modern theory to bridge the gap between the two domains.

Rodolfo Llinas, New York University: Llinas went right to the core of the matter when he asked and then answered the question "How does the brain work then?" (p. 8) as follows:

> It works by organizing the electrical activity of its neurons in time into coherence patterns, not unlike the spectacular choreographic of a complex dance. . . . To do so millions of neurons must be active together and keep pace with each other at a rhythm of their own making, the so-called neuronal electrical oscillation. (p. 9)

One can hardly deny this allegorical statement; it rings true about the "spectacular choreographic" of the neurons. However, there are two residual problems. First, it invokes a coordinated oscillation, a topic discussed and found wanting in chapter 4. Second, and much more to the point being made here, however satisfying and elegant the poetry may be, it ignores the issues of complexity and tractability that are at the heart of the matter. Llinas's poetry is of no more use to science than the classic metaphor of the "enchanted loom" enunciated by Sherrington (1940/1963) 70 or more years earlier:

> The brain is waking and with it the mind is returning. It is as if the Milky Way entered upon some cosmic dance. Swiftly the head-mass becomes an en-

> chanted loom where millions of flashing shuttles weave a dissolving pattern, always a meaningful pattern, though never an abiding one; a shifting harmony of subpatterns. (p. 178)

Llinas went on to acknowledge the limits of our knowledge in the face of these beautiful allegories by noting:

> And what don't we know that is crucial? We don't know how subjectivity (qualia) comes to be. That is, the ability to feel as opposed to simply act without feelings, like biological robots. (p. 9)

"Aye," as Shakespeare had Hamlet say, "there's the rub." It is consciousness, awareness, qualia, and the subjective states that pose the great mysteries and we haven't a clue to as to how they emerge from the "enchanted loom."

The overarching conclusion that can be drawn from virtually all of these commentators, as aptly done by Blakeslee, is that we do not yet know the answer to the great question of how the brain makes the mind. Unmentioned, but looming like a dark specter on the horizon, is the possibility that an answer or valid theory is not obtainable. This issue must, at the very least be objectively and actively considered, rather than being passively accepted without criticism or controversy just because some feel it is "pessimistic." To accept (or more accurately "hope for") tractability without thinking about the possibility of intractability may challenge the entire future of a truly scientific psychology.

3.4 ON SUPERNATURAL SUBSTITUTES FOR SCIENTIFIC THEORY

At this point, it is important to inject a few words about "nonscientific theories," those especially subject to Rescher's problematic category (see p. 104). Everything that is said in mind–brain theory must be constrained within the context of observable phenomena and laws that are consistent with the main body of scientific knowledge. Scientific theories are bounded and constrained by empirical anchors and hopefully by logical consistency.

The present discussion, therefore, specifically rejects any theories of the untestable supernatural as alternatives to scientific ones. The laws of science must take priority if we are to strive for a rational, logical, and lawful world. Supernatural, nonscientific thinking creates havoc in science by subliminally exerting a distorting influence on what should be purely natural theories.

Furthermore, any effort to find a means of reconciling the supernatural and the natural must be eschewed since it can only lead to a diminishment in the integrity of a true scientific theory, characterized by criteria of corrigibility and comprehensiveness. By definition, the supernatural is not bounded by empirical results and is therefore, free to invoke concepts and entities for which no evidence is available or likely to become available. If the most fundamental property of the rational enterprise we call "science"—publicly observable empirical observations—is violated, then the entire enterprise can be compromised.

The major factor leading us down the slippery slope from science to nonscience is that there exist, in fact, mysteries and intractable problems in the natural world that have not been solved and may not be solvable. Human cravings for answers to questions that are either extremely difficult or impossible to answer all-too-often stimulate the creation of spurious answers that transcend the scientific method. However, the existence of mysteries is, not by itself evidence supporting supernatural events and entities; many of the persisting mysteries of modern science are the result of complexity and or the randomness of natural processes, not of Gods, angels, or some magical mystery. Unresolved mysteries are more likely to come from uncontrolled complexity.

Rescher (1998), for example, pointed out that as science progresses it uncovers more and more complex interconnections in "reality." As this complexity increases, so too must the technology and information processing of science, but the complexity always runs ahead of our ability to catch up. As a result, he goes on:

> Existing science does not and never will embody perfection. The cognitive ideals of completeness unity, consistency, and definitive finality represent an aspiration rather than a coming reality, an idealized *telos* rather than a realizable condition of things. Perfected science lies outside history as a useful contrast-case that cannot be secured in this imperfect world. (p. 119)

Some problems, especially the exact relationships between the network of neurons of the brain and mental processes (themselves, at best, indirect inferences from behavior) are the ultimate expressions of Rescher's concerns. They are unlikely to ever be understood because of (a) the sheer number of interconnections and problems emerging from such natural processes as chaotic and thermodynamic irreversibility and (b) their inaccessibility. They remain, nevertheless, well within the range of natural phenomena.

3.5 VERIFICATION AND REFUTATION

The topic of the verification of theories has been a major concern to philosophers of science for centuries. The classic version of science was that it collected facts and then inductively gathered these together into a theory that was subject to confirmation or rejection as new data became available. Popper (1959), however, revolutionized thinking concerning verification when he argued that theories could never be confirmed; indeed, he suggested just the opposite—that a good theory was one that could be falsified when he stated:

> These considerations suggest that not the verifiability but the falsifiability of a system is to be taken as a criterion of demarcation. In other words: I shall not require of a scientific system that it shall be capable of being singled out, once and for all, in a positive sense; but I shall require that its logical form shall be such it can be singled out, by means of empirical tests, in a negative sense: *it must be possible for an empirical scientific system to be refuted by experience*. (pp. 40–41)[9]

Popper's falsification proposal, however, has come under extreme criticism from other philosophers of science who argue that falsification is not realistically possible for all but the most trivial of theories. Such a counterargument has a long history. The philosopher of science Kockelmans (1968) pointed out that at least a century ago physicists such as P. M. M. Duhem had argued that

> physical theories were not able to teach anything about the very nature of reality; they did not give a genuine explanation of natural phenomena. A physical theory is, rather, a system of mathematical propositions deduced from a small number of principles with the aim of representing as simply, as completely, and as exactly as possible a whole domain of experimental laws. (p. 296)

Duhem (1914/1954) was among the first to assert that theories were constrained and limited in their significance. He stimulated later philosophers, including Quine (1960), to propose that since all theories were undetermined, no theory was sufficiently closed that it did not have enough slack to incorporate virtually any contradictory finding. It is only when observations become so glaringly inconsistent with the predictions of a theory, that a kind of major paradigm shift would occur as described by Kuhn (1970). It should be emphasized that this is not a matter that concerns only physics. Although Duhem was originally interested in the physical sciences, Rakover (2003) makes it clear in his discussion that it is also totally relevant to the psychological sciences.

---

[9]By "demarcation," Popper means the distinction between science and pseudoscience, but without the pejorative connotation usually associated with the latter term. Rather, a scientific theory is a correct one and a pseudoscientific theory is just a false one.

The problem of validation, either by confirmation or falsification, was also considered by Kaplan (1964). Arguing from the point of view that no theory can be definitively proven or disproven, he went on to note:

> What must in any case be taken into account in assessing a theory is the set of alternatives to it in conjunction with which it is being considered. That a theory is validated does not mean that it is probable, in some appropriate sense, but only that it is more probable than the other possible explanations. . . . Truth may be eternal, but science requires no more of a theory than that it be sufficient unto the day. (p. 315)

Kaplan, thus, expresses a pragmatic approach to theory that is shared by many other scientists, among them my colleague Peter Killeen of Arizona State University. Proponents of this point of view are concerned less with the ultimate truth or validity of a theory than with its utility as a schema for interpreting observations for some immediate purpose. Although there is a certain practical sense to this viewpoint, it must not be allowed to distract us from the ultimate purpose of science—to describe reality in as truthful and complete manner as possible, whatever the ultimate limits of science may be. To substitute a "useful" interpretation for a more "valid" one for some practical purpose can only lead to a diminishment of the eventual progress of any science toward the ideal of explaining ourselves and our world as fully as possible. (I must reiterate my conviction that the qualifying phrases "as fully as possible" and "complete manner as possible" implicitly accept the notion that a complete theory of anything is unlikely ever to be attained.)

Even more precise in his criticism of the power of theories in general was Gödel (1931) in what has become a classic interpretation of the constraints encumbering all theory building efforts. He argued that no theoretical system could be shown to be internally consistent for two quite distinct and different reasons. First, Gödel proved that at the least there were always some propositions in any axiomatic theory that were *undecidable* (i.e., the axioms of the system cannot prove or disprove some propositions of the theory). Second, he showed that all axiomatic theories had to be *incomplete* (i.e., all theoretical systems will always contain some statements that are mutually contradictory). Therefore, according to him, the much-desired internal consistency criterion used to designate a "good" theory is an idealization that can never be achieved.

Gödel's ideas and proofs provide a firm foundation for the idea that theories, in general, would be extremely hard to either confirm or falsify. Because of the ubiquity of undecidability and incompleteness in all theories, all are always open-ended enough to incorporate many new observations simply by adding additional axioms. Furthermore, even the robust demonstration of an inconsistency cannot be used to invalidate a theory, he argues, because all theories, even the best, contain them.

Gödel's proofs have many other ramifications suggesting that even what appear to be the strongest axiomatic theories are limited in their robustness. Chaitlin (1982) expanded on the argument to show that theoretical incompleteness is "natural and widespread rather than pathological and unusual" (p. 941). An exceedingly serious implication of incompleteness is, I believe, that there are many problems that cannot be solved. One example of an insolvable problem cited by Chaitlin was Turing's classic analysis that implied that even as simple a question as "Will a computer program eventually stop?" (the so-called halting problem) couldn't be answered! How much less likely, then, is a complete analysis of a system as complex as the mind–brain?

The implications of Gödel's theorem to the cognitive neurosciences have been debated for some years. Some believe that this is merely a mathematical formalism that is not relevant in this field. Others believe it has direct implications. Most of this controversy is somewhat premature because most formal theories of the organization of the nervous system and how it might engender mental processes are too primitive to even be evaluated in this stratosphere of mathematical or logical epistemology. However, given some of the other concerns I have raised, it seems likely that when such theories appear (and, as the remainder of this book attests, they do with surprising frequency) there must necessarily be residual doubts about their completeness, their decidability, their falsifiability, their uniqueness, and their robustness. In addition, there remain many doubts about what mathematical or neuroscientific theories of the mind mean in terms of the inferences that are drawn from them (i.e., the degree to which they are neutral or not), and how we must go about choosing from among alternative theories.[10]

This epistemological interlude brings us to the main part of this book—a critical review of the many modern theories of the relationship between the mind and the brain. The penultimate point being made is that none of the theories yet proposed meets the criteria required for their acceptance as an explanation for how this amazing phenomena occurs. The ultimate point is that it is unlikely any such theory can ever be complete for reasons that are dictated by the nature of the material world of which the brain is a part.

---

[10]I have discussed the neutrality problem extensively in Uttal (1998) and the problem of choosing among theories in Uttal (2003) and do not replicate those discussions here.

CHAPTER

4

Field Theories—Do What You Can Do When You Can't Do What You Should Do!

4.1 INTRODUCTION

One set of persistent alternatives to the idea that the proper level of analysis at which the psychoneural equivalent of mind was to be found is the complex web of local neuronal interactions is characterized by the rubric—field theories. Field theories minimize the microstructural details of the nervous system and concentrate on global patterns of electroneural, electrochemical, or even quantum activity. For example, the electroencephalogram (EEG) and the evoked brain potential (EVBP) or, as the latter is known nowadays, the event related potential (ERP), represent the cumulative activity of uncountable numbers of individual brain cells.

The details of how these global, relatively low frequency, electrical fields arise from the action of individual cells has not been definitively established. However, it is thought they are most likely the accumulation of synaptic slow potentials from oriented pyramidal cells (Martin, 1991) rather than superimpositions of neuronal spike activity. Field theorists do not, in general, deny that these globally measured electric fields are generated by accumulating the electrical activity of the multitude of discrete cells (possibly including both neurons and glia) that make up the tissue of the brain. However, rather than considering the microscopic details of the intercellular interactions to be the psychoneural equivalents of mental activity, they believe it is the field itself that is the key bridge from brain to mind.

Other field theories do not dote on the EEG or the ERP, but rather are extrapolations from abstract mathematics, sometimes developed for fields of scientific endeavor that are far removed from the physiology of the brain.

As we see in this chapter, the extraordinary intellectual development of quantum theory has also become a mainstay of some highly interesting, but highly problematic, field theories of the mind.

There are several reasons for the persistence of field theories in the current neuroscientific epoch that otherwise largely focuses on the anatomy and physiology of individual neurons. The first is the incontrovertible fact that we cannot (either practically or theoretically) simultaneously cope (by simulation, experimentation, or analysis) with the actions and interactions of the multitude of neurons that is most likely involved in creating mental activity. To do so runs into a computational explosion that would challenge not only the best available computer these days but also the best conceivable computer in the future.

Therefore, some cognitive neuroscientists have turned to signals from the brain that can be measured and are, at least at first glance, much more amenable to analysis. Given that we have available such molar measures as the EEG and the ERP, why not look to them as the psychoneural equivalents of cognitive processes? In short, if you cannot do what you should do, do what you can do!

The second reason for the popularity and persistence of field theories of cognition can be found in the historical record. It concerns fundamental ideas, concepts, and, to be frank, wishes about the nature of mind. The central controversy encountered throughout the history of the problem was the debate between holistic and elementalist approaches to understanding psychological processes.

For what are primarily phenomenological reasons, mind has long been assumed to have global or holistic properties that are analogous to measurable electrical fields. The mind or consciousness (take your pick) is essentially a unitary phenomenon. That is, all of the introspective reports of what it is like to think suggest that our minds are, in the main, single-track processes. We can pay attention to only one thing (or to a very few) or perceive one state of a given ambiguous stimulus (e.g., the reversible Necker cube) at a time. Everything is melded into a singular, molar, whole of conscious experience. We neither are aware of the activity of the individual neurons that collectively produce our minds nor of the components of mind so assiduously sought by cognitive scientists today. Thus, the parallel between the molar action of the mind and the overall, widespread electrical fields of the brain seem at first glance to be greater than any parallel between the mind and the details of the activity patterns of the myriad of individual neurons.

The third reason for the continued popularity of field theories is that there was (and continues to be) a long-standing conviction that things or processes that exhibit the same form (i.e., that are isomorphic to each other) are functionally as well as structurally identical. Therefore, there is considerable intellectual pressure to assume that a holistic and unitary mind should be based on neural underpinnings that are also unitary and holistic. Although the raw kind of mental–neural isomorphism championed by Gestalt psychology's early theories has long been rejected by psychologists, a kind of subtle isomorphism still pervades current thinking. An unwritten, but probably incorrect, rule of neuroreductionism states that—"If the time course of an neuroelectric signal and some measure of behavior are comparable, then the latter is a plausible explanation of the former."

Fourth, it has been suggested that neuroelectric fields might provide an answer to the long-standing "binding" question (i.e., how do the individual activities of the many centers, nuclei, and neurons of the brain combine to produce the singular and unified experience of the mind). By the 19th century it was clear that the nervous system was not homogeneous; rather it was made up of parts that had different macroscopic and microscopic properties. Since the beginnings of the 20th century, it was also clear that this lack of homogeneity extended down to the level of individual neurons. As the realization that neurons were discrete and interacted with each other became more widely accepted, the question of how these numerous cells could produce a unitary mental process became salient.

The binding question continues to bedevil modern cognitive neuroscience. Nevertheless, it may not be a meaningful one. To at least some modest degree, it resurrects the old canard of the homunculus. That is, the binding problem may represent nothing more or less than the continuation of the classic challenge—Who or what reads out the neural code to produce mental experience? The effort to combine or bind isolated modules may represent a similar kind of fallacious quest. Our search for an explanation of how distributed components are linked together ignores the possibility that the distributed state itself may be sufficient. On the psychological side, it is not at all certain that cognitive modules exist.

Fifth, and in a related vein, during the late 19th and early 20th century, a radical, elementalist approach dominated psychological thinking, particularly in Germany and the United States. Wilhelm Wundt (1832–1920) and E. B. Titchener's (1867–1927) empiricist and structuralist psychology assumed the mind was made up of tiny units that had to be teased apart experimentally and which collectively represented human mentation. This elementalism foundered on a number of intellectual shoals, not the least of which was the increasing number of components that had to be incorporated in any theory. The holist point of view of such scholars as Immanuel Kant (1724–1804), Ernst Mach (1838–1916), and Christian von Ehrenfels (1859–1932) was revitalized in reactive response to this hyperelementalism. Thus, there was a trend toward psychological unity and holism during the period that the EEG technology was becoming popular. This confluence of intellectual forces had a profound effect on holistic field theories.

Sixth, a long tradition, dating as far back as Roger Bacon (1214–1294) and Rene Descartes (1596–1650) argued that to understand any complex system it is necessary to take it apart into its components and examine each part while holding the others constant to the maximum extent possible. Current psychological research methodology has taken this admonition to its very core. However, in spite of this widespread belief, there is a considerable argument that things cannot be dissected in this manner without losing much of their meaning and function. Certainly in today's world in which we understand the complex interactions between the components of nonlinear systems, this centuries old admonition may be totally inappropriate in the cognitive neuroscience context. This point of view also contributes to the remaining popularity of field theories.

Seventh, there is a purely physiological question to which field theories seem at first glance to provide a possible answer. That question is—How do the distant parts of the brain interact for what is a very long distance for an individual neuron? The parallel processing power of the brain is so great that action at relatively distant sites seems to occur almost simultaneously. Given the finite speed at which neurons actively conduct due to their electrochemical nature, there is an a priori pressure to consider high speed, electrical, passive spread of activity by fields to account for this "action at a distance."

Eighth, given the problems encountered when one tries to deal analytically with the huge numbers of discrete neurons and the fact that the mathematics of continuous fields offers at least approximate solutions, a number of mathematical biophysicists have found it desirable to examine how individual neurons can collectively give rise to neuroelectric fields. An early version of this idea was attributed to Wilson and Cowan (1973) and the idea has been pursued by many current workers in the field (e.g., Martin, 1991; Igel, Erlhagen, & Jancke, 2001; Giese & Xie, 2002). Other interesting and modern discussions of how the EEG and the ERP may be generated by the cumulative active of the neurons in the brain can be found in McFadden (2002) and Nunez (1995). Each of these authors discusses the possible ways in which the EEG might be generated from localized neuronal activity, unfortunately in ways that do not always overlap. Nunez (1995), especially, was extremely cautious in considering how global neuroelectric fields may be associated with cognitive activity. Nevertheless, his work is one of the most compete theoretical discussions of the physics and origins of the EEG now available.

Fields, therefore, are popular mathematical constructs in an area of considerable interest these days and, best of all, they meet some of the superficial conditions of process similarity that permit them both to describe brain activity and to represent cognitive processes. Although many of these studies (e.g., Nunez, 1995) are purely biophysical and do not explicitly attempt to explain cognitive processes, they do establish a milieu in which fields offer the promise of special advantages over theories that are based on discrete neurons.

Thus, there is and has been for many years substantial pressure to support the developments of field theories of the mind. This is so despite the increasing attention given to individual neurons by neurophysiologists and the current popularity of such alternative approaches as the connectionist or neural net theories.

This brings us to a related issue, something I referred to (Uttal, 1967) as the sign-code distinction some years ago. The point of this concern is that there exists a class of genuine neuroelectric signals,[1] indisputatively originating from the electrophysiological activity of the brain, that can be shown to correlate, sometimes quite highly, with cognitive processes of one kind or another. One possible example of such a correlated but irrelevant signal is the EEG itself! However, these correlates need not necessarily be the "psychoneural equivalents" of the cognitive processes or exert any causal force on the brain or, for that matter, the mind. Rather, they could be neural epiphenomena (signs) generated by some physiological processes other than those that are the true equivalents (codes) of mind.

Over the years, such an admonition has not been taken seriously by those who continue to happily use field signals of one kind or another as global models of mind. Indeed, the very availability and ease of accessibility of these signals, and their correlation with some behaviors, has been taken by some to authenticate their role as psychoneural equivalents. The possibility of a gross misunderstanding of the meaning and significance of the EEG and other global electrical measures of brain activity, however, cannot be discounted.

In the sections that follow, I discuss a variety of these global or field models of the mind. None disagree with fundamental assertion of Proposition 1 expressed in chapter 3. Whatever the fields are, their origins are likely to be found in the cumulated activity of individual neurons. The ultimate question is, however: Which is the essential psychoneural equivalent of mind—the discrete and local activity of individual neurons and their interactions—or the global activity of the continuous electrical fields? A corollary of this fundamental question is: Do the components of the brain interact purely by means of local synaptic activity or, alternatively, can they communicate by means of the broadly distributed and continuous fields that arise from their cumulative activity?

---

[1]By genuine, I mean that the measured electrical activity is a real product of the brain's neural activity and not due to some physical artifact. It had been suggested that the EEG might be such an artifact. For example, Kennedy (1959) proposed that the EEG might possibly be produced by impulsive perturbations of the brain's gelatinous material by the heartbeat in the same way that any other electromagnetic signal is produced by acceleration of charge.

There is no better place to begin this review than with the classic holistic cognitive neuroscience–Gestalt field theory.

4.2 GESTALT FIELD THEORY[2]

The history of Gestalt neuroscientific theories of the mind had its roots in preexisting philosophical speculations about the nature of cognitive processes. Kant, for example, stressed the idea that the act of perception was not a passive concatenation of individual events to produce perceptions but rather an active processing of the overall organizational pattern of the information communicated by the stimulus. In other words, he stressed the "melody" rather than the "notes" of the symphony of perceptual experience. In doing so he explicitly emphasized the vital importance of the global pattern itself without rejecting the fundamental elementalism implicit in the associationist philosophy of Wundt and Titchener. Similarly, Mach and von Ehrenfels made important contributions to the foundation assumptions of a holistic cognitive neuroscience by suggesting, more or less independently, that, in addition to the elemental sensory qualities and properties so strongly emphasized by the associationist psychologists, there were other significant global properties that could influence our perceptions and thoughts. These additional properties were lost and, therefore, could not be discerned during an examination of the parts of a stimulus. However, they could be defined and even measured in terms of the overall spatial and temporal form of stimulus patterns and sequences.

Both Mach and von Ehrenfels alluded to the increasingly popular idea of emergentism, the concept that these global properties contained more information than did the sum of their parts (i.e., new holistic properties "emerged" that were not predictable from the properties of the parts). Thus, they argued that the properties of the whole transcended any simple summation of the properties of the separate components. Of course, we now appreciate that if we could understand all of the properties of the parts–including the rules by means of which they interacted with other parts–then even the so-called emerged pattern was implicit in the "properties of the parts." It is only a practical epistemological difficulty (due to the ancient enemies of reductive explanation–numerousness and nonlinearity) that prevents us from pursuing this ontological truth and assigning mysterious "emergence" to the ash heap of science.

The essence of this new configurationist or holist school of thought, therefore, revolved around the radically different assumption (compared to the associationist–structuralist tradition) regarding the nature of the rela-

[2]This section on Gestalt Field theory is adapted and updated from Uttal (1981).

tionships between the whole and the parts in determining experience. This line of thought ultimately crystallized in the Gestalt (best translated as "pattern" or "structure") theories under the leadership of Max Wertheimer (1880–1943), Kurt Koffka (1886–1941), and Wolfgang Kohler (1887–1967) in the first half of the 20th century, first in Germany and then after the dismal days of 1933 in the United States.

The essential premise of this new Gestalt school of thought, which most sharply distinguished it from the structuralism of Wundt or Titchener, was its vigorous adherence to the notion that the global configuration of the stimulus was neither just another property of the stimulus nor just the sum of the parts of which it was composed. Rather, the central dogma of Gestalt psychology was that the overall form of a pattern was the essential causal influence on perception, the substantive field of psychology most emphasized by them.

The Gestalt psychologists carried out a large number of experiments demonstrating the important role of the global pattern and what they believed to be the lesser role played by the individual components on perception. However, many of the classic Gestalt experiments were nonquantitative, in that they were often unique demonstrations that made some point concerning the global pattern. Typically, however, they were not suitable for parametric experimental manipulation or a high degree of control over the full range of the salient stimulus dimension. "Form," unfortunately, was as poorly quantified then as it is now, and, therefore, this centerpiece of Gestalt theory was never adequately defined in most of their experiments. As a result, this configurationist approach was at odds in many ways with the quantitative and reductionist tradition of modern science. The difficulty in defining "a form" persists. (For a fuller discussion of this problem, see Uttal, 2002.)

What the Gestalt psychologists did contribute, and what remains their major gift to modern perceptual theory, was their emphasis on a holistic approach in a science that had previously been and was later to be totally dominated by elementalist assumptions. They developed a system of laws and principles that are, at the very least, accurate and powerful descriptors of the way humans report what they perceive or think.

Beyond this descriptive set of perceptual principles, the pioneers in Gestalt theory also proposed one of the first brain field theories. The idea was first suggested by Wertheimer as early as 1912 but became a mainstay of the later Gestalt psychologists including Koffka and Kohler. Kohler (1920, p. 193) has been cited (Ehrenstein, Spillmann, & Sarris, 2003) as the first time that the idea was formalized in the following manner:

> [E]very phenomenal (perceptual) state is linked to a structurally identical (isomorphic) neural process that occurs at a central level of the brain, the so-

> called *psychophysical level* (Kohler, 1920, 1938). The search strategy underlying this analogy may be phrased as follows: At which level of the brain can we identify a pattern of neuronal activity that matches the percept more closely than the physical stimulus? (p. 446)

According to both Boring (1950) and Luchins and Luchins (1999), the earliest versions of neuroelectric field theory emerged more as a result of the Gestalt psychologist's observations of the field-like properties of their perceptual observations and the prevailing neurophysiological Zeitgeist (the newly discovered EEG was becoming increasingly popular as a noninvasive means of measuring brain activity) than from an explicit experimental program. It was not until the late 1940s that any of the founding Gestalt psychologists observed such fields electrophysiologically.

Nevertheless, their theory, in the absence of a supportive body of empirical findings, became extremely specific in suggesting that perception (in particular) occurred because there was a similarity between the phenomenal experience and the concurrent brain field. This similarity was not based on a precise replication of shape, as is misleadingly suggested by their oft used term—*isomorphism*. Rather, it was only in a topological manner—a rubber sheet kind of similarity—that the brain field and the experience were supposed to exhibit common forms. That is, for topological constancy, the distances between equivalent points on the field might vary but the order in which they were laid out had to remain constant.

The first physiological evidence for even this limited topological kind of isomorphism was highly equivocal. Kohler and Held (1949) used EEGs and visual stimuli to describe what were the electric fields of the brain supposed to encode perceptual responses. They reported that substantial voltage shifts in the EEG as a result of stimulation with moving lights. After dispensing with the idea that their findings were just a result of the low band-pass of their amplifiers, they argued that the recorded signal represented:

> an approximately steady potential and an equally steady flow through and around the cortical counterpart of the image . . . from a psychological point of view this is the main issue. (p. 419)

Much to their credit, they immediately went on to note that ". . . our results must be interpreted with some caution, just because they are related to important problems" (p. 419). It was not until much later that retinotopic mapping of the visual field in the primary visual regions was described and, by then, classical Gestalt electrical field theory was more or less completely discarded.

The main conceptual point of the classic Gestalt topological theory of brain representation, in accord with the general adherence to holistic processes, was that it was the overall electrical field of brain activity, rather than the action of individual neurons,[3] that was critically important in the representation of psychological function.

In spite of the rather vague formulation of the Gestalt neuroelectric field theory by its founders and its extremely weak empirical basis, it was felt necessary by a number of contemporary researchers to put it to rest definitively. Electrical field theories were attacked by several novel experimental procedures shortly after the Kohler and Held (1949) paper was published. Lashley, Chow, and Semmes, (1951) and Sperry, Miner, and Myers (1955), for example, showed that the hypothetical fields of electrical activity in the brain could not possibly account for what seemed to be some of the closest behavioral correlates. Metal foils and pins inserted into the brain in a way that would certainly have short-circuited any neuroelectric field seemed to have little effect on any behavioral measures of perceptual responses in experimental animals.

Pribram (1971) reported another type of experiment that used chemicals instead of surgical insults to consider the plausibility of field-type theories. In this report, he described how pattern discrimination was not affected by the application of aluminum hydroxide directly to the visual areas of an experimental animal in spite of the fact that EEG was substantially disrupted (pp. 110–111).[4] Thus, the grandfather of the electrical field theories perished.

The idea that the relevant brain responses were isomorphic to the associated psychological processes, however, still exerts a powerful, though usually unacknowledged, influence on thinking with regard to models of perceptual process. The Gestalt theoreticians were not willing to accept any coded or symbolic representation of perceptual responses in the brain, an alternative that is necessarily introduced by the network theories that were to follow. On close examination, the idea of isomorphism is fundamentally antagonistic to the ideas of neural coding and symbolic representation that have become popular in interpreting modern cognitive neuroscientific data. Yet, a kind of conceptual isomorphism still apparently leads many experimenters to believe that whenever a spatial or temporal similarity in any kind of neural response, on the one hand, and reports of a temporal or spatial experience, on the other, occurs, then the former is ipso facto the psychoneural equivalent code of the latter. Fortunately, as cognitive neuroscientists are becoming more sophisticated in their appreciation of the meaning of "a code" and its distinction from an irrelevant "sign," this point

[3]The idea that the cumulative action of many individual neurons was the source of the fields was, however, accepted by Kohler and Held (1949) as it is by virtually all other field theorists. To deny such a link would be tantamount to accepting a nonphysical source of the electrical fields.

[4]As we see shortly, however, Pribram later proposed another field type theory of brain activity.

of view is diminishing in influence. Nevertheless, vestiges of the conflict between the concepts of isomorphic and symbolic coding remain prevalent in contemporary psychobiological theory.

Around 1970, field theories went through a kind of renaissance. Several new and interesting versions were proposed based on exciting new developments in the physical sciences. One of the most interesting and persistent was based on the development of the optical hologram.

4.3 PRIBRAM'S HOLOGRAPHIC FIELD THEORY[5]

As I just noted, Karl Pribram had participated in one of the key experiments challenging the classic electrical field theory proposed by the Gestalt psychologists. At about the same time, however, he was also beginning to formulate another version of a global neuroelectric field theory. Pribram reports (see Pribram, 1971, p. 9) that he was still influenced by Lashley's early assertion that memory of specific events seemed to be distributed widely throughout the nervous system. On this basis and other experiments in which he had participated, Pribram proposed a model of the brain that was based on new developments in optical holography that were percolating to the surface of physical science about that time. Like other field theories, the neural basis of this model was that continuous fields distributed across the entire brain's surface interacted in a way that encoded mental activity. Holography added the essential idea that *memory and perception are simultaneously encoded in all portions of the brain.*

The notion of interacting fields of neuronal activity had been around for a remarkably long period of time. The original idea actually predated the optical hologram by many years. Goldscheider (1906), according to Pribram, was only one of many scientists who proposed interference-type theories as possible explanations of perceptual phenomena almost a century ago. Pribram and his coworkers (see, e.g., Pribram, 1969; Pribram, Nuwer, & Baron, 1974) extended the idea of interference patterns as the key means of representing perceptual and learning processes. They accomplished this by merging new information concerning cellular plasticity with the mathematics developed to describe holograms developed by Gabor (1948, 1949).

The key to understanding Pribram's conjecture is to appreciate that it depended upon the sensitivity of individual neurons to the amplitude and phase components (measured in the frequency domain) of the Fourier transformation of an image or memory rather than to the raw form (meas-

[5]This section is also an updated extract from my longer discussion of the holographic theory in Uttal (1978).

ures in the spatial or temporal domain) of the image. Two-dimensional Fourier components or basis functions are distributed over broad regions in any mathematical analysis. (See Section 4.9 later in this chapter.) According to this mathematical formularization, local components are produced by the superimposition of many different spatial frequencies and depend on the proportion of each spatial frequency component added at that locale. Coupled with what is interpreted to be a substantial amount of information rejecting precise localization of any cognitive process in the brain, further support seemed to be provided for the idea of a distributed coding scheme such as analogized by a holographic theory of memory representation.

Two features of optical holograms are particularly important to their proposed use as a possible model of the neural basis of cognitive processing, in general, and of memory, in particular. First, the hologram is a totally distributed form of recording images; all portions of an original scene are represented everywhere in the hologram. For example, if a holographic image was imprinted on a glass plate and the plate is subsequently broken, each shard, no matter how small, would contain the entire picture; the smaller the shard, however, the more blurred the reconstructed picture. Thus, the retention of some memory after specific localized trauma to the brain is modeled. Second, a hologram is intrinsically three-dimensional. Three-dimensional objects are recorded in a form that allows their stereoscopic shapes to be reconstructed from two-dimensional records. This, too, analogizes a property of human perception.

The holographic theory of learning and perception proposed by Pribram makes a huge logical leap that is rarely made explicit. That is, they propose that the fields and the dimensions of their measurements *are* the psychoneural equivalents of the cognitive processes with which they correlate. It is not just a matter of these fields serving, at best, as indicators or, at worst, as epiphenomena, but rather these global patterns of neuroelectric activity *are identifiable with our thoughts*! This is an important and ubiquitous aspect of field theories—the idea that the psychoneural equivalents of our mental lives are none other than these neuroelectric fields.[6]

It is important to note that Pribram's approach should not be misconstrued to suggest he believed there is actually an optical hologram in the head. Rather, Pribram was quite clear that the optical hologram is only a functional analog, if not just a metaphor, subject to the same mathematical principles governing the neural mechanisms of the brain. Both the optical hologram and the neural one, he argued, must exhibit the same distributed

[6]It is also, it must be pointed out, a basic part of any reductive theory of mental activity. Each and every neuroreductive theory of mind discussed in this book implicitly assumes that the measured bioelectric activity, whatever it may be, *is* mind!

transformational properties. It is the concept of interacting and distributed fields of neural activity rather than the particular physical mechanisms by which the fields are implemented that is the essence of his argument.

Pribram's holographic field theory, like virtually all other field theories, therefore, does not deny an underlying neural microstructure. The essence of Pribram's theory is that once a neural pattern has been established by alterations in the microscopic connectivity pattern, its retrieval is triggered by an input that produces a field of nervous activity in the brain acting very like the reference wave[7] in an optical hologram. My readers who may be interested in more of the details of the holographic theory are directed to Pribram's updating of holographic theory in his book (Pribram, 1991).

4.4 JOHN'S STATISTICAL THEORY[8]

Another early field theory of mind was proposed by John (1972). However, rather than being based on the notion of interfering waves of the EEG, it was aimed at explaining learning and memory by means of global evoked or event related potentials (ERPs). As in other field approaches, John did not deny the role of individual neurons; rather, he, in turn, emphasized that it was the integrated waves produced collectively by huge arrays of neurons in the brain that permitted information to be distributed to distant parts of the brain. His unique slant on the problem was to suggest that the manner in which these fields were generated was statistical in nature. That is, as John (1972) put it:

> [T]he informational significance of an event is represented in the average behavior of a responsive neural ensemble rather than by the exclusive behavior of any specifiable neuron in the ensemble. (p. 854)[9]

He then went on to argue:

> The critical event in learning is envisaged as the establishment of large numbers of neurons in different parts of the brain, whose activity has been affected in a coordinated way by the spatial temporal characteristics of the stimuli present during a learning stimulus. (p. 853)

---

[7]Readout of an optical hologram is accomplished by passing a light though the holographic medium. The transformation of this reference light is what produces the rich three-dimensional image.

[8]This is an updated abstract from a more extensive discussion presented in Uttal (1978).

[9]This is clearly a challenge to single cell theories of the type discussed in chapter 5.

John's contribution in emphasizing the statistical ensemble as the basis of the origin of the molar compound waves recorded from the brain was very important for its time. However correct or incorrect the idea that the key issue equivalent was the statistical tendencies of many neurons may have been (and it is almost certain that this concept was partially correct), it must be distinguished from his corollary suggestion that the cumulative ERP wave actually was a means of communication among distant neurons.

However, John went even further than just suggesting the importance of the statistical properties of the neuron and the role of the cumulative response as a means of communicating between different parts of the brain. Specifically, he was explicit in speculating that these "coherent temporal pattern [i.e., the fields] . . . may constitute the neurophysiological basis of subjective experience" (p. 863). By so asserting, he joined with other field theorists in suggesting that the psychoneural equivalent of mind was to be found at this molar level. Although John (1972) provides us with an alternative way in which the global neuroelectric fields such as the EEG may be measured (cumulative ERPs), he also asserted that these global fields *are* the neurophysiological equivalent of our mental activities.

In a later article, John (1990) elaborated on the meaning of this central idea of mind–brain equivalence when he said:

> The modulation of the random neural activity generated in a way inherent in our human nervous systems by the nonrandom neural activity, which is generated in a way uniquely determined by our personal histories and our interaction with our present environment, constitutes the content of consciousness, a continuous and internally consistent subjective experience, and self-awareness. The anatomical distribution of the participating ensembles, together with the discontinuous characteristics of neuronal activity, makes it clear that consciousness, subjective experience, and self-awareness cannot be attributed to any process localizable to any discrete set of neurons, connected to all other neurons so as to assess nonrandomness in all remote neural ensembles and responsive continuously. (p. 54)

The key words that identify John as a field theorist here are "modulation," "continuous," and [not] "localizable." The key idea that he champions along with most modern cognitive neuroscientists is that there is some, as yet unidentified, kind of neural activity that is the material equivalent of mental phenomena. Unfortunately, this particular field theory shares a lack of any direct empirical validation with all other theories of the mind. What is even worse is that each and every such theory, based on whatever driving metaphor or analogy motivates it, will always be bedeviled by the likelihood that such validation can never be forthcoming.

4.5 FREEMAN'S MASS ACTION THEORY

About 60 years ago, Adrian (1942) observed that when odorous stimuli were presented to the olfactory mucosa of a hedgehog, macroelectrodes applied to the animal's olfactory lobe detected midrange frequencies centered at approximately 40 Hz in the measured electrical field. This band of frequencies had been designated as the gamma band.[10] For many years, Freeman (1975, 2000) pursued Adrian's original observation of these fields on the rabbit's olfactory lobe. This model preparation provided a fertile ground for the development of a model of human thought based on neuroelectric fields measured by means of the EEG and ERP and either regulated or communicated by what was assumed to be ubiquitous 40 Hz EEG signals.

Freeman, again in agreement with most other field theorists, accepted the view that the integrated signal represented by the electrical field is produced by the cumulative extracellular currents generated by a large number of discrete neurons. He actively pursued both empirical and theoretical studies to explain how these microscopic local potentials could accumulate to produce the macroscopic (or as he refers to them, "mesoscopic") fields. However, the focus of his work that now draws our attention is the role played by the EEG in the representation of cognitive experience itself.

The essence of Freeman's (2000) approach, more or less typical of field theories, is expressed in his book. Speaking of the response of the olfactory lobe, he said:

> [T]he surface EEG is by far the better measure of the output of a cortical population, whereas the activity of individual neurons is the better measure of cortical response to its input. (p. 6)

Here, Freeman was explicitly proposing that while individual neurons respond each in its own manner to a stimulus, the overall pattern of the "population" is the true code or psychoneural equivalent of the phenomenal experience of olfactory quality. Furthermore, he suggested that the spatial pattern of the electrical field measured over the entire lobe (rather than the temporal pattern) that encodes different odors. Freeman (2000) stated the following in a discussion of the results of an experiment carried out by Viana Di Prisco and Freeman (1985):

> The hypothesis was that, between the time of inhalation and the performance of a correct response, odorant information existed in the bulb as a pattern of

---

[10]The value of 40 Hz is only approximate and actually denotes signals that occur within a spectral range of 20 to 60 Hz. The exact value of this frequently observed waveform varies with the conditions of the experiment and the species of animal on which the work is carried out.

> neural activity, on the basis of which the animal made the discrimination, that this information would be detectable in as some as yet to be determined properties of the EEG. The results showed that the information sought was indeed manifested in the [20–80 Hz] EEG. (p. 8)

The idea that the 40 Hz component of the EEG played an especially important role in experience has gained surprising acceptance among biophysicists in the last 25 years. Based on both analogy and other research (e.g., Basar, Gonder, Ozesmi, & Ungan, 1975) the idea that the spatial distribution of the 40 Hz fields played an equally important coding role in other parts of the brain has become widely accepted. The clincher was the demonstration by Galambos, Makeig, and Talmachoff (1981) that external electrodes could pick up similar 40 Hz frequencies in the EEG from the human brain. This result added apparent support to the hypothesis that the 40 Hz component of the EEG had much to say about how the brain represents cognitive processing. Whether evoked by repetitive impulsive stimuli (ERPs) or by more complex instructions, the 40 Hz signal seemed to be ubiquitous in our brains as well as other species.

Freeman also agreed that the cortex, like the olfactory lobe, had the function of producing neuroelectric spatial fields that are critical to our awareness of many different sensory experiences. Unfortunately, as in so many other theories concerning the bridge between the activity of the brain and cognitive or behavioral phenomena, there is a kind of studied ambiguity inherent in Freeman's use of the word *manifested*. It is possible that he meant the gamma wave literally encodes or represents the odorant stimulus. However, with this phraseology, it seems to me that he avoids a firm commitment to the exact nature of the relationship between the 40 Hz wave and the mind. Perhaps this is a necessary property of any theory of the mind and brain.

Interestingly, although "40 Hz" is defined by the temporal properties of the EEG, the actual temporal pattern of the waves was considered by Freeman to be chaotic and unpredictable (Freeman & Skarda, 1985). This chaotic property, according to them, permits rapid changes of state as the brain is sequentially influenced by different attractors.[11] Rather, as Freeman has repeatedly emphasized, it is the *spatial attributes* of the 40 Hz signals as they are distributed across the brain that play the key role in representing sensory and cognitive processes.

The study of the 40 Hz and other EEG frequency bands, despite some epistemological concerns to be discussed momentarily, has become a topic

---

[11]For a discussion of the nature of attractors in the neurophysiological context, see Uttal (2003).

of considerable interest in cognitive neuroscience. Some of the researchers pursuing this topic have concentrated on the biophysics of its origin from localized neuronal responses (see, e.g., von der Malsburg, 1981, and Basar's, 1998, and Freeman's, 2000, recent books).

The idea that the 40 Hz Gamma wave is of particular importance in the representation of cognitive processing has, furthermore, become supported by a number of researchers in fields other than olfaction. A brief sampling of the cognitive functions that have been associated with 40 Hz signals includes:

1. Sheer (1976, 1989) was one of the first to associate the 40 Hz wave with psychological functioning, in particular cortical arousal.
2. Galambos, Makeig, and Talmachoff (1981) were the first to observe 40 Hz oscillations in auditory ERPs.
3. Ingber (1985) and Ingber and Nunez (1995) associated 40 Hz signals with short-term memory. The 1985 paper also suggested that Miller's (1956) 7 +/− 2 law might be explained by the encoding of 40 Hz signals.
4. Tiitinen et al. (1993) described how selective attention could modulate the 40 Hz transient response.
5. Joliot, Ribary, and Llinas (1994) observed that 40 Hz signals (recorded with a magnetic probe) correlate with the ability of human observers to resolve two closely spaced acoustic clicks.
6. Kissler, Muller, Fehr, Rockstroh, and Elbert (2000) used the 40 Hz signal to distinguish between normal and schizophrenic subjects' abilities to carry out mental arithmetic.
7. Haig, Gordon, Wright, Meares, and Bahramali (2000) associated 40 Hz signals with task relevant stimuli.
8. Pulvermuller and his group (Pulvermuller et al., 1996; Pulvermuller et al., 2001) implicated 40 Hz signals in lexical processing.
9. Elliot and Muller (2000) suggested that short-term visual memory is correlated with 40 Hz signals.
10. Finally, Crick and Koch (1990) suggest that the 40 Hz oscillation is the "basis of consciousness."

Furthermore, the 40 Hz hypothesis has now become a major candidate as a putative answer to the binding problem: How are the individual components of mental processing bound together to produce the unified sense of conscious experience reported by humans?

It seems, however, that these associations are based on a critical logical error (among others of lesser import) expressed when a special meaning is ascribed to the EEG. Much of this work is based on an implicit assumption that was made overt by Freeman (1991) and is implicit in other field theories of this genre:

> The [EEG] tracings detect essentially the same information that neurons assess when they "decide" whether or not to fire impulses, but an EEG records that information for thousands of cells at once. (p. 80)

This assertion, however, is fundamentally incorrect! Whenever information from a group of individual elements is integrated or statistically accumulated, information is indisputatively lost! The details of the response patterns of the individual components disappear. Furthermore, those individual properties cannot generally be recovered from the final accumulation. Indeed, this is the very reason that statistics are carried out on systems containing variable components—to reduce the amount of information provided by the raw data to a level at which it can be practically analyzed. The determination of the "central tendency" of a group of idiosyncratic components erases all evidence of their individual values. Thus, it follows that there is less information in an EEG than in all of the neuronal responses that contributed to it.

At best, then, the neuroelectric fields, on which theories such as Freeman's are based, represent a substantial reduction from a full description of the state of the nervous system at the moment a cognitive process occurs. This is not to say that the cognitive process itself may not represent a comparable kind of information reduction. Rather, it is to illustrate that the nervous system operates at a much richer level of informational complexity than is represented by these conveniently measured electrical fields.

4.6 McFADDEN'S *CEMI* FIELD THEORY

McFadden (2000, 2002) recently proposed another neuroelectric field theory in a specific effort to explain the nature of human consciousness. In this regard his approach is somewhat different than many of its predecessors in that it does not concentrate on either perception or learning. Rather, his interest, not unlike other currently popular cognitive neuroscientists, is concentrated on the arguably ineffable and certainly indefinable stuff of sentience or awareness itself.

Like other field theorists, McFadden sees the brain's overall electromagnetic field as being generated by the superimposition of the firing patterns of a large ensemble of individual neurons. Neurons that are sufficiently near each other to influence each other's local fields of electromagnetic energy. These local fields, according to his theory, cascade into the voltages that we record in the form of EEGs detectable over the entire head. In turn, these low frequency, but widely distributed, voltages feed back onto individual neurons to modulate their activity.

The essence of McFadden's (2002) theory is found in his proposition that:

> [T]he brain's em [electromagnetic] field *is* consciousness and that information held in distributed neurons is integrated into a single conscious em field: the *cemi field*. (p. 31)

The basis of this assertion is that:

> [I]nformation in em fields is analog, integrated, and distributed . . . characteristics are those usually ascribed to the phenomena of consciousness that are most difficult to account for in neural identity theories of consciousness. (p. 31)

McFadden (2002) succinctly summed up his theory with the following statement:

> *Conscious electromagnetic information field (cemi field) theory:* Digital information within neurons is pooled and integrated to form an electromagnetic information field in the brain. Consciousness is the component of the brain's electromagnetic information field that is transmitted to motor neurons and is thereby capable of communicating its state to the outside world. (p. 37)

McFadden's field theory thus represents a much deeper commitment to a classic monistic identity theory than other field theorists who equivocate at this critical point in their logic and allude only to the field's "influence." No hesitation or equivocation here; he forcefully argues that the em field *is* the mind.

However vigorous his commitment to this identity position, there are still major logical difficulties with McFadden's approach that are shared with other field theories. His approach to answering the complex question of how the brain and its constituent parts produce mental activity (specifically consciousness) is, as usual, based mainly upon the temporal and spatial analogy that exists between what are believed to be the properties of the conscious mind and those of the electromagnetic fields of the brain. Reasoning by analogies of this kind is, as I have already noted, widely appreciated in philosophical circles to be a flawed road to understanding.

We have learned in the modern world of information-processing machines and Turing theorems is that symbolic representation is an entirely plausible way to represent even the most intangible of concepts or personal experiences. The idea that isomorphic encoding (i.e., spatiotemporal congruence) has any priority over symbolic representation flies in the face of our ability to encode such parameters as the hue of a 700 nm light or the aroma of a flower's chemical mix. Qualitative experiences such as hue and odor obviously must be encoded by parameters of the neural response devoid of any reproduction of the wavelength or the chemistry of the stimulus. Why then, one must ask, could not such a symbolic encoding be used for any other conscious experience? If the answer to this rhetorical question is "yes," then all analogical allusion to similarity of the time course or spatial extent of two functions becomes a fragile argument indeed.

There is another very important and likely to be erroneous assumption that both McFadden and Freeman (1991) made explicit (as discussed in the previous section) but which is implicit in virtually all of the other field theories discussed here. That assumption is that the information content of the em field and the states of the neurons are identical. McFadden (2002) puts it in the following manner: ". . . the brain's em field holds precisely the same information as neuron firing patterns . . ." (p. 31).

The assertion of equivalent information in the EEG and the myriad of discrete neuronal responses is entirely incorrect; any accumulation of the responses of many component units into a single global measure represents a vast reduction in the amount of information. Thus, the EEG is not equivalent to the ensemble activity of the brain's neurons.

McFadden went on to justify this logical error by drawing an analogy to Einstein's $E = mc^2$ equation. I presume his idea was that there was equivalence in the information content of an EEG and the individual responses of the array of involved neurons, respectively, in the same way that energy and matter could be interchanged. However wonderful was Einstein's contribution to cosmology and basic particle physics, in no way does it justify the extrapolation that em fields contain the same information as the "sum total of the information in the discrete neurons." The information in accumulated EEG signals (or, for that matter, reduced and summarized data of any kind), as I have already indicated, is less than in the components that it summarizes.

First, at a general level, Einstein was speaking of matter–energy equivalence and not information equivalence. Second and more specifically, the essence of Einstein's equation is the bidirectionality of the equal sign. Mass could be converted to energy but so too could energy be converted to mass. There is no such bidirectionality possible between the em wave and the action of neurons. Although it is, in principle, possible to develop an EEG from the aggregate neural responses, it is not possible to go backwards from the EEG to the details of individual neural responses. (For an early proof of this conjecture, see Cox and Smith, 1954.) Thus, the allusion to the famous and valid Einstein equation of mass–energy equivalence is totally irrelevant in this context.

4.7 LEHAR'S HARMONIC RESONANCE THEORY

Lehar (2003b) offered another version of a field theory with a different twist. Rather than emphasizing the neuroelectric fields so popular among most field theorists, he uses as his material base the electrochemical standing waves that are produced by biochemical actions occurring in the brain. Nevertheless, his argument, like that of most other field theorists, is mainly based on the analogy drawn between the global properties of brain responses and cognitive processes.

In Lehar's theory, the brain's actions are analogized by mechanical oscillators—Chladni plates—that are presumed to operate in the same overall manner, as does the brain when it produces perceptual responses. Chladni plates are metal sheets that resonate to produce characteristic standing wave patterns (depending upon their shape and the properties of the metal of which they are constructed) when vibrations are applied to them. Their popularity is based on the fact that if small grains of sand or metal filings are placed on the surface of the plate, these grains physically assume the shape of the standing wave patterns. Lehar proposed that similar neurochemical standing waves occur on and in the brain.

The key neuroreductionist argument made by Lehar is that regardless of how it is instantiated in the brain, there must be a topological, if not isomorphic, recapitulation of the stimulus pattern by a harmonic resonator in the brain. That is, the brain, either by virtue of its physical or chemical properties, has intrinsic resonant patterns that are activated to produce cognitive activity. This argument is most clearly expressed in a delightful and interesting medium for expressing complex scientific ideas—an Internet comic strip (Lehar, 2003a). Whether one agrees with his theory or not, and I do not, the dialog in this series of cartoons is interesting, compelling, and fun.

Topological or quasi-isomorphism of the kind invoked by Lehar holds the seed of another important idea—that of reification. Lehar suggested that once the neurochemical standing wave pattern has been determined, there is no need to seek further decoding, interpretation, or homunculus to evaluate its state. Rather, the pattern so produced itself "reifies" the perceptual experience; in other words, it becomes or *is* the perceptual experience!

Such a process, he argues, can act as a kind of associative memory, reproducing an image from an incomplete stimulus. This idea of the momentary brain state as the equivalent of cognitive process without the intervention of any binding or further interpretation is a notion with which I am very comfortable and have expressed my support of it in Uttal (2002).[12]

[12]The only theory of neural encoding of cognitive processes in which the state of the unaggregated neurons itself was the distinguishing code for a mental process (form recognition) with which I am familiar was the one proposed by Fukushima and his colleagues (Fukushima & Miyake, 1978).

However, the notion that the state of the global resonant patterns represents the actual instantiation of the brain state is not one that satisfies other criteria. The appeal of a false isomorphism obscures the possibility of other much more likely and more symbolic kinds of encoding.

To support his idea that a resonant field pattern could encode such processes as reconstruction of an incomplete pattern, Lehar (2003b) went on to point out:

> Therefore if a noisy or irregular or incomplete pattern of damping is applied to the plate, [or the neural substrate] the resonance from that input pattern will set up the nearest matching standing wave pattern. . . . (p. 30)

Lehar makes it very clear he is not suggesting that the Chladni plates, no more than an optical hologram, are physically instantiated in the head; these metal plates are just metaphorical devices that are presumed to be subject to the same mathematical principles as the biochemical resonant patterns in the brain. However, his argument, like other field theories, is based on the spatial isomorphism of this global brain activity and the supposed perceptual phenomenology. This is an analogy that leaves much to be desired.

Lehar bellieves that his Harmonic Resonance model gains credibility from the similarity of the hypothetical neurochemical fields and many of the old Gestalt psychophysical findings. Lehar suggested that such perceptual phenomena as multistability (the ability of a single stimulus to be perceived in more than one way) and invariance (the ability to perceive an object in its standard configuration even though it may be rotated, magnified, or translated) are characteristics of both resonant systems and human perception. Mainly on this basis, the former becomes a conceptual model of the latter.

The component of Lehar's Harmonic Resonance theory that places it in this chapter on field theories is that regardless of the details of the particular material mechanisms invoked, harmonic fields and human cognition are presumed to be similar in their temporal and spatial properties. He is particularly emphatic in specifying that this conceptual model is an antagonist of any theory based on the action and interaction of discrete neurons. Whatever is happening at the microscopic level of neurons is not, he argues, the psychoneural correlate of consciousness; instead the emphasis is on the global, whole, and cumulative chemical action of the brain and their propensity to produce standing wave patterns.

Physiological evidence supporting Lehar's model, based on standing waves of chemical action in the brain, is sparse. More significantly, it is challenged by the classic experiments that debunked the traditional Gestalt "isomorphic neuroelectric field theories." Presumably, Lashley, Chow, and Semmes (1951) and Sperry, Miner, and Myers (1955) results would disrupt

Lehar's hypothetical chemical standing waves as well as the electrochemical fields invoked by Kohler and the other Gestalt field theorists.

4.8 QUANTUM FIELD THEORIES OF MIND

Among field theorists in general, the mind cum consciousness cum soul cum ego is characterized by certain spatial properties that have stimulated imaginative and ingenious theories of how it might be generated by the brain. Prominent among these properties are nonlocality (distribution) and wholeness. Although there are many cognitive neuroscientists who would argue that these characteristics do not properly denote either mind or brain, field theories have typically concentrated on these supposed common characteristics. In addition, there are other characteristics of mind that are germane to this discussion that have indirectly influenced the development of a new kind of field theory of cognitive processes. One is the personal impression enjoyed by each of us that we can make choices and have a modicum of "free-will." In other words, the hope or desire that our mental activity is not strictly determined by forces beyond our personal control.

Another factor that contributes to some particularly long leaps of logic must be repeatedly acknowledged. This additional stimulus for misdirection to irrelevancies is the lack of progress that has been made in explaining the great conundrum—How does the brain make the mind? Since no one has a good answer, there is no obstacle to the wildest speculative suggestion.

This situation, filled with analogies, hopes, and the unfulfilled promise of a solid answer to the mind-brain question stimulated the generation of new theories of the mind that are based on metaphors with the prevailing scientific and technological milieu. In chapter 2, we saw how hydraulic thinking dominated Greek and Renaissance theories. With the advent of electricity, came the electrical theories of the 19th century. The rise of telephone and computer technologies in the 20th century gave rise to metaphors based on switching circuits and program algorithms. Now a new field theory of mind has evolved that is based on one of the most abstract and counterintuitive fields of modern science—quantum physics.

One of the most important, interesting, influential, and visible scientific developments of the 20th century has been the transition from classical Newtonian physics to a quantum theoretical view of the universe based on several theory-shaking, but nonintuitive, ideas. These include: (a) stochastic *probabilities* (rather than certainties) define the existence of everything in the universe; (b) objects and entities can exist simultaneously at distant locations and are thus *nonlocal*; and (c) matter can exist simultaneously in both wave and particle states (physical duality), which state is manifested depends on the particular measurements made. In the course of normal events, this strikingly different modern physical theory, in its turn, generated some novel theories of mind and consciousness. Like earlier field theories, much of the logic supporting these quantum theories of consciousness was based on what appeared to their originators to be similarities and analogies between the properties of quantum fields and mental activity.

To understand how quantum field theories came to be associated with human consciousness and their current popularity, it is necessary to expand upon the meaning of some of the critical concepts just mentioned that guided the development of what has come to be called "Quantum Consciousness." Nonlocality, to begin with one of the central ideas, has two meanings. The first refers to a property of the mind such that it seems not to be located in any particular place or time, an idea that dates back at least as far as the Roman philosopher Plotinus (205–270 CE). Thus, in principle, according to this view, our thoughts could run far afield from our brain. Thus, too, was a seed of another kind of dualism planted: Our wandering minds might not be so firmly attached to the brain as materialist monism suggested.

Second, nonlocality refers to the idea in quantum physics that objects cannot be definitively placed at a specific point in space, but may have a extensive distribution of probabilities of being located simultaneously anyplace in space and time.

Another property of mind to which we are all privy is *wholeness*. Our mind does not appear introspectively to be a conglomerate of individual components but rather is unified into, what is in practical experience, a global or molar experiential whole. Quantum physics is also based on an analogous model of the physical world. That is, since everything is everywhere (in a probabilistic sense), then everywhere must contribute some portion of the existence of everything.[13] In this quantum mechanical context, wholeness refers to the fact what is experienced at any time or place is the result of actions and forces that are distributed throughout the entire universe.

The analogies and metaphors surrounding the two properties of nonlocality and wholeness provided a fertile bed for the germination of some highly ingenious and interesting theories that combined quantum mechanics with psychological concepts of mind and consciousness. Such a

[13]The particular analogy to the holographic theory is clear at this point. However, it must be appreciated that this is a theme that runs throughout all field theories. It is, therefore, both possible and likely that, regardless of their specific instantiations, all have a common conceptual root in Fourier analysis, even those not formulated in that specific mathematical process. In other words, all mathematical field theories are duals of each other, even if they have different methods of neural instantiation, and may be intertransformable.

combination seemed to offer some possible solutions to some of the most challenging problems of mental activity—for example, the binding problem: Since our brains are arguably compartmentalized and specialized for different functions, how are all of these functions unified into the wholeness of our conscious phenomenology? Specifically, it was proposed that since quantum physics, unlike the physics of the scale at which humans operate, is also based on properties of nonlocality and wholeness, that the probabilistic field equations that underlay this arcane field of physics may also describe mental activity. As previously noted, a probabilistic universe also suggests a way in which free-will could conceivably be implemented. The residual uncertainty of whether or not a synapse will conduct or a neuron will fire provided an opportunity for other personal, immaterial, nonphysical, even supernatural, influences to be exerted.

The quantum consciousness field theory attempts to extend certain ideas that had been extremely important in our understanding of the microscopic world of basic particle physics to the macroscopic world of psychology. According to initial interpretation of the work of such giants of physical theory as Niels Bohr (1885–1962), Erwin Schrödinger (1887–1961), and Werner Heisenberg (1901–1976), material objects in the microcosm could no longer be considered to be little bounded "billiard balls" that were confined to a particular place and time. To the contrary, objects, in the view of the early quantum theory, were nothing more than probability distributions[14] that could extend over vast distances and times. This idea was interpreted to mean that objects were not localizable in principle and that, rather than discrete, they were actually overlapping.

This new interpretation of the nature of energy and matter raised many complex quasi-philosophical issues. First, it led to the nonintuitive idea that objects and events could not be precisely located in space, in time, and that their momentum and position could not be determined simultaneously—an idea that was formally defined by Heisenberg as the "Uncertainty Principle."

Second, it implied that science might be incomplete, that is, it might not be possible to "explain" natural phenomena because they could only be resolved in terms of probabilities and not certainties or hidden variables that had not, and possibly could not, be measured.

Third, it raised anew the issue of the meaning of physical properties prior to their being measured. This ghost of Bishop Berkeley's (1710/1998) idealism, the view that the material world existed only because it was per-

[14]The probability distribution in this case represents a function that indicated the likelihood that an object would be detected at a point if a measurement were made there. The probability distribution is assumed to extend infinitely far in all directions in space and time. Although the probability that an object is at some distant location might be very small, it is not nil.

ceived (or measured), runs strongly counter to both intuition and to the prevailing view of an existing, even a pre-existing, reality in modern science. Nevertheless, the priority of the measuring or perceiving process over the physical reality of objects is considered by many to be one of the most significant implications of quantum theory. It is also the basis of the idea expressed by Eccles (1994) and others such as Wolf (1989) that mental events instantiated as probability fields can "cause" neural events. Wigner (1961) took this idea even further proposing that consciousness might actually guide its own evolution and that its interaction with the material world would be different than that of an insentient machine.[15]

Furthermore, because all events and objects had some probability of being represented at any point in time or space, the possibility of action at great, even infinite, distances, a concept strongly rejected by Einstein's relativity theory, could be envisaged.[16] There was no need to explain how or when isolated events, no matter how far apart, could interact with each other since, on this theory, no events were actually "distant" from each other; rather all such entities overlapped with what might be an infinitesimal, but still nonzero, probability. Events and objects were, therefore, not separated from each other as in the Newtonian or even Einsteinean framework. Rather, they were connected because of the overlap of their intrinsically nonlocal distribution, a property implied by the wavelike properties of matter built into quantum wave theory.

Extrapolating from this view of the physical world, many psychological processes supposedly became understandable in terms of their nonlocal and probabilistic nature. Thus, too, the binding problem was essentially finessed. Nothing had to be bound because everything intrinsically overlapped with everything else.

The physicist David Bohm (1917–1994) is usually given credit for both stimulating the modern emphasis on the nonlocality implications of quantum physics and for initially proposing that such a mathematically complex system could be used as a model for consciousness. The analogical basis of his argument was that since matter was nonlocal, so, too, would the mind have to be. The field in this quantum model of mind was the wavelike probability distribution. Action at a distance was achieved not because information or energy had to be transmitted from place to distant place by neural connections or neuroelectric fields, but rather because the necessary information for integrating the components of mind was already contained at all locations.

---

[15]It is only fair and appropriate to note that Wigner later changed his mind on this issue.

[16]Einstein's relativity theory placed an absolute maximum of the speed of light in a vacuum. He argued that it would take a measurable amount of time for any kind of interaction to occur. Largely for this reason, he rejected the idea of instantaneous action at a distance.

In what has been considered by some to be a major contribution, Bohm (1952a, 1952b) focused attention on a new interpretation of quantum physics in which a

> precise and continuous description of all processes . . . determining the actual behavior of each individual system and not merely it probable behavior [was possible]. (Bohm, 1952a, p. 166)

This, in technical parlance, is the equivalent of Albert Einstein's famous remark "God does not play dice with the universe." Einstein would prefer to make quantum physics at least potentially deterministic and attribute the incompleteness to as yet undiscovered hidden principles. He was very concerned about the inelegance of an "incomplete" and "probabilistic" universe.

However, Bohm's new interpretation that quantum physics was a complete theory contrasted with the then prevailing interpretation that only the probabilities of a quantum description could be obtained from quantum physics. From this perspective, there was an inescapable uncertainty about where things were and what they were doing at any particular time. Einstein's disapproving thoughts on the matter were expressed in one of the classic articles in physical science (Einstein, Podolsky, & Rosen, 1935).

The complete mathematical details of the locality–nonlocality controversy are beyond the scope of this book. However, to sum it up briefly, the locality–nonlocality issue became focused by a theorem presented by Bell (1964) in which he proposed a set of mathematical "inequalities." Bell's inequalities were interpreted as providing a foundation for a localized universe in which the "simultaneous action at great distances," the concept so despised by Einstein, was not possible. Surprisingly, many physicists believed that Bell's inequalities were not only empirically testable, but the obtained results (Aspect, Dalibard, & Roger, 1982; Aspect, Grangier, & Roger, 1982) actually contraindicated them and, thus, to the surprise of many physicists, supported the idea of nonlocality.

Bohm was not only a distinguished physicist but developed a reputation as philosopher of the mind by extrapolating from the underlying principles of quantum mechanics to the nature of consciousness. The main conclusion he drew from his studies was that the world was a unified wholeness in which everything was interconnected. Based on these ideas, Bohm (1980) suggested that both matter and consciousness were subject to the same rules and that both were just momentary manifestations of a more fundamental "implicate order." He argued that both were just eddies in an otherwise continuous flow of reality. His words elegantly expressed this idea:

> The best image of process is perhaps the flowing stream, whose substance is never the same. On this stream, one may see an ever-changing pattern of vortices, ripples, waves, splashes, etc., which evidently have no independent existence as such. (p. 48)

It was in the 1980 book, some of us believe, that Bohm diverged from physics to a point at which fancy and imagination took the place of mathematical proofs and harder kind of science. The discussion of such issues as Bell's inequalities, the mathematics of the quantum field theories, or the Einstein, Podolsky, and Rosen (1935) incompleteness argument (i.e., that quantum mechanics was an incomplete description of reality that had to inject probability to fill the gaps) was replaced with distant analogies and an almost poetic interpretation of the nature of consciousness and material reality.

This brings us to the thoughts of another notable figure in the history of the quantum field theory of consciousness—Roger Penrose. Penrose (1989, 1994), especially as expressed in his 1994 book, was also concerned with the relation between quantum fields and consciousness or mental activity. The first part of his book considered the implications of Gödel's famous proof of inconsistency and incompleteness (see p. 112). Using this theorem as a starting point, Penrose argued that consciousness could not be based on algorithmic principles comparable to those controlling the behavior of a digital computer. Speaking of Gödel's theorem, Penrose (1994) said:

> Gödel's argument does not argue in favor of there being inaccessible mathematical truths. What it *does* argue for, on the other hand, is that human insight lies beyond formal argument and beyond computational procedures. (p. 418)

In other words, according to Penrose, consciousness is not algorithmic nor can it be simulated by a Turing type machine of the familiar kind. The problem, as we see shortly, is that it is not entirely clear what "nonalgorithmic" actually means.

The next stage of Penrose's effort to conjoin quantum mechanics and consciousness was based in large part on collaboration with Hameroff (Hameroff & Penrose, 1996; Penrose & Hameroff, 1995). Hameroff had originally suggested that microtubules[17] might be a possible means for the microscopic quantum fields to interact with matter at the macroscopic level of neurons. In brief, Penrose and Hameroff argued that the transformation in the state of these quasi-crystalline microtubules is sensitive to the quan-

---

[17]Microtubules are quasicrystalline structures that are now known to form the skeleton of cells including neurons. In addition to providing structural support they also serve as channels for the transfer of even smaller nutritive materials from one part of a cell to another.

tum field and, furthermore, that the initial structural changes in the microtubules produced by quantum level forces corresponded to "precognitive changes." As the microtubule self-organize, consciousness appears when the quantum fields "collapse" producing a sequence of mental events—a "stream of consciousness."

I have gone into the detailed history of the quantum theory of consciousness for several reasons. It is important to appreciate that there are many speculative steps underlying this proposed bridge from the microcosm for which quantum theory appears to offer a possible answer to the otherwise intractable macroscopic problem of the origins of human thought and consciousness. Quantum theory, however, is still a very long shot. Even Penrose (1994) himself, was very careful to delimit what he was attempting to do. He pointed out the limits of his theory in two ways. First, he issued the following caveat to disabuse us of the popular idealistic idea that the mind can influence the physical world:

> No doubt some readers might expect that, since I am searching for a link between the quantum measurement problem and the problem of consciousness, I might find myself attracted by ideas of this general nature [that mind can influence matter]. I should make myself clear that this is *not* the case. It is probable, after all, that consciousness is a rather rare phenomenon throughout the universe. . . . It would be a very strange picture of a "real" physical universe in which physical objects evolve in totally different ways depending upon whether or not they are within sight or sound or touch of one of its conscious inhabitants. (p. 330)

Second, Penrose argued against the idea that quantum consciousness *currently* explains the great mystery of how mind could be produced by some combination of the properties of the physical world. In this regard, he stated:

> How is it that consciousness arises from such unpromising ingredients as matter, space, and time? We have not yet come to an answer, but I hope that at least the reader may be able to appreciate that matter *itself* is mysterious, as is the space-time within whose framework physical theories now operate. (p. 419)

Thus, Penrose modestly delimited the preliminary nature of his work and the limits of progress toward the solution of the mind–brain problem.

Serious scientific criticisms of the quantum approach have appeared, even if often overlooked in the crush of uncritical acceptance of some of the more fanciful aspects of the theory. One compelling critique by Grush and Churchland (1995) specifically attacked the Penrose–Hameroff argument and is of special interest here as it raises questions about the entire quantum consciousness movement.

The first of Grush and Churchland's criticisms of quantum consciousness, in general, and of Penrose and Hameroff's interpretation, in particular, was based on the tremendous difference of scale between the microcosm of quantum theory level and the relative macrocosm of the neuron. Grush and Churchland pointed out that "quantum-level effects are generally agreed to be washed out at the neuronal level" (p. 11).

Second, they attacked the foundation idea of "nonalgorithmic" processing extrapolated from Gödel's work by Penrose. They argue that it is still a moot point whether or not any such condition as "nonalgorithmic" processing actually exists.

Third, they challenged the original Hameroff suggestion that microtubules are the mediators between quantum fields and consciousness. They argued, in this regard, that the hypothetical microtubule link to quantum fields was simply incorrect from a purely technical and empirical perspective. For example, Grush and Churchland pointed out that microtubules are not found near the synaptic junctions, the purported locus of their impact on the neuron. Finally, it was their judgment that there still was no physiological or physical evidence that quantum effects are functionally linked to microtubule activity.

Grush and Churchland (1995) made an important point about the sociology of science, one I vigorously supported in a recent book (Uttal, 2004). They stated:

> Some people, who intellectually, are materialists, nevertheless have strong dualist hankerings—especially hankerings about life after death. They have a negative "gut" reaction to the idea that neurons—cells that you see under a microscope and probe with electrodes, brains that you can hold in one hand and that rapidly rot without oxygen supply—are the source of subjectivity and the "me-ness of me."
>
> . . . Quantum physics, on the other hand, seems more resonant with those residual dualist hankerings, perhaps by holding out the possibility that scientific realism and objectivity melt away in that domain. . . . Perhaps what is comforting about quantum physics is that it can be invoked to "explain" a mysterious phenomenon without removing much of the mystery, quantum-physical explanations being highly mysterious themselves. (pp. 27–28)

To which I can only add—Amen!

Indeed, the mystery remain so great, the human "need to know" so powerful, and the fear of the termination of one's conscious existence so profound, that the idea of quantum consciousness has drawn to it more than the usual list of crazies, fanatics, religious extremists, and fringe scientists who see it as an explanation of everything from free will to reincarnation.

Unfortunately for this approach (and for many other comparable reductive theories of mind), the main link between quantum theory and consciousness is the supposed analogy between the apparently holistic and distributed (i.e., nonlocal) properties posed by theories in each domain.

Arrayed alongside this functional analogical similarity is a set of fragile hypotheses that permit even the most fragile theories to garner some support. For example, the allocation of primitive forms of consciousness to all components of the material universe (an idea inherent in the work of Bohm and many of his followers) reminds us of the primitive animisms that characterized early religious beliefs. Most of all, however, the seeming perpetuity and enormous extent of quantum fields also provides another, albeit quasiphysical, means by which our nonlocal and whole personal consciousness might persist even though the local brain structure does not.

As I have already noted, the indeterminate nature of the quantum wave equations also provides a crutch for notions of choice and free will. On this perspective, the world (including our behavior) is not *determined* by rigid algorithmic rules but is sufficiently indeterminate or probabilistic for small forces to be exerted by quantum fields on neurons in a way that permits us to express our true will. All of this comes indistinguishably close to a kind of spiritualistic antiscience.

Quantum theories of consciousness are one of many highly speculative ideas, some more and some less plausible, some more or less well expressed in the opacity of mathematical formalisms, that like other quasi-religious beliefs are hard to eject from main stream thinking. I particularly enjoyed the final statement by Grush and Churchland (1995):

> Our view is just that it [quantum consciousness] is no better supported than any one of a gazillion caterpillar-with hookah hypotheses. (p. 28)

Much the same can be said for most of the rest of the field models of the mind.

4.9 FOURIER FIELD THEORY[18]

This brief review of some of the more interesting field theories now comes to its conclusion with consideration of the granddaddy of them all. All field theories owe at least a modicum of debt to J. B. J. Fourier (1768–1830), the inventor of Fourier analysis. Fourier analysis and its mathematical deriva-

[18]The following discussion of Fourier analysis is adapted and updated from a much more extensive discussion in Uttal (2002). The topic is so germane to the present discussion that I feel it is necessary to include it at this point to make this book self-inclusive.

tives all operate on the foundation assumption that complex functions can be "analyzed" in to a series of basis functions, a set of mutually independent primitives or basis functions that spread nonlocally across what ever domain is being modeled. In classic Fourier analysis, the basis functions are one-dimensional sinusoidal functions of the form $\mathbf{a_n sin\ nx}$ or $\mathbf{b_n cos\ nx}$ or comparable functions that can be expanded in two- or three-dimensions.[19] The mathematical trick involved in Fourier analysis is to allow the complex function that is being analyzed to determine the amplitudes (i.e., the coefficients $\mathbf{a_n}$ and $\mathbf{b_n}$) and the frequencies of a set of extended (across the entire frequency space) sine and cosine basis functions that, when added together, reproduce the original function $f(x)$as expressed ina the equation:

$$f(x) = \frac{1}{2}\boldsymbol{a}_0 + \sum_{n=1}^{\infty}(\boldsymbol{a}_n \cos n\boldsymbol{x} + \boldsymbol{b}_n \sin n\boldsymbol{x}). \qquad \text{(Eq. 4.1)}$$

Fourier theories of visual perception have been particularly popular. My readers are directed to the work of DeValois and DeValois (1988)[20] for the most complete statement of a Fourier theory of spatial vision. An excellent, articulate, and thoughtful modern history of the developments in Fourier theories of vision was written by Westheimer (2001).

As with all other mathematical field theories, the basis functions are assumed to extend infinitely far in the frequency space. Although an object is present at a local point in its own space, it is represented by a superimposition of a widely distributed set of particular basis functions. If one thinks about it a minute, this is also the same metaphor of communication at a distance expressed by the quantum theory of consciousness. What exists locally, according to quantum theory, is the sum of the myriad of probability functions at that point.

This brings us to the great conceptual flaw of all field theories—the fact that these mathematical tools may not represent reality. Although Fourier analysis has made many powerful contributions to science and engineering, including the neurosciences, its great mathematical power is, at the same time, its most significant vulnerability as a source of psychological theory. The problem is that this technique is so general that its suitability as a reductive explanatory theoretical model of mind or brain should have been questioned from the beginning. *This is so because it works (mathematically) to reduce a function to a set of basis functions regardless of whether or not the underlying processes or neural machinery represented by the basis functions ac-*

---

[19]Readers interested in higher dimension Fourier analysis are directed to the premier text in the field—Pratt (1991).

[20]Sadly, Russ DeValois died in 2003. His dedication to scientific rigor and scholarship will be missed.

tually exist! In other words, it is, too general and too powerful or, in another terminology, it is neutral with regard to the actual underlying mechanisms.

Furthermore, however satisfactory and convenient the sinusoid function-based (for example) Fourier transform may be as a means of uniquely representing a set of data, it is not the only analytic method or set of hypothetical basis functions capable of doing so. Stewart and Pinkham (1991, 1994), for example, have shown that all mathematical procedures (including the sinusoid-based Fourier analysis, Gaussian modulated sinusoids [Gabor functions], quantum fields, wavelets, etc.) that have been proposed as neuroreductive "explanations" are actually equivalent to (i.e., duals of) each other; they can all be shown to be special cases of a more general form of mathematical representation called Hermitic Eigenfunctions. Each special case is usually associated with distinctly different physiological assumptions that are quite separable from the mathematical ones. However, as already noted, the physiological and mathematical assumptions can easily be separated from each other.

As a result of their mathematical equivalence, any of the particular mathematical formulations is capable of modeling the actual biology of the nervous system equally well (Stewart and Pinkham's point) and none, therefore, is capable of discriminating between any of the neurobiological assumptions regarding internal mechanisms. Therefore, whatever the mathematical formulation of a field and however successfully it may describe a form or a function, any such mathematical method is absolutely, fundamentally, and "in principle" neutral with regard to the specific underlying mechanisms. Any of these methods may perfectly describe any form or function and yet there may be no mechanism corresponding to the chosen set of basis functions physically present in the cognitive or neural domains.

Similarly, if there is any sensitivity to the Fourier components evident in the psychophysical data, it should be possible to demonstrate sensitivity to the basic functions of any of the other methods. The problem, to recapitulate, is that these analytical methods—Fourier (and similar) analyses—are too powerful! They work perfectly in a mathematical sense that is completely independent of the nature of the internal neural mechanisms. However useful, they become a frequent source of psychomythical mechanisms—in particular, the hypothesis that actual physiological frequency-sensitive components are actually instantiated in the visual system.

Westheimer (2001) expressed the same problem in a somewhat different way when he asked the rhetorical question:

> Another deeply searching question concerns the sufficiency of an analytical framework. No one is surprised if complexity has to be introduced in the modeling of a biological system, especially where the brain is involved. But one

> also has to examine whether in principle a model can account completely for the phenomena under its purview. (p. 536)

He summed it up well when he pointed out:

> Allowing nonlinearities or even substituting other types of basis functions does not eliminate the difficulties faced by any theory of visual perception that is based on the notion of fixed spatial filters. (p. 531)

Others have raised similar caveats. Wenger and Townsend (2000) concerned themselves with the problem of the relevance of the Fourier model to psychological studies of face recognition. Their particular concern was with the popular idea that low frequency information encoded the configural attributes of faces. They raised three specific counter arguments to this hypothesis:

- First, and possibly most important for present purposes, the validity and coherence of the mapping between ranges of spatial frequencies and those aspects of the stimulus that support performance indicative of configural, holistic, featural, and so on, processing is compromised by a lack of definitional precision with respect to the latter constructs. . . .
- Second, the heuristic [of low spatial frequencies coding configurations] oversimplifies the distinction between global and local processing. . . .
- Third, in some applications it overlooks the degree to which various spatial frequency ranges might function to support performance in task-specific ways. (p. 126)

Wenger and Townsend (2000) concluded that their work cannot "answer the question of whether there exists *any* critical spatial frequency band for faces" (p. 138). Thus, they provide no support for either the low frequency hypotheses or the high frequency precedence hypothesis in face processing. Rather they argued for a task-dependency hypothesis (i.e., that those aspects of a stimulus that were used by the nervous system depended on the task at hand).

The powerful analysis method proposed by Fourier adds an enormous amount of precision and quantification to anyone interested in studying or manipulating stimuli, responses, and databases. However, the practical utility and the indisputable power of the method also meant that it could be misused if invoked neuroreductionistically to "explain" some cognitive process. The fact that mythical or artificial components could be produced by mathematical analyses led many unwary scientists to presume the components actually existed in the brain. Many vision scientists reported the presence of "Fourier channels" in the brain. However, even these physiological observations could be illusions, the generality of the mathematics used to describe them being so powerful and general.

4.10 SUMMARY AND CONCLUSIONS

Field theories of mental activity, regardless of their specific mathematical and neurophysiological assumptions and postulates, have certain common properties and are driven by certain common motivations. They mainly arise as putative explanations of cognitive processes, mind, or consciousness, because of the intractability of the task of explaining brain action at the discrete neural level. They provide a seductive and possible entrée to an explanation of mental processes in the same way the concept of "gas pressure" finesses the horrendous number of calculations that would have to be executed if one tried to track the positions and momenta of the individual gas molecules in a tank. Just as "pressure" substitutes for the details of the uncountable number of gas molecules, EEGs seem to offer a composite measure of the activity of innumerable neurons. However, both gas pressure and the EEG obscure vast amounts of information concerning the detailed states of the microscopic components that produce these global measures. With gases this is not such a terrible problem since each molecule is presumably indistinguishable from another and its individual momentary velocity and momentum really don't matter. The properties of all of the molecules in the tank simply sum to produce the overall measure we call pressure. However, the brain is quite a different structure. Here the local information-processing aspects of the individual neurons may be quite idiosyncratic and the loss of detail in creating the aggregate global EEG waves may obfuscate and obscure what these remarkable cells are actually doing individually. Unfortunately, it is at this complex level—the action and interaction of discrete neurons—that mind is most likely to be encoded.

Another impetus to the generation of field theories of the mind is that a powerful and compelling metaphor is at work subtly guiding our thinking in what may be a gross misdirection. The global and distributed properties of a field seem superficially to mimic the corresponding properties of mental activity. Both mind and fields seem to exhibit distributed, global, and unified properties. What, it is argued, could be a better fit than that potentially existing between two domains, each of which has a superficial isomorphic relation to the other. Indeed, from the earliest Gestalt theories to the most modern quantum field approaches, similarity in these global properties was the cornerstone of all such theorizing. Unfortunately, this is a form of arguing by analogy that has proven to be a treacherous base for any kind of theory development. Unfortunately, similarity of form expressed by any kind of correlation or isomorphism does not necessarily imply the kind of homologous psychoneural identity that cognitive neuroscientists seek. I believe that much of the persistent popularity of field theories is based on nothing more than an uncritical extrapolation of the original analogy–the temporal and spatial similarity of our unitary and holistic minds and the global measures of brain activity such as the EEG.

Next, in the list of motivating forces driving field theories of the mind, is the fact that there is rapidly evolving progress in the mathematical handling of fields. The last century has seen field theories emerge as a very important and increasingly potent means of describing physical systems. Mathematical tools are available on which to base theories that did not exist earlier. Schrödinger and Maxwell's equations provided a means of representing fields that vastly exceeded the capacity of algorithmic formalisms to describe the many interaction of huge numbers of discrete neurons.

It can be argued in this context that the neuroelectric field theories of mental processes are persistent and still popular approaches because of an overly ambitious utilization of what are assumed to be related and effective theories in physics and/or mathematics. On this point of view, field theories represent uncritical extrapolations of a neutral mathematics that is capable of describing (without reductively explaining) some extremely difficult ideas and concepts. Physics is increasingly comfortable dealing with waves and fields of all kinds and a formidable armamentarium of powerful mathematical tools has been developed to handle such phenomena. There is, therefore, a tendency to imitate the success of the physical sciences by attacking the mind–brain problem with these same techniques. This effort continues regardless of other considerations such as the absence of any direct or even indirect empirical evidence that quantum forces or neuroelectric fields can actually influence mental activity.

The tendency to think of fields in this domain is enhanced simply because we still have not yet determined how the mind is constructed by processes in the brain. Thus, almost any far-fetched hypothesis, however unverifiable or however it may run counter to normal science, garners an audience. To the degree that it provides some semblance of hope for the residual dualism that permeates human society, even the most abstract proposal becomes grist for parascientific and spiritual fantasies.

The urge to solve the so-called "binding problem" provides another incentive for theorizing about fields. There is, however, a subtle flaw in the formulation of the binding problem. The syllogism goes something like this:

- Our brains and minds are made up modular components.
- Our phenomenological experience is holistic and continuous.
- Therefore, there is a need to explain how the modules are combined in the unified experience.

The problem with this syllogism is that the first assumption may be false, especially with regard to mental modules. In other words, the binding problem may be a false query. Thus, epiphenomenon such as the 40 Hz signal or overlapping quantum probability fields may have been invoked to answer an ill-posed or, in Rescher's (1984) terminology, an improper question. It is at least arguable that the overall state of the high information state of a myriad of discrete neurons encoding a thought may collectively, but still individually, represent such a unified process equally as well as a global, information deficient field. Given that there is no solution yet available (nor likely to become available) wildly imaginative theories are unconstrained.

On this point of view, the quasimythical binding process may be an artifact of the way in which we do our experiments and some interesting, but irrelevant sensory and motor processes in the peripheral nervous system. The discovery of separate channels for the separate dimensions of a visual experience, for example, in the lateral geniculate body and the primary visual cortex may have inspired cognitive neuroscientists to put back together again that which was never asunder. However, the coding mechanisms used by the actual regions of the brain where the psychoneural equivalents of vision (as opposed to the communication of afferent information) are likely to be found are not known. It is not necessarily the case that modularity exists either physiologically or psychologically at those levels.

There are other forces of the current scientific Zeitgeist that drive us to field theories of mind and to a quest for solving what may be a nonexistent "binding" problem. The computer metaphor, so popular in cognitive psychology, is one of these forces. Contemporary computer models of cognition are constructed on the basis of an accumulation of the action of separate program modules, each supposedly representing a separable module of information processing. The concept of the separate processing of the features of a visual image centrally, to cite one popular example, is reinforced by the undeniable existence of separate channels for different stimulus features in the peripheral sensory pathway. Both the computer metaphor and the functional anatomy of the ascending sensory pathways lead us, therefore, to think of and then model partitions. This algorithmic, step-by-step (or feature detection) approach creates a conceptual need to explain how the steps are combined into a unified experience. By doing so, an alternative approach to the solution of the great mind–body problem is obscured—the possibility that the momentary state of the entire system itself is the psychoneural equivalent of mental activity.

What about the purported empirical evidence for fields? Each field theory discussed in this chapter invokes observations from neurophysiological or psychophysical laboratories to support its case. Even here, there is residual uncertainty that should not be ignored. Given the complexity of the relationship between the brain and cognitive domains, there is a huge amount of evidence available. By carefully selecting among this vast database it is possible to find some research that seems to support any particular speculation.

Furthermore, the attribution of a particular meaning to a piece of data is, itself, an act of judgment and interpretation. As one reads the literature and observes the kind of evidence offered in support of field theories of the mind, one is left with the feeling that a priori theoretical assumptions determine the meaning of the data rather than the converse. The very ease with which the EEG and ERP methods can be noninvasively applied gives them a superficial appearance of transparency into the neuroelectric activity of the brain. Even the possibility of their epiphenomenal nature is often ignored as work on this type of theory continues.

The EEG and the ERP both vary in their magnitude and timing across the surface of the skull and even, when exposed, across the brain. This modulation by the physical properties of the brain and skull can be so extensive that the signals can be hugely distorted and, more to the point, often not even detectable. Thus, what is measured often provides an incomplete picture of the global electrical fields. As one peruses the EEG and ERP literature, there is a constant itch of doubt caused by the small and idiosyncratic differences between conditions that are often offered up as "evidence" for one or another hypothesis.

The continuing uncertainty of how EEGs and other neuroelectric fields are generated by the brain remains an important constraint on any interpretation of them as psychoneural equivalents of mind. The possibility that they might be nothing other than concomitant epiphenomena no longer reflecting (because of their cumulative nature) the true details of the truly salient neural processing remains a substantial constraint on the acceptance of any such theory. To emphasize this point, it is entirely possible that EEGs, for example, might correlate, even very highly, with some psychophysical function even though they are not causally related to the cognitive processes under investigation. The warning that "correlation does not imply causation" enunciated by Yule (1926) three quarters of a century ago remains a fundamental conceptual challenge to casual acceptance of any field theory.

Another problem repeatedly encountered in this discussion of field theories is the widespread unwillingness on the part of their originators to accept the fact that neuroelectric fields represent a highly reduced amount of information compared with the amount encoded by the array of individual neurons. There is no reason to believe that the EEG contains the equivalent or the same amount of information that would be included in a tabulation of the individual states of an array of billions of neurons. The main advantage that a neuroelectric field has over such a tabulation is that fields are much more accessible than an exhaustive compilation of individual neural responses. Furthermore, the basic fact that EEGs and other widespread low frequency waves do measure some electrical activity of the brain gives them a certain face validity. Nevertheless, the fact that they represent such a highly integrated and, thus, reduced amount of information may mean that crucial information underlying mental activity is not present in these cumulated signals.

In conclusion, field theories do not seem to represent a promising road leading to understanding how the brain produces mental functions. Tenuous analogies, flimsy bridging assumptions, and inadequate experimental support argue against their future utility to this central scientific problem. We now turn to another traditional answer to the mind–brain question—one that proposes that single neurons rather than neuroelectric codes are the key to cutting through the world knot.

CHAPTER

5

Single Neuron Theories of the Mind–The Undue Influence of a Point in Space

5.1 INTRODUCTION

Chapter 4 discusses how a substantial amount of theory concerning the mind–brain issue was motivated by an analogy drawn between the spatio-temporal characteristics of available global neuroelectric measures and the supposed experiential dimensions of cognitive activity. In this chapter I consider another major theoretical movement that attacks the problem from a totally different direction and at a totally different scale of magnification. Rather than considering macroscopic global signals that are distributed over large parts of the brain, this alternative strategy–single neuron theory–bases its argument on the electrophysiological properties of individual microscopic neurons. Theories of this class are based on knowledge obtained during what was one of the most exciting and fruitful times in the history of neurophysiology–the period in which we were able to look inside a neuron. The major breakthrough enabling this extraordinary capability was the development of a technology utilizing high impedance, microscopic recording electrodes. These tiny electrodes made it possible to examine the electrophysiological potentials across the cell membrane. It was by this means that neuroscientists were able to understand the chemical processes that underlay the activity of these cells. However, like so many other technical breakthroughs, the microelectrode technique and the otherwise indisputably important empirical knowledge gained led to a misadventure in theory building. This technological achievement and the theories it stimulated are the topics of this chapter.

Before starting, however, one cautionary comment must be introduced. In many ways the different theories discussed in this book are not entirely in conflict with each other and often overlap. There is no sharp line of demarcation, other than their respective emphases, between single cell theories and the others dealt with elsewhere in this book. Single cell theorists no longer make the literal argument that the activity of one neuron is the encoded psychoneural equivalent[1] of a pondered thought or a recognized pattern.

On the other hand, few current field theorists are such radical equipotentialists that they would argue there is no microscopic differentiation between different parts of the brain. They are also concerned with the manner in which the field signals emerge from the aggregate neuronal activity. Network theorists, as well as field theorists, strongly accept the contributory role of individual neurons and single cell theorists always seem to appreciate that each individual neuron is heavily interconnected within some kind of a functional network. What has happened is that now the quibble is over rather ill-defined notions of sparseness, distribution, and tuning width.

The key distinction among the various theoretical types, therefore, concerns what happens to an afferent neural signal as it ascends the nervous system. Does it converge on ever fewer neurons until a relatively small number (as small as one) encodes complex features? Alternatively, does the signal diverge to activate huge numbers of neurons in a vast shower of activity driven by even the simplest and least energetic stimulus? Clearly the different theories fuse into each other. However, on one point there is no question among neuroscientists; no currently viable theory denies the basic proposition—that it is some aspect of the brain's activity that *is* our cognitive activity.

Nevertheless, there are sufficient differences of emphasis and interpretation to distinguish the single cell theories from the others. The purpose of this chapter is to make clear exactly what is being proposed by this class of theories. To understand the foundation concepts of present day single cell theories of the mind, however, we have to look back over the history of neuroscience in the past century.

---

[1]The term *psychoneural equivalent* is very important in this discussion. To assure that it is understood, I now reiterate my intended definition of this phrase. A psychoneural equivalent is the neuronal response (or responses) that is (or are) the necessary and sufficient cause of a cognitive process. As we see later, a neuronal response may transmit information without being manifested as a mental event. In that case it may be a transmission code. On the other hand, the activation of the psychoneural equivalent *IS* the mental process, according to the intended meaning of the term.

5.1.1 Neuron Doctrine ≠ neuron doctrine ≠ Single Neuron Theory[2]

The Neuron Doctrine, introduced and described in chapter 2, is universally accepted now. It states a fundamental truth about the anatomy of the brain and its components; that truth is that the brain, like all of the other organs of the body, is composed of an assemblage of isolatable cells or "neurons," each of which is separated from its neighbors by a semipermeable and continuous cell membrane. As important as the Neuron Doctrine is to modern theory in neurophysiology, there is a major misunderstanding concerning its applicability in the development of theories of the mind. Accepting, without reservation, the unarguable anatomic and physiological axioms of the Neuron Doctrine, it does not logically or necessarily follow, that these individual, encapsulated, discrete neurons are, by themselves, satisfactory explanations of the mechanisms of mental processes. Indeed, it takes some slippery logic to slide from the *Neuron Doctrine* to the completely different idea that single cell activity is the psychoneural equivalent of our perceptions, cognitions, and other thoughts, an idea that has come to be called the *single neuron theory.* In addition, there is a third category to be considered—the *neuron doctrine as a* philosophical stance. Let us now distinguish these three distinctly different ideas from each other.

The classic and currently fully accepted Neuron Doctrine is a very specific statement about the anatomy and physiology of neurons. The Neuron Doctrine neither confirms nor is confirmed by any observation that demonstrates correlations between activity recorded with a microelectrode and behavior or a stimulus pattern. It deals solely with the structural continuity or discontinuity of neurons, an anatomical issue that is not directly assayed by such physiological tests, and their interaction via the gaps between these cells. Its proof depended upon the development of ingenious staining and ultimately electron magnification techniques that finally and unequivocally demonstrated the reality of the continuity of the cell membrane and of the intercellular gaps between neurons.

The *neuron doctrine* of the mind, on the other hand, deals with a completely different issue—the general assumption (which is, as I have noted, undisputed by cognitive neuroscientists of all theoretical stripes) that the representation of cognitive processes is fully accounted for by brain components and their activity. It argues that if it is at all possible, mental processes will ultimately be explicable only in terms of the anatomy and physiology of the nervous system and its components. The neuron doctrine

---

[2]In this section I distinguish between the *Neuron Doctrine* (the anatomical statement that the nervous system is made up a discontinuous array of individual neurons) and the *neuron doctrine* (the philosophy that a more or less complete explanation of the mind can be achieved by the use of biological concepts) by the use of capital or lower case letters respectively.

rejects any other non- or supernatural influence. Psychology, it is further argued, can be completely explained in the language and data of neurophysiology—in principle if not in fact.

The third member of this oft-confused triumvirate—a *single neuron theory*—can also be distinguished from the Neuron Doctrine as well as from the neuron doctrine; it is a specific and hypothetical association of single neurons and cognitive processes going far beyond the anatomic proposition of the Neuron Doctrine and the reductionist philosophical statement of the neuron doctrine. It is studied by showing associations or correlations between a particular impaled neuron's activity and behavior and then drawing inferences about representational processes from that behavior.

Another introductory point must be emphasized here. The demonstration of an association or correlation between a mental process and the activity of a single neuron may be empirically correct without providing any compelling proof of the single neuron hypothesis. When a single neuron is being studied it is obvious that other neurons are active and deeply involved in the process, although their activities are not being recorded. Thus, the recorded responses from a single neuron may represent only the smallest fraction of the full extent of associated activity. A single neuron theory of psychoneural representation is no more confirmed by such correlations than is the anatomical Neuron Doctrine. In the case of single neuron theory, the reported associations of single cell and mental activity are so incomplete that we count on them for answers to the mind–brain problem only at our theoretical peril.

The phrase "Neuron Doctrine" has, because of this linguistic confusion, become encumbered with many other meanings than the original anatomical one asserting that the nervous system was made up of discrete neurons rather than a continuous syncytium. For modern neuroscientists, far distant from the work of Cajal and Golgi, the lower case version of the phrase—neuron doctrine—has come to represent nothing more or less than an expression of the monist philosophy that the mind is a process of the brain. However justified such a philosophy may be, this is not what was originally meant by the concept of the Neuron Doctrine. Gold and Stoljar (1999), for example, defined the neuron doctrine cum philosophy as:

> Roughly, the neuron doctrine is the view that the framework within which the science of the mind will be developed is the framework provided by neuroscience; or, as we shall put it, that a successful theory of the mind will be a solely neuroscientific theory. (p. 809)

Gold and Stoljar went on to distinguish between two versions of this neuron doctrine. First, they consider a "trivial" version arguing that the ultimate explanation of how mind is produced will emerge from a mélange of psychology, chemistry, physics, and the neurosciences. They are, in the context of this definition, essentially invoking the range of activities incorporated these days by the term "cognitive neuroscience." The important aspect of this first and less radical definition is that psychology and other sciences will persist, each providing their own insight into how the mind emerges from the brain.

The second and more radical version of the neuron doctrine, according to Gold and Stoljar, is the one offered by the eliminativists (e.g., Churchland, 1981; Churchland & Churchland, 1994). This version is far more damning for the future of psychology and the other behavioral sciences; it argues that neurobiological terms and processes will ultimately explain everything and lead to the disappearance of such "folk" sciences as current day psychology.[3]

The radical version of the neuron doctrine can be criticized on a number of counts including those encompassed within the discussions of this book and others raised by Gold and Stoljar themselves as well as their critics.[4] However, all of these fine slices are mainly epistemological and do not speak to the fundamental naturalism of either version. The future will determine if the eliminativists are correct or if some intractable nonreductive aspects of the problem will eventually block the achievement of their goals. I suspect, however, that there is sufficient evidence from mathematics and psychology already existing to suggest that the goal of a totally neurophysiological explanation of mind and cognition will never be achieved. (This argument is detailed in chapter 6.)

The two definitions proposed by Gold and Stoljar are followed by citations of a substantial number of neuroscientists and philosophers who agree with the trivial version and a few who would carry the radical view even further. It is well that they should, because whichever version one accepts, the neuron doctrine, in any of its forms, is an expression of the fundamental naturalist approach to scientific explanation. For the mind, furthermore, there is no other game in town than the brain unless one is willing to

---

[3]The dichotomous teasing apart of the meaning of the neuron doctrine continues. For example, Byrne and Hilbert (1999) suggest that Gold and Stoljar's radical version actually comes in two forms—weak radical and strong radical. The weak radical says that "... the mind—psychological phenomena—can be (wholly) explained by neurobiology. The strong radical version says that "... *only* neurobiology can explain the mind" (p. 833). I leave it to my readers to further extract these additional meanings of the term.

[4]An interesting example of how the phrase *neuron doctrine* has many alternative meanings is to be found in a comment on the original Gold and Stoljar (1999) article by Hameroff (1999). Hameroff slams the original article because in his view "The N[n]euron D[n]octrine is an insult to neurons"! By this he means that it does not take into account the even more microscopic substructure of the individual neurons. Hameroff's definition of the neuron doctrine is that it is a statement of the activity of the whole neuron and does not include the cytoskeletal structures and functions going on within the cell. Although none of these subcellular activities are explicit in most of the neuronal reductive theories, in principle they are not rejected by any modern neuroscientist. "What we have here is a failure of communication" of the meaning of the words we are using; something that goes on all the time in this field.

adopt supernatural explanations that are quite beyond the pale of an acceptable materialist monism. I include myself among those totally dedicated to the trivial version of the neuron doctrine as stated by Gold and Stoljar. My rejection of the radical, eliminativist version is equally complete, but for the purposes of the present discussion, irrelevant.

The reason for this irrelevancy is that neither of Gold and Stoljar's versions of the phrase "neuron doctrine" is a valid extrapolation from the original Neuron Doctrine. Virtually the same monism, either in its trivial or radical form, could have been based on totally different neuroanatomical foundations. For example, prior to Golgi and Cajal's times, with a few exceptions, most neurophysiologists thought that the nervous system was a giant syncytium—an interconnected, continuous, protoplasmic mass that, although endowed with many nuclei, was actually a single glob—an individual superneuron. In other words, the nervous system consisted of a single, albeit huge and multinucleated, cell surrounded without interruption by a huge and continuous membrane.

There is no question nowadays, as Cajal so forcibly demonstrated, that the syncytium idea was wrong. It also seems likely that it had some deleterious effects on thinking in the field. Nevertheless, neither the monist philosophy of brain–mind identity nor the single neuron theory would be in any fundamental conceptual conflict with the syncytium idea.[5] The neuroanatomical and physiological details of the theory might well have been different. In all likelihood, they would eventually have had to be changed in the light of new discoveries. However, but such changes in the anatomic axioms of the Neuron Doctrine would not have affected the neuron doctrine in any fundamental way—local regions of the syncytium could have been as good components as separate neurons for the development of mind–brain theories. Indeed, although not generally appreciated, both the trivial and the radical versions of the neuron doctrine are neutral with regard to the specific anatomical implementations and instantiations implied by the Neuron Doctrine.

This does not mean that the Neuron Doctrine did not have strong theoretical and even philosophical effects on the development of cognitive neuroscience. What the Neuron Doctrine did accomplish so strongly was to emphasize the role of the individual, discrete neuron as opposed to the mass activity of the nervous system. Of course, it had to compete with other theories, but that is another part of the tale.

Then came another critical influence—the technological one of the invention of the microelectrode—as discussed in the next section. The combination of the most basic anatomic rule of modern neurophysiology—the Neuron

---

[5]I say this with an appreciation of the fact that other empirical data would have to be made compatible with some aspects of the syncytium idea. However, theoretical accommodations of this kind are entirely possible and have characterized all such theories.

Doctrine—with its emphasis on discrete neurons with the most powerful tool for studying the activity of those discrete neurons—exerted a compelling and powerful effect on the point of view of cognitive neuroscientists.

In large part, as it must always be and as it has always been, theoretical perspectives are constrained and limited to the available technologies and the data forthcoming from their application. With the development of microelectrodes, the activity of individual neurons could be compared with stimulus or behavioral response parameters and the correspondences between the two domains determined. The effect was to focus attention on the single neuron and to extrapolate the findings to a theory of how the brain produces cognitive processes. Unfortunately, the forced shift of attention led to ideas that were not eventually sustainable.

To summarize, the Neuron Doctrine can be distinguished from the neuron doctrine and both can be distinguished from—the single neuron theory.

- The Neuron Doctrine is an anatomical statement of cellular discontinuity.
- The neuron doctrine is a naturalist ontological conjecture that mind is essentially the result of neural activity.
- The single neuron theory is the presumption that the embodiment of the mind is to be found in the behavior of single neurons as opposed to cumulated activity fields or neural networks.[6]

The great flaws in the interpretations that led to the mid 20th century misemphasis on single cells as the representative equivalents of cognitive processes can be identified.

1. Although there is currently no question that the brain is made up of individual cells or neurons, there is no direct linkage from this Neuron Doctrine to the role they are purported to play in representing or encoding psychological processes. The Neuron Doctrine, an anatomical and physiological axiom, was incorrectly extrapolated into theoretical statements about the single neuron representation of cognitive processing. Essentially it was a pun.

2. The invention of the microelectrode technology directed research attention strongly to the action of the individual neuron. As with so many other technological developments in the past, it became the analogy à la mode of mind–brain interaction.

[6]The situation was even further complicated by the fact that Barlow (1972) has designated his single cell theory as a "[N]neuron [N]doctrine," but with a different meaning than the one used here.

3. Early success in showing that information is encoded and transmitted by the activity of individual neurons led to the confusion of peripheral transmission codes with higher level cognitive–neural representations. Our attention was thus directed away from the study of complex neural nets to the activity of individual neurons.

4. Finally, the technology did not and does not exist for the study of neural nets of a complexity sufficient to represent cognitive processes.[7] Given that the mind–brain problem was not (and is not yet) solved, free rein was given to hypothetical conjecture.

I now turn to a brief review of the early discoveries in single cell neurophysiology using microelectrodes that so powerfully impacted 20th-century theories of how the brain makes the mind.

5.1.2 The Compelling Influence of the Microelectrode Technology

The initial technical problem faced when the Neuron Doctrine became firmly established around the end of the 19th century was the microscopic size of neurons relative to the macroscopic measuring equipment that was available to measure their electroneural activity. In particular, given that neurons could be as small as 10 μ and fiber diameters as small as a fraction of a μ, it was extremely difficult to connect a single neuron to a recording electrode.

[8]Compound nerve activity (i.e., cumulative signals from nerves composed of many fibers) had been recorded as early as the middle of the 19th century. Hermann von Helmholtz (1821–1894) had actually made quite good measurements (Helmholtz, 1850) of the speed of conduction of the mixed fibers in frogs' nerves. However, the ultimate neuroscientific goal was to measure the activity of single axons, preferably from inside the cell so that the transmembrane potential could be measured.

In the 20th century, with the development of electronic amplifiers and oscilloscopes, the task of recording neural activity from single neurons from the outside was first accomplished in motor fibers (Adrian & Bronk, 1928). In the 1930s, a few investigators, like these pioneers, were able to dissect out a single active sensory fiber, free from the compound nerve of which it was a part. If they laid the single fiber across a relatively large electrode (e.g., a saline-soaked cotton wick), it was possible to pick up highly attenuated records of the neuronal action potentials. This technique was

[7]See chapter 6 where the ontological truth of neural net theories is supported but their epistemological intractability accepted.

[8]This section on the history of intracellular recording from single neurons is adapted and updated from Uttal (1975).

used by Hartline in two important studies (Hartline, 1935, 1938). The initial article reported recordings from a single optic nerve fiber from a vertebrate for the first time. The second article was an important study in which the concept of the receptive field was first enunciated.

However, these extracellularly recorded potentials were only weak reflections of the intracellular voltages across the cell membrane. Most workers in the field by that time realized that explanatory neurochemical theory would have to remain speculative until it became possible to record transmembrane potentials. To do so required that one of a pair of bipolar electrodes be placed inside the neuron.

The heroic task of getting a recording electrode inside a neuron was finally accomplished because of an anatomical freak. Young (1936) described a most unusual neuron, a giant cell in the squid nervous system that had an axon that could be as great as 1 mm in diameter. This axon was sufficiently large that the open end of a small glass tube could be inserted into the intracellular space from a cut end of the axon. If this glass tube contained a salt solution, it acted as an internal electrode referenced to an external electrode positioned in the saline-filled dish holding the giant neuron. Tubular electrodes of this type were used to record transmembrane, intracellular potentials first by Hodgkin and Huxley (1939) and then shortly afterwards by Curtis and Cole (1942).

This technique, based as it was on an anatomical rarity, had an astonishingly influential impact on theory from virtually the first observation. Among the earliest discoveries was that the electrical potential across the membrane went slightly positive (rather than simply retreating to zero) during the production of a spike action potential. This meant that the electrical activity of the neuron could not be an entirely passive discharge. This single fact necessitated a drastic reformulation of the then prevailing theory of membrane action in terms of active metabolic processes. It led to what is still the prevailing theory; namely that neurons carry out their activities by means of metabolically energized ionic transport mechanisms (Hodgkin & Katz, 1949) as well as by some passive conduction across the semipermeable cell membrane.

As productive as the squid axon procedure was, it required a freak neuron that was big enough to permit a relatively large glass tube to be pushed into it. This required that the axon be cut and, therefore, that the intracellular fluids could leak out. The transmembrane potentials could, under these conditions, change over a short period of time. The study of the neurophysiology of single neurons could advance only if a procedure for the intracellular recording of neuronal action potentials of broader applicability and less traumatic intervention could be developed.

The important invention of nondestructive penetration of a cell by a tiny electrode was accomplished by Gerard and his colleagues (Graham &

Gerard, 1946; Ling & Gerard, 1949) on muscle fibers, but the technique is identical to that currently used on neurons. Their procedure involved the use of a fluid-filled glass tube that actually penetrated the membrane of the cell itself. Tiny open tips (approaching one μ) were required so that the damage to the neuron would be minimized and the fluid inside the electrode could come into electrical contact with the fluids in the neuron's interior. These exceptionally fine electrodes were made by heating tubes of soft glass at an intermediate point and then pulling the tube apart evenly from both ends until it thinned and broke at the heated portion. The process worked because the fluid characteristics of molten glass act as a "demagnifier" to produce a replica of the original tube, but of a very small size.[9]

Microelectrode technology over the years has advanced substantially. Electrolytically polished platinum-iridium coated with glass or tungsten coated with lacquers (Hubel, 1957) has been used for some preparations. Other newer versions have been made by the same techniques developed for etching the tiny components used in computer chip manufacturing. Indeed, amplifying circuits can now be created right on the microelectrodes themselves (and vice versa).

The glass or metal microelectrodes are so small that they can be literally pushed through the membrane of even very small neurons without destroying the integrity of the cell. The membrane apparently forms a seal around the micropipette, in the same manner as a self-sealing tire. This seal is sufficiently robust to allow the neuron often to continue operating for hours or even days after being impaled.

The impact of these new *intracellular* microelectrodes was huge and led to a rush of discovery that was so vast that it is impossible to even begin to summarize it here. It is only necessary to point out that an enormous amount was learned about the function of individual neurons and new understanding about the electrochemical bases of neuronal activity rapidly accumulated. Once again, a pathway into the action of the brain seemed to be at hand. Buttressed by this accumulated flood of data on the physiology of single neurons, another rush of ingenious theoretical creativity ensued. This new wave consisted, in large part, of single neuron theories of the mind.

The general result that motivated the vast expansion of single neuron theories of mental activity was that, in undeniable fact, individual cellular activity could be found that correlated with psychological function. In this case the analogy was not drawn between the global signals (e.g., the EEG)

---

[9]This is the same process used to produce the beautiful Venetian glass patterns known as "Mille Fiore" (a thousand flowers). Relatively large bundles of glass are bound together in flower like designs and then heated and pulled to produce highly reduced replicas of the original bundle.

as was done by field theorists or complex networks of discrete neurons and the mind. Instead, the basic comparison of mind and brain was made between individual neuronal responses and mental processes. In the sensory domain, in particular, extraordinary correlations appeared between physical stimuli and neural response dimensions, on the one hand, and perceptual experiences, on the other.

Two theoretical missteps followed, however. First, these highly correlated peripheral neuronal responses were, rather cavalierly, assumed to be psychoneural equivalents rather than simply transmission codes. That is, the response of the neuron was interpreted as both the necessary and sufficient representation of psychological experience. Second, the fact that single *peripheral* neurons coded distinguishable properties of the stimulus was extrapolated to mean that single *central* neurons also encoded complex experiential phenomena or complex cognitive processes. The impact of these two logical errors on neuroreductionist thinking, particularly among psychologists, was enormous.

It takes no deep analysis to appreciate that the single neuron theory of cognitive representation runs into a major handicap at the outset. That handicap is the huge number of other brain cells also active at the same time as the one under investigation. If one examines the logic of this situation critically, it quickly becomes clear that *all such experiments are, in principle, totally uncontrolled.* That is, the microelectrode produces a time function of activity at a single point in space. It ignores the activity going on at all other points! Activities at all other points may or may not (and probably are not) using the same codes as the impaled neuron but may be equally deeply involved in the mental activity under study. Thus, the microelectrode tells us little about the overall state of the network of neurons that make up the brain as it goes about its business of producing experience from physical stimuli.[10]

There is, therefore, a profound bias in all microelectrode studies of single neuron correlates of mental experience. That bias led inexorably to the unjustifiable reification of whatever coded responses happened to be found in the small sample of neurons that could be probed in any practical experiment. It leaves knowledge about the activity within the much larger number of unprobed neurons uncontrolled and unknown. Clearly, there are many more of the latter than the former, almost certainly by orders of magnitude.

This problem of the uncontrolled sampling of neurons is difficult enough when one is studying sensory or motor transmission codes in which case

---

[10]Again, it is necessary to reiterate that such an experimental paradigm does tell us much about the coding of transmitted information in the peripheral nervous system. However, transmission of information is not the same as the psychoneurally equivalent representation of mental process by neural nets.

the stimuli are well anchored to physical measures. It is vastly compounded when a correlation between the activity of the impaled neuron and some aspect of some unanchored, difficult-to-define, putative cognitive function is sought. When confronted with a seductive correlation between a thought and a responsive neuron, it is extremely easy to come to the fallacious conclusion that the sampled neuron, either by itself or as member of a small sparsely distributed group of its fellows, fully represents the neural equivalent of a particular cognitive process.

In summary, single neuron theories of cognitive processes do not provide a solid idea of how the central nervous system encodes our percepts and cognitions. The basic problem is that these fundamentally uncontrolled experiments make for an extremely underdetermined and ambiguous situation when it comes to evaluating and comparing theories of mental activity. This ambiguity leads to the opportunity for data to be very loosely interpreted and theories to be glibly formulated.

To overcome this fundamental handicap, some investigators have turned to indirect means of evaluating whether a single or a few neurons are likely to be a sufficient code for a perception or a memory. For example, Lennie (2003) suggested that it might be possible to resolve this issue by calculating the "cost" of having a neuron respond—where cost is measured in energy consumption. He cited calculations that he contended supported the argument that only a small proportion of the neurons in the brain can be active when our minds are active. The residual question, however, is—How few are a "few"? Indeed, indirect information like this must contend with data that show broad tuning, thus suggesting the involvement of "many," rather than a "few," neurons and widely distributed activity involving large numbers of neurons, rather than limited neural responses.

If nothing else, such arguments highlight the uncertainty of the language that we use in evaluating this kind of empirical data. Ambiguity and vagueness take the place of precise definition and agreed upon units of measurement. Nevertheless, there is no question that there are many indirect arguments that can be invoked to either reject or support single neuron theory. It is, therefore, especially useful in such a case to study the history of these theories to determine what were the various influences that led to their development and how thinking in the cognitive neurosciences developed.

5.1.3 Early Neurophysiological Discoveries Leading to Single Cell Theories of the Mind

The previous section presents the history of the development of the microelectrode and its major contribution to our understanding how neurons work. This was a scientific invention of the first magnitude; the accomplishments from Ling and Gerard's (1949) invention and their application to muscle cells and its subsequent use as the tool par excellence for the study of neurons have revolutionized neuroscience.

There was, however, a new revolution lying just over the horizon that was to overshadow even that remarkable technological development. The old revolution was characterized by the ability to observe the detailed behavior of individual neurons and to control the intensity or magnitude of stimuli. The new revolution was a conceptual one that extended our appreciation of the dimensionality of brain responses and radically changed both the obtained data and their interpretations.

Traditional neurophysiology up until the 1960s had largely been based on the assumption that the energy of a stimulus was the sole determinant of its response. The stimuli that were used up to that time were simply bursts of light, acoustic, or mechanical energy that were known to be adequate stimuli for the activation of a neuron. It had been known since Adrian's (1928)[11] time, for example, that when recordings were made from the optic nerve of an amphibian, that the response would vary with the amount of light falling on the animal's eye. One of the first reports to show the generality of this coding scheme was Hodgkin's (1948) classic study in which electrical stimuli were applied to a crab's nerve and the frequency of the response measured. The fact that the response was functionally dependent on the stimulus intensity was characteristic of the kind of data being collected prior to mid century.

By the 1950s and 1960s, a large number of other supporting studies[12] had been published that demonstrated there was a strong positive correlation between stimulus strength and the frequency of firing of individual neurons. Thus, this fact was widely accepted by neurophysiologists and remains one of the basic laws of neural information transmission encoding.[13] Indeed, until the 1960s it was generally assumed that the intensity of the stimulating light was all that counted in determining the response of a visual neuron. However, things were about to change.

The second neural coding revolution and the impetus for many ingenious single neuron theories of cognition lay in the emerging realization that it was not just the stimulus energy that mattered but also its spatial and temporal properties. The first suggestions that intensity–frequency coding was only part of the story came around mid century. Hartline (1940a, 1940b) elaborated on his early identification of the receptive field by sug-

[11]Adrian's 1928b book, among other things, summarized the results of a four part series of experiments that were originally published in 1926.

[12]See chapter 6 in Uttal (1973) for a complete review of the many studies showing the relationship between neuronal spike frequency and stimulus intensity.

[13]However, the work on the opponent coding schemes of the second and higher neuronal levels of visual information coding by DeValois, Smith, Kitai, and Karoly (1958) was later to remind us that, while general, this law is not universal.

gesting the concept of spatial summation—a process in which stimulus energy is accumulated or integrated across an area bigger than a single receptor cell. Later, Hartline and his colleagues (e.g., Hartline, Wagner, & Ratliff, 1956; Ratliff & Hartline, 1959), while studying the response of the horseshoe crab eye, discovered that the frequency of neural responses was not only dependent on the raw intensity of the light but the spatial pattern with which it was projected onto this compound eye. If two light spots were projected side by side within the receptive field of an ommatidium, it was possible to generate a response in either that was actually *less* than that generated by stimulating one alone. Their explanation for this "subtractive" response pattern was a simple one: Lateral inhibitory interactions between the adjacent receptor units were mutually modulating the frequency of each neuron's response.[14] This was one of the initial suggestions that complex information processing occurred in the eye itself.

Somewhat later, Barlow (1953), working with the frog's eye, reported confirmation of earlier work by Hartline that "on" and "off" neurons existed that were excited by appropriate onset and offset timing patterns of the stimulus. Thus, there were clear indications that both the spatial and temporal patterns of a stimulus could determine the magnitude of a neuronal response. Then, in what was perhaps the marker between the "bolts of lightning and crashes of thunder"[15] purely energy-based theories of the past, Barlow (1953) made the following prescient remark:

> Perhaps the idea of sensory integration has been pressed too far, but the distortions [in firing rates of neurons] introduced by the retina seem to be meaningful; the retina is acting as a filter rejecting unwanted information and passing useful information. (p. 87)

Others may have thought the thought, but it fell to Barlow to enunciate it in a way that captured the flavor of the neural net as an information processor par excellence for decades to come.

It is of historical interest to note, however, that at that time Barlow did not make the leap from potential information processing to the notion of special purpose neurons sensitive to particular spatiotemporal stimulus patterns. He came very close when he (Barlow, 1953, p. 87) discussed how the visual response to a fly's movement patterns could be determined by the on–off properties of a frog's retinal neuron. However, it was for others

---

[14]This was not a new idea. Ernst Mach (1838–1916), based on some psychophysical phenomena that had been immortalized as the "Mach Band," suggested on purely speculative grounds that lateral inhibitory interaction existed in the visual system.

[15]This dramatic phrasing of the energy dependent hypothesis has been attributed to H. L. Teuber (1916–1977).

to make both the empirical discoveries and the conceptual leaps that set the course of sensory neuroreductionism in the decades to come.

Other harbingers of what was to come were published by Kuffler (1953) who discovered the center–surround organization of the cat's retina. Here the argument was made that the invertebrate results observed by Hartline and his colleagues represented a simple example of what could also occur in the more complex vertebrate nervous system.

The real breakthrough and full enlightenment that energy alone did not determine the nature of sensory neurons response came in 1959 when two exceedingly important papers were published nearly simultaneously. Although each group of researchers worked on different animals, used different techniques of stimulation and recording, and published in very different journals, the conclusion to which each group independently came shook modern neurophysiology and ultimately theories of the mind to their conceptual roots.

That seminal idea was that single neurons of the visual system were not sensitive to the raw energy of the "bolts and crashes," but to behaviorally "meaningful" spatiotemporal patterns of light energy falling on the receptors of the eye. A dim stimulus representing a moving fly or mouse meant more than a very bright stationary light!

"What the Frog's Eye Tells the Frog's Brain"[16]

In 1959, Lettvin, Maturana, McCulloch, and Pitts published an exceedingly important article that powerfully influenced research for the next decade. The major impact of this article (and that of Hubel and Wiesel considered in the next section) lay in its suggestion that since the stimuli, with which the organism usually dealt, are not simple impulsive events, there was no reason to assume that the neural organization had evolved to deal only with energetic "bolts and crashes" either. That is, it was not the raw energy distribution alone that determined how much information was conducted from the retina to the brain; rather, the spatiotemporal pattern of the stimulus was also critical. This central assumption implied, that the nervous system, in Barlow's prescient terms, acted as an information processor more than a simple energy detector and measurer.

Lettvin and his colleagues, two of whom (McCulloch & Pitts, 1943) had been participants in the seminal earlier MIT work on the processing of information by neural networks, took a very unorthodox approach to the problem. Their research utilized the responses recorded from single cells of the optic nerve and of the superior colliculus of the frog. Most insight-

[16]The following two sections on the work of Lettvin, Maturana, McCulloch, and Pitts (1959) and Hubel and Wiesel (1959) have been abstracted, adapted, and updated from my much more extensive discussion of their work in Uttal (1973).

fully, they entitled their article "What the Frog's Eye Tells the Frog's Brain," a whimsically anthropomorphic title that emphasized the idea of complex processing in the peripheral nervous system, rather than merely passive reproduction and transmission of a mosaic signal conveying the distribution of stimulus energy. Their work stimulated an enormous amount of follow-up research, in which the temporal and spatial properties of the stimulus came to be considered as important, if not more important, than its intensity, extent, or even its onset and offset times. There is no question of the fundamental importance of this new idea, and it is instructive to quote specifically the sort of thinking that led Lettvin, Maturana, McCulloch, and Pitts (1959) to this most significant conceptual breakthrough:

> The assumption has been that the eye mainly senses light, whose local distribution is transmitted to the brain in a kind of copy by a mosaic of impulses. Suppose we held otherwise, that the nervous apparatus in the eye is itself devoted to detecting certain patterns of light and their changes, corresponding to particular relations in the visible world. If this should be the case, the laws found by using small spots of light on the retina may be true and yet, in a sense, be misleading. (p. 1992)

Moving Stimulus Detectors in the Cat's Brain

About the same time that work was going on in Lettvin's laboratory at MIT, down the street at the Harvard Medical School a pair of researchers were making equally important and influential discoveries concerning the organization and specific sensitivities of visual cells in the mammalian nervous system. Hubel and Wiesel had quickly moved to take advantage of the new tungsten electrode (see p. 161) that allowed very long and stable periods of observations from single cells in the central nervous system of a cat. Their published articles, which initiated a joint collaboration lasting for many years following the key 1959 report, established that mammalian neurons, as well as the frog's, displayed fine sensitivities to the spatiotemporal patterns of visual stimuli. They, too, were selective information processors and filters.

Hubel and Wiesel (1959), in this now classic article, observed specific sensitivity to spatiotemporal features of stimuli in neurons of the visual cortex of the cat. They reported large numbers of cortical neurons that were unaffected by the general level of retinal illumination, but that produced large amounts of spike activity when an elongated, but still relatively small, bar of light was moved across the retina. Not only was the movement of the spot necessary, but those neurons also seemed to have preferential directions of movements for maximal activation. When they mapped out the shape and polarity of the receptive fields of these neurons, Hubel and Wiesel (1959) discovered that antagonistic regions of excitation and inhibition were usually arranged in side-by-side patterns. Although not all mapped cells required movement to elicit responses, responses were greatly enhanced when the stimulus was moving in a particular direction rather than remaining still.

It should be emphasized that the response of many of these brain cells seemed to be dependent not only on movement and preferential direction, but also on the shape of the moving stimulus. Whereas bars of light were effective for some cells, dark bars or moving edges were found to be the best stimuli for other cells. Presumably, the effectiveness of these elongated stimuli is associated with the shape of the neuron's receptive field and the way in which its adjacent regions of inhibitory and excitatory interactions with other neurons were organized.

In likely their most important and influential contribution to theories of perception, Hubel and Wiesel proposed a hierarchical theory of sensory encoding. This idea was generated by their continuing series of discoveries of the increasing complexity of the response sensitivities of the visual neurons as one ascended the afferent pathway. They (Hubel & Wiesel, 1965) offered the following hierarchical classification of the cells they encountered as they probed to higher levels of the cat's visual brain.

- Simple Cells–The sensitivity of which resulted from interactions of the inhibitory and excitatory regions of receptive fields.
- Complex Cells–The sensitivity of which resulted from integration of the outputs of several simple cells.
- Lower Order Hypercomplex Cells–The sensitivity of which resulted from the integration of several inhibitory and excitatory complex cells.
- Upper Order Hypercomplex Cells–The sensitivity of which resulted from the integration of several lower order hypercomplex complex cells.

The impact of this ascending system of ever more selective neurons, above and beyond the magnificent empirical discoveries themselves, was to introduce the concept of a convergent hierarchy in which the responses of neurons lower down the afferent chain converged on those higher in the chain. This concept suggested the encoding of ever more complex and specific meanings by an ever-smaller number of neurons. Although Hubel and Wiesel never carried this idea to the extreme version in which very complex cognitions were encoded, as we shortly see, other cognitive neuroscientists did make that leap.

Thus, these two independent and exceedingly influential investigations by Lettvin, Maturana, McCulloch, and Pitts (1959) and by Hubel and Wiesel (1959) established what are the undeniable temporal and spatial sensitivities of neurons in different species and at different levels of the visual nervous system. They initiated an era in which neurophysiologists began to consider a number of important facts. First, even peripheral neurons are capable of responding differentially to complex stimulus patterns in a manner transcending simple energy registration, encoding, and transmission. Second, complex stimulus patterns may produce responses that are not simply predictable from the mosaic of energy distribution on the receptor lattice. Third, the types of responses that are observed neurophysiologically in the visual system, at least, are associated in a meaningful way with the environmental tasks faced by the animal. Neither frogs nor mammals live in a world of static spots of light or of diffuse fields. They live in a world of flies and dragonflies and mice and other small animals. These stimuli are better modeled by moving spots or edges (in other words, by complex spatiotemporal patterns) than by briefly exposed stationary forms that had been traditionally used in earlier research. The surprising result that emerged from subsequent contributions was that this sort of specific pattern detection mechanism appeared to be a general property of all sensory modalities in all species.

Other Early Supporting Research[17]

It is impossible to review here the huge amount of research that contributed to the realization that stimulus energy alone was insufficient to determine the response of a neuron. I can only apologize to the many other important contributors that must remain unacknowledged in the following list. Nevertheless, there are a few mileposts that are especially notable.

1. Galambos and Davis' (1943) demonstration that single auditory nerve fibers displayed a selective sensitivity to the intensity–frequency pattern of an acoustic stimulus.
2. DeValois, Smith, Kitai, and Karoly's (1958) discovery of opponent cells in the lateral geniculate body in the visual pathway.
3. Mountcastle and Powell's (1959) demonstration of the antagonistic and reciprocal center–surround arrangement of somatosensory cortical cells in the monkey.
4. Barlow, Hill, and Levick's (1964) study of directional sensitivity in the ganglion cells of the rabbit retina.

---

[17]It is obvious that this list of "important" discoveries comes, in large part, from studies of vision and visual perception, a subfield of cognition. There are several reasons for this selectivity: First, sensory topics provide a very high level of control because they are so well anchored to physical stimulus dimensions. Second, the largest portion of cognitive neuroscience empirical studies, until recently, has been in this field. Third, this is my field of research specialization and there, I am most familiar with these studies. It must not be overlooked, however, that research in audition, somatosensation, and the other senses was also carried on during this seminal period in which novel ideas were being germinated.

5. The demonstration by two independent groups of the trichromatic nature of the retinal cones. Brown and Wald (1964) and Marks, Dobelle, and MacNichol (1964) accomplished this task by direct photometric readings of the light absorbed by a cone.
6. Rodieck and Stone's (1965) discovery that the position of the stimulus and the shape of the receptive field interacted to produce particular kinds of responses (On, Off, On–Off, No response).
7. Gross, Rocha-Miranda, and Bender's (1972) discovery of neurons in the monkey's inferotemporal cortex that were specifically sensitive to pictures of the animal's hand and the subsequent discovery of face specific cortical neurons by Bruce, Desimone, and Gross (1981).[18]

The Subsequent Logical Misstep

Research supporting the idea that the neurons in the sensory pathways were selectively sensitive to the spatiotemporal pattern of the stimulus, even more so than its intensity, was repeatedly replicated and validated. Such findings must be counted among the most important developments in neuroscience; it is likely that the physiological processes identified by these pioneering cognitive neuroscientists are as they indicated.

An even larger body of relevant research, however, was going on in the closely related field of psychophysics. For more than a century, studies of the relationships between physical stimuli and cognitive phenomena had also been growing with ever increasing vigor. The literature, in this case, is also too extensive to be reviewed here. One has only to look at the many handbooks and texts of experimental psychology published just in the 20th century to appreciate the huge number of these contributions. In the same sense that the corpus of neurophysiological findings is now acknowledged to be solid and irrefutable, so, too, are the general findings from these psychophysical studies.[19]

However, there was another implicit step in the development of single cell theories of cognitive processes during which these two fields of knowledge were brought together that largely went unnoticed. A conceptual, but cryptic, leap surreptitiously crept into thinking about the relationship of

[18]As we shall see, this conclusion has been challenged by subsequent research, but it was an influential and significant step in influencing thinking about the role of single neurons in coding complex concepts.

[19]Of course, the theoretical interpretation of all of this data, both psychophysical and neurophysiological, is subject to enormous controversy. Debates between behaviorists and mentalists, between reductionists and nonreductionists, between empiricists and rationalists, and between elementalists and holists (among others) rage on. None of these great controversies, however, reduce the quality or validity of the vast amount of factual knowledge that cognitive neuroscience has gathered.

the neuronal to the psychophysical data. This leap was necessary to set the stage for the full-blown theories of single neuron representation of cognitive processes that were to follow. Based on a number of experimental findings and analogies, *it was subsequently assumed that the correlations between the stimulus and the neuronal responses could be assumed a priori to be tantamount or equivalent to associations drawn between neuronal responses and perceptual experiences.*[20]

In other words, an implicit, but unspoken, hypothesis evolved that argued that any correlated single neuron response *was* the encoded psychoneural equivalent of the co-varying perceptual experience! The neural response and the mental experience were not only correlated—an empirical observation—but the former was assumed to be the equivalent of the latter! This was the essential assumption underlying all single neuron theories of cognition that once again ignored the basic admonishment that "correlation does not establish causation" (Yule, 1926).

As seductive as this erroneous logical conclusion may have been and continues to be, it must be emphasized and reemphasized that such an intimate association of the activity of the individual neuron and the perceptual experience is a hypothesis based on several assumptions and logical leaps, some of which, in retrospect, seem incorrect. This conclusion was heavily influenced by the microelectrode zeitgeist, by the compelling, but misleading, pressure of functional isomorphism, and the seeming ubiquity of stimulus selectivity on the part of neurons. However, the assumption of a tight linkage between individual neuronal responses and global experience ignores other significant parts of the scientific milieu. Two of these logical counter arguments are now reviewed.

First, as noted earlier, there is the major problem that a microelectrode is sampling only a miniscule portion (usually a single neuron) of the many millions or billions that must be involved in representing an experience. Since much more than the activity of this single neuron is going on in the brain during even the simplest cognitive process, the huge variety of neural responses probably made it likely that one would always find some correlated responses. Indeed, this statement can be further strengthened by noting that so much is going unobserved in the brain on that almost anything, however implausible or improbable, can be found should the experimenter seek it.

Second, it should be obvious to my readers that almost all these studies were carried out for the sensory systems. There was, however, an uncritical tendency to extrapolate from these explorations of the nature of these pe-

---

[20]This was an assumption almost all of us made. My book *The Psychobiology of Sensory Coding* (Uttal, 1973) is filled with comparisons of the results of neurophysiological experiments and human psychophysical studies. Mea Culpa!

ripheral transmission codes to quite a different level of activity—the psychoneural equivalents of perceptual experiences.[21]

A number of experiments helped make this (il)logical leap from the similarities between the stimulus and the peripheral neural response (as well as the similarities between the stimulus and the experienced perceptual phenomena) to the association of the single neuronal response and experience all too easy and seductive. A host of correlative studies in which neurophysiology and psychophysical findings were compared were quickly carried out following the discoveries of the specific sensitivities of neurons to the same stimulus properties known to affect human perception. Unfortunately, many of these early neurophysiological experiments were not carried out simultaneously with the associated psychophysical studies. Rather, in large part (with only a few exceptions), psychophysical results were compared with preexisting neuronal data or vice versa. Psychologists compared the human psychophysical data they observed with neuronal responses collected by neurophysiologists, usually from other species. Physiologists compared their laboratory findings with published records of psychophysical experiments. Sometimes the comparison was carried out by a third cognitive neuroscientist unbeknownst to the psychophysicist or neurophysiologist who actually collected the two sets of original data.

A few of the most interesting of these comparative or correlative experiments are tabulated in the following list.

1. Jung and Spillmann (1970) recorded from the cat's cortex and found cells that were correlated with the human visual experience of the Hermann grid.
2. Blake and Bellhorn's (1975) study of visual acuity in the cat was compared with that of the human (Berkley, Kitterlee, & Watkins, 1975).
3. The work of Ratliff and Hartline (1959) on lateral inhibitory interaction in the horseshoe crab (Limulus) has been compared to any number of studies of the perceptual phenomenon known as the Mach Band. Among to the first to make this comparison, other than members of Hartline's group themselves, were Fiorentini and Radici (1957). Ratliff (1965) and Fiorentini (1972) provide full histories of this type of comparison.

---

[21]I have previously pointed out that there is no definitive way to show that even the primary receiving areas of the brain (e.g., V1) may not be the locus of the neural activity that was presumed to be the psychoneural equivalent of a cognitive process. That is, neural activity in the primary cerebral occipital receiving area may better be considered a part of the transmission pathway than a part of the representational system where this activity becomes, for example, the phenomena of visual perception. Others (e.g., Crick & Koch, 1995) have recently supported this suggestion. Crick and Koch put the proposition in a very straightforward manner when they proposed, "the activity in V1 does not directly enter awareness" (p. 122). However, we all agree that this assignment of a transmission role to a region of the cortex must be considered to be, at best, a speculative hypothesis that at present can be suggested but not confirmed.

4. Hurvich and Jameson's (1957) psychophysical data were quickly compared to DeValois et al.'s (1958) findings concerning the opponent nature of the response of the monkey's lateral geniculate body.

5. Metacontrast, a curious paradoxical phenomenon in which a following stimulus affects the perception of an earlier one has also been linked to neuronal responses. Werner (1935) first described the phenomenon that was later to be compared with neurophysiological data by Schiller (1968) among many others.

This list just begins to sample a few examples from the history of a correlative science in which superficially similar physiological and psychophysical experiments were compared. The recent literature is crammed with other more modern examples. All of these studies, either explicitly or implicitly, were guided by the assumption that the response of a single neuron was the psychoneural equivalent of mind simply because it seemed to follow the same time course as the psychophysical phenomenon. In so doing, they represented a meaningful and influential part of the development of theories that attributed the foundation of cognitive functions to a single or a few neurons. It is this group of theories to which we now turn our attention.

5.2 THE HISTORY OF SINGLE NEURON THEORIES OF THE MIND

The idea that activity in a single neuron could represent a complex cognitive process first emerged around the beginning of the 20th century. It was, as already noted, motivated in part by the Neuron Doctrine (the concept that the nervous system was made up of discrete neurons and was not a neural syncytium) and the neuron doctrine (the idea that the mind could ultimately be explained by the activity of neurons). The strength of the idea was enhanced by the development of techniques that appeared to show correspondences between the activity of single neurons and perceptual phenomena, the lack of any methods to deal with the complex interactions of a realistically large array of those same neurons, and a conceptual confusion of transmission codes with representational equivalences.

In short, the single cell theory of mental activity was another approach to modeling the mind that was "not inconsistent" with a good portion of the knowledge that was available during these exciting times. However, at best, what had been shown was concomitancy; certainly not the kind of causal relationship that single neuron theories proposed. Consistency, although suggestive, can also be terribly misleading.

To understand more completely the assumptions and concepts of single neuron theories, it is necessary to explore their historical evolution and the key players who formulated specific, as opposed to vaguely formulated, versions of them.

5.2.1 The Origins of the Single Neuron Theory

It is not clear from the historical record where the term *pontifical* neuron was first used or when the idea was first enunciated. Kinsbourne (2003) and Gross (2002) alluded to the origin of the term by William James. Gross, in particular, directs our attention to the following comment by James (1890) in which he supports the idea of single "pontifical cell," strongly influenced by inputs from many other cells, yet to which "consciousness" is uniquely attached:

> Every brain-cell has its own individual consciousness, which no other cell knows anything about, all individual consciousnesses being "ejective" to each other. There is, however, among the cells one central or pontifical one to which *our* consciousness is attached. But the events of all the other cells physically influence this arch-cell; and through producing their joint effects on it, these other cells may be said to "combine." (p. 179)[22]

James went further on this same page to suggest some concepts that still attract a great deal of attention. In his next sentence he refers to "fusion or integration" anticipating the currently popular idea of binding. Similarly, he then mentions "a sequence of results" that has within it the germ of the idea of a convergent hierarchy or of Hebb's "phase sequence," also influential modern concepts.

Later, Barlow (1972) referred to Sherrington (1940) who was (perhaps) the next to consider the possibility that the many neural signals from the senses merged onto "one ultimate pontifical neuron" (p. 390). Sherrington, however, rejected the pontifical neuron idea and expressed his enthusiasm for the "enchanted loom" (p. 78) idea in which the brain operated as a "million-fold democracy" (as quoted in Barlow, 1972, p. 390)—a poetic metaphor the neural network theories so popular currently. From then, the term seems to have lain dormant until the middle of the 20th century where it became synonymous with the single neuron theory of mental representation.

---

[22]The idea that there is a single neuron to "which *our* consciousness is attached" is certainly the most extreme possible version of this type of theory. Given that the idea of a syncytium was just in the process of being refuted, one can only imagine what James meant by this expression. Since there is nothing in his book that suggests awareness of the microscopic arrangement of the brain, it is possible that he was referring to some more macroscopic chunk of the brain, the gross anatomical structure of which he does discuss in detail.

5.2.2 Konorski's Gnostic Units

Konorski (1967) proposed what appears to be the first modern single neuron theory of mind. Like all his predecessors and successors, he was searching for an answer to the question of how the brain generates mental activity. His argument was largely based on the concept that we, as whole humans, are not sensitive to the individual features and elements of the stimulus object even though the individual neurons of our sensory systems do have specific trigger features. In this regard, he noted that he was trying to resolve some of the issues that were generated by observations based on Gestalt theory in the previous half of the 20th century. In particular, Konorski was deeply concerned about those psychophysical findings that showed a holistic unity of experience rather than any sensitivity or awareness of the parts of a stimulus or of the experience. Here, we can also see another harbinger of the erroneously formulated "binding problem" that has so mystified and motivated cognitive neuroscientists for decades.

In his 1967 book, Konorski leaned heavily on the Hubel and Wiesel experiments of the 1960s, particularly with regard to their proposal that there was a continued hierarchical convergence of the feature encoding signals onto certain high level neurons, the activity of which corresponded to the combined effect of all of the transmitted features. In Konorski's (1967) own words:

> [W]e can assume that perceptions experienced in humans' and animals' lives are represented not by the *assemblies* [proposed by Hebb, 1957] of units but by single units in the highest levels of the particular analyzers. We shall call these levels *gnostic* areas and the units responsible for particular perceptions, *gnostic* units. (p. 75)

Konorski then made a very important distinction between the *transit* and *gnostic* portions of the nervous system corresponding to the transmission and representation distinction I previously mentioned. It is only in the gnostic areas that neural activity becomes mental activity, or, as he puts it, this is where the gnostic units:

> represent the biologically meaningful stimulus patterns which are used in associative processes and behavior of the organisms. (p. 76)

Activity in the transit areas, on the other hand, according to Konorski, loses any significance in the "associative processes" once they have communicated the sensory information to the gnostic areas. Nor can the gnostic unit decompose anything about the transit information; all it "knows" is the final effect.

This inability to decompose a final effect is an important idea. It once again highlights the enormous difficulties encountered when one tries to decompose the function of a huge assemblage of units. There is, as the chaos and combinatorial people tell us, no way to go back from the final state of a complex system to its initial conditions or, to put it in the vernacular, to unscramble an omelet.

Konorski (1967), whose reputation suffers in modern day cognitive neuroscience because of what is believed to be his extreme position in invoking "gnostic" units, nevertheless did appreciate that this was, at best, only an interesting hypothesis. For example, he stated, quite frankly, that:

> There is so far no direct electrophysiological evidence that perceptions are really represented by the units of gnostic areas. (p. 76)

He was obviously aware of the near absurdity of any literal idea that a single neuron might be the sole and immutable repository of some idea or concept when he said:

> [E]ach unitary perception may be represented in a given gnostic field not by a single gnostic unit but by a number of them, because, if in a state of arousal of that field a new stimulus pattern is presented, all unengaged units which potentially include its elements are capable of becoming the actual gnostic units representing that pattern. (p. 90)

In the absence of direct data, supporting the necessity and adequacy of a single unit's ability to represent a complex idea, the main arguments raised by Konorski to support his argument were based on the Gestalt concept of "unitary nature of perception." In other words, he used the reported molar responses of subjects introspectively describing their experiences as a main source of arguments for the representation of high-level concepts by individual units. This was a very long logical leap, indeed.

Jerzy Konorski (1903–1973), like most of the other single neuron theorists, ultimately fell back on some kind of network theory. His imaginative theory of gnostic units embedded in particular gnostic areas of the brain was also clearly influenced by ideas of localization that had been percolating through cognitive neuroscience for many decades. His development of the hierarchical idea (first introduced by Hubel and Wiesel's observations) was among the first to appreciate the implications, however correct or incorrect they may have been, of that conjecture. Furthermore, many of his ideas anticipated aspects of "network" theories that were yet to come.

Clearly the brilliance and insight of Konorski deserved far more attention than he has received in recent years outside of his native Poland. There, he is still (as of 2003) honored in the annual proceedings of the Polish Neuroscience Society.[23]

5.2.3 Barlow's Misuse of the "Neuron Doctrine"

Without question, the single most influential paper in the history of the "single neuron" theory of cognition was the one published by Horace Barlow in 1972. His contribution was not only the presentation of a new version of single neuron theory, but also the first modern statement of what such a theory actually meant and what were its implications.

Before I begin my discussion of Barlow, it is important to note that he has undergone an evolution of his thoughts over the years. The first article (Barlow, 1972) was a very strong statement of a highly specific theory of single neuron representation. In it, however, there are some harbingers of doubt; a few questions raised here and there; an intelligent and scholarly expression of "criticisms and alternatives of his point of view" (p. 388); and a willingness to appreciate that his theory is, at best, "incomplete" (p. 390). Indeed, in Barlow (1995)—also a very influential publication in this field—he approached the problem as if it were much more controversial than the 1972 paper suggested. Furthermore, by the time Barlow (2001) was published, he was speaking about statistics and redundancy in a much different way than originally. His new view can be interpreted as an even further deviation (than the 1995 article) from the original single neuron theory he enunciated in 1972. It differs in fundamental concepts very little from some versions of network theory

However, to trace this intellectual Odyssey, it is necessary to start back in Barlow's scientific past. What may have been his first speculation about single cell theory is to be found in Barlow (1961). This article was published in a one of the first books (Rosenblith, 1961) that sought to unite new ideas in information theory with classic ones concerning sensory processes. The main thrust of Barlow's article was aimed at three key issues: (a) selective sensitivity on the part of sensory signals to particular aspects of the stimulus; (b) the control of sensory input by other parts of the nervous system at relay points—synaptic interfaces; and (c) reduction of sensory signal redundancy by coding mechanisms. This third hypothesis led him to make the following statements:

---

[23]Just how much respect is still shown to Konorski in current meetings of the Polish Neuroscience Society can be observed in their 2003 program at: http://www.ptbun.org.pl/congress2003/pns2003_prog.htm

> It is amusing to speculate on the possibility that the whole of the complex sensory input we experience is represented, at the highest level, by activity in a very few, and perhaps only a single neural unit at any one instant. (Barlow, 1961, p. 232)

And shortly, thereafter:

> The present speculation is that the sensory image that is thus disseminated consists of a very few impulses and perhaps only a solitary one, in a very large array of nerve fibers. But whether this particular speculation is right or not, it offends one's intuition, and one's experience of the efficiency and economy of naturally evolved mechanisms, to suppose that sensory messages are widely disseminated through the nervous system before they have been organized in a fairly non-redundant form. (p. 233)

Although Barlow proceeded in his summary to state that these speculations are "for entertainment only" (p. 233), this was the germ of what was to become one of the most significant and popular cognitive neuroscientific theories of modern times. It remained for the much more influential article that followed a decade later (Barlow, 1972) for his "entertaining speculation" to be formulated in an explicit manner and taken very seriously, indeed. The 1972 article was another significant milestone in the development of not only his specific thoughts, but of the single neuron theory in general. However, as I have already mentioned and will expand upon later, it was not the theoretical end point either for Barlow or for this particular theoretical orientation.

Barlow (1972) is an extremely interesting article quite unlike so many of the bare bones empirical efforts usually published in the neurosciences. In it, he went far beyond the empirical data and the usual hand-waving vagueness of previous theorizing to formulate specific hypotheses and axioms concerning his theoretical point of view. Barlow characterized his new formulation of a single neuron theory in the following terms:

> The central proposition is that our perceptions are caused by the activity of a rather small number of neurons selected from a very large population of predominantly silent cells. (p. 371)[24]

Of course, there is nothing new here, others such as James, Sherrington, and Konorski had previously raised this possibility in the form of hypothetical pontifical or gnostic neurons. What Barlow (1972) did next, however,

---

[24]Although Barlow used the word "perceptions" in this context mainly because his work was in this field and the data base was primarily to be found in the visual literature, he quickly went on to generalize his ideas to include "human thought processes" on this same page.

was quite novel. He proposed five specific axioms, statements, or "dogma" that he hoped would make the argument specific enough to be empirically "clear and testable" (p. 380). It is useful for the remainder of this discussion to quote them in their entirety.

First dogma

A description of that activity of a single nerve cell which is transmitted to and influences other nerve cells, and of a nerve cell's response to such influences from other cells, is a complete enough description for functional understanding of the nervous system. There is nothing else "looking at" or controlling this activity, which must therefore provide a basis for understanding how the brain controls behaviour.

Second dogma

At progressively higher levels in sensory pathways information about the physical stimulus is carried by progressively fewer active neurons. The sensory system is organized to achieve as complete a representation as possible with the minimum number of active neurons.

Third dogma

Trigger features of neurons are matched to the redundant features of sensory stimulation in order to achieve greater completeness and economy of representation. This selective responsiveness is determined by the sensory stimulation to which neurons have been exposed, as well as by genetic factors operating during development.

Fourth dogma

Just as physical stimuli directly cause receptors to initiate neural activity, so the active high-level neurons directly and simply cause the elements of our perception.

Fifth dogma

The frequency of neural impulses codes subjective certainty: a high impulse frequency in a given neuron corresponds to a high degree of confidence that the cause of the percept is present in the external world. (Barlow, 1972, pp. 380–381)

Here in a concise and specific form is the essence of Barlow's 1972 theory of representation of "human thought processes" by the single neuron. The rest of the paper is filled with a review of the preceding scientific literature, explaining how he felt that literature supported his theoretical argument, and elucidating the implications of these bare bone dogmatic statements.

Later in this seminal paper, Barlow went on to express some caveats that moderated the role of single cells, per se, and suggested that *unity* might better be replaced by *small multiplicity*. He distinguished between his concept of the "cardinal cell" and Sherrington's rejection of the idea of "pontifical cell":

> First notice that the current proposal does not say that each distinct perception corresponds to a different cell being active. . . . It says that there is a simple correspondence between the elements of perception and unit activity. Thus the whole of subjective experience at any one time must correspond to a specific combination of active cells, and the "'pontifical cell" should be replaced by the by a number of "cardinal cells." Among the many cardinals only a few speak at once; . . . (p. 390)

Thus, even in 1972 Barlow was clearly not expressing an extreme single neuron theory but, as he later noted, the cardinals "must include a substantial fraction of the 10^{10} cells of the human brain" (p. 390). This accommodation to the unavoidable physiological facts of wide spread activity throughout the brain when even the simplest kind of stimulus is sensed is especially evident in the next significant milestone publication (Barlow, 1995). It was here that he described the further development of his version of single neuron theory.

From one point of view, it can be argued that the data used to support Barlow's theory were more appropriately aimed at the observed sensitivities of single neurons than at how "thought processes" are represented in the nervous system. The sensitivities could be evaluated empirically and have been over the years to show that neurons are rather more broadly than narrowly tuned. The ability of these neurons to represent or by themselves to signal the meaning of these responses, however, cannot be proven in the laboratory because of the unknown contribution of the host of other responding neurons.

By 1995 Barlow was clearly aware of the difficulties that the single neuron theory of human thought processes must inevitably face. In Barlow (1995), the tone of his writing changed in a way that might be described as less dogmatic and more eclectic. This new hesitation can be best expressed by recapitulating his list of "unresolved questions about neurons in perception" that, from some point of view seem to replace the dogma of Barlow (1972).

1. What is the best measure of the short-term average activity of a single neuron?

2. Why is the dynamic range of a single neuron so small compared with that obtained from psychophysical just-noticeable difference experiments?
3. Can measures of oscillation, synchronization, or correlation among neurons improve the relation between psychophysical and neural performance?
4. When comparing single-unit and behavioral thresholds, how does one take into account the problem of false-positive responses resulting from the very large number of neurons in the brain?
5. How sparse is the distributed representation in the brain?
6. Is the relation between unit activity and input pattern tight enough to support population or ensemble coding?
7. Can a single neuron mediate a perceptual discrimination? (Barlow, 1995, p. 425)

Unfortunately, the expression of these seeds of doubt reflect a continuing reluctance on Barlow's part to accept that some of these questions have already been answered, and had been, decades before 1995. For example, Barlow still seems to accept the concept of sparse coding—the idea that "progressively fewer active neurons" are activated at "progressively higher levels." Closely related to this was his assumption that neurons are "... much more pattern selective than was formerly believed ..." (Barlow 1995, p. 430).

However, both sparse coding and finely tuned neurons are now known to be false assumptions. It has been acknowledged for many years that many central neurons are, in general, broadly tuned.[25] Furthermore, some of the assumptions on which the questions were based were incorrect; for example, the proposition that false positives are due to the "very large numbers of neurons in the brain." False positives, as signal detection theory tells us, are due to the ambiguity and overlap of the noise and signal plus noise distributions and the arbitrariness of criterion levels, not large numbers per se.

In the 1995 article Barlow also asserted that the incoming information converged on an ever-smaller number of cardinal neurons was, in fact, the opposite of what we now know to be the situation.

Furthermore, Barlow remains deeply bedeviled with a nonissue—the confusion of the Neuron Doctrine with his single neuron theory of "human thought processes" (see p. 154). Neuron Doctrine considerations offer lit-

[25]Of course, words like *broad* and *narrow* are relative and, thus, subject to interpretation. Even so, neurons are never sharply enough tuned to individually correspond to psychophysical data. Therefore, the central tendency (or some other statistical estimate) of many neurons is required for precise discrimination. See page 125 where I expand on this point.

tle support for single neuron theory. The anatomical discreteness of neurons is irrelevant to the concept that single neurons represent "thought processes."

Barlow (1995) clearly reflected the inconsistencies and difficulties involved in adhering to the single neuron theory of the mind when he drew his conclusions. Two remarks, in particular, seem to represent principles antithetical to his core argument. First he champions distribution and interactive processes:

> Advocates of grandmother cells, cardinal cells, ensemble encoding, and dense distributed representations all agree that the elements of perception are used in combination, as are words in a language: Perception certainly uses a distributed, not a mutually exclusive, representation. (p. 430)

Nevertheless, only a few sentences later he retreats to the original extreme single neuron hypothesis:

> A psychophysical linking hypothesis is proposed which states that a single neuron can provide a sufficient basis for a perceptual discrimination. This appears to be necessarily true if neurons are the only means available to the brain for making a decision based on evidence from other neurons. (p. 431)

Finally, in Barlow (2001) another one of the foundation assumptions of single neuron theory—the need to reduce redundancy by progressive reduction of activated neurons—is rejected by Barlow himself.

> Therefore, I now think that the principle is redundancy *exploitation,* rather than *reduction*, since performance can be improved by taking account of sensory redundancy in other ways than by coding the information onto channels of reduced capacity. (p. 604)

In this manner, the basic conceptual foundations of the original single neuron theory were cast into deeper doubt by one of its main proponents.

To sum up this all too brief discussion of one of the most important contributors in the history of neuroreductionist theory, I would like to take advantage of an author's prerogative to quote himself. In a conference held in 1979 dedicated mainly to considering how neuroscience could account for pattern and form perception, I made some critical points about single neuron and other neuroreductionist theories. The first three of my criticisms were specifically in response to Barlow's (1972) early dogma, although the rest ranged over some of the other theory types discussed in this book. The point here is that many of the problems with single neuron theories were already appreciated at that time, at least by a few of us. The following extended excerpt (Uttal, 1982) is from the proceedings of that meeting. They are formulated as responses to Barlow's first, second, and fifth dogmas, respectively. As they are particular to Barlow's dogma, I present them here in advance of other critiques of single neuron theory presented later in this chapter.[26]

Questionable Dogma Number 1

The action of single cells encodes or represents complex perceptual behavior. This very general dogma, most explicitly expressed by Barlow, (1972), is the keystone of a substantial portion of contemporary neuroreductionist theory. In spite of the fact that neurons responding to specific trigger features of the stimulus are ubiquitous in the nervous system, there are many logical and empirical counterarguments that argue against the validity of such a dogma. . . . The identification of individual neuronal feature sensitivity with perceptual experience is simply not justified on logical grounds. . . . There are several empirical arguments that can be made against the single cell hypothesis. Even Horace Barlow, the arch proponent of the neuron dogma, sees some counterindications to the single cell hypothesis. His (Barlow, 1978) inability to find any differential sensitivity to form in a texture discrimination task, even he quite flexibly acknowledged, is a possible argument against a single cell theory of form perception.

Similarly, Timney and MacDonald (1978) raised an important question concerning feature detectors in the visual nervous system. They sought to determine whether curvature detectors per se, as opposed to multiple line detectors sensitive to the tangents of curves, were responsible for the adaptive desensitization to curved gratings by prolonged exposure to other curved gratings. They concluded that their experiments did not distinguish between the two hypotheses and also alluded to the fact that the overall structure of the pattern, and thus, "higher" levels of processing, must be involved. Pomerantz, (1978) also raises another difficulty for a simplistic single cell feature detection theory in his experimental findings that show that stimuli varying in slope alone are difficult to discriminate. . . . The most complete body of empirical evidence counter indicating this dogma, however, is the large amount of classic evidence dealing with the effect of the configuration or global pattern of a stimulus on many different phenomena. Features, unless redefined to a point of generality at which they are no longer local "properties" but rather, global aspects of the stimulus, are woefully inadequate in explaining such phenomena.

Questionable Dogma Number 2

The nervous system operates by greater and greater degrees of feature extraction and abstraction and the mapping of concepts of ever-greater complexity onto the responses of an ever-decreasing number of neurons. This proposition, Barlow's (1972) second dogma, unlike the first, seems clearly to be incorrect on a strictly

---

[26]I have deleted some material from these excerpts that is totally redundant with previous discussions in this chapter.

> empirical basis. The mass of neurophysiological evidence indicates that activity initially elicited in even a single peripheral receptor neuron is magnified and distributed by neural divergence in time and space in such a way that an unaccountably large number of neurons are activated in the brain by even the most localized peripheral stimulus. Rather than an increasing specificity and contraction to a small number of neurons, just the opposite seems to be happening; responses to stimuli, mediated by both the ascending reticular formation and the classic sensory pathways are generated in widely distributed regions of the brain. . . . The call for some kind of "neural economy" made by Barlow is a spurious one in a system that has many neurons (and, perhaps more important, synapses) to spare and in which individual neurons can be involved in so many different circuits simultaneously.
>
> **Questionable Dogma Number 5**
>
> *High frequency in neural responses rate encodes high stimulus certainty.* This proposition, Barlow's (1972) fifth dogma, stating that high frequency nerve action potentials (or large ones etc.) encode higher certainty of a stimulus being present, can also be criticized on empirical grounds. The weight of evidence now suggests that strong stimuli may be encoded in several parts of the nervous system either as increases or decreases from the resting level of spike action potential firing rate, as differential rates of firing in adjacent loci, or by the absolute magnitude of the response. The opponent color mechanism in the visual system is one obvious example of this differential encoding as is the differential responsivity of binocularly sensitive neurons in the visual cortex. Such opponent or differential mechanisms probably occur in many other portions of the nervous system. The inherent isomorphism of positive correlations between neural and mental responses is simply not justified by current neurophysiological knowledge. A strong negative correlation may be just as "significant" as a strong positive one and ample evidence suggests that the nervous system is capable of encoding signals in just this way. (Excerpted from Uttal, 1982, pp. 194–197)

It appears that Barlow (e.g., Barlow, 2001) is also beginning to accept many of these criticisms of the single neuron theory that he supported so eloquently and so vigorously three decades ago. His ideas have clearly gone through an evolution from "amusing speculation" to dominant perspective to what seems much more congruent with contemporary ideas. This does not diminish either his work or the general point that we still do not understand how the brain makes our perceptions and our thoughts. Indeed, it seems he has joined some of us in the skeptical feeling that the quest for neuroreductionist solutions may be, at the very least and in some cases, questionable when he said:

> The third problem [concerning the specific issue of motion perception] is even more basic: we do not understand the neural basis for subjective experi-

ences of moving objects, so it is risky to try to relate the experience to mechanism. (Barlow, 2001, p. 606)

Thus, is progress made.

5.2.4 Feature Detector Theory

As more and more problems developed with the raw form of the single neuron theory other approaches were tried. Among the most prominent of these was the feature detector approach in which the entire "grandmother" was not encoded but only certain features and parts. Thus, for example, the features or components of a square would presumably be stored in the relative amount of activity of a set of neurons with sensitivities similar to those Hubel and Wiesel had observed in the cerebral cortex of the cat. This approach is conceptually identical to the single neuron theory; it just uses a larger set of less specific details rather than the entire object to represent that object. As usually formulated, the feature detectors typically converge on some highly specialized decision cells, thus closely the loop between features and single cell psychoneural equivalents.

The feature detection type of model was extremely popular from the 1960s on. It became the basis of many different models, some of which invoked individual neurons and others of which invoked examples of neural network theoretical types. Some of these are discussed in the next chapter. Many hypothetical "feature detectors" are, at best, speculative extrapolations from psychophysical data with absolutely no neurophysiological supportive evidence. Others are convenient transfers of ideas from computer algorithms that have been developed to simulate some human cognitive process. In the latter case, there is no reason to believe (other than a remote kind of plausibility) that similar processes are carried out in the human brain. A more complete discussion of feature detectors can be found in Uttal (2002).

The hierarchical arrangement of a system of feature detecting neurons, remains, however, a compelling line of thinking in the development of theories of the visual system in particular. Riesenhuber and Poggio (1999), for example, have proposed such a theory to explain to the representation of different views of the same object in a set of neurons. In their model, they propose that the usual hierarchical hypothesis in which separate features are sequentially pooled until a set of high-level neurons is arrived at, each of which may represent a different view of the same object. Clearly this approach still exerts considerable influence these days on theories of the mind. In the next section, I consider further why any approach that reifies the activity of single neurons, either in the form of pontifical or quasi-pontifical cells that encode a complete object or a set of feature detecting cells that encode only components of it, is not likely to provide a satisfactory explanation of how the brain makes the mind.

5.3 COUNTERARGUMENTS

Single neuron theories still abound both explicitly and implicitly in cognitive neuroscience these days. Often these are embedded in the discussion of results from electrophysiological experiments or, conversely, psychophysicists invoke some cellular neurophysiological data to "explain" the cognitive phenomenon. The important general point that must be repeatedly made is that such associations represent conclusions drawn from uncontrolled experiments that do not justify the theoretical inference that the single cell is the representation of the cognitive process.

What microelectrode, single neuron studies do very well is to define the sensitivities of a particular neuron to certain conditions and stimuli. They also define the response capabilities of the neuron; however, they do not speak directly to the problem of how the activity in one or many neurons represents or encodes our mental activities. Mind may be the result of sparse (i.e., individual) neuronal activity or it may be the result of the activity of huge numbers of neurons working in collaboration or in the aggregate: The problem is that the studies of the individual neuron do not and cannot resolve this issue.

Microelectrode studies have, thus, been a powerful means of describing the activity of individual neurons. We have learned an enormous amount through the application of this method and neuroscience can be justifiably proud of these accomplishments. Nevertheless, The inherent difficulty of interpreting the meaning of the response of a microelectrode impaled single neuron that correlates with some cognitive process has not deterred many recent investigators from proposing what are explicitly or implicitly single neuron theories of perception.

The main problem is that comparison is just too easy! One has only to compare the results of the electrophysiological experiment with the observed behavior of a model organism, or even better, with the introspective report of a human observer. The next step is to assume that any observed correlations testify to the necessity and sufficiency of the encoding or representation of the "thought process" by the activity of the observed neuron. This fallacious logic tends to misidentify the latter as the former's psychoneural equivalent. Of course, not all cognitive neuroscientists are unaware of this potential for logical error, but a host of studies have been published in the last 50 years in which the assumption of a direct psychoneural correspondence between an individual or a few neurons and cognition is implicit. The effect was subtle, but influential, and still percolates along just under the surface of a major portion of cognitive neuroscience research.

As usual, the various sides in a contentious issue such as this tend to move toward each other as the years go by. Rather than supporting a raw form of single neuron theory, on the one hand, or a totally distributed network concept, on the other, the contenders have now converged on a modified and reduced form of the debate. The present controversy nowadays concerns the *relative* sparseness of the cells that might be encoding some concept or perception. Barlow, as we saw earlier, has framed his new position in terms of relatively sparse neurons with highly specific tuning sensitivities. Others have carried out studies that they believe suggests that individual neurons are broadly tuned and widely distributed across the brain. As I now discuss, recent data seems to have moved current thinking toward the broadly tuned and widely distributed side of the argument.

In this section, some of the historical criticisms of single neuron theory are presented and discussed. Collectively they make the case that the neuron theory of cognition in its classical forms (pontifical or cardinal) is theoretically bankrupt and cannot be extended to answer the great question of how the brain makes the mind.

There was little discussion in the literature about the single cell theory until Sherrington's (1940) invocation of the "enchanted loom" metaphor. After Barlow (1972), however, the issue became quite contentious. Some others who have argued against single neuron theories, either in their original or modified from (where the degree of sparseness has become the issue) include:

1. Colin Blakemore: The year after Barlow's 1972 paper saw the first explicit criticism of the single neuron idea. Blakemore's (1973) argument was the common sense one that it would require a huge leap from the general idea of convergent visual signals emphasized by Hubel and Wiesel (1965) in their pioneering studies to the specific idea proposed by Barlow and Konorski that every image and concept was represented by a single or very sparse number of cells. Although, neither of these scholars actually supported the "pontifical cell" argument in its most extreme form, Blakemore (1973) identified the conceptual difficulty as follows:

> But there is a logical problem in this argument. Surely animals cannot have individual detector cells for every conceivable object they can recognize? The great debate has become known as the question of the "grandmother cell." Do you really have a certain nerve cell for recognizing the concatenation of features representing your grandmother? (p. 675)

Blakemore (1973) then went on to suggest that several kinds of evidence provided negative answers to these rhetorical questions. First, he noted that brain injuries do not produce highly specific recognition deficits. Thus, it does not seem that if you lose a small, localized number of cells, you loose recognition of a particular object. Rather, the visual processing of classes of objects or relations is degraded. This criticism can be expanded to point out that a single neuron based equivalent of a thought would leave our perceptual systems in a terribly vulnerable state. The fortuitous accidental or maturational disruption of the function of only a few neurons would drastically disrupt our recognition abilities. Second, he noted that our increasing knowledge of brain region interconnectedness argued against particular regions, much less single neurons operating independently. Data like these, he concluded, suggested that although it is possible that some cells might be specialized for something as familiar as hand detection, more usually, the brain generally encodes attributes of an image rather the image itself.

2. Charles S. Harris: A few years later, Harris (1980) suggested that the extreme "pontifical" concept of the "Yellow Volkswagen Detector" (p. 130) (which he had earlier invoked in talks as a straw man argument against single neuron theories) was severely challenged by the contingent aftereffects such as the one proposed by McCollough (1965).[27] The level of interaction between different dimensions of the visual response was so great that there was no plausible way to account for them in terms of single neurons.

3. David Marr (1945–1980): The magnum opus of the late David Marr *Vision* (Marr, 1982) was extremely influential in championing a computational model of the vision system. During the course of the book, Marr eloquently argued against the older models epitomized by the single neuron theory and, according to him, its linear descendent—feature detector theory. His main argument was that the world is too complex to be encoded by the single neuron or feature detection theories (p. 341). Marr proceeded to invoke other arguments, not so much as critiques of single neuron theories, as arguments in favor of his computational approach. In doing so he raised an important point about symbolic representation. Many of the single cell and feature detector theories emerged from studies of the visual system. However, many cognitive concepts are not so neatly linked to spatial dimensions. How does a predominantly spatial kind of thinking deal with such properties? In such situations, he concluded, no amount of simple zero crossing-type computation can capture the network of relationships among even a simple set of nonspatial ideas.

4. Edwin Land (1909–1991): Another strong argument can be found in the work of vision scientists such as described by Land (1977). Land showed that

---

[27]The McCollough Effect, discovered by Celeste McCullough, 1965, is a contingent effect on colored afterimages that is determined by the geometry (specifically, line orientation) of a preexisting visual stimulus. The difficulty of having a single neuron encode two different experiences as the result of such a contingency raises questions about the role of a single neuron.

the perception of color or lightness depends strongly upon the relationships between different areas of the visual scene. Such a complex interaction indicates that it is not the absolute response of any single neuron or local area of the brain that determines the perceptual response but a complex processing of the spatial relationships of the stimulus information that determines what we see. Since spatial relationships are, by definition, distributed, the key codes for color are not likely to be sparsely encoded.

5. Semir Zeki: The theme of complex interaction has also been championed by Zeki (1993) as an argument against simplistic single neuron theories of perception. Based on his anatomical and physiological studies of the brain, he came to the conclusion that the brain has no particular locus that must be activated to produce conscious experience. Rather, he argued that:

> A review of the experimental and clinical evidence suggest that for the conscious perception of a visual stimulus and thus for acquisition of knowledge about the visual world, the simultaneous activity of many visual areas is necessary and that a stimulus will not reach visual awareness unless this condition is satisfied, even if signals reach the specialized areas indirectly. (Zeki, 1993, p. 356)

Although this point speaks mainly to any theory attributing mind to a particular region of the brain, it also argues strongly against any extreme theory in which a single or a few neurons are the psychoneural equivalent of mental activity.

In recent years, neurophysiological evidence has begun to accumulate that challenges the fundamental assumption of narrow tuning (i.e., that only very specific stimulus properties will activate a neuron) in single neuron theory. The classic idea was that the sharper the tuning, the more specific the neuronal response could presumably be. However, it has been repeatedly shown from as far back as the original studies of Hubel and Wiesel that neuronal activity does not turn off sharply when the stimulus was shifted away from the cell's preferred orientation. New data also contravenes the idea that other suggestions of narrow tuning are not valid. Nevertheless, the argument of sharp tuning has continued to be used by proponents of single neuron theory.

Before presenting a few examples that speak to the issue of sparse versus coarse distribution and narrow or broad tuning of individual neurons, it is important to point out that the issue is not completely settled. The problem, of course, is the persistent one that even in accord with the most extreme "single neuron" theories, there is still a great deal of flexibility concerning the acceptable number of neurons involved in the representation of a cognitive process.

Furthermore, the problem is not going to be solved easily: A conclusive answer to the question—Are neuronal representations sparse or distributed?—would require an enormous neurostatistical effort. Even then, there are no fixed criteria for what constitutes sparseness or distribution. However, there is a trend that seems to reflect the idea that distribution and broad interaction are winning the field over fine-tuning and sparseness. Some recent evidence relevant to this argument is now presented.

6. Edmund Rolls and Martin Tovee: In the 1990s some classic papers that had so influenced thinking in the earlier decades began to be challenged. In particular, the "face" validity of the face detecting neurons was subject to a renewed scrutiny. The impact of the original papers by Gross, Desmione, and others had proven to be remarkably persistent. However, the picture began to change in the last decade of the 20th century. Rolls and Tovee (1995), for example, carried out an impressive examination of the idea that single neurons encoded specific faces by stimulating temporal neurons in the monkey with a collection of faces and other objects. Their goal was to compare the selectivity of the monkey's temporal neurons to this variety of stimulus forms after they had been highly trained to fixate on a display. They observed that some neurons could be identified that responded to face-like stimuli more vigorously then to the non-face stimuli. This finding suggested that the neurons that were responsive to faces could collectively distinguish between faces. However, their results also indicated that this discrimination could not be carried out by an individual neuron; it required the collective action of a large set of them. That is, no single cell responded uniquely to a particular face even though it was a part of a set that could. Their concluding comment is worthwhile quoting in full:

> This discussion on the sparseness of representation provided by these face-selective cells runs counter to the possibility that they are very specifically tuned and provide a "cardinal" or "grandmother cell" type of very sparse representation (Barlow 1972). Instead, the data presented in this paper indicate that they are very selective, in that they respond rather selectively to stimuli within the class faces, and provide little information about stimuli that are not faces. However, within the class for which they encode information (faces), the representation is very distributed, implying great discriminative ability, including the representation of small differences between faces presented simultaneously. (p. 724)

Thus, they argue (a) that there are some neurons that respond selectively to face-like objects. However, the task of discriminating between faces cannot be carried out by an individual cell–it requires many interconnected and interacting neurons.

7. Kenneth Britten and William Newsome: The problem of tuning bandwidth was examined by studying neurons in visual area 5 (the middle temporal area) by Britten and Newsome (1998). A very important aspect of their study was their use of streams of dots as a stimulus in which the spatiotemporal pattern could be controlled independently of the stimulus intensity. By manipulating the direction of motion of the dot patterns they were able to measure the relative tuning of these neurons. The conclusion of their study, which is germane to the present discussion, was that the tuning curves remained broad (over an orientation range of 90 deg) even when the induced motion was near threshold. At higher levels of the induced motion, the breadth of tuning approached 240 deg. They concluded that these data counterindicated any theory of sparse or individual neuron theories by noting:

> Thus, large numbers of neurons carry signals appropriate for performing the task, even near psychophysical threshold. This pattern of results appears consistent with coarse coding models of the representation of stimulus direction in MT. (p. 767)[28]

8. Keiji Tanaka: So much of the neurophysiological literature, even those that have just been presented as counterarguments to single neuron theory, have accepted without deep consideration that the critical stimulus for certain responding neurons is a "face." The conjecture is that if a "face" stimulus activates a "face-sensitive cell," the key is the "faceness" of that stimulus. However, on close examination, this is little more than a hypothesis driven by a stimulus protocol or a stimulus protocol driven by a hypothesis. The problem is that a "face" may not be a "face" but rather a concatenation of certain subfeatures that are present in faces as well as in other types of stimuli. Injudicious selection of stimuli or a misappreciation of the effective attributes of a stimulus may then produce what appears to be face sensitive neurons, but which in reality are cells that are sensitive to more general kinds of either individual or collections of geometrical features. How does one resolve this possible artifact of interpretation? The best way to do so is to strip away the extraneous parts of the stimulus until one reaches the core attributes that truly describe the sensitivity of the impaled neuron. The main proponent of this reductive analysis into residual or optimal features has been Keiji Tanaka (1993) who had insights into this potential misinterpretation

[28]Britten and Newsome (1998) also cited a number of other research reports in which direct neurophysiological measurements of tuning curves supported the idea that broad tuning is the rule, rather than the exception, in the medial temporal area.

over a decade ago (Tanaka, Saito, Fukada, and Moriya, 1991). Early on he and his colleagues had appreciated that:

> Although responses of anterior IT [inferior temporal] cells were thus selective to particular features, the features coded by the individual cells were not complex enough to indicate a concept of particular real objects. (p. 187)

Tanaka and his colleagues went on to discuss the problem of face codes, in particular, in this pioneering study. They pointed out that even though they could find cells that seemed selectively sensitive to faces, they "responded to virtually all different faces with only broad tunings" (p. 187). This finding led Tanaka to develop his reductive technique[29] and to observe that cells that seemed to be highly selective to particular stimuli (such as faces) actually were activated by much simple attributes of the stimulus included in, but certainly not conveying, the full information of the original object. Based on his work, Tanaka (2003) concluded: "representation by multiple cells with overlapping selectivities can be more precise than a mere summation of representations by individual cells" (p. 98). This approach also overcomes the logical difficulty of imagining a system in which every concept or object is represented by individual neurons. The work of Tanaka is especially important. In addition to providing some significant neurophysiological data, it illustrates how our preconceptions concerning the nature and selection of the stimuli we use in experiments themselves may be seriously flawed.

5.4 SUMMARY

Single neuron theory has been a persistent and popular explanation of how the brain produces mental activity for much of the last half century. It is largely, it can be argued, an intellectual product of one of the main technologies—microelectrode recording—that is available to cognitive neuroscientists. Just as the availability of the EEG stimulated the growth of the field theoretical perspective, so, too, did the enormous amount of information obtained in many exciting and important studies of the activity of single neurons focus attention on the possibility that the origins of the mind may

[29]The reductive technique involves the selective removal of various attributes of a stimulus and the observation of the continued response of a cell until the stimulus has been reduced to a primitive that no longer activates the cell. For example, Tanaka found neurons that apparently were selectively activated by an image of a man in a white coat or that of a cat. Selective reduction of the stimuli showed the key stimulus in either case was not the "concept" of "a man in a white coat" or of a "cat." Rather the essential attribute of the stimulus was a much simpler attribute—a white circle underneath a smaller black circle or two striped fields, respectively.

lay there. There is no question that our understanding of the functions of neurons—the building blocks of the nervous system—has been extraordinary. The problem, however, is that, because of this success, our attention has been focused on too microscopic a level of the structure of the brain. Both logic and recent findings from this same kind of microelectrophysiological investigation now strongly argue that the original extreme idea of narrowly tuned, sparsely distributed, neurons representing complex concepts is no longer sustainable.

Logically, the problem runs up against the imponderably large number of different objects and concepts that would have to be represented. Even the very large number of neurons in the brain does not seem sufficient to accommodate such a simplistic code.

If one steps back a little from the excitement and objectivity of the empirical findings, it becomes obvious that the method (locating and recording from a neuron that responds to an object or concept) is deeply flawed as a guiding paradigm. Such an experiment is fundamentally an uncontrolled experiment! Even with several, a hundred, or a thousand microelectrodes (the latter task not yet achieved), it is not possible to account for the codes and activities of all of the other neurons that might be involved or activated, but which are not examined.

Furthermore, it is often forgotten that "neurophysiological data are not the same as neurophysiological theories."[30] Substantial, although, implicit and cryptic, assumptions must be made to bridge from the "spike counts" of an impaled neuron to the assertion that such a measure is the psychoneural equivalent of a thought. Closely related to this crypto-logic is the equally important caveat that misconceptions about the true nature of the key attributes of a stimulus may confuse and confound both the design and interpretation of experimental studies.

Looming over all these logical considerations is the inescapable problem that even if a correlation can be demonstrated between a neuronal response and some percept or concept, this association does not necessarily support a causal link between the two domains. A particular neural response might as well be a concomitant and correlated, but functionally irrelevant "sign" (Uttal, 1967) or a transmission signal as well as the true psychoneural equivalent or "code."

Finally, we must appreciate that the only uncontroversial kind of experiment to support single neuron theory would be to find a neuron whose response to a stimulus is unique. Then, by some electrical or chemical means, turn off that single neuron's activity and determine that the awareness or conscious experience of the encoded concept also disappeared. A good control would be to reactivate the neuron and observe whether or not the

[30]A comment originally attributed to Charles S. Harris.

experience reappeared. Such a Gedanken Experiment, of course, is impossible to implement. Thus, inferential leaps from suggestive data from this kind of uncontrolled experiment to comprehensive theories are literally unconstrained.

Notwithstanding the caveat that the variety of neuronal electrophysiological responses in the brain is great enough to allow an intrepid investigator to find almost anything, it does seem that the trend of recent findings has been shifting to support broad tuning and distributed responses rather than sparse and narrow tuning. Therefore, the very empirical foundations of single neuron theory are evaporating just as some of the logical problems are becoming more evident.

Another thing that cognitive neuroscience has come to appreciate is that the terminology we use is often arbitrary and judgmental. Terms such as *narrow, broad, localized, distributed,* etc.) are flexible and their exact denotation is very uncertain. The same observation may be categorized by different investigators by totally different terminologies solely on the basis of preexisting theoretical views. A few investigators (e.g., Rolls & Tovee, 1995) have attempted to quantify the terminology. However, there is still ample room for disagreement in terms of the criteria used once a "quantitative measure" has been made.

The point is that even the hardest cellular neurophysiological data is underdetermined. This is especially true of any data obtained from experiments that are confounded by the undeniable presence of unobserved activity. Rather, what the single neuron theory and the field theories share in common is their dependence upon concepts and ideas (emerging in substantial part from their respective technologies) that themselves are at best imaginative inventions rather than compelling empirical proofs or sound logical arguments. In fact, both approaches may be considered to be displacement activities that are substituted for the neural activity that is the true psychoneural equivalent of mind—the widely distributed, overall state of the huge numbers of interconnected neurons—the neural network.

I now turn to this other great class of mind–brain theories—the neural network. There is widespread agreement that, in principle, this level of analysis is the most likely form of representation of cognitive processes by the nervous system. However, the problem of analyzing such a network may be intractable because of nonlinear complexity and the huge number of neurons involved in even the simplest cognitive mental act. We may be forever prohibited from understanding how the mind may emerge from the action of the huge array that makes up our brain. It is this intractability that led us to the "displacement" theories, such as those discussed in chapters 4 and 5. If I am correct that the neural net model is both the correct one and that it is, in principle, unsolvable, then the goal of a neuroreductive theory of the mind is unobtainable.

CHAPTER

6

Network Theories—Truth Denied

6.1 INTRODUCTION

If there is any single axiom of brain organization that we can depend on to remain inviolate in the future it is that the brain is an elaborate mesh of interconnected neurons. That is, the mass of neurons, communicate and interact in complex ways. As I discuss in earlier chapters, our knowledge of the behavior of individual neurons has reached high levels. We have a deep and profound understanding of how the metabolic chemistry of the neuron accounts for the ionic flows that drive the electro-potentials across the cell membrane that we call "spike" or "local" action potentials. The mechanisms of interconnection between *individual* neurons are also increasingly well known each year; synapses, transmitter chemicals (e.g., GABA, Acetylcholine, etc.) and their associated electro-potentials (e.g., psp, ipsp, etc.) are among the vocabulary of even introductory students of neuroscience. We also know a considerable amount concerning the interconnectivity of the various areas of the brain and the brain's connections with other relatively distant areas within the nervous system.

Progress has also been made in understanding the coded languages by means of which afferent and efferent neurons convey information from and to the periphery–the world of stimuli and responses. However, there is another level of analysis about which we know much less. That level concerns the detailed arrangement of the innumerable interconnections among the large numbers of neurons that makes up the central nervous system. Among the great central areas of the cerebral cortex, in particular, the neuronal interconnections are complex and irregular to the point of inscrutability. Yet, it is here, in the momentary states of these myriad neurons and their interconnections, that mind is most likely to be embodied. The "state" of this vast array of neurons, heavily processed and integrated from sensory inputs, most likely is the psychoneural equivalent of mind so diligently sought by cognitive neuroscientists.

The key phrase in this sentence, however, is "most likely." There is still no definitive empirical data linking mental processes and neural network organization. Indeed, as we have seen, there is no accepted solution to the mind–brain connection of any kind. In spite of this lacuna in our knowledge, network theorists take this hypothesis as their foundation assumption.

The overarching handicap to analysis at the network level is the very condition that makes it possible for mind to emerge—the high level of complexity of a lattice capable of carrying out the computations that lead to our sense of awareness, our thoughts, even our subliminal processing of afferent information. Unfortunately, the detailed nature of the salient interactions among neurons—at the level necessary for the production of mental processes—has not proven to be attackable at other than the most reduced level with any of the standard techniques of modern science.

Is it possible that some means of studying networks of the complexity of the brain will be found in the future? Other sciences have made progress in the study of systems with large number of components by introducing some reasonable simplifying constraints when formulating their problems. Can we do the same? The answer to this question lies at the heart of the future of neural network theory in cognitive neuroscience as well as our future ability to solve the mind–brain problem.

Simplification is always possible, however it must be done with care not to lose the essential nature of the problem at hand. The important thing is that simplification, however it is done, must reflect the inherent properties of the mechanism under study. The study of the structure of crystalline matter, for example, is made comparatively easy by the regular and repetitive arrangement of the constituent atoms. This allows x-ray diffraction methods to explore their structure without concern for idiosyncratic irregularities. Statistical mechanical studies of the behavior of contained gases are similarly constrained by the fact that the individual behavior of individual molecules can be simply averaged to produce insights into the unified behavior as expressed by such measures as pressure and volume. Even in the peripheral nervous system, the relatively simple structure of the receptor plexuses has permitted us occasionally to study their arrangement and coding schemes with promising results.

It remains uncertain, however, if the arrangement of the neurons in the cerebral layers enjoys a comparable capability for simplifying constraints. The problem facing neural network theorists and the mathematicians who study these networks is: What kinds of simplification methods, if any, may be applicable to the analysis of such structures? Unfortunately, the preliminary evidence is that complexity cannot be reduced in synthetic neural networks without loosing their essential ability to produce mental processes. The arrangement of a neural network that is the "most likely" psychoneural equivalent of cognitive processes raises the complexity level to new heights. Conventional mathematics, therefore, is usually inadequate to describe anything more detailed than either the overall behavior of an organism or the action of a highly simplified neural network composed of a relatively small number of simulated neurons. Such highly reduced models are often described in the same context as more complex neural networks. On closer analysis, however, they often turn out to be conceptually identical to the block or modular diagrams favored by earlier generations of cognitive psychologists. Worst of all, although they appear in the guise of networks of neurons, they may actually represent something quite different.

The problem, thus confronted, is hugely frustrating. On the one hand, most cognitive neuroscientists agree that it is "most likely" that the details of the activity of the heavily, albeit irregularly, interconnected network of neurons in the brain is the source of mental, cognitive, and consciousness processes of all kinds. On the other, the sheer number of the brain components (neurons, as well as more macroscopic regions) and the irregular complexity of their interactions are likely to make any analysis unobtainable. From one point of view, the truth can be said to have been revealed; yet its details are still denied to us. Philosophers distinguish between what is a consensual *ontology* (we generally agree that mind is embodied in the vast pattern of interconnections of the brain's many neurons—the neuron doctrine) and the *epistemological* barrier (we have no way of unraveling this tangle).[1]

In spite of the inherent and inescapable frustration of dealing with such a situation, the sheer ontological face validity of assuming that the neural network of the brain is the foundation of mind has directed the efforts of many cognitive neuroscientists to develop synthetic or computational neural network theories. Indeed, the presumption that this approach is the "correct" one has led to the dispersal of similar ideas into the applied technological field of computer science. "Neural network modeling" is a staple of the AI field as well as of the cognitive neuroscientific one.

This enthusiasm, however, has to be tempered by three important caveats. First, it is essential it be understood that not all neural network theories are, in fact, "neurophysiologically" coherent. That is, many so-called neural

---

[1]Of course, there are many proposals for crossing this epistemological barrier. This book considers some of the biological theories that attempt to make this leap. Each is flawed in some fundamental way. There are also many "theories" invoking dualistic ideas of a nonmaterial bond between mind and brain. To accept any of these would be to ignore the most basic foundations of a naturalist scientific approach altogether. That dualistic trail is clearly not the way to go.

network theories are "network" theories, not in any biological or neurophysiological sense, but only in the sense they are implemented in the form of distributed, parallel processing structures. It is a general property of many such models that they introduce a kind of unrealistic, nonbiological, pseudo-crystalline regularity to make it possible for traditional computational or mathematical techniques to be applied. Many such theories and simulations are far removed from any physiological axioms, constraints, or presumptions. In fact, the underlying logic of many exemplars of neural network "theories" or AI simulations comes not from the physiological laboratory but from the abilities, methods, and limitations of computer technology! If these computer attributes once had roots in the basic brain fact that neurons are arranged in three-dimensional lattices, this foundation assumption is long submerged under the technological abilities and limitations of the electronic systems on which they are programmed.

Clearly, the early (c. 1950s and 1960s) idea that computers operated by similar laws and rules as does the brain (or vice versa) has long been replaced by a general appreciation that the two system types probably have wildly different characteristics and operate by substantially different logics. This dissimilarity shows up in many ways, not the least of which is that the typical computer program goes through a *serial* sequence[2] of processing steps to select a specific outcome. The brain, on the other hand, goes through a series of nearly simultaneous processing steps and ends up with a final distributed state that, I argue, is the most likely psychoneural equivalent of mind. One neural network theory operating in this mode is that of Fukushima and Miyake (1978). I return to discuss this model in detail later in this chapter.

Second, even those computational models that closely imitate or simulate some cognitive process need not do so by incorporation of the identical logic carried out by the organic brain. Behavioral functions that may be the same as those observed in organisms can be (and probably are) achieved with computer programs, but by means of algorithms that are totally different than those used by brains or even simpler nervous systems. There is a tendency in this field to underestimate the mechanisms and rules by which the brain operates because similar results can often be obtained by much less complex machines. This is another manifestation of the continuing potential for analogs to mislead and deceive us concerning the true nature of underlying mechanisms.

---

[2]During the 1980s and 1990s computers based on parallel processing by a large number of simultaneously active computational elements was proposed and some actually built. In recent years, however, there has been a gradual diminishment in interest in such fine grain systems of this kind as well as a reduction in the number of companies marketing them. This retreat is mainly accounted for by their intrinsic difficulty of programming. This is another indication of how difficult it is going to be to analyze the action of a full-scale parallel system like the brain.

Third, and perhaps most important, is the fact that all neural network models are oversimplifications that are incapable of dealing with the number of neurons and interactions that must be involved in instantiating the simplest cognitive process. Some, indeed, are so oversimplified that they cannot simulate cognition. Much is lost in the shift from reality to theory.

This is not the place to inquire into what seems to be an unending, but in my opinion pointless, controversy: Is the brain a computer? (Or, vice versa, does the computer have the potential to artificially produce human-like cognitive processes?) In any event, it is clear now that whatever it is, the brain is not a classic serial von Neumann computer with input, central processor, memory, and output functional units. Furthermore, I hope to avoid the intellectual tangle that certainly will continue to exist concerning the question of consciousness in animals, other people, or computers. My strong conviction is that there is no way to distinguish between a clever automaton and a sentient being that is amenable to scientific research because of the fundamental inaccessibility of mental processes (see Uttal, 2000).

Others will make those arguments—pro and con. The argument I make in this book is that all psychobiological theories of mind are, *in principle,* incapable of providing a satisfactory explanation of how the mind is actually instantiated in or produced by brain mechanisms. In this chapter, I extend this argument to include the type of theory—the neural network—that has the greatest degree of face validity and widest acceptance.

The intricate pattern of cellular activities that Sherrington described so well as the "enchanted loom" only begins to capture the true challenge to analysis provided by the real neural network. The nut of this argument is, because of the irregular structure of and huge number of connections in any realistic neural net, the mind–brain conundrum is an example of an unsolvable or intractable problem. The argument supporting this view is based on modern thinking in combinatoric and solvability theory. This intractability, it is emphasized here, is not just a temporary matter of inadequate methods, incomplete data, or insufficiently powerful computers; to the contrary, the case is made that the problem is unsolvable not only by any means available to us today, but by any conceivable one in the future!

What all the theories and models described in this chapter have in common is discrete, multinodal, *parallelism.* That is, unlike field theories, they assume that the neurons of the brain operate in a quasi-independent manner as modulated by the way in which they are interconnected. Furthermore, it is argued that these interactions work to determine the specific response of each neuron in a way that is profoundly nonlinear. In addition, unlike the emphasis of single cell theories, a basic assumption of neural network theories is that many neurons are simultaneously involved in processing and representing a cognitive process. They do so by establishing an overall pattern of activity in the network rather than the activation of a single "pontifical" neuron. A final corollary of this network point of view is that there is no special output evaluator or homunculus that interprets the network state; rather, each of the many involved neurons represents one small part of the overall final system state that itself *is* cognition.

Once again, to fully understand the assumptions under which the neural network models work, we have to look back on the history of this theoretical approach to explaining how the brain makes the mind.

6.2 THE ORIGINS OF NEURAL NETWORK THEORY

Prior to the work of Cajal and Golgi near the end of the 19th century, the nervous system was dealt with mainly at the level of the macroscopically observable nerves and large brain parts. The role of the cells that made up the nervous system was only infrequently alluded to in discussions of the time. By the mid-19th century, it was fully appreciated that the brain was the locus of our minds. It was further hypothesized that different parts of the brain served different cognitive processes. The key aspect of the then popular theories of brain and mind was the way that the compound nerves communicated and how the "chunks" of the brain might represent thoughts. Although some of the most extreme "bumpology" ideas expressed in Spurzheim's (1832) phrenological theory were discredited as early as 1840, the strong localization theme, which attributed cognition to chunks of the brain, was and still is popular. The idea of a network or assemblage of interacting neurons existed only in a rudimentary form. Some of the early localization theorists (e.g., J. Hughlings Jackson, 1835–1911) suggested that the way in which these major regions interacted could explain how cognitive processes worked. However, the ideas were very primitive and not well developed. Originally, they did not even invoke individual neurons.[3]

This misdirection was not due to a complete lack of knowledge of the microanatomy of the brain. Ferrier's (1886) great book on brain function presented a set of plates illustrating the microscopic arrangement of the tissues of several parts of the brain; he specifically referred to the observed components as "nerve cells" (p. 40).

By the end of the century, however, Cajal (1900), as discussed in chapter 2, had published drawings using the Golgi stain that graphically illustrated the network-like arrangement of the neurons in the visual cortex and then

[3]Recently, I had the privilege of reviewing the draft of a new book to be published in 2005. Its author, Brian Burrell (2005), presents one of the most lucid and fascinating accounts of the history of cerebral "chunkology"—the idea that mind could be explained by the shape, size, of fissure pattern of the brain. This book is a must read!

later in the superior colliculus (Cajal, 1911). Thus, it was the concept of a functional network that was missing, not the anatomical facts, in the continuing emphasis on the macroscopic components of the brain.

Where allusions to the possible role of the more microscopic parts of the brain were made, it was almost in poetic or allegorical sense. For example, Binet (1907) discussed the relation between perception and brain function in an effort to counteract strong dualistic tendencies in the philosophy and psychology of his day with the following language:

> I look at the plain before me, and see a flock of sheep pass through it. At the same time an observer, armed with a microscope *ǎ la* Jules Verne, looks into my brain and observes there a certain molecular dance which accompanies my visual perception. Thus, on the one hand is my representation; on the other, a dynamic state of the nerve cells. (p. 267)

Binet went on to suggest that this "molecular dance" was the same stuff as perception, thus expressing a material monism that can be considered to be an early expression of a neural network theory.

Nevertheless, poetry and microscopic and neuroanatomical knowledge aside, there was little appreciation of the quasi-computational role that the neurons of the brain might play in concert with each other. A few glimmerings could be observed in the work of such neurophysiologists as Lorente de Nó (1934, 1938a) who examined reflex arcs and the conditions for the activation of one neuron by others. However, in the main, the modern idea of a network of neurons underlying mental processes had simply not dawned. Technology and genius combined in the work of Warren S. McCulloch and Walter Pitts to provide a theoretical bridge for the grand leap from microscopic neuroanatomy to a new kind of organizational logic.

6.3 PITTS AND MCCULLOCH'S PROTOTYPICAL NEURONAL NET[4]

The terms *classic* or *seminal* may never be more appropriately used than when describing the outstanding work of Warren S. McCulloch and Walter Pitts.[5] Their contribution sharply defined the border between two periods of research into theories of mind—one in which the macroscopic functions

---

[4]This section on the work of McCulloch and Pitts's seminal work is abstracted and updated from a similar discussion in Uttal (2002).

[5]Walter Pitts was at the very least a brilliant eccentric. His full story is told in the *MIT Encyclopedia of Cognitive Science*. Suffice to say he died in obscurity, possibly in 1969, after participating in one of the most important developments in modern cognitive neuroscience's history.

of the brain were emphasized and the other in which the discussion shifted to the computational role of networks of neurons. (The former, of course, has had new life breathed into it by modern imaging devices.) Two of their articles stand as milestones in the development of the neural network models that were to follow (see McCulloch & Pitts, 1943 and Pitts & McCulloch, 1947).

The McCulloch and Pitts (1943) article was an exercise in formal logic. In that milestone contribution, they proposed a propositional logic based on an interacting system of simple binary neurons as the basis of cognition. Given that they were both on the staff of the Research Laboratory of Electronics at MIT, it is not surprising to note that this logic was very similar to the ideas actively being considered at that laboratory during World War II. Discoveries and developments concerning digital logic, cybernetics, and on information theory later to be published by such luminaries as Norbert Wiener (1948) and Claude Shannon (1948), respectively, were shaking up technology as well.

McCulloch and Pitts' work had an immediate and major impact. Rashevsky (1948) had a chapter (XLVI) in his book in which the McCulloch and Pitts work was discussed. Others, such as Culbertson (1950), were also moving in the same intellectual direction. Simple neural nets began to be analyzed in novel, and even more important, quantitative ways that made exciting promises to those who sought to build bridges between mind and brain. The anatomy and physiology of the nervous system became a much hotter topic as information theory excited many researchers at the time. Most of all, however, the digital computer was going through its birth throes. What had been, at best, impractical conjectures now seemed as if they might become practical implementations.

The McCulloch and Pitts (1943) article invoked a conceptual nervous system of considerably less complexity than one that would satisfy neurophysiologists these days. For example, it acknowledged only all-or-none responses, postulated a system of delays restricted exclusively to synaptic functions, and assumed a rigid structural stability on the part of the nervous system. These assumptions are no longer accepted. However, at that time these neurophysiological simplifications permitted the kind of logical analysis of networks that McCulloch and Pitts pioneered.

The 1943 article offered a model of a neural network that was initially based on the propositional logic of "all-or-none neurons." It operated on the basis of Boolean laws that were extremely specific. (Not surprisingly, the drawings presented in their Figure 1, look just like the standard depiction of the gates of a typical modern electronic logical system.) Inhibition and excitation were total or not at all. A single inhibitor could deny the action of a neuron and specific patterns of input were required to fire particular neurons. Time played a role in that information could be stored in reverberatory circuits; a simple form of memory could thus be instantiated. The introduction of such feedback loops made the system much more complicated and potentially more powerful. With the addition of this kind of memory, however, the mathematics became extremely complicated—a harbinger of things to come. Nevertheless, the essential components of one kind of a hypothetical nervous network are there and the idea that such a network could be an "explanation" of cognitive function became a mainstay of contemporary mind–brain theory.

Their second article (Pitts & McCulloch, 1947) was primarily concerned with a specific kind of cognition—form recognition. Here, too, these two extraordinary men were pioneers in shaping a field that has become one of the main targets of cognitive-brain theorizing in recent years—how we recognize objects. Not only was their perceptual vocabulary modern, but so too was the general neural network approach they used.

Once again, from our current perspective, the neurophysiology expressed in the Pitts and McCulloch article seems antique: They identified the superior colliculus as a site of one of two possible form recognition processes and invoked a kind of feedback to motor systems as the source of their method for computing stimulus invariance. Nevertheless, their ideas about the plausible nature of networks were novel and contributed to many later developments in the field. If one ignores the physiological assumptions and considers only the mathematics and the basic assumptions of their approach, it is clear their two models were the first to deal with networks of neurons that might possibly carry out specific logical and computational processes in a way that was supposed to realistically simulate mental activity. More up-to-date neurophysiology could only alter the neural assumptions of subsequent theories and not the basic network concept described by Pitts and McCulloch's mathematics.

In the second article, McCulloch and Pitts (1947) reverted to a more conventional kind of mathematics to account for some of the specific features required for form recognition. This decision was probably based on their emerging appreciation that continuous processes were likely to be involved—conventional analysis meeting the need for a solution to the form recognition problem better than the Boolean type logic that had served so well in the first article. Indeed, an entirely new idea was about to be introduced in the thought processes of the neural network theoretical community that both made this hypothesis of continuity much more respectable and the problem of properly representing the activity of such nets far more reasonable. That idea was the ability of interneuronal connections to change their value and efficiency as a result of experience. No longer were the interconnections fixed and immutable, but dynamic and variable.

6.4 HEBB AND THE CELL ASSEMBLY

Donald Hebb (1904–1985) was a distinguished Canadian psychologist and one of the early supporters of the cognitive approach to theory in psychology. Hebb was, at his most fundamental conceptual roots, however, a neuroreductionist. That is, he was interested in "reducing the vagaries of human thought to a mechanical process of cause and effect" (Hebb, 1949, p. xi). He pursued this reductionist view to develop a concept that has long been identified as the next major step in the evolution of neural network theories.

Hebb's great contributions were incorporated in ideas expressed in a book, the persistent influence of which can hardly be understated. *The Organization of Behavior: A Neuropsychological Theory* (Hebb, 1949) was published within a few years of McCulloch and Pitts' (1943; Pitts & Mcculloch, 1947) enunciation of the idea of a computer-like neural net as a putative theory of mental activity. However, these two earlier articles had only briefly been concerned with the problems with which psychologists must contend everyday. Learning (more precisely, memory) had been dealt with by McCulloch and Pitts only in terms of reverberatory circuits. In addition, they considered form recognition either to be integration across an image or a template kind of matching. How the hypothetical neural nets arrived at the state that would allow these process to grow and change as a result of their experience with a number of input forms was a question unasked and unanswered by McCulloch and Pitts.

Hebb, however, was a psychologist and the dominant psychological zeitgeist of his times can be characterized by the desire to understand learning and other cognitive processes that changed over time as a result of maturation or experience. His thoughts were thus directed to mechanisms that could account for the dynamic changes that occurred during the functioning of a neural network. The existence and role of a neural network of the kind suggested by McCulloch and Pitts was a foundation assumption on his part.[6] However, Hebb's approach was very different. Rather than extolling the mathematical approach that characterized the Cambridge group, Hebb (1949) argued that using mathematical methods forced the theoretician to drastically simplify the "the psychological problem almost out of existence" (p. xi). In this regard and from our current viewpoint, he was exactly correct. Hebb's principles of neural network organization did not provide any detailed explanation of the functions of neural net. What it did do so effec-

[6]Surprisingly, Hebb does not directly cite either of the two McCulloch and Pitts papers. Rather, he alludes to them indirectly listing the work of "Rashevsky, Pitts, Householder, Landahl, McCulloch, and others" as representatives of those who studied "populations of neurons mathematically" (Hebb, 1949, p. xi).

tively was to provide a set of general principles by means of which the brain was likely to operate. The most significant of these principles was the idea that synapses changed their effectiveness (their "weight") as a function of usage. In point of historical fact, the adaptive "Hebbian synapse" became the core idea of virtually all of the neural network models that were to follow.

To account for the dynamic ability of the nervous system to adapt to past experiences, Hebb turned to recent discoveries (e.g., Lorente de Nó, 1938b) concerning the action of synapses. His intuitive leap was that the neuronal networks subserving cognitive processes were continuously modified by changes in the ability of the synapse to conduct information from one neuron to the next as a result of experience. The causal force underlying these changes, he proposed, was simply repetitive activity—an extrapolation of the "law of effect" originally proposed by Thorndike (1931).[7] This is such a fundamental idea for current cognitive neuroscience that it is appropriate to quote his assumption in its entirety:

> When an axon of cell A is near enough to excite a cell B and repeatedly or persistently takes part in firing it, some growth process or metabolic changes takes place in one or both cells such that A's efficiency, as one of the cells firing B, is increased. (Hebb, 1949, p.62)

Hebb went on to suggest that the obvious way in which this increase in efficiency takes place is by growth of the synaptic knobs that Lorente de Nó had recently diagrammed.

Before continuing with later stages of Hebb's dynamic synaptic theory of network change, it is important to appreciate that virtually all modern neuroscientific theories of experience-driven changes in the neural network attribute long-term learning to changes in synaptic efficiency. However, despite nearly universal acceptance of this concept, there remains no direct evidence that such microscopic synaptic changes underlay equivalent changes in human behavior or thought. However clear it is to all of us that synaptic conductivity changes are the only plausible reductive hypothesis available to explain the changes that occur during learning, the kind of experiment required to confirm or disconfirm such a hypothesis is clearly impossible to carry out. Indirect evidence, logical necessity, and the absence of a plausible alternative, support this fundamental idea. Even Hebb acknowledged in his book that the synaptic growth or metabolic change that might occur during learning was only a suggestion generated to provide a

---

[7]Thorndike had originally proposed a Law of Effect in which the "effect" had to be not only repetitive but also experientially positive at the macroscopic level to persevere. Hebb's corollary was simpler and assumed that any repetitive process would produce a persistent effect at the microscopic level.

plausible mechanism for learning and other kinds of adaptive behavior. Nor, for that matter, are we able to disentangle the relative contributions of experience and maturation in the development of these synaptic knobs. Hebb (1949) spoke directly to this issue when he said:

> It is implied that the knobs appear in the course of learning, but this does not give us a means of testing the assumption. There is apparently no good evidence concerning the relative frequency of knobs in infant and adult brains, and the assumption does *not* imply that there should be none in the newborn infant. The learning referred to is learning in a very general sense, which most certainly have begun long before birth. (p. 66)

In context of the debate between learning and maturation there still is no definitive way to distinguish between these two sources of altered states of neural networks. Concomitancy and complexity breeds a kind of misleading obscurity in this situation.

Having assumed how synaptic changes might operate to change the state of a nervous network, Hebb (1949) next considered how a previously unrelated set of neurons might begin to operate in concert. The concept that he developed was a *cell-assembly*—a group of neurons that were interconnected in such a way that activity in one stimulated the others to respond in a coordinated way at the same time and in the order in which they were originally activated. The key to this coordinated activity is the arrangement of the neurons by means of convergent and divergent connections. As Hebb put it:

> Any frequently repeated, particular stimulation will lead to the slow development of a "cell-assembly," a diffuse structure comprising cells in the cortex and the diencephalon (and, also, perhaps, in the basal ganglion of the cerebrum), capable of acting briefly as a closed system, delivering facilitation to other such systems and usually having a specific motor facilitation. (p. xix)

In this manner, he proposed that a simple stimulus would be capable of producing coordinated activity in a network sufficient to embody much more complex concepts than could be instantiated in a single neuron. His argument was that this coordinated activity could produce a state of the network that could persist for prolonged periods after the original stimulus was gone. Such a process of sequentially triggering a chain of thoughts and memories is well known in psychology (e.g., in the priming process). Once again, however, keep in mind that this is an analogical argument about the way the brain must work. It is an inferred general principle, not the result of confirming empirical findings.

Hebb (1949) went on to propose that there was another level of coordination among the cell assemblies to which he referred as "phase sequences." The key idea expressed there was that each cell assembly could trigger another to produce a series of neurophysiological activations (the phase sequence) that collectively would be the psychoneural equivalent of a cognitive process leading to appropriate motor responses. As he put it:

> A series of such events constitutes a "phase sequence"—the thought process. (p. xix)

There is no equivocation here; to Hebb, the phase sequence was the stuff of the mind!

In light of the modern acceptance of the natural, material explanation of mind as a brain process and our current knowledge about the microanatomy of the central nervous system, Hebb had to be correct, in principle, about the general way that the nervous system instantiates mental activity. There is no question that experience produces some kind of a change, most likely expressed in physical growth of or change in some metabolic processes at the synapse. It seems logically uncontestable that neurons must act together to produce mental phenomena in some manner that is indistinguishable from the general Hebbian concepts of cell assemblies and phase sequences.

Unfortunately, in the splendid imagination of Donald Hebb also lies the germ of the difficulty that any neural network theory must contend. He was correct then, and we understand more deeply now, that the constraints applied by available mathematical and computational methods to the analysis of neural nets limit the range of psychological processes that can be examined. Mathematics breaks down rather quickly in its ability to handle the complex, nonlinear systems of which the three-dimensional array instantiated in the brain is a classic example. He was, perhaps, not so much aware a half century ago, that concepts like the cell assembly and phase sequence were so unconstrained and so unstructured that they could not in fact be tested—either mathematically or neurophysiologically—thus violating one of the premier criteria of a good theory. Although the general metaphor expressed by Hebb is likely to be far closer to psychobiological truth, it is, from another point of view, even further from testability and confirmation than a single neuron theory.

Nevertheless, the impact of Hebb's thinking, as revealed in his 1949 book has, been, without question, profound for all subsequent neural network theories. No computational or neural network theoretical expression since his time fails to include some aspect of his ideas on the dynamic change of synaptic efficiency as a result of experience. The notion of a cluster of interacting neurons, which he designated as a cell assembly, is also closely modeled in most modern theories of network activity.

Unfortunately, it was and continues to be difficult to go beyond Hebb's general ideas to more specific details in real brains. There are just too many neurons, too many unobservable situations, and too many synaptic connections to develop a neural network theory that is both specific enough and closely enough related to a cognitive process to be tested in the neuroscientific laboratory. Although the number of research articles implying that this is actually being done is large, all such contributions are characterized by unsubstantiated inferential leaps. Simply put, all such studies are confounded, constrained, and to a degree, incapacitated by the actual complexity of a realistically sized neural network.

The only possible alternative, therefore, has been to develop mathematical, computational, or simulation models of "toy systems" that bear a superficial resemblance to real neural or psychological observations. Often, such "toys" produce behavior that is comparable to human cognition. On close inspection, however, it always turns out that the formal mechanisms and algorithms used to implement the pseudo-cognitive process do little more than describe, analogize, or imitate cognition. The mechanisms they invoke to simulate a particular kind of behavior are, most likely, vastly different than those actually embodied in the organic brain, however close the functional analogy may turn out to be.

Clearly, the relation between neurophysiology and neuroanatomy and our thoughts is an incompletely described, incompletely determined, and ill-posed problem. Hebb's ideas, although influential, must, therefore, be considered to be speculative and ingenious, probably correct, but untestable. That caveat holds true for all other neural network theories that have been constructed between his time and the present.

6.5 ROSENBLATT AND THE PERCEPTRON

One way that scientists have of dealing with complex systems is to apply what are now called "Monte Carlo" techniques. Such methods are designed to handle problems involving such high levels of complexity or numerousness as to preclude any kind of an exact, deterministic solution. The *Monte Carlo* approach is based on the assumption that the values associated with components and values of a complex system can be approximated by a random distribution. Therefore, by assigning random values to the various parameters, allowing the system to run its course, and observing what it does, approximate solutions to problems that are otherwise mathematically intractable or computationally prohibitive can sometimes be obtained.

The next significant step in the historical development of neural network theories introduced this concept of randomness to the emerging neural network tradition. Rosenblatt (1958, 1962) wrote from the point of view of a critic of both the McCulloch and Pitts type of logical modeling and the unquantifiable psychobiological thinking implicit in the Hebbian approach. With regard to the former, he noted that no matter how refined the deterministic methods, they could never solve the problems of biology and psychology:

> The proponents of this line of approach have maintained that, once it has been shown how a physical system of any variety might be made to perceive and recognize stimuli, or perform any other brain like functions, it would require a refinement or modification of existing principles to understand the working of a more realistic nervous system . . . (Rosenblatt, 1958, p. 388)

To which he added:

> The writer [Rosenblatt] takes the position, on the other hand, that these shortcomings are such that a mere refinement or improvement of the [determinist] principles could never account for biological intelligence; a difference in principle is clearly indicated. (p. 388)

Rosenblatt then turned to consider the Hebbian position and those of the others who followed. He said:

> [T]he lack of an analytic language comparable in efficiency to the Boolean algebra of the network analysts has been one of the main obstacles. . . . The contributions of this group should perhaps be considered as suggestions of what to look for and investigate, rather than as finished theoretical systems in their own right. (p. 388)

From this perspective, Rosenblatt (1958) went on to propose a network model based on random values that has become the foundation for much of the theoretical developments that were to follow. His goal was to show how a mechanism could both store information gained through experience and how that stored information could exert an effect on subsequent activity.

The initial Rosenblatt perceptron model consisted of a three-dimensional lattice comprised of four stacked two-dimensional arrays of processing units—referred to as "cells" or "units" in his discussion. The most peripheral layer was a matrix of receptors that did nothing more than translate the spatial pattern of a stimulus form presented to a simulated retina into a mosaic of electrical signals. He defined the second two layers as association layers I and II, respectively.[8] The fourth layer was a set of response units,

---

[8]Rosenblatt suggests that association area I may not be necessary in all systems. This suggestion was to haunt the impact of his work since it was later shown by Minsky and Papert (1969) that a simple three-layer perceptron, among other configurations, was intrinsically incapable of solving even some relatively trivial problems.

the action of each particular one being determined by the pattern of activity in the two association layers. The task assigned to this model of a brain was to examine the input, train the system, and, by modifying the connectivity in the association layers, to associate a particular input pattern from the receptor layer with a particular output cell in the response layer.

In Rosenblatt's perceptron system, there were several novel innovations that went beyond both biological speculation and solvable mathematical formulation. First, particular points on the input array were not connected to spatially corresponding points in the association layers. Rather, units in the input array were randomly connected to units in the association layers.

Second, the connections between the second association layer and the response layers were bidirectional. That is, the signals traveled from the response units to association level II as well as from that association level to the response units.

Third, the retrograde or centrifugal signals from the response units had distinct effects on the association units depending on whether or not the association units were transmitting to the response units. If an association unit sent signals ahead to a response unit, then the response unit would return a signal that enhanced or excited that response unit. On the other hand, the response unit would send an inhibitory signal back to all of those association units that did not send signals to it.

This idea of sending signals back from the response units was, perhaps, the most important initial feature of the perceptron theory described by Rosenblatt (1962). It forms the basis of what was later to become a main theme of neural network research—error correction through backpropagation.[9] If the errors made by the response mechanisms were sent back to the association units, their weights or values could be adjusted to enhance the task at hand. A considerable amount of later work (as summarized by Werbos, 1988.[10]) was aimed at this problem by network theorists. In general, this process has come to be referred to as the *delta rule*, which asserts that the change in the weight of a synapse will be proportional to the difference between the current state of that synapse and the desired state (as determined by some predetermined criterion of the output).

Rosenblatt suggested that the "value" or strength of the connections between the association units and the response units should continuously be

---

[9]It has been pointed out to me by Alan Pavio that the idea of back propagation may have had an even earlier introduction. Although the word was not used by Hebb (1949), the concept was discussed as a major factor in his formation of cell assemblies.

[10]Werbos (1974) was among the first to formally implement a "backpropagation" method in his dissertation. However, the idea was a part of work as early as that of Rosenblatt and, as mentioned, implicit in Hebb's thinking.

adjusted by means of this specialized feedback or *backpropagation* system. He tried a number of different algorithms that could adjust the values of the connections between the association and response units. As the system experienced new input patterns at the receptor layer, the effect would be to associate each input pattern with a particular response unit.

The backpropagation system was supposed to work spontaneously and automatically in Rosenblatt's scheme. There was an initial pre-learning or "pre-dominant" (Rosenblatt, 1958, p. 392) phase in which the input pattern produced some ill-defined activity in the association layers but did not activate particular response units. Then, after a period in which the response units randomly began to fire, specific connections were made between a given stimulus pattern and a particular response unit as guided by the feedback rules. The process was to presumably continue until it achieved a "post-dominant" phase (p. 392) in which each response unit was "tuned" not only to a specific input pattern, but, less strongly, to a set of similar patterns This ability to respond preferentially to similar but not identical inputs, according to Rosenblatt, simulated the powerful human cognitive process of stimulus generalization.

In addition to generalization, Rosenblatt also believed that his computational model simulated other aspects of the observed psychological processes of human perception. The following list, paraphrased from his conclusions summarizes the outcome of the computer experiments that he carried out to test the model.

1. A network of randomly connected units can learn to make specific associations between stimuli and responses. Trial and error learning is possible to a certain degree in a multilayer system of this kind.

2. However, randomness is not a cure all. The system works better with connections that had some order to them.

3. Depending on the type of connections proposed and the nature of the stimulus classes, a system may either increase or decrease the probability of a correct response as the number of input stimuli increases. (In general, however, the larger the number of stimuli, the poorer the performance, beyond some point of diminishing returns.)

4. A major factor in determining the behavior of the system is the statistical separability of the stimuli. Only a set of linearly separable stimulus patterns can be discriminated by a simple system such as a perceptron.

5. The more units available, the better that system performs. However, adding more units increase the computational load and eventually one encounters the scaling problem (see p. 234).

6. Temporal patterns can also be simulated by a perceptron using only a modest extension of the proposed system.

7. The storage of information in this system (memory) is distributed. That is, no single connection matters; rather the overall, distributed pattern of the strengths of the connections determines what information is stored. Thus, a perceptron is relatively insensitive to the destruction of some modest number of the units in multiple layers.

(Paraphrased from Rosenblatt, 1958, p. 405)

However, there were many practical problems encountered in Rosenblatt's early experiments. His data also showed that in many cases the learning process deteriorated, rather than converged on a stable solution as the number of trials (as well as the number of input stimuli) in the experimental runs increased. This deterioration in performance was due to the fact that some of the "synaptic" weights assigned to some connections became so large that they swamped out the effect of others.

Rosenblatt was well aware of the limitations of his perceptron theory from the outset. Others were quick to point out that the original perceptron idea was incapable of generalization to other kinds of problems than the ones he had originally proposed. Nevertheless, his accomplishment was the first quantitative neural network model that actually was evaluated in terms of specific physical parameters such as the number of units, the strength of connections, and the interconnectivity pattern. It differed greatly, he noted, from the descriptive mathematical theories of learning that had been popular up to that time. It also differed from the physiological "concepts" of Hebb and the conceptual neural net of McCulloch and Pitts in that it was tested by simulation and computation. Herein, lay what many consider to be Rosenblatt's most important contribution–his was the first model actually to be tested. The experiences, both the successes and failures he encountered set the stage for virtually all future research in this field of neural network theory.

Rosenblatt was clearly aware that future neural network models would eventually fall victim to their own complexity as attempts were made to scale them up to realistic numbers of simulated neurons. In the years that followed it became increasingly clear that some superficially simple problems existed that could not be solved by neural networks.[11] The demon-

[11]One of the simplest problems that a classic perceptron could not solve was the "exclusive or," an example of a problem that is not linearly separable. (Exclusive OR Boolean functions are those that are true when either one of the inputs are true but not both.) A linearly separable problem is one that does not have any overlap in the classification space; the two regions of classification can be separated from each other by an appropriately directed straight line. Even some simple problems are not so separable and, thus, are intractable tasks for a simple perceptron. More complicated perceptrons can in some cases, however, solve such problems by adding additional intervening association layers.

strated limits of the early formulations of relatively simple neural networks (Block, 1962; Minsky & Papert, 1969) led to a hiatus in this kind of research. Ultimately, there was resurgence in thinking about neural nets. Some critics, however, would be so bold as to suggest that the new wave of activity in this field made only modest further conceptual innovations. None of this diminishes the contribution made by Rosenblatt. He was the first to carry out specific experiments on a neural network and also the first to appreciate some of the problems that would ultimately emerge with this popular and ubiquitous kind of theorizing about how the brain generates mental processes.

6.6 THE NEXT GENERATION OF NEURAL NETWORK THEORETICIANS

McCulloch, Pitts, and Hebb's ideas not only influenced the fertile mind of Rosenblatt but also stimulated a number of others who added to what became a crescendo of neural network theories. However, a schism continues to this day. On the one hand are the cognitive neuroscientists seeking an answer to the psychobiological mind–brain problem; on the other are information scientists and engineers whose interests were practical rather than psychobiological. In fact, the emerging awareness of the limits of the neural network method has led to what arguably is an understandable diminishment in the purely psychobiological goals. The main corpus of work today is to be found in the enormous amount of reasonably successful work simply intended to carry out some practical task or in the formal studies of the computational properties of these "neural" networks. Thus, the neural network concept played a seminal role in Artificial Intelligence (AI) by providing the metaphor of a real parallel and distributed system (i.e., the brain) that was clearly capable of prodigious cognitive problem solving.

Although some skeptic may argue that it is unnecessarily contentious even to suggest the following, neural network approaches to theorizing about the mind seem to be much less frequent nowadays than only a few years ago. My readers are directed to the discussion of "nonneural" network theories later in this chapter (see p. 224) to justify what I am sure will be a vigorously disputed opinion.

Thus, the engineers cum AI researchers went off on their own. When it became clear that there were fundamental barriers to reproducing cognitive processes with the simple neural networks that could be analyzed, other nonbiological metaphors began to dominate AI work. Special computer languages (e.g., Lisp as developed by McCarthy and his group in the late 1950s) that bore no resemblance to neural nets but simulated conceptual similarity in cognition by propinquity in list structures emerged as popular models of the mind. Other programs used conventional mathematics or computational algorithms to imitate game-playing behavior such as chess, mathematical proof solving, or even psychotherapy. Most of these theoretical efforts, however, are less implementations of neural networks than they are clever conventional programming efforts.

In general, therefore, there has been a reduction in the original hope that computers could produce behavior on the basis of neural networks in a biologically realistic manner. Computers could be made to imitate human cognitive processes, but by vastly different rules and logics than those originally proposed by the neural network pioneers.[12] The AI engineer's goal was to build machines that would serve some useful function but not necessarily in the same way the organic brain does. Practical robots and the computer skills necessary to control came to dominate the AI world sometimes to the exclusion of the search for the fundamental theories of mind that had originally stimulated neural network theories. Furthermore, above and beyond the difficulty of constructing computer versions of realistic neural nets, it also became clear that the necessary neurophysiological information required for a meaningful simulation was not only not currently available but was not likely to become available in the foreseeable future–if ever.

6.6.1 Selfridge's Pandemonium

Although Rosenblatt was the first[13] to actually carry out computations of his model, other scientists were already becoming concerned about some of the same issues. Selfridge (1958), for example, presented a speculative article about how learning might occur in a multilayered network that had many similarities to Rosenblatt's perceptron. The main goal of Selfridge's system was to learn a means of recognizing patterns by an automatic (i.e., not guided by the external experimenter) adaptive process.

[12]The computational algorithms currently used in computer chess machines, for example, are improving every year. However, all still work in part by an exhaustive analysis of future moves and not by the subtle pattern recognition procedures based on neural net activities it is believed that humans use. Even then, the analysis cannot be fully exhaustive for simple combinatorial reasons and must be truncated by simple decision criteria. To do otherwise, would lead to never-ending analyses.

[13]Rosenblatt's (1958) article in the journal *Psychological Review* was a detailed and moderately complete analysis of the problems posed in neural net simulations. It involved computer analysis as well as the construction of a special purpose machine to simulate the perceptron. Considerable preliminary work preceded the publication of this article. Selfridge's (1958) work, although indisputatively ingenious and significant, did not involve such an extensive analysis, nor a concomitant simulation experiment.

Selfridge's theoretical model proposed a regular (i.e., nonrandom) array of four levels—a receptor level, a computational level, a cognitive level, and a decision level. The receptor level performed the same task as the one in Rosenblatt's model. At the computational level of Selfridge's model there were units that were sensitive to particular geometrical features of the input pattern. These computational units sent signals to the cognitive units that evaluated the relative strength of the feature detecting computational units. Finally, at the top level, decision level units determined which one of the cognitive units had the strongest output signal and, thus, which response unit was appropriate to be assigned to a given input pattern. The application that Selfridge used to exemplify the function of this method was the printed alphabet. An entire character was acquired by the image level; its features (e.g., horizontal, vertical, or oblique lines) were separately acquired by specialized units of the second level; the third level units evaluated the relative amount of activity from combinations of the group of feature sensitive units; and the decision units responded to the highest amount of activity and selected the appropriate character.

Selfridge (1958) personified ("anthropomorphized" or "biopmorphized," in his terminology) his model by drawing attention to the fact that its function was based on which of the units at the various levels was "shouting the loudest." The entire array of units was analogized as a system of "demons" whose collective "shouting" would sound like a "Pandemonium"—the name he gave to his system. Only the loudest—the most active—would be singled out to be heard above the "clamor." It was this collective *clamor* that Selfridge proposed to use as the core concept of the method by which this type of machine might automatically learn to improve its recognition skills.

The key to learning how to improve Pandemonium's function lay in the behavior of the cognitive units. Their output was the sum of the outputs of all the units that fed into them, each of which was multiplied by a weighting function. The task in the learning process was to adjust these weighting functions to an optimum set. Selfridge's (1958) proposal to make this adjustment was to arbitrarily try a number of randomly selected sets of weighting functions and see which worked the best—a randomized hill climbing process. Then, using the new values of the weighting functions, iterate the process until the selection process converged on a best final set.

Selfridge's work was an important conceptual step forward, but a reexamination of it from the perspective we have today suggests his alternative version of a neural network model cannot deal with networks of the complexity of those encountered in the brain any more than could the perceptron. As the number of units increased, the problem of trying a random number of combinations would increase exponentially. The relatively minor problems involved in any hill climbing procedure involving a small number of units would be quickly swamped out by the sheer number of interactions between the various levels in a realistically sized network. In retrospect, we must look back upon Pandemonium as an interesting intellectual exercise, but not one that was any more promising than any other contemporary neural network theory.

6.6.2 Other Learning Algorithms

Problems with the perceptron and Pandemonium quickly became evident. Although they might work in ideal, highly reduced situations, in practice the amount of computation and time it took for them to converge on an ideal set of weights for the interconnections would quickly become astronomical as the number of involved units increased. Indeed, this is a classic admonition that is all too often ignored by purveyors of AI systems such as face recognition systems. What works in the lab with a few faces, quickly succumbs to false positives or missed recognitions when applied in the field to the realistic number of faces that would be encountered in, for example, an airport. No such system has yet been shown to work in a practical, real-world environment.

A number of efforts were proposed in the following years that sought to overcome the combinatorial numerousness or complexity handicap by accelerating the rules for converging on the best set of weights. Nevertheless, the Hebbian principle—learning by changing effective weights of the inputs to the simulated neurons as a result of activation experience—continues to exert a strong influence on neural network theorizing. Many recent attempts to develop neural network theories have been aimed at the elusive goal of developing an automatic self-organizing or self-tutoring learning system. A few of the most prominent examples are now briefly discussed.

Widrow and Huff. Widrow and Huff (1960) proposed to speed up the learning process by giving the simulated network examples of the correct answers. This was one of the first applications of "reinforcement" feedback (a common technique in behavioral laboratories) to error correction, in what was to become a main theme as the neural network field continued to develop. Widrow and Huff's implementation of an adaptive system was, however, based on a manually adjusted simulated neuron. Their model was not, therefore, an automatic learning system. Rather, it was one in which the training was "supervised" by an external agent—the experimenter. The notion of supervised error correction, implicit in most neural network theories since Rosenblatt's, remains a central theme of current research. The ideal, of course, is to simulate an entirely unsupervised and automatic error correction system that leads to the desired organization of the neural network as a result of repeated stimulation in imitation of human learning.

Von der Malsburg. In an effort to solve a fundamental difficulty of the early neural network models, Von der Malsburg (1973) also implemented Hebb's principle, but in a novel way. Up to this time, most of these adaptive learning models had permitted the strength or weight of the simulated synaptic connections to increase without bound. This property led to some of the problems that Rosenblatt had discovered, in particular the deterioration of performance as the number of trials increased. Von der Malsburg's solution was to introduce the concept of *synaptic weight saturation*, thus putting a cap on the value of any particular connecting link. He stated his saturation-modified learning principle as follows:

> If there is coincidence of activity in an afferent fiber I and a cortical E-cell K, then s_{IK}, the strength of the connection between the two, is increased to $s_{IK} + \Delta s$, Δs being proportional to the signal on the afferent fiber I and to the output signal of the E-cell K. Then all of the s_{JK} leading to the same cortical cell K are renormalized to keep the sum $\sum_J s_{JK}$ constant. (p. 88)

The first step is this process is nothing more than another expression of the delta rule—a change gauged by the difference between the actual and desired values. The second step, the renormalization, is necessary to avoid neural saturation according to von der Malsburg: saturation reflecting a maximum physical size for a synapse or the exhaustion of receiving space, sites, or molecules on the postsynaptic neuron.

Kohonen. Pioneering efforts in face recognition using neural network theories were carried out by Kohonen (1977). In his book, Kohonen describes a simple one-layer lattice that is supplied with a pattern of feedback signals from each of the cells on to all of the others in the horizontal lattice of which it is a part. This is expressed as:

$$\boldsymbol{O}_i = \boldsymbol{I}_i + \sum_j \mu_{ij} \boldsymbol{n}_j \qquad 6.1$$

where $\boldsymbol{O}_i$ is the output of the **i**th cell in the lattice, $\boldsymbol{I}_i$ is the input to the **i**th cell, μ_{ij} is the strength of the connection from cell **j** to cell **I**, and $\boldsymbol{n}_j$ is the output of the **j**th cell.

The key Hebbian aspect of this model was its ability to change the strength of the connections between the constituent neurons as a result of its experience. Kohonen simulated this dynamic property by calculating the rate of change of the strength of the connections, in accord with the following rule:

$$\frac{d}{dt}\mu_{ij} = \alpha \boldsymbol{n}_i(\boldsymbol{n}_j - \boldsymbol{n}_{jb}) \qquad 6.2$$

where n_{jb} (the only new term) is a threshold beyond which n_j does not produce any change in μ_{ij}. This also tends to constrain the explosive growth of the weight of the synaptic junction and, thus, avoid saturation. Equation 6.1 was then evaluated by an iterative process assuming an initial condition in which all μ_{ij}, the strengths of the connections, were zero.

Kohonen's (1977) computer simulation consisted of 510 "neurons." Six hundred and forty connections were randomly selected from among the possible connections between the simulated neurons. The system was tested by "teaching" the system the proper responses to a training set of 100 face images. After this training, the system was able to determine which of these images was represented by a partial stimulus such as a half of one of the previously experienced faces. The association was based on determining the highest correlation between members of the training set and the partial face. In this manner, Kohonen believed that he was modeling a process analogous to associative recall.

Although the model did work reasonably well in this limited universe of face stimuli, it quickly became clear that it was a poor imitation of the human ability to recognize complex forms. Kohonen (1977) himself alluded to these limitations when he said:

> Currently, it appears impossible to model any significantly more complex neuronal system in all of its details. (p. 150)

Nevertheless, Kohonen's theory of "associative recall" had a number of important features. First, its use of a random set of interconnections (similar in concept to the original Rosenblatt suggestion) helped to overcome the rigidity, limits, and computational demands of a strictly regular network. Second, it embodied a primitive kind of self-organization as the system stepped through the iterative evaluation of Equation 6.1. Third, as the parameter weights of the system evolved through experience, it did not reproduce the input pattern in a simple isomorphic form. That is, the activity pattern of the simulated neurons could be arranged in various ways other than one that was retinotopically identical to the original stimulus. Fourth, there is an element of automated learning or self-organization in this model. The achievement of even this primitive form of automatic learning drastically reduced the need for experimenter supervised learning. Fifth, Kohonen demonstrated that at least a primitive form of generalization and associative recall were possible in systems as simple as the one he had implemented.

Amari. Another important step in automating the learning process in accord with Hebb's rule was provided by Amari (1977). He also noted a counterintuitive result comparable to the saturation effect wrestled with by von der Malsburg. In many kinds of neural networks, the simulated memory (i.e., the network state that solved the problem) tended to fade with the number of iterations and not remain permanently inscribed in the neural network. In other words, the system not only failed to improve but also degraded as a result of too many trials. This phenomenon was also due to the unconstrained growth of some of the interconnecting weights of the simulated synaptic weights over the course of the operation of the network. Amari introduced another significant idea to overcome this degradation—temporal forgetting—into the theoretical expressions. The effect of this technique, like that of von der Malsburg's renormalization, is to counterbalance experience-based saturation. That is, by introducing an automatic and progressive diminution in synaptic strength with the passage of time, the problem of unconstrained growth could be reduced and a limit placed on synaptic weight. This is an extremely interesting idea from the point of view of psychological science. It suggests that forgetting is not just a progressive failure of the brain's function. Rather, it is necessary for the acquisition and retention of new information.

Fukushima and Miyake. The backward propagation of information from higher levels to lower levels was also a central feature of the work of Fukushima and Miyake (1978). Unlike the prototypical effort of Selfridge, their work did not involve any local feature analysis nor did it require a decision about which of a set of responders had to be chosen on the basis of the input signals. Indeed, Fukushima and Miyake made a remarkable, though not generally appreciated, step forward. Early versions of their systems were designed to produce a particular overall pattern of activity for each input stimulus, not a particular localized output response of the kind sought by Rosenblatt and Selfridge. To the best of my knowledge this was the first instance in which the *overall global state* of the simulated neural network was considered to be the end product of the executed computations rather than the selection of a specific output pattern!

Fukushima and Miyake's neural network model shared with some of Kohonen's simulations what was essentially a symbolic means of encoding stimulus forms. The overall pattern of responses in the simulated array of neurons need have no discernable spatial relation to the input stimulus. Rather, it was a new pattern that automatically responded to translated, distorted, or incomplete versions of the original stimuli on which the system was trained. Generalization is, thereby, imitated. However, most important was their suggestion that the overall state of the neural network was the essential factor as opposed to what may better be considered to an unnecessary selection of a particular response unit. This, it may be noted, is equivalent to exorcizing the homunculus from their model. No longer was it necessary to evaluate the state of the system to generate a local output response; the state itself was the solution to the recognition problem.

The importance of this suggestion cannot be underestimated. The overall neural network state has the possibility of representing a very large amount of information in much the same way that a computer register can encode many more numbers than there are available bits. The potential information content of a set of singular "output units" is much less than that possible with an array of simultaneously evaluated units. Considering the number of neurons available to the brain, the number of and complexity of such encoded "concepts" can be very large. Unfortunately, at the same time, the possibility of its analyzability and explanatory reduction becomes increasingly remote.

Fukushima and Miyake's theoretical approach, therefore, is constrained by its own difficulties. The challenging question remains: How do investigators capture the nature of that multineuronal state other than by an exhaustive tabulation of the condition of each participating neuron? One way would be to use such psychological measures (e.g., perception, emotion, etc.) in a way that is analogous to the use of "pressure" and "volume" in gas dynamics. However, such an approach negates any hope of solving the mind–body problem in a neuroreductionist way; no measurable subset of the involved neurons could adequately represent the state of the entire system. It seems clear that many of the strategies implemented by neural network theorists (e.g., the postulation of a layer of response units) are efforts to finesse this essential combinatorial handicap.

Although Fukushima and Miyake's (1978) model, like all others, eventually ran into problems as the number of simulated neurons increased, they raised an extremely important conceptual point in this early paper. Biologically, their suggestion is extremely interesting, however discouraging it may be for neural network theory building. It is interesting because it suggests a highly plausible way in which the nervous system might work to produce our thought processes simply by means of adaptive and heavily encoded processes that lead to an overall, yet still discrete, pattern of brain activity. It is discouraging because it reminds us that a detailed neuron-by-neuron examination of such a distributed state is not likely to be realizable.

Hopfield. Hopfield (1982, 1984) also picked up on the suggestion from Rosenblatt that both afferent (inward going) and efferent (feedback signals) were important in determining the behavior of a neural network. However, he (Hopfield, 1982) pointed to an important caveat about feedback; introduction of this essentially nonlinear process drastically complicates the problem mathematically. Indeed, the addition of feedback almost certainly exceeds the capacity of any conventional perceptron to converge or "solve" the problem for which it was designed.

Nevertheless, feedback or backpropagation is a realistic and expected property of biological neural nets. Therefore, Hopfield built this feature into his theories in the form of a level of simulated neurons that had both inhibitory and excitatory inputs from either the receptor layer or from higher level neurons. The first of his two papers (Hopfield, 1982) modeled the system with two-state neurons; the second (Hopfield, 1984) did so with simulated synaptic weight values that could be continuous, thus adding to the realism of his theory.

In addition to the emphasis on backpropagation, Hopfield (1984) also elaborated on the critical idea of a state space as originally suggested by Fukushima and Miyake (1978). Specifically, he suggested the use of the concept of a continuous energy field to represent the overall state of the system. He, thus, introduced the techniques of energy minimization that have proven to be so useful in physics into neural network theory. Physicists had long used specialized mathematics to solve very difficult problems by seeking solutions that minimized the internal stress of a structure—a structure that could be either a steel bridge or a network of neurons—the neutral mathematics would work equally well for both systems. The *calculus of variations* is the general term for these minimization procedures; specific examples include *Hamilton's principle.*

Hopfield allowed each of his simulated neurons to change its effective value by checking on its set of inputs in what was essentially an irregular or random schedule. This incorporated the Monte Carlo idea originally suggested by Rosenblatt. Each neuron changed its value depending on whether or not it exceeded a threshold difference between the last and current value. This change would affect all others to which it was connected. Thus, there was a continuous readjustment of the overall state of the system in which the distributed pattern of interneuronal connection values modeled the system's distributed energy. The system was designed by Hopfield to minimize the overall system "energy," that is, the sum total of the differences between the values of all of the neurons. The "solution" to the problem proposed by the neural network with a specific pattern of input stimuli was the development a minimum energy surface representing the most stable equilibrium state of the system, not the selection of a single response output.

Hopfield's models, although making a major contribution by suggesting that the behavior of a neural network could be simulated by a continuous energy field, did have a major deficiency. That deficiency was that once having found a point at which the energy of the system was at a minimum, there was no way to determine if an even lower energy level would have been found if the calculation had continued. Although this *false minimum* problem was severe, as we see momentarily, it could be overcome by other mathematical methods.

The introduction by Hopfield of the concept of an energy minimization as a result of interactions between neurons broadly distributed across a discrete or continuous surface was to play an increasingly important role in later research. Several methods proposed to further develop this approach and to overcome the false minimum problem are now considered.

Kirkpatrick, Gelatt, and Vecchi.[14] Following the development of Hopfield's ideas (in which energy functions were minimized), there was a transition from discrete "neural network" models to ones that used the same mathematics as that describing how glass or metal cooled. *Simulated annealing*, for example, originally proposed by Kirkpatrick, Gelatt, and Vecchi (1983), is a straightforward application to neural network theories of the classic idea that an agitated surface cools to a final, stable state in a way that is dependent on the cooling rate and the nature of the material. The key idea is that high energy or "hot" locations will give up energy in a systematic way to low energy or "cool" locations. In a simulated annealing program, the probability of altering the strength of an internodal connection is a joint function of the input to that node and the simulated "temperature"—a variable indicative of the activity of the system at that point. As the "temperature" is lowered, the system tends to converge on an equilibrium state representing a minimum energy distribution or lowest stress level within the system. This relationship can be represented by the expression:

$$P = \frac{1}{1+e^{-\frac{I}{T}}} \qquad 6.3$$

where P is the probability that a connection to a node changes, I is the input to the node, and T is the simulated temperature (i.e., energy or activity level). As T declines, the probability of changing the strength of a connection is reduced, and the system settles down into what it is hoped is a stable final state determined by the goal of minimizing internal stresses.

Since P is a stochastic term, the final outcome of the annealing process is not entirely predetermined. Here, therefore, is one solution to the challenge raised by Hopfield's false minimum problem. The random factor built into this formulation permits the system state to occasionally move (i.e., jump) out of that false minimum. The probability, therefore, is increased that it will ultimately arrive at the true minimum.

A key idea inherent in the simulated annealing approach is, therefore, the introduction of stochastic (i.e., random) factors into the energy mini-

[14]Some of the discussions in this section and the next sections on Hinton and Sejnowski are abstracted and updated from a similar discussion in Uttal (2002). Fuller details of these two important developments in neural network theory can be found there and in the original publications.

mization analysis, an idea that had been ubiquitous since Rosenblatt's time. However, probabilistic algorithms require much more processing than do deterministic systems. This tends to make such models operate relatively slowly.

Hinton and Sejnowski. Another closely related method incorporating stochastic ideas that has recently enjoyed enthusiastic support in the neural network community is one based on the "Boltzmann machine"—a modification of the annealing technique. The Boltzmann machine concept, originally proposed by Hinton and Sejnowski (1986), is based on the analogy between a "hot" thermodynamic system moving toward a final equilibrium "cold" state by an energy minimization process, on the one hand, and the activity of a neural network, on the other.

The central mathematical idea in the Boltzmann model is the same as that underlying the statistical analysis of gases. Although a high degree of variability in the energy of each particle in the system characterizes the initial state of the system, there is a tendency for the system to settle down into a stable state in which the energy is much more evenly distributed (i.e., in which the internal stresses are minimized). The foundation assumption is that high-energy particles give up energy to the low-energy particles and this transfer provides a force driving the system toward a final stable state.

Like the simulated annealing method, the Boltzmann machine concept incorporates probability principles (specifically the Boltzmann probability distribution) that allow it in many cases to solve network problems that would confound a deterministic system. The probabilistically controlled sequence of states through which the system progresses is not predetermined, but can vary randomly. Such a system is also much less likely to become "stuck" in some erroneous intermediate state such as a false minimum. The Boltzmann probability distribution is defined as an exponential function in the following way:

$$P(S) = Ke^{\frac{-E_s}{BT}} \qquad 6.4$$

where $P(S)$ is the probability of finding a component of a multi-component system in a state S; K is a constant; $-E_s$ is the negative of the energy of the energy of the State S; T is the temperature; and B is the Boltzmann constant—1.3806503 x 10^{-23} Joules per degree Kelvin.

A major benefit arising from the statistical distribution of the original Boltzmann approach was that it allowed physicists to describe the macroscopic behavior of a system of microscopic elements without paying attention to the idiosyncratic behavior of the individual components that make up the system. The hope was that these same stochastic principles could be used to describe the macroscopic behavior of a system like the organic brain without resorting to an exhaustive determination of the behavior of each neuron.

However, there is a major difference between these probabilistic energy minimization models and the brain. The energy state theories are not, in fact, of the same genre as the original neural networks proposed by McCulloch and Pitts or Rosenblatt; those early theories literally dealt with discrete units. Rather, they are similar to the gas laws that seek to describe complex systems by integrated measures. There is a real difference, therefore, between the relatively simple continuous interactions of a molecule in a gas or in a cooling piece of glass, on the one hand, and the true functional discreteness of the neurons in the brain. By seeking mathematical simplicity, the newer methods may have moved backwards from the goal of understanding the neural network to a situation in which the applied mathematics are no more analytic than the molar descriptions of human cognitive processes typical of psychological theorizing.

6.7 A NONNEURAL "NETWORK" THEORY—CONNECTIONISM

In the previous section, I review a history that was strongly dominated by the assumption that the neural network of the brain could be modeled and studied in the form of reduced networks of entities that intentionally simulated the properties of real neurons and their myriad synaptic interconnections. This brief history indicates a progressive realization that the computational and mathematical requirements of such an approach might exhaust any plausible tools and introduce ever more remote approximations from neurobiological reality. The larger the number of input stimuli, in general, the less effective were these pioneering theories of one aspect or another of cognition.

As the evolution of ideas in this domain progressed, there has been an implicit retreat from the original hope that a true discrete *neuronal* network model could ever fully simulate even a constrained example of human recognition, learning, or any other cognitive process. As one reviews this history, it becomes increasingly clear that the mathematics of a system such as the brain might be, in fundamental principle, intractable. The inventions of the simulated annealing and Boltzmann machine techniques were expressions of an emerging realization that a network of discrete neuron-like nodes might never be analyzed in terms of individual neurons and specific connections. The organizational complexity of the neural networks, not to mention the huge number of involved components, posed what appeared to be insurmountable barriers to either simulated or analytic solutions. The introduction of these methods, which after all were originally designed to deal with continuous surfaces, partially overcame these conceptual barriers.

However, the network idea was still extremely influential and other lines of research in which the basic idea of a formal model of a network of nodes was preserved emerged from this frustration. The details of the approach, however, had to change in some quite remarkable ways to preserve this strategy. From the perspective of this new approach, the nodes and elements of classic neural network theory came to mean something entirely different than the original idea of imitation neurons suggested by McCulloch and Pitts (1943).

In the following section, a major development in network thinking is discussed that I regard as no longer "neural" in the classic theoretical sense. Rather, mathematical models of networks are invoked that do not depend on the biological roots shared with the explicitly neural theories of the past. To the contrary, the nodes of these new network theories are often the traditional modules and faculties of psychological science.

It is not usual that the specific origins of a new paradigm in science can be identified and isolated to a particular event. However, modern *connectionism* dates exactly from the publication of two of the most influential books in the history of scientific psychology (Rumelhart, McClelland, and The PDP Research Group, 1988, hereafter referred to as Volume 1; and McClelland, Rumelhart, and The PDP Research Group, 1988, hereafter referred to as Volume 2). This two-volume set broke upon the psychological scene with an enormous impact.

Connectionism introduced a kind of thinking that was timely and useful to a cognitive psychological community that was becoming increasingly disenchanted with the preexisting computer metaphor and aware of the limits of theories based on more explicit neural networks. The complexities of behavior simply did not seem to be able to be modeled either by the standard von Neumann computer or by the McCulloch and Pitts logical networks. Furthermore, the older neural network models were increasingly running up against the problem of mathematical intractability; the formal problems (as opposed to the verbal metaphors and analogies) posed by these theories simply could not be solved.[15]

[15]The word "solved" in this context can take on several different meanings. Some mathematical problems were simply so ill posed that they did not in principle contain sufficient information to be solved. Others were unsolvable because they required so many computational steps that they were in practice unsolvable. Even others were mathematically so difficult, typically involving complex and nonlinear feedback mechanisms, that normal mathematics was not able to solve them. In other cases, the solution was supposed to be a stable state onto which the model was supposed to converge. Some systems, did not converge, or converged for a while and then diverged. In short, intractability comes in many guises; all neural net models are subject to one or the other forms of computational intractability.

One of the most comprehensive statements of the attractiveness of what was to be called connectionism was offered by Fodor and Pylyshyn (1988). They listed some of the major reasons that parallel-distributed connectionism was considered to be superior to the conventional cognitive computer theory based on the serial von Neumann computer. Among the most notable reasons for the transition they highlighted were:

1. Cognitive process are so fast and neurons so slow that some kind of parallel organization of the brain is required.
2. Pattern recognition has not worked in conventional computers; therefore, some kind alternative (i.e., parallel) processing is necessary.
3. Conventional computers do not handle "exceptional" behavior well. They do so by adding special rules to the usual rules for each idiosyncratic instance. Connectionist networks seem to offer an opportunity to handle both the usual and the unusual better by a single theory.
4. Conventional computer systems cannot handle nonverbal or intuitive processes.
5. Conventional computer models are drastically affected by damage and noise: They do not degrade gracefully.
6. Memory in conventional computers is totally passive and does not change with experience.
7. Conventional computer-based theories are rigid and deterministic rule followers that cannot account for human behavior with all of its randomness and uncertainty.
8. Finally, conventional computer models overemphasize characteristics of the computer rather than those of the biological and behavioral systems.
   (Abstracted from Fodor & Pylyshyn, 1988, pp. 51–53)

Into this mélange of seductive attractions and failures of the older conventional computer approach to models of the mind came something that was at once familiar and novel. Rumelhart, McClelland, and their colleagues had been well aware of the previous developments in neural network modeling. In fact, in Volume I on pages 41 and 42,[16] they provide a minihistory that includes many of the same contributors I have already described in this chapter.[17] Modern texts in the neural network field (e.g., Anderson 1995;

---

[16]Citations from Volume 1 and Volume 2 are referred to by their respective page numbers in each book as required. It should be remembered, however, that each of the many chapters in both volumes was written by a different set of authors.

[17]They suggested there that the first modern use of the word "connectionism" should be attributed to Feldman and Ballard (1982). The word, of course, had a much longer history being a part of James (1890) and Thorndike's (1913) psychological principles expressed much earlier,

Levine, 2000) also exhibit this same vestigial residue acknowledging the historical origins of neural network theory. In fact, this supplementary material is largely irrelevant to their otherwise quite informative discussion of the mathematical methods used in connectionist theory.

However, after a tip of the hat to the neurophysiological origins (comparable to Hippocrates' and Descartes' courtesies to their respective Gods) a close inspection suggests that, in fact, the founders of connectionism appropriated only one major idea from the biology of the brain. That was the general idea of a parallel and distributed network of interconnected nodes. In other words, in concert with the older neurophysiologically inspired neural network theories, their most general and prototypical model was considered to be a three dimensional lattice—layers of receptor units feeding into layers of processing units which subsequently fed into higher response layers. The processing executed by the connectionist network, like that of the original neurally inspired network theories, was not carried out at a single point in this lattice; instead it was the joint result of actions carried out in many places (i.e., in a parallel and distributed fashion).

The major idea introduced by the new connectionist tradition was that the nodes were no longer intended to model or represent synthetic neurons per se; rather the nodes could themselves represent microcognitive elements, each of which could represent processes far more complex than those likely to be carried out by a single neuron. Thus, it was the idea of distributed information processing rather than the idea that these elements of this essentially parallel distributed processing (PDP) units were real or approximations to biological neurons that characterized this new endeavor.

Rumelhart, McClelland, and their colleague's major contribution, therefore, was actually to de-physiologize neural network theory. They transformed "neuronal" networks into "cognitive" networks. I argue here that connectionism was and still is an essentially psychological theory—one with its distributed and parallel processing roots in the distant physiological past but one that shed those origins as it evolved into a molar psychological approach.

In Volume 1, Rumelhart, McClelland, and their colleagues laid out the properties that a parallel, distributed processor must have. It is interesting to note that none of these properties make any reference to biological neurons per se. According to them, a PDP system must consist of:

- A set of processing units
- A state of activation

---

albeit with a different meaning. It is interesting to speculate that the scene may have been set for modern connectionism by the persisting influence of the concept, if not the word.

- An output function for each unit
- A pattern of connectivity among units
- A propagation rule for propagating patterns of activities through the network of connectivities
- An activation rule for combining the inputs impinging on a unit with the current state of that unit to produce a new levels of activation for the units
- A learning rule whereby patterns of connectivity are modified by experience
- An environment within which the system must operate.

(p. 46)

Although this set of properties subsumes truly neural nets, it by no means requires that "process units" be neurons or even chunks of the brain. Rather, the core of connectionism is parallelicity and this can include intangible ideas as well. In shedding the biological or neurophysiological constraints or properties and dealing with cognitive modules as nodes, they transformed *neural network* theory into a *cognitive network* (i.e., psychological) theory with all of the epistemological problems about mental accessibility and analysis that such an approach entails. Although the mathematics may have been the same or related, this was a profoundly different approach than the one McCulloch and Pitts had originally conceived.

Contemporary cognitive scholars may dispute this interpretation—the de-physiologizing of neural network theory by the connectionists. However, a close inspection of the topics and approaches presented in Volumes 1 and 2, makes it clear that the book is concerned more with discussions of relevant mathematics (e.g., linear algebra on p. 365 of Volume 1) and with psychological problems (e.g., language processing and learning) than with the simulation of truly neural networks. Even those chapters in the sections dealing with "Biological Mechanisms" are recapitulations of standard neurophysiology or discussions of methods that might be useful to study them (see Vol. 2). It is infrequent throughout the two volumes that the so-called constraints of neurophysiology are invoked by any of the connectionist theoreticians. Rather, most of the models are presented at a higher level of abstraction, one of interaction of cognitive modules, not neural ones. Neurophysiology peers over the shoulders of the players, but does not participate in the new game.

The biological sections of these important two volumes are presented mainly as an expression of the prevailing monistic ontology—the neuron doctrine—that the mind is entirely explicable (in principle) as a product or function of the brain. Beyond that ontological expression (with which I totally agree), it is difficult to find any theoretical bridge between the general connectionist approach and the physiological material presented in the fifth part of Volume 2.

McClelland and Rumelhart, themselves, expressed the disconnect between connectionism and neurophysiology in several excerpts from their introduction to Part 5 of Volume 2:

> All [PDP theories] share in common that they are "neurally inspired" models and are explorations of "brain style" processing. (p. 328)

and

> Other PDP models . . . attempt more directly to build accounts of human information processing capabilities, at a level of abstraction somewhat higher than the level of individual neurons and connections. (p. 329)

Connectionism, we all agree, is "neurally inspired." However, currently these origins are obscured by its essentially mathematico-cognitive nature. McClelland and Rumelhart did go on to argue that some PDP models still attempt to study realistic neural nets. They refer to the last three chapters of Part V as examples of this approach. However, although these models are specifically linked to physiology and are peppered with a neural vocabulary, on close inspection even these so called neural theories would work equally well without that linguistic connection to explain place recognition, neural plasticity, and amnesia respectively. In fact, these minitheories are really just mathematical simulations of cognitive processes under a thin veneer of neurophysiological terminology.

By no means should the contribution of Rumelhart, McClelland, and their colleagues be minimized by this reinterpretation of the meaning of their work. It represents a critical transition point from network approaches constrained and limited by the biological facts and computation complexity to those in which the nodes represented something very different—cognitive modules. It is in this regard, however, that their impact may have had unanticipated consequences! The entire idea of cognitive modules represents what some of us feel is at least an unanswered question and at most a serious misdirection.[18]

Connectionism is intimately tied up with acceptance of concepts of cognitive modularity, representation, and the accessibility of these modules. All of these assumptions are, arguably, incorrect and misleading for the future of a true scientific psychology.

What modern day connectionism does share with previous kinds of neural modeling is that it is computational. The computers available to current

---

[18]See Uttal (2001) for a full discussion of the problem of cognitive modules.

cognitive psychology are of such enormous power that it is now possible to invent and implement theories and models of a level of complexity that was beyond the wildest dreams of early connectionist psychologists such as James or Thorndike. However, this advantage is not without its own intrinsic perils. Even the most powerful computers have not been able to evaluate any cognitive process at a level of complexity that must certainly occur in the human nervous system.

Connectionism, descended from, albeit very different than, neural network theory, has been criticized by proponents of a number of different perspectives. One of the most salient counterarguments is the one just made–the bridge that it proposed to make between connectionist nets and neural nets is but the palest form of metaphor. The apparent connection with neuroanatomy and neurophysiology is, according to this point of view, only an illusion arising from the common properties of heavily interconnected lattices. It is not, however, adequately linked to biology;[19] on the one hand are the relatively objective properties of neurons and on the other are the inferred properties of entities that in many cases are nothing more than hypothetical constructs.[20]

It fell to Fodor and Pylyshyn (1988), who were so authoritative in describing why connectionism had such appeal at a critical point in psychological history, to point out that the deficiencies in this new approach:

1. The argument for parallel computation as a means of producing high-speed processing is spurious since parallelism is a matter of implementation and not of the basic idea of how the brain is organized. The only thing such a criterion validly rejects is ". . . the absurd hypothesis that cognitive architectures are implemented in the brain in the same way as they are implemented on electronic computers." (p. 55)

2. The argument for resistance to noise and inability to gracefully degrade with damage are also issues of implementation and could affect a serial computer as well as a parallel one.

3. The argument that such "soft constraints" as continuity and randomness are better represented by connectionist systems than by serial type-computer models is also a matter of implementation. Either a serial or a parallel process could, in principle, be implemented on either type of computer system as well as on even simpler devices such as a Turing machine.

---

[19]It must be remembered that the link from connectionist nodes to neurons, as already discussed, is not a tenet of classic Rumelhart and McClelland connectionism.

[20]As Landredth and Richardson (2004) correctly remind us, hypothetical constructs (MacCorquodale and Meehl, 1948) are part and parcel of the scientific method. Their use cannot be dismissed completely. However, it seems clear that the use of this "tool" should be linked to some operational method for carrying them forward from inference to observation. A point I try to make in this book is that psychology has special problems with hypothetical constructs.

4. The argument that rules are less explicit in a connectionist system than in a conventional computer is "contentious" as well as "ubiquitous" (p. 60). In fact, conventional computers can represent implicit rules just as well as explicit rules. Creating a network requires the same kind of assumptions as does expressing a "rule."

5. The argument that connectionist networks are more like brains than conventional computers is simply false. In actuality, current connectionist models embrace only the passive and distributed property of a brain, but the nodes are no longer neurophysiological.

(Abstracted from Fodor and Pylyshyn, 1988, pp. 54–64)

In summary, what connectionism has become is a new machine metaphor for cognitive processes. It provides some advantages in that it provides an organized point of view and a formal structure that has many advantages over verbal models and speculation. It also mimics some highly reduced abstractions of human thought processes, but at a level that almost always has to be characterized as "toy" or highly reduced models.

Most important in the present context is that connectionist models née neural network theories are metamorphing into something akin to the very psychological level theories they were intended to replace. The continuing effort to link them to neurophysiology becomes increasingly strained as the conceptual nodes of a connectionist network deviate further and further from neurons.

Finally, there are other approaches to brain and mind theory that are arguably neither neural nor networks. I refer here specifically to the work of Stephen Grossberg. Grossberg has offered an enormous corpus of information. However, his work is framed in terms of continuous differential equations rather than the discrete language of networks. Much of his work is illustrated by block diagrams in which the modules are not neuronal-like. Instead he invokes functional modules such as the Boundary Completion System (BCS) or Feature Contour System (FCS) that might be combined to produce a pattern recognition system.

Little of Grossberg's work is actually presented in the form of network-like simulations (i.e., computer programs that instantiate the network idea). To the contrary, in most of his publications, he evaluates differential equations and shows how a few exemplar neurons can be interconnected in a manner that behaves in the same way as the cognitive process being modeled. Although the mathematical sophistication of this important corpus of work is undeniable and Grossberg must be complimented in his quest for a unified theory of a wide range of psychological processes, it is not at all clear that his paradigm should be classified as either a neural or a network paradigm.

6.8 MATHEMATICAL ARGUMENTS FOR THE INTRACTABILITY[21] OF NEURAL NETWORKS

6.8.1 Mathematical Intractability in General

It should be obvious to my readers that this review of neural network theories and some of its fellow travelers such as connectionism is incomplete. The books by Levine (2000) and by Anderson (1995), among others, provide a fuller treatment of recent work. Indeed, the amount of activity in this field has been enormous.[22] My goal in presenting the mini-review provided in this chapter has been to filter out the fundamental assumptions, axioms, advantages and disadvantages, and the sequence of theoretical ideas that have characterized neural network theory's history. My purpose has been to provide a foundation for the argument that, to a degree that is not usually appreciated by students of this field, neural network models are demonstrably incapable of achieving their ultimate goals.

It is now appropriate to consider the specific arguments for what I have only suggested before—that the search for underlying neural network mechanisms of the mind represent an intractable challenge for any research technique, be it computational, mathematical, behavioral, or neurophysiological. My thesis in this regard is based on ideas that are becoming increasingly well known among mathematicians and computational theorists, but remain largely outside the ken of cognitive neuroscientists.

The problems of computational complexity and the intractability of what seem at first glance to be relatively simple problems have been of interest to mathematicians for years. Classic (i.e., precomputer) problems relevant to this topic were concerned with proving that some theorems are undecidable. The most famous of these undecidable problems was whether or not the Diophantine equation (i.e., an equation in which the solution has to consist of integers) equation of the form

$$x^n + y^n = z^n \qquad 6.5$$

had any non-zero integer solutions for x, y and z when $n > 2$. The classic answer to this question was that it did not. However, this conjecture went unproven for centuries. Although it was originally suggested that a proof ex-

[21] *Intractable = Unruly, fractious, indocile, indomitable, recalcitrant, undisciplined, ungovernable, unmanageable, wild.* Unmanageable and unsolvable are the operational meanings in the present context.

[22] The Arizona State University library responds with 192 titles when asked to search for the key word "neural networks" many of which are application oriented, but many of which are introductions to the field.

isted in 1637 by the great mathematician Pierre de Fermat, this conjecture was not finally proven until the 20th century by Andrew Wiles (1995) in an article that spanned 108 pages and depended upon other proofs in what initially seemed to be unrelated fields of mathematics. Even then, Wiles' proof was limited. It had been known since 1970 that there could be no general proof, like that of Wiles, that could resolve the issue for all kinds of Diophantine polynomial equations. The point, however, is that proofs of what appear to be relatively simple mathematical questions are sometimes very difficult to obtain.

With the rise of digital computers, many other problems became of interest concerning the computational capacities of these powerful machines. I have already mentioned the halting problem for a computer program. Another of the most important theorems concerning the computational complexity of programs was proposed by Meyer and Stockmeyer (1972). Their work was described more fully and expanded to probabilistic systems in a recent report by Stockmeyer and Meyer (2002). The point made in these highly important articles was that there were some relatively simple logical circuits (comparable to a neural network composed of only a few dozen neurons) that could not be solved because of the enormous numbers of logical units required for their solution.

The specific logic circuit that Meyer and Stockmeyer modeled was in the form of a truth table that was characterized by 63 input variables, each of which could be encoded by six bits of information. A "sentence" was considered to have a length of 610, equivalent to a specific pattern of 3660 bits. The device that was to evaluate this truth table was to give a logical "1" as an output only if a particular "sentence" was presented as the input to logical device. Although the numbers of elements and possible states involved in this proof are relatively small (63, 610, and even 3660), Meyer and Stockmeyer (1972) showed that the device would need *more than* 10^{125} *logical gates* to evaluate this logical expression and produce the single bit of output information asserting that the input was true (i.e., that the particular pattern had been introduced!). Since they also calculated that "the known universe could contain at most 10^{125} protons," obviously this device could not be built.

The point of this anecdote in combinatorial history is that superficially simple problems can demand such horrendous amounts of computer time or mathematical power that their solutions are either in practice or in principle unobtainable. The corollary of this assertion is that neural networks have all the characteristics of the class of intractable problems that combinatorial and computational complexity theorists have dealt with in recent years. The practical impact is that most of the neural network models that have been proposed are incapable of adequately representing that which they are supposed to model. There is no deep mystery here; it is a matter of the number of nodes in a network, the complexity of their interactions, their intrinsic nonlinearity, and the dynamic condition under which all such simulations must be run.

The intractability argument is both a strong and a pessimistic generalization. I have no doubt there will be a reflexive negative response on the part of practitioners of the neural network approach to such a pronouncement. Nevertheless, it is essential that cognitive neuroscientists approach their work with an appreciation that all is not well at the most fundamental conceptual level of the neural network idea.

This potential difficulty is exacerbated by the fact that neural networks have been applied to such an enormous number of psychological problems. Networks have been proposed that learn some appropriate response, recognize different forms, or solve some logical problem. The "problem to be solved," however, is special to each proposed neural network experiment. Despite this enormous breath and the acknowledged dangers of overgeneralization, it is important to keep in mind that the difficulty of combinatorial complexity is universal whatever the problem being attacked.

The question is–Why is this so? The answer to this question is that the difficulty in solving a mathematical problem goes up with the number of variables.[23] For a psychologically realistic network, the number of variables is so large that the simulation problem becomes intractable or unsolvable for practical rather than theoretical reasons. That is, although there may be no intrinsic barrier to the solution of a given problem (as there is in the case of Fermat's last theorem), it would take what is effectively an infinite amount of time to solve it. This combinatorial barrier is known by many names. One is the scaling problem; another is the NP complete classification;[24] another alludes to the information content of the neural network. All fall within the general rubric of combinatorial complexity and all, ultimately, fall victim to either simple numerousness or nonlinear complexity.

6.8.2 The Scaling Problem

The simplest indication that a problem of this type, no matter what its particular task is, will be unsolvable is that its computational complexity (i.e.,

---

[23]The term *variable* should be construed to be synonymous with a number of other equivalent words. Variables are also known as parameters, dimensions, factors, independent measurements, nodes, or operations. The point is that whatever they are called, there is a vast increase in the number of calculations that must be made for even relatively simple problems or for neural networks with relatively few units.

[24]It should be pointed out that it has not yet been proven that a NP-complete problem is necessarily intractable in a formal, in principle, sense. In all likelihood, however, mathematicians agree that intractability and NP-completeness are synonymous, for practical if not for theoretical reasons.

the number of variables) increases exponentially with an exponent greater than 1.[25] For any such exponential growth function, eventually the problem will become too complex or require too many steps to be solved. The tension then becomes a race between having a number of neurons that is sufficiently large to adequately represent some prototypical mental activity and the increasing tendency to explode into a situation in which the network cannot be evaluated in a realistic amount of time.

The effect of combinatorial explosions in neural network theorems for modest numbers of neurons has been criticized for many years, but without sufficient impact. Minsky and Papert (1988), for example, warned repeatedly that the jump from "toy" problems involving only a few synthetic neurons to realistically sized neural networks was not always feasible. They pointed out that there is a quantitative progression from solvable simplicity to intractability. What is not generally appreciated by neural network theorists and connectionists alike is that some problems, including many of the neural networks that are the topic of this chapter, are "inherently exponential" (Stockmeyer and Chandra, 1979).

For reasons that are both arcane and obvious, no one has ever run a computer simulation of a neural network that even begins to approximate the number of neurons involved in even the simplest cognitive process. Depending on the particular problem, computers have been capable of running a simulation consisting of a hundred or so neurons, each of which is interconnected to a relatively small number of other neurons. The reality of the human brain, however, is quite different: Billions of brain cells each with as many as a thousand interneuronal interconnections are probably involved in producing even the simplest cognitive process. All simulations, without exception, thus have necessarily been designed to demonstrate some principle of network organization that can reproduce some basic process such as learning or form recognition by means of a relatively modest number of simulated neurons. The undeniable achievement of this approach has been to produce behavior in the network that is analogous to the cognitive process under study. The equally undeniable disadvantage of this approach is that there is no way to assure that the simulation actually instantiates the same mechanisms that account for the behavior produced by a full-scale biological system such as the brain. The very fact that such simulations also fail, often very ungracefully, suggests that neural networks of the complexity level used by current theorists are, at best, process analogs and not true reductive explanations of mental activity.

---

[25]However, any other growth function in which the dependent variable grows faster than the independent variable will also exhibit this combinatorial explosion, albeit at a relative speed that will be determined by the power of the exponential function and the other growth function respectively. The traveling salesman problem, for example, which seeks to find the minimum cost travel schedule for a given number of cities, explodes at rate determined by the factorial expression $\frac{(n-1)!}{2}$ as n, the number of cities increases (Karp, 1986).

Thus, toy problems may be useful and provide interesting insights and heuristics, but they are in no way definitive, no matter how similar their behavior may be to a seemingly related psychobiological response. This problem is exacerbated by the fact that there is no guarantee that the mechanisms programmed into a particular "toy" neural network will prove to be of the same kind as those that might be effective in a full-scale system. The much more usual situation, as already discussed in this chapter, is that virtually all such toy simulations collapse when attempts are made to increase the number of units beyond the minimal levels of the toy. This may be due to the rapidly increasing number of interactions as the number of nodes increases. Furthermore, simply increasing the number of input stimuli typically leads to a collapse of even those successful models that worked for small numbers of test stimuli. In general, it is always uncertain that the "toys" will scale up in a way that is meaningful before they collapse for combinatorial reasons.

This brings us to another issue. In principle, mathematicians know that it is possible to solve any problem by exhaustive search techniques: However, Minsky and Papert (1988) pointed out that, in practice, the number of steps necessary to carry out such an exhaustive search for anything other than a very reduced problem quickly becomes enormous (p. 262). They further noted that such a relatively simple game as chess prohibits an exhaustive search and a determinist solution to the problem of beating an opponent simply because of the number of steps required to carry out the search.

The formidable obstruction to valid theory construction faced by neural network aficionados is that their algorithms also tend to diverge so quickly that the proposed tests would quickly require a number of steps that would be indistinguishable from the number required for exhaustive search. Minsky and Papert (1988), therefore, expressed their conviction that neural network theorists have a responsibility to be sure that the scaling issue would not make their own favorite model collapse under the weight of its own proclivity for intrinsic exponential growth. Furthermore, even the use of random or Monte Carlo procedures is not certain to overcome the scaling problem. They said, in this context:

> Moving from small to large problems will often demand this transition from exhaustive to statistical sampling, and we suspect that in many realistic situations the resulting sampling noise would mask the signal completely. We suspect that many who read the connectionist literature are not aware of this phenomenon, which dims some of the prospects of successfully applying certain learning procedures to large-scale problems. (p. 264)

Minsky and Papert emphasized, despite the superficial biological relevance of neural networks and despite the preliminary successes some small "toy" problems have had, efforts should always be made to determine the effects of scaling before leaping to the conclusion that a particular toy theory was upwardly scalable and, thus, enjoyed a modicum of realism.

An important corollary of this admonition is that it is not merely the engineering capability of computers that is the issue. Rather, it is often the intrinsic nature of the simulated neural network that blocks a successful solution. Simply seeking another model or theory or a faster computer is not likely to overcome the "in principle" barrier to solution exhibited by many problems of this genre.

Simply increasing the speed or memory capacity (or even the degree of parallelicity) of the computational engine does not offer any way to overcome the scaling problem. Instead of suggesting that all that is needed is a better computer with higher processing speed or larger memory capacity, what has to be appreciated is that most attempts at upward scaling of neural network models are likely quickly to swamp any conceivable computer design. The requirements for a device implementing even a relatively simple (compared to the processes required to produce mental activity) logical truth table described by Stockmeyer and Meyer (2002) emphatically made this point.

6.8.3 NP-Completeness

The same limit on the solvability of some classes of neural network models arises under a different name—NP-completeness. Combinatorial complexity theorists have suggested a taxonomy in which mathematical problems are classified in terms of their intrinsic difficulty and amenability to solution. "P" problems are those that can be solved by an exhaustive search in a determined amount of time;[26] "NP" problems are those that probably can be solved but only in a undetermined amount of time; "NP-hard" problems are those that are at least as hard as NP problem but may be more difficult to solve; and "NP-complete" problems are those that cannot be solved in any determined amount of time; NP-completeness being signaled by the fact that a problem is both NP and NP-hard. NP-complete problems are, therefore, problems that cannot be solved, not because they are in principle unsolvable, but rather because they would take a length of time that is, for all practical purposes, infinite even if it is not literally so. The point being that neural nets have a strong propensity to scale up very badly to become NP-complete problems even though they may be P problems in their "toy" state.

The difficulty strikes close to home when we consider problems that are specifically psychological. Speaking specifically of the problem of loading

[26]A "determined amount of time" is also referred to as "polynomial time" (i.e., a number of steps that is a polynomial function of the size of the problem).

information into a neural network, Judd (1991) made the same general point about the intractability of a particular kind of problem that connectionist theorists repeatedly attempt to solve. He said:

> The learning (memorization) problem in its general form is too difficult to solve. By proving it to be NP-complete, we can claim that large instances of the problem would be wildly impractical to solve. There is no way to configure a given arbitrary network to remember a given arbitrary body of data in a reasonable amount of time. This result shows that the simple problem of remembering a list of data items (something that is trivial in a classical random access machine) is extremely difficult to perform in some fixed networks. (p. 7)[27]

Judd went on to prove the NP-completeness of several different versions of the learning problem for several different kinds of logical interconnection schema. He also proceeded to show that many problems of this class remain intractable even if some kinds of constraints are applied. For example, it does not help to simplify the problem by limiting a neural network to two layers. Reducing the complexity in this way only introduces other impediments to "solving" a neural network problem, a caveat that was also pointed out by Minsky and Papert.

Orponen (1994) surveyed a wide range of different neural network theories and also came to the conclusion that many of the neural network algorithms that have been proposed so far by ambitious neural network theoreticians have already been determined to be NP-complete by mathematicians. He reports, for example, that it is not possible to determine if a "given symmetric, simple network" (p. 12) of the Hopfield type has more than one stable state, a property that would preclude its solution. In this example, a "stable state" means a single deterministic solution. "Multiple stable states" alludes to ambiguity, false solutions, and, ultimately, intractability.

Orponen additionally points out that the task of synthesizing a neural network by comparing their inputs and outputs (as would occur in a backpropagation systems) is in many cases (depending upon how the problem is formulated) also an NP-complete task. This is an important observation providing formal proof of the dictate that both mathematics and behavior are neutral with regard to internal structures and mechanisms.

Parberry (1994) provided a formal treatment of the challenge created by combinatorial complexity specifically in the context of neural networks. Although, he notes that not all neural network problems are NP complete, the fact that so many instances of familiar psychological theories are should be a strong warning to those who would seek to model mental functions with

---

[27]However, Judd (1991) also makes the point that some problems can be solved by constraining the task to a reduced form (see p. 241).

neural networks. Among the many instances of what are usually considered to be standard problems that Parberry found to be NP-complete were:

1. "Simple" two layer logical structures in which the two layers either perform AND or OR logical functions, but not both (the layers are alternating in function) and for which there is considerable convergence (i.e., fan in) from one layer to another.
2. Most forms of neural networks with feedback such as the Hopfield model. Such systems are referred to as "cyclic" and may be unstable or fail to halt in any reasonable amount of time.
3. The problem in which the computer must learn a sequence of input–output pairs (the loading problem) even when the number of nodes was relatively small.

Parberry did acknowledge that some problems could be simplified to the point they do become solvable (i.e., in a determined amount of polynomial time). For example, he pointed out:

> One way of avoiding the intractability of learning [demonstrated earlier] is to learn only limited task sets on simple architectures with limited node function sets. (p. 239)

However useful this advice is, it appears to be merely a recipe for testing "toy" problems and leaves open the challenge faced when attempts are made to scale a problem upward beyond "limited task sets" and small network sizes. For those interested in the history of the complexity problem, an interesting rendition of the story is told by Karp (1986).

6.8.4 Information Measures

Another way to frame the problem of neural network complexity is in terms of its information content. Information content was formularized by Shannon (1948) by means of the following expression:

$$I = \sum_{1}^{a} \boldsymbol{p}_i \log_2 \boldsymbol{p}_i \qquad 6.6$$

where I (also known as H in recent terminology) is the amount of information in a message, $\boldsymbol{p}_i$ is the probability that any one of a possible alternative messages is sent. (With the logarithm taken to the base 2, the unit of information measurement is the familiar "bit" used as the unit of information). The important thing about this equation is that as the probability of guessing a particular message value goes up when the information content is relatively low (e.g., in the task of choosing the lightness of a checkerboard square when all of the squares are black). When the probability of guessing a particular value of lightness for a square goes down (e.g., when the squares in the checker board all have different lightness values) the information content escalates very rapidly. In other words, the more regular a picture is, the less information, and the more irregular, the more information it contains. Depending upon the number of states, the information can go up substantially, to the point of combinatorial intractability for a relatively simple system (e.g., a checkerboard of only 64 squares.)

Furthermore, information is inversely correlated with the measure known as entropy. Low information means high entropy and high entropy means a great deal of uncertainty about the behavior of the components of a system such as a neural network. In a highly entropic situation all of the irregularities have been smoothed out and the predictability of the behavior of any one of the components or units would become high. In this case the information content is reduced.

Thus, a neural network made up of identical units interconnected in simple and repetitive ways would have very little information and thus a high degree of predictability or entropy. However, a network made up of idiosyncratic neurons interconnected in a virtually random manner would be high in information but very low in predictability or entropy. This means that the state of a system would have to be evaluated on what would be a unit-by-unit basis, a demanding requirement even for a system with only a few units (remember the three-body problem?), and an impossible requirement for a biological system of a realistic level of complexity.

Information and entropy are just another way of expressing the computational complexity of a problem. The predictions of information theory jibe with those from other fields. They all suggest there will be a huge growth in the computational requirements to solve neural network problems for anything other than the trivial toys now being studied. A few simple computations of the information inherent in even a simple neural network (framed in terms of number of nodes, numbers of interconnections, and their values) will help one to appreciate the enormity of the problems lurking just beyond the toy models of neural network theorists.

The easiest way to get an intuitive feeling for how quickly complexity (in the form of fantastically large numbers) can develop is to consider the possible combinations of **n** things taken **p** at a time. (A standard formula for combinations can be found in any handbook of mathematics.) The number of different combinations quickly rises to huge exponential values even for relatively small numbers not at all unlike the number of synthetic neurons or nodes used in most connectionist or neural network models.

6.8.5 The Limits of Computational Simplification for Network Theories

Current efforts to use neural networks as theories of mind, therefore, have had to turn to simplifying constraints. The most successful have been simplified lattices in which all components were identical and the interconnections between components all functioned in the same way. The earliest successes in neural network modeling (e.g., the work of Ratliff and Hartline, 1959) were for models of this kind. Happily, the model accurately represented the simple nature of the anatomy of the eye of the *Limulus polyphemus*—the horseshoe crab. Each ommatidium was identical to each of its neighbors and each interconnection exerted a simple, reciprocal, and inhibitory effect on its neighbors.

However, most of the neural networks proposed so far are not of this highly simplified genre. Nor are we able to take full advantage of the simplification used by the gas dynamicists or the cosmologists, because the networks used in the brain are intrinsically irregular. Indeed, the goal of most of the learning type networks is to differentiate the weight or strength of the connections between nodes in a dynamic way dependent upon the inputs. The trend is, therefore, toward increasing structural (i.e., synaptic weight) diversity and, therefore, away from the kind of simplification that even initial estimates of regularity would offer. In other words, it seems increasingly likely most of the proposed neural network theories simulating the learning process are NP-complete.

In some cases, it is possible to develop short-cut mathematical techniques that can take advantage of this regularity. For example, Fast Fourier Transforms have been developed that permit the application of this powerful techniques by compartmentalizing the calculations to avoid high level and long distance interactions. My colleague, Sriram Dayanand (1999) developed a surface reconstruction method that works by breaking the whole task into a series of small tessellated triangles. The triangles were then interconnected by assuming that the slopes of the triangles must be identical at the points of intersection. What had been an enormously difficult problem of many variables had been reduced to local and almost trivial computations. Of course, the combinatorial problem still remains. There is a practical limit to the number of triangles that can be dealt with for any given surface.

What else can be done to permit solutions to some subset of the seemingly intractable problems attacked by network theorists? One possibility is to apply the method that was originally proposed by Rosenblatt (1958, 1962)—apply random or Monte Carlo techniques. Although randomness is not a universal solution (see the comment by Minsky and Papert cited on page 236), it can overcome some obstacles to a correct solution such as the false energy minimum one. Nevertheless, there remain barriers to the glib application of stochastic methods. For example, Stockmeyer and Meyer (2002) showed that their theorem demonstrating the impracticality of deterministic logic circuitry also applies to randomly interconnected logical units. As a warning to any overly optimistic futurist among us, they have also extended their proof to quantum computational circuits, another gleam in the eye of ambitious computer engineers.

Another simplification strategy that is ubiquitous, but which is fraught with its own problems, is to break up the problem into a set of component modules (i.e., to partition it into subtasks). This has the possible advantage of simplifying the task at hand by solving parts of the brain–mind problem independently. However, at the same time, such a strategy introduces a kind of component or faculty type of thinking that has bedeviled scientific psychology since its origins (Uttal, 2001). Furthermore, the proposed components may not be separable without losing their essential identity.

Finally, another means of simplifying a complex problem is known as *regularization*. The modeling of a complex process with many variables can, as we have seen, become very complex, very quickly. One way to think of regularization is as the imposition of an artificial requirement for a smooth solution. One kind of regularization helps to reduce complexity by adding a cost factor that increases with the deviation of a particular value from a smooth or locally average function. In some cases this artificial smoothing may permit a solution to be obtained where none had been possible before.

In some cases neural networks themselves may provide the means of solving some problems that are intractable to conventional mathematics. Shams (1997) discussed how combinatorially difficult problems could, in some cases, be attacked by the use of parallel neural networks. This approach does not work all of the time; intractability is a general feature of many kinds of problems. However, alternative strategies of the kind mentioned here can in some instances overcome the otherwise insurmountable barriers introduced by unsuitable formulations.

Judd (1991) also dealt with the value of parallelism, per se. He pointed out, however, that it just will not work in many cases. His argument went as follows:

> This [intractability] is true whether the algorithm is conceived as a nodal entity working in a distributed fashion with other nodes or as a global entity working in a centralized fashion on the network as a whole. (p. 43)

He then went on:

> The parallelism inherent in most neural network systems does not avoid this intractability. An exponential expression (c^x) cannot be contained by dividing

> it by a linear expression (cx). In many connectionist approaches to learning, there is a strong reason why large numbers of computing elements will not accomplish the loading problem in feasible time. . . . Naïve attempts to exploit parallelism can actually be counterproductive. (p. 43)

The key in all of these approximation methods striving to solve "intrinsically difficult problems" (Stockmeyer & Chandra, 1979) is adequately constraining the problem under attack to a simpler condition. However, it must be appreciated that whatever gains one makes in simplification comes at a cost. The cost may be in accuracy of the solution, uncertainty in the produced probabilities, and approximate rather than deterministic solutions. There is no free lunch! At the worst, one may lose the essential nature of the problem under attack!

Clearly, we do not yet have a coherent and complete proof of the tractability or intractability of neural net theories of mind. The suggestion, however, is that they are similar to other problems that are demonstrably intractable. As Karp (1986) pointed out in his Turing Award Lecture:

> The NP-completeness results proved in the 1970s showed that, unless P = NP, the great majority of the problems of combinatorial optimization that arise in commerce, science, and engineering are intractable: No methods for their solution can completely evade combinatorial explosions. (p. 105)

The facts that such an explosion can happen with relatively few nodes and that, in many if not most cases, simplifications or approximations cannot be applied without losing the crux of the problem, argue strongly that neural network models, although the most relevant ontologically, are epistemological dead ends.

6.9 AN INTERIM SUMMARY

This selective and brief history of a few of the milestones in the history of neural network theories depicts a stream of ideas, some novel and some persistent, dating from the earliest days of McCulloch and Pitts' enormous insight. Most of these theories described here came from the fields of visual perception, memory, and learning. The reasons for this selection from among the much wider variety of human experience are crystal clear. The isomorphic relationships between the function of the spatially organized visual stimuli and the neural array are specific enough to make the relevance of a simulation self-evident. Learning is also a process that presumably occurs in parallel with well-defined changes throughout the simulated neural network. The logic of learning studies is that this distributed change directly corresponds to measurable aspects of the experiences to which the network is exposed. More subtle emotional and cognitive processes are harder to describe in their own right, not being associated with specific behavior changes. It is difficult to suggest comparable network properties that would correspond to these intangibles.[28]

As we scan this history, a number of significant points can be identified at which key ideas were introduced. The very idea that an information-processing network might be capable of simulating psychological process was a profound paradigm shift. Subsequently, with the availability of programmable digital computers, the art of neural network theorizing exploded. Specific developments followed in rapid order; backward connections, randomization, feature analysis; supervised and unsupervised (i.e., automatic) learning; overall state spaces, and, perhaps the most drastic theoretical mutation of all—the transition from discrete networks to continuous energy surfaces.

All activity in this field of theory notwithstanding, it is clear that the hope that the mind might be explained by studying networks has not fulfilled its promise. There appears to be an increasing realization that the complexity of the problem, specified in terms of the number of units, the irregularity of their interconnections, their nonlinearity, and simple combinatorics may forever preclude our ability to solve the mind–brain problem using this approach. Unfortunately, the realization of the problem has not been accompanied by specific attempts to evaluate the combinatorial complexity of neural networks by the neural network theoretical community itself. The significant work in this domain has come from mathematicians interested in combinatorics and computability. It is distressing to examine the major theories of psychobiological neural networks and to discover that problems of tractability are in large part ignored. Terms such as *computability*, *tractability*, *scaling*, *combinatorics*, *NP-completeness*, and so forth, are notoriously absent from texts and treatises in this field.[29] The inadequate attention paid to this problem is exemplified by the contents of the otherwise comprehensive *Handbook of Neural Computation* (Fiesler and Beale, 1997). Only one index item deals with "complexity" and I have found just a few references to the topic scattered throughout the book.

It seems to me that in answer to the question—Can the proposed neural network theories solve the mind–brain problem?—is most likely to be "No"!

---

[28]The issue of whether or not such a simulation would experience consciousness or self-awareness is beyond the scope of this book. However, it should be noted in passing that there is no way to determine if another entity is conscious or not. This is the classic "other minds" problem of philosophy. Despite the hopes of some that a "Turing test" might provide a means of determining whether or not consciousness is present, the hope of achieving accessibility and thus confirming the presence of other's consciousness appears to be dim.

[29]The one notable exception being the work of Minsky and Papert (1988) whose admonitions have all-too-often been ignored.

Certainly, past efforts to extend "toy" systems to real life situations have been universally disappointing. The evolutionary changes that have occurred in the original neural network approach seemingly have occurred without explicit attention to the challenges introduced by the combinatoric explosion that occurs when nodes and connections multiply beyond the absurdly reduced levels of most theories of this type.

We are thus left with a totally unsatisfactory state of affairs. On the one hand, we have a pretty good idea of the nature of the truth regarding the way in which mind emerges from the brain. Every scientific fact we have tells us that mind is a result of the complex interaction of a huge number of discrete, but heavily interconnected, neurons. Yet, on the other hand, we are prohibited by the nature of this explanation from understanding how such a remarkable process happens. The most frustrating aspect of this conclusion is that this dilemma is not a temporary problem that might be overcome by new equipment or algorithms. Rather, it seems likely that we will be forever denied access to a solution of the mind–brain problem based on the one type of theory that must, ontologically speaking, be true.

CHAPTER

7

Summary and Conclusions

7.1 INTRODUCTION

So far in this book, I have considered three main types of psychobiological theory to explain how the brain produces the intrapersonal mental states that we call mind, self-awareness, consciousness, or cognitive processing.[1] After introducing the history and current status of each of three theoretical approaches–field, single neuron, and network–I critiqued each one in order to buttress the argument that each was logically or empirically inadequate to the task they set for themselves. In this chapter, I draw together these threads, briefly mention a few alternative approaches, draw some general conclusions, and propose what I believe is the best way to pursue studies in this field. This summary chapter also examines how well the various theoretical types meet the standards expected of an ideal theory as described in chapter 1.

7.2 OTHER APPROACHES

Although the three types of theory discussed in chapters 4, 5, and 6, respectively, represent the main theoretical thrusts in the search for a neurobio-

[1]It is imperative that I once again reiterate one of the greatest impediments to understanding in this field. It is very difficult, if not impossible, to objectively define any of these terms. Thus, subjective and connotative interpretations and enormous, although usually empty, debates rage over what we mean by mind or consciousness and their measurability. Everything said in this book has to be tempered by this fundamental lacuna in our knowledge.

logical explanation of the mysterious process we call mind, obviously they do not exhaust all possible and plausible explanations. Indeed, there is a substantial corpus of research in which other basic assumptions have been invoked and other lines of theory pursued. In this section, I briefly mention and describe a few of this second tier of theories.

Throughout the long history of the mind–body problem, a repeated theme has been to attribute our mental activity to a particular place in the body, a place that may not always have been the brain. The heart, of course, was the classic Aristotelean locus. However, as traditional neuroscience evolved and we learned more about the anatomy and function of the brain, the predominant approach has become the assignment of mind to a specific organ—the brain. In the 19th century, studies of the influence of brain injury on behavior and an emerging trend to modularizing both the brain and the mind (both phrenology and faculty psychology have long histories), particular functions were attributed to specific portions of the brain. In particular, that period saw the postulation of what were believed to be empirical links between such high level cognitive processes as speech and local areas of the left hemisphere. In the presence of only minimal information about the microscopic structure of the brain, the absence of good definitions of mental processes, and the continued influence of the Cartesian method, this kind of "chunkology" became the consensual view.

In the 20th century, the theoretical situation evolved such that ever more specific locales in the brain were associated with a generalized concept of consciousness itself. What was probably the earliest work in this context was reported by Bremer (1935). He discovered that if the reticular system of the brain stem, through which most of the ascending sensory signals passed, was cut in an experimental animal, it appeared to be continuously asleep. Moruzzi and Magoun (1949) subsequently showed that electrical stimulation of the reticular system would keep an animal constantly awake. Consciousness, in the guise of wakefulness, therefore was attributed to the reticular formation. However, whether this was merely a facilitating influence or whether the psychoneural equivalent of consciousness was to be found in the reticular formation remains controversial.

In the 1990s, however, the spotlight of localization theory was redirected in a major way; consciousness, however, ill defined it may be, replaced the simpler idea of arousal and currently has emerged as a substitute for the vaguely defined concept of mind. Thus, for example, Gray (1995) implicated the hippocampus, Cotterill (1994) suggested the anterior cingulate, and Bogen (1995), identified the thalamus as possible sites for the encoding of consciousness. Furthermore, Baars (2001) suggested that there is a role for both the thalamus and the inferotemporal cortex on the basis of research by Sheinberg and Logothetis (1997). Van der Werf (2000) also suggested that the thalamus played a very important role in activating memories in the medial temporal and frontal regions of the brain. More complex schemes have been offered; Dehaene and Naccache (2001), for example, proposed that consciousness is a function of the interaction "of prefrontal cortex and the anterior cingulated regions, and the areas that connect to them" (p. 2).

Recently it has become popular to assign consciousness to widely distributed, but strong, interactions among many areas of the brain. Baars (1996), for example, suggested there are active feed forward and feedback interactions between the cerebral cortex and the thalamus. This theory attributes consciousness to the interaction of a number of the macrostructures in the brain. Unfortunately, this approach is likely to run up against complexity problems as the number of cortical regions increases or as the interactions drive the system toward increasing degrees of nonlinearity.

In addition to these general associations of consciousness with various regions of the brain, there has been an enormous amount of activity linking particular functional components of the mind (i.e., cognitive modules) with particular regions of the brain by means of functional Magnetic Resonance Imaging (fMRI) or Positron Emission Tomography (PET) techniques. In an earlier book (Uttal, 2001), I reviewed a portion of the enormous corpus of findings that has emerged from this type of research. In that work I raised serious concerns about the general validity of this "localization" approach based not only on the bases of methodology and the fragility of the empirical data, but also on the general grounds that it was implausible to separate cognitive analysis into modules.

Brief mention should also be made of a number of other theoretical approaches that are not specifically biological in the same sense as the ones described in this book. Psychologists have for many years developed various kinds of models of mind based on various forms of mathematical analysis or computational methods. There is no denying that this approach has been successful. However, its success must be tempered by the understanding that such models are not reductive. Rather they are descriptive; although capable of adequately tracking the course of some process or even predicting its future, in no way do they explain (or intend to explain) how the neural processes of the brain produce psychological entities. As mentioned here and in greater detail elsewhere, mathematical models are neutral with regard to the kind of neural processes that must produce the indefinable, inscrutable, mental roots of our behavior.

7.3 THE STANDARDS FOR A SOUND THEORY

In chapter 1, on pages 13–14, a list of the characteristics of a good theory is presented. In brief, these criteria or properties are:

1. Accuracy
2. Consistency
3. Synoptic breadth
4. Simplicity
5. Fruitfulness
6. Testability
7. Linguistically and Methodologically Scientific

The present task is to determine how well the four types of psychobiological theories (field, single neuron, network, and localization) discussed in this book meet these qualifications. First, there is no question that all these theories are framed in the vocabulary and the methodology of an objective neural science. None invokes any supernatural or immeasurable force or entities that would transcend the methods of science. Therefore, we can stipulate that all are "scientific" or materialist in their general orientation.

Second, all seek to interpret the processes that produce mind by reference to a set of general principles or processes that incorporate substantial numbers of individual empirical observations into a broader context. Each, therefore, has some degree of intended synoptic breadth—but only within its own domain. As discussed later, when considered in the light of the whole science, all of these theories are relatively narrowly configured and none exhibits the breadth of vision that should be the foundation of unification into a grand theoretical scheme. It seems obvious that none of them adequately incorporates the empirical database of the others

Third, accuracy is in the eye of the beholder. Simple correspondence between behavior and neural measurements is often cited as a sign of a theory's validity. However, this correspondence is often based on comparisons between dimensions that may not be drawn from the same domain. In such cases, the similarity may be nothing more than analogical and be devoid of the precision that is implied by the need for accuracy. None, therefore, has yet been proven to be "accurate" if precision of prediction is implied by the term.

Fourth, as we have seen, internal consistency and completeness are not features that can be attributed to any theory (Gödel, 1931). Therefore, a demand for consistency should no more be expected of these psychobiological theories than any other. However, even beyond this mathematical subtlety, there are inconsistencies aplenty in virtually all of the theories. Often, these inconsistencies are found in the foundation assumptions on which each theory is based. Sometimes, they are simply illogical steps in the links of an argument.

Most theories, therefore, have to be evaluated on the basis of their simplicity, fruitfulness, and testability. As now shown, all four of the theories fail to satisfactorily meet one or more of these criteria.

7.3.1 Field Theories

Field theories are built on the analogy between the spatial and temporal properties of observed behavior and those of the integrated neural activity of the brain's neurons. The latter are measured with relatively low frequency, global (i.e., widely distributed) signals such as the EEG or the evoked brain potential. The supposed advantages of such an approach are in large part determined by this particular recording technology (it is easy to record these wide spread signals) and the metaphor that has been provided by modern gas or quantum physics (overall pressure can substitute for the details of the components). Furthermore, the concept of a global voltage seems to provide an answer, superficial though it may be, to the ever present, but problematic, binding problem. Unfortunately, the binding problem itself may be more of an artifact of our failed theories than a true problem itself. It represents a hypothetical conundrum that is generated by the need to put back together that that had been incorrectly separated into parts.

There are many difficulties with all field theories. The compound voltages–the empirical data–used in the development of this type of theory are highly variable and the differences recorded under different conditions are notoriously small.[2]

The question then arises–How well do such signals meet the accuracy standard? Although, as I just noted, accuracy is relative, examination of the literature suggests that EEGs and ERPs are neither accurate nor consistent from trial to trial, from subject to subject, or from experiment to experiment. Although the use of integrated signals such as the EEG may seem to simplify the task of measuring the individual responses of a huge number of individual neurons, in fact this kind of simplification tosses out what actually may be the essential information concerning the origins of the mind in the brain.

The main weakness of the field neuroelectric theories, however, is that they are based on tenuous analogies and flimsy bridging assumptions. These failures, at the most fundamental level of their logic, mean that they cannot be fruitful in a scientific sense. Furthermore, there is a ubiquitous failure to meet the testability standard for all field theories. This fact alone would force a critic to conclude they do not meet the criteria of a sound theory of how the brain might make the mind.

To summarize, field theories utilize easily available, but possibly irrelevant, global electrical voltages, rather than the difficult (or impossible) to

---

[2]The major exception to this generalization is to be found in the large difference between the EEGs associated with the various stages of sleep and waking or attention and inattention, respectively. Alpha blockade due to inattention, for example, was first observed in the human brain by Hans Berger in the 1920s. Sleep obliterates the P300 wave of the event related potential (Uttal & Cook, 1964).

record full range of individual neuronal responses. The convenient availability of those measures of brain activity has spurred the development of field theories of the mind. Unfortunately, these theories operate at the wrong level of analysis.

7.3.2 Single Neuron Theories

If the field theories err in directing their attention to a level of analysis that is too macroscopic (largely because of the available technology of EEG recording) the single neuron theorists err in the opposite microscopic direction (largely because of the available technology of single cell recording). The main problem with single neuron theories of mental process is that any data obtained from a microelectrode (or even a practical size array of microelectrodes) is the result of an uncontrolled experiment. The penetration of a single or a few neurons leaves totally unanswered the question of what is going on in other regions of the brain that might be involved in the representation of a salient cognitive process. It is simply impractical to record with a few microelectrodes at a sufficient number of sites to determine the overall pattern of activity of a cognitively significant number of neurons.[3]

This basic limitation—the essentially uncontrolled nature of the single neuron recording technique—leads to a generic failure on the part of microelectrode technology to meet several of the criteria. The attribution of mind to a small number of neurons is essentially an untestable hypothesis; no matter how strong the correlation between the cognitive process and an individual neuron's response, there are too many uncontrolled variables to take any such theory as more than a metaphor for the mind. Although we continue to learn much about the operation of single neurons, it is not possible for such a theory to be fruitful or accurate in any sense of the meaning of these standards. Therefore, the application of the single neuron hypothesis represents another misdirection of theoretical attention from what should be done to what conveniently can be done.

7.3.3 Neural Network Theories

The aspect of brain function that is the most plausible psychoneural equivalent of all aspects of mind, consciousness, or cognitive processing is the adaptive interaction within the huge lattice of neurons operating collec-

[3]A related problem is that even a few microelectrodes can record so many individual neural responses that it quickly becomes impossible to determine their sequential firing relationships. Virtually all such multiple microelectrode studies now only use some cumulative count of the recorded responses as their measure. The hope that multiple arrays of electrodes would allow us to unravel the functional interactions among many neurons has not yet been achieved.

tively by means of modifiable synaptic junctions. This network hypothesis is adhered to by the majority of currently active cognitive neuroscientists. The central idea is that no single neuron is determinative; the emergence of mind is the result of the coordinated activity among what are, for all practical purposes, uncountable large numbers of neurons operating in a coordinated manner—the "enchanted loom" of Sherrington (1940, p. 178).

However valid the conjecture, neural net theories cannot be validated any more than can any of the others. If the number of neurons involved is even moderate, then the numbers of combinations and interactions are beyond practical measure. Added to this combinatorial explosion is the nonlinearity of a system composed, as it must be, of complex interactions between units with lateral and feedback connections. Together, these factors specify an emerging supercomplexity that means there is no hope of a complete neural network theory with available or conceivable network analysis methods. For the reasons discussed in chapter 6, the levels of complexity and numerousness dealt with in the study of the cognitively relevant portions of the brain make any kind of analysis or simulation belong to the frustrating class of intractable problems. Far simpler tasks have been shown to be unsolvable; therefore, there is no reason, other than a kind of naïve optimism, to hope that the tools we have or will have, are going to be capable of "solving" the mind–brain problem.

As a result, all simulations of neural networks are necessarily either toy problems (of inadequate complexity to produce or simulate even relatively simple cognitive processes) or computationally or combinatorially intractable. Neural net theories, therefore, are intrinsically untestable. Other than perhaps providing some heuristic metaphors (e.g., parallel, distributed processing) network approaches are unlikely to solve the mind–brain problem and, therefore, are not fruitful. Whatever superficial simplification may be achieved by dealing with such a toy system, neural network theory at this trivial level has the undesirable property of not adequately representing the entity that it is supposed to describe—the mind. It is a sad state of affairs; although the neural network is most likely to be the proper level of analysis of the mind, neural networks of a suitable level of complexity are beyond our analytic ability.

7.3.4 Brain Chunk (Localization) Theories

Although I have not discussed the localization theory of the link between the mind and the brain extensively in this book, it has been a topic of considerable concern with which I dealt in an earlier book (Uttal, 2001). This type of theory, which assigns modular cognitive functions to localized regions of the brain, has been a dominant idea throughout the history of psychology. Macro-localization, however, is a seriously flawed foundation on which to search for an answer to the mind–brain problem.

From the days of Bacon and Descartes, the strategy of breaking a complex task up into its parts for independent examination has been one of the most widely accepted strategies for dealing with real-world problems. In recent years, however, the emerging realization of the difficulty inherent in the partitioning of nonlinear systems and high-level combinatoric problems has raised serious concern about the appropriateness of this strategy. The debate vying localization ideas against holistic concepts is still an active issue in modern psychology.

Despite this continuing uncertainty, the issue is assumed, without due consideration, to have been resolved by those who would seek to locate functionally specialized cognitive modules in particular regions of the brain. That psychological processes are separable into modules is a required premise if localization in the brain is to serve as the cornerstone of a neuroscientific theory of the mind. Unfortunately there is a strong argument that such a compartmentalization of mental activities is not an adequate description of how the mind works.

Earlier methodologies (e.g., comparisons of behavior before and after surgical lesioning of brain regions) in a search for specialized locations of psychological modules have slowly fallen from favor for several reasons. Ethical and practical concerns (animal research is getting very expensive) are the usual explanations, but there may be a subtler and more effective reason for this decline. The technique of seeking indisputable and uncontroversial changes in an animal's behavior that can be strongly linked to an experimental brain lesion just did not work. Too many equivocations; too complex a system; too many uncontrolled factors; too much recovery of function; and an imprecisely defined brain anatomy all contributed to a diminution of interest in this severely invasive technique.

In recent years, however, the localization approach (otherwise known as "chunkology" or "neophrenology"—pejorative intended) has taken on a new life with the application of modern brain imagining techniques in which the metabolism of localized regions of the brain is shown to vary as a function of assigned cognitive tasks. However, repetition from one laboratory to another and even from one session to another has not been encouraging in producing the kind of stable and replicable scientific evidence that must serve as the broad foundation of a theory. In one of the few meta-studies of brain imaging correlations with cognitive processes, Cabeza and Nyberg (2000) showed that there was an enormous amount of variability in the regions of the brain that were associated with what were relatively well-defined (by psychologists) cognitive processes. The further one moved from sensory processes to higher level cognitive functions, the more dispersed were the brain regions reported as being activated. For example, for working memory, activated regions scattered across virtually the entire brain were reported by different laboratories. Clearly, the empirical foundation for a localization-based theory based on narrowly defined brain regions and mental modules based on brain imaging techniques is not yet sound.

Because of the obvious conceptual misassumptions and the fragile replicability of the database, a modular localization theory of the relationship between the brain and the mind is neither accurate nor empirically consistent.

7.4 SOME GENERAL SOURCES OF THEORETICAL MISDIRECTION

Now that the frailties of the four major mind–brain theories have been considered individually, it is possible to distill the common difficulties they share. The totally understandable human compulsion to explain the magnificent conversion of the functions of a tangible piece of brain matter into the intangible mind is handicapped by a number of conditions and artifacts of our existence and of our science. This section considers some of the main impediments to the development of a satisfactory theory of mind.

7.4.1 Influence of Technologies

Throughout this discussion of the major brain–mind theories proposed in modern times (as well as in the historical past), there has been the recurrent, albeit usually, cryptic background theme—available technology inordinately determines theoretical concepts of the mind–brain relationship. Whatever technologies are momentarily popular at any point in history strongly influence the fundamental analogies, metaphors, and assumptions, of contemporary mind–brain theories. Classic neuroscientific history is filled with allusions to hydraulic, telephonic, and telegraphic stimulants to theoretical ingenuity. The traditional serial computer became the metaphor of choice for those who supported a theory of mind made up of independent cognitive modules. Network approaches, obviously, sprouted from the work on parallel logic circuits carried out during World War II.

The point is that whenever a new technology emerged, a new theory of the relationship between the brain and the mind was born. This effect was particularly noticeable whenever a new technology (e.g., EEGs, microelectrode recordings, brain scanning, etc.) provided a novel means of examining the workings of the brain. To the extent that any new investigation methodology permitted the noninvasive studies of the brain, there were no limits on speculation by psychologists in particular.

An important caveat must not be overlooked. Although every theory must be based on an empirical foundation, concern should be raised when the methodologies rather than the evidence determine the nature of the theory. That the technology or the methodology has historically had such a strong influence on the nature of theory strongly suggests that the mind–body problem is not yet sufficiently constrained by the empirical data. The drastically different and largely incompatible assumptions of the different theories suggest that the connection between the material and immaterial is still moot. Consider the following nutshell statements of what those basic assumptions are:

- Field theories assert that the mind is encoded by continuous, global waves of electrical or chemical activity.
- Single cell theories assert that mind is encoded by the action of one or a very small number of neurons.
- Neural network theories assert that mind is encoded in the coordinated activity of a very large number of heavily interconnected neurons.
- Localization or brain "chunk" theories assert that the isolatable modules of mind are separately encoded in specific interconnected regions of the brain.

Obviously, the four theoretical efforts differ in fundamental ways. At this point, there seems to be no way that a rapprochement among their basic assumptions is likely to occur. Each has gone off in its own direction, depending on its own technology, independently choosing what it assumes to be its own salient corpus of empirical results, and largely ignoring the implications of data obtained with other instruments. Such a situation does not bode well for the unification of these theories in the future.

7.4.2 The Absence of Breadth

Narrowness of vision results directly from the constraints imposed by the limited view of cognitive neuroscience on each theoretical perspective. Indeed, the most egregious limitation of all is their collective inability to provide the one property that is most necessary for the acceptance of a valid theory—breadth. None of these theories offers a depth of explanation that goes beyond their initial, technology driven, assumption. None deals adequately with the wealth of knowledge of any of the others.

7.4.3 Information Loss

Another major problem with all four of the mind–brain theories is their collective information loss. In the case of the localization and field theories, this deficiency is explicitly an intended part of their formularization. These two intentionally smooth over the micro-anatomical details of the brain by concentrating on macroscopic measurements and features. The microdetails are, thereby, finessed. Yet, it is likely that understanding lies in the very microdetails of neuronal interactions being ignored. They are the essential parts of any explanation of the production of mental processes by the brain. To the extent that this assertion is correct, the neural network theory is a closer approximation to ontological truth than any of the other theoretical approaches.

Unfortunately, the neural network theories, themselves, are not immune to this kind of information loss; they, too, represent what is at best a degraded form of representation simply because of our inability to evaluate anything more complicated than a simple “toy” model. The degradation is this case is not in terms of their fundamental assumptions but, rather, is a consequence of the intractable combinatiorial requirements of the computational or mathematical formulations that are necessary to simulate the critical processes that must be invoked to account for the transformation from brain to mind.

Single neuron theories also lose immense amounts of information, not by pooling microresponses, but by ignoring them. A microelectrode records from only one or a few of the many neurons that must be involved in instantiating a cognitive process.

In sum, all neural theories of mind operate in an informationally deprived environment.

7.4.4 The Empirical Inaccessibility of Mind

There is another somewhat cryptic theme underlying virtually all experiments that are invoked to support one or another of the theories discussed in this book. The prototypical procedure in this type of research is to compare some aspect of mental activity with what is assumed to be some corresponding aspect of neural activity. The brain measurements are generally sound and solidly anchored to measurements from other biological, physical, and chemical sciences. However uncertain are the implications of what they may mean, there is little dispute that an EEG or a microelectrode response is measuring what it purports to be measuring with regard to the brain. Bioelectric signals of this sort are direct enough so that we can have confidence that, whatever they may mean, they are accessible to our instruments and probably do not represent artifacts of measurement.

Unfortunately, mental processes are not so directly accessible or so solidly anchored to the dimensions of the physical world. In fact, all our interpretations of mental processes are indirectly inferred from what are the presumed effects of some set of stimuli or from what we construe a given overt behavior to signify about covert mental processes. The difference in accessibility of mental and neural measurements creates a logical imbalance between the two domains. It also raises serious concerns about the ubiquitous strategy of comparing the two kinds of responses.

Because of the intrinsic inaccessibility of mental processes, there may be no way to overcome this imbalance. All too often in our science, we may be comparing ill-defined phenomenological phantoms, accessed through fallible introspection or marginally effective stimulus control, with objective physical measurements.

7.4.5 The Pressure of False Analogies

The imbalance between well-anchored physiological and anatomical measures and vaguely defined mental states makes any such comparison extremely susceptible to potentially misleading reasoning by analogy, that is, by emphasizing what are, at best, superficial similarities of form or process. Although it is clear that science proceeds in large part by the use of metaphors and analogies to stimulate new ideas, it is by no means equally certain that analogies can be used to confirm or deny a given neural theory of the mind.

A false analogy is defined as one in which two events appear to be similar in behavior, but for totally different reasons. The error occurs when a property of one event is attributed to another superficially similar one although they may be the product of entirely different causes. To the extent that the underlying causes cannot be known, any such theory built on analogies would be untestable in the sense required of a sound theory.

The question now arising is—Are the various types of theories that are described here based to an unacceptable degree on analogical reasoning? The answer to this question seems clearly to be "yes." The analogy of slow waves invoked by field theories and the holistic nature of human thought processes (the latter fact authenticated to at least a partial, although admittedly unsatisfactory, degree by our own personal experiences as well as from introspective reports from others) is obvious enough and was discussed in chapter 4.

Furthermore, if one closely examines the strategy used by single cell theorists to support their point of view, it becomes equally clear that the empirical argument in that case depends on a similar analogy drawn between the time course of the response of an impaled neuron and some comparable cognitive process. Neural network theories, to the extent that they simulate behavior in toy systems, also depend on the analogy between the observed microstructure structure of the brain and that of the lattice structure programmed into a computer model. The respective details of the two systems suggest, however, that although the behavior of the two systems may be similar, their underlying causes may be quite different.

The residual problem, therefore, is that each of these comparisons of neural and inferred cognitive processes is only an unprovable analogy. The assumption that they are causally identical is fragile at best, if not completely erroneous. However fragile or uncertain, little or no effort is usually made to establish possible causal links. Thus, for reasons of deep principle, an analogical argument cannot authenticate proposed relationships between the mind and the brain.

There is an unfortunate lack of appreciation throughout cognitive neuroscience that such analogies are based on superficial functional descriptions and not reductive explanations. Even our most powerful tool, mathematics, is incapable of doing more than describing the action of a system. It, like all other analogical methods, remains neutral with regard to the underlying mechanisms of the events it so effectively describes.

7.4.6 Other Conceptual and Logical Errors

It is as easy in the intricate and complex field of cognitive neuroscience for one's premises to dictate one's conclusions, as it is for available tools to specify one's theoretical orientation. The database of this science is replete with examples of how the posing of a question can lead to an empirical answer that is preordained by the selection of stimuli or the construction of the experimental protocol. Logicians refer to this as "affirming the consequent"; a logical fallacy more present in a wide variety of cognitive neuroscience protocols than we may wish to accept.

This situation, of course, is exacerbated when the premises of an argument are incorrect. However, it should also be clear that logical errors could occur even when the premises of the argument are unassailable. In that case even the most impeccable axioms or premises can lead to fallacious conclusions. The prototypical cognitive neuroscience example of such a cryptic logical error occurs in those experiments in which a stimulus is assumed to represent one class of objects (e.g., a face) when, in fact, deeper analysis shows that it actually represents some subcomponent that was fortuitously included in the complete object (e.g., a T shaped arrangement).

In many instances, enormous conceptual gaps between the logical premises and conclusions are crossed, not on the basis of solid evidentiary foundations, but on imaginative, if not fanciful hypotheses or far-fetched bridging assumptions. This kind of specious logical leap is especially prevalent in correlative studies based on superficial similarities between observations of the time courses of two very different functions.

7.5 SOME BARRIERS TO SOLVING THE MIND–BRAIN PROBLEM

The mind–brain problem constitutes what is arguably the most extreme challenge to science. As I review the discussion in this book, it becomes clear that many of my readers may feel it is a pessimistic view of the future. Such a judgment, however, is not warranted. Science of all kinds is replete with constraints, boundaries, and intractable problems. Some of our most fundamental conceptual and technical limits have not only been found to be true but have provided the basis for an ever-deepening understanding of our universe and ourselves. To mention only a few of the best known:

- the speed of light
- the conservation of energy
- the irreversibility of time
- the impossibility of perpetual motion
- the insolvability of certain mathematical problems
- the incompleteness and undecidability of all theoretical systems
- the uncertainty principle

Given this array of widely accepted limits to what can be known about the physical world of which we are a part, one wonders why there is such reluctance to accept that there are going to be equally profound, and yet equally fruitful, limits in the mind–brain sciences? The answer to this rhetorical question mainly lies in the fact that we really do not yet have the barest glimmerings of how the brain produces the mind. Therefore, the mind–brain problem remains susceptible to wild speculation, no matter how inconsistent the arguments and no matter how incomplete the supporting data. Some of the most fundamental and controversial issues, therefore, remain open to what is essentially a matter of scientific *belief* rather than scientific *rigor*.

As the empirical data accumulate, cognitive neuroscientists should have become increasingly aware that their neuroreductive science has limits similar to those found in the sciences of the physical macrocosm and the microcosm. In the future, the ultimate appreciation of these limits on brain–mind reductionism are likely to be as revered as those comparable principles in the physical, chemical, and biological sciences.

The argument made here is that comparable barriers to theoretical progress, if not completeness, exist in the cognitive neurosciences as they do in the physical sciences. It is further argued that these limits should not be faced with scientific despair but with the same appreciation that they, too, might help to stimulate cognitive neuroscience to further understanding.

Among the most relevant of these fundamental barriers to cognitive neuroscience theory building encountered when we deal with systems as complex as the brain are:

1. *The combinatorial explosion:* Many formal theories are incapable of dealing with the huge numbers of components or transformations that exist when dealing with the brain with its enormous numbers of heavily and idiosyncratically interconnected neurons.

2. *Nonlinear systems:* The response to some of the nonlinearities introduced into systems in which there is extensive feedback, feed forward, and lateral connections have not been developed. In some cases, mathematicians have already proven that analytic solutions are not possible. In particular, the hierarchical arrangement of the heavily interconnected regions of the brain, at its most fundamental level, is indeterminate and no unique solution is possible (Hilgetag, O'Neill, & Young, 1996; 2000).[4]

3. *Chaotic Randomness:* Although the general characteristics of a random or quasi-random process may be specified by the nature of its attractors, the details of the behavior of the components of such a system will always be obscured by the fact that a small early event may have a profound later effect. That is, it is impossible to either deterministically predict the future of a chaotic system because of the influence of innumerable small (however deterministic) perturbations or to run the system backwards to its initial conditions. In other words, systems with high entropy (i.e., low information content) are not reversible. It is not possible to unscramble eggs for the simple reason that the historical information is lost!

4. *The Black Box Problem:* The inner mechanisms of a closed system cannot be deduced from the changes that occur between its input and its output. This caveat holds for mathematical models and for behavior observed with psychophysical methods; both of which are neutral with regard to inner mechanisms. This constraint holds true for the brain sciences in a curious way. Although it is possible to open the "black box" of the skull to carry out physiological experiments on the brain, one encounters another kind of functional black box whenever experiments get down to the essential level of psychoneural equivalence. This second level of black box impenetrability

---

[4]In a personal communication to me, C. Hilgetag (Summer, 2004) pointed out that the conclusion to which he and his colleagues were led is widely misunderstood. It is an interesting side issue that even when an irrefutable mathematical proof is provided concerning a completely germane situation, neuroscientists do not always accept it. One of the corollaries of Hilgetag, O'Neil, and Young's (1996, 2000) articles is that no amount of additional data collection can overcome the fundamental barrier to determining the unique hierarchy of a system that can otherwise be shown to be hierarically organized. Hilgetag reports that many of his colleagues ignored this point and argued—"We just need some more data and then we can do what you believe is impossible." The power of our preconceptions is enormous!

is the enormous complexity of the great neural networks of the brain. The brain may be anatomically exposed but it is still closed to examination and analysis by complexity, entropic, and chaotic considerations.

5. *Incomplete Nature of Theories:* Theories, indeed models and maps of all kinds, are incomplete representations of the system being represented. Not only do they not "explain" everything, but they also may add conflating and superfluous information to the description of the system because of their own properties. In some cases, therefore, the properties of the model or map itself may be introduced into the interpretation of the system under study. In cognitive neuroscience, this kind of erroneous "super-completeness" is as serious as a map's incompleteness.

6. *Incomplete Nature of Data:* However hard we work, it is, of course, not possible to collect all of the information needed to authenticate a theory for all possible conditions. Thus, many theoreticians are forced to extrapolate from what is actually an inadequate knowledge base to flesh out the details of their theories. In some situations, specifically the neurophysiological use of the microelectrode (a device that is incapable of measuring distributed neural activity) the inadequacy of the data is so extreme that it leads theory in entirely the wrong direction. An implication of this concept of incomplete data is that meta-analyses of whatever available data are available is essential. Unfortunately, it is rare to identify idiosyncratic and theoretically misleading results by broad scale meta-analyses of the kind especially needed in the cognitive neurosciences.

7. *Elusive Definitions of Mind:* One of the major problems in developing a theory of mind is the elusive nature of the mind itself. Defining mind, mental processes, cognitions, awareness, or consciousness is an enormously difficult, if not impossible, task. Despite many and diverse definitions proposed over the years, there still is great difficulty in simply arriving at a consensus for what these words mean. One reason for this lexicographic intransigence is the intrapersonal privacy of our mental activity. It is not at all certain that the nature of mind can be inferred from behavior in spite of the near universal acceptance of this assumption by mentalist psychologists of many different persuasions.

8. *Impossibility of Verification:* As much as we would like to believe that our theories can be tested and accepted or rejected, there is considerable debate concerning whether or not we will be able to do so. For example, interpretations of Gödel's theorem of the incompleteness and undecidability of any logical or mathematical system have suggested to some philosophers that it is impossible for the human mind to understand itself.

9. *Misallocation of the Meaning of Empirical Results:* Although we cannot measure everything, there is already such a huge mass of data available, that it is always possible to find some result that seems to support virtually any

theory. One of the most surprising effects of this difficulty is that contesting theories, even when speaking about the same issue, do not allude to the same empirical database in their search for support.

7.6 A FUTURE COURSE OF ACTION

If one accepts the fact that there are barriers and limit to theory building in cognitive neuroscience, it is fair to ask, what should we do in the future? The first answer to this question has to be that the current empirical course of this science should continue pretty much as it has in the past. There is much to be learned in the laboratories of psychologists and neurophysiologists with their conventional armamentarium of methods and tools. However, I am convinced there is a sustainable argument that the mentalism of cognitive psychology is a dead end. In its place, a revitalized and reconstructed version of a positivist, objective behaviorism that does not seek to accomplish the impossible, should be the preferred course of scientific action. This new version of behaviorism should have the following characteristics, a list with which I have concluded all of my recent books.

1. Psychophysical: It must utilize the well-controlled methods of psychophysical research.
2. Anchored Stimuli: Stimuli must be anchored to independent physical measures.
3. Simple Responses: Psychophysical responses must be limited to simple (Class A as defined by Brindley, 1960) discriminations such as "same" or "different" to minimize the cognitive penetration effects that distort functional relationships.
4. Operational: It must define its concepts in terms of procedures, not in terms of unverifiable, ad hoc hypothetical mentalist constructs.
5. Mathematically descriptive: Its formal theories must be acknowledged to be only behaviorally descriptive and to be neutral with regard to underlying mechanisms.
6. Neuronally Nonreductive: It must abandon any hope of reducing psychological phenomena to the details of neural nets because of their computational intractability.
7. Experimental: It must continue to maintain the empirical tussle with nature that has characterized the best psychology in the past.
8. Molar: It must look at behavior in terms of the overall, unitary, integrated process it is and avoid invoking a false modularity.
9. Empiricist$_1$ and Nativist: It must accept the compromise that both experience and evolved mechanisms motivate and drive behavior.

10. Empiricist$_2$ and Rationalist: It must accept that compromise that behavior accrues from both stimulus determined (automatic) and logical (inferential) causal sequences.
11. Anti-Pragmatic: Psychology must accept its primary role as a theoretical science and base it goals on the quest for knowledge of the nature of our nature rather than on the immediate needs of society or the utility that some of its findings may seem to have. *Useful* theories do not necessarily have the same validity as *true* explanations.

However this new science may deviate from the current zeitgeist, there is no need to invoke any supernatural mysteries. Complexity alone provides an insurmountable barrier to analysis and understanding. It, along with mental inaccessibility, is the most compelling argument for a new look at behaviorism.

References

Adrian, E. D. (1928). *The basis of sensation*. London: Christophers.

Adrian, E. D. (1942). Olfactory responses in the brain of the hedgehog. *Journal of Physiology (London), 100*.

Adrian, E. D., & Bronk, D. W. (1928). The discharge of impulses in motor nerve fibers. I Impulses in single fibres of the phrenic nerve. *Journal of Physiology (London), 66*, 81–101.

Amari, S.-I. (1977). Neural theory of association and concept-formation. *Biological Cybernetics, 26*, 175–185.

American Psychiatric Association. (1992). *Diagnostic and statistical manual of mental disorders* (4th ed.). Washington, DC: Author.

Anderson, J. A. (1995). *An introduction to neural networks*. Cambridge, MA: MIT Press.

Anonymous. (2003). *The experts respond*. nytimes.com. Retrieved November 10, 2003, from the World Wide Web: http://www/nytimes.com/2003/11/10/science/BLAKESLEE.html

Aristotle. (1976). *De Anima/Aristotle* (R. D. Hicks, Trans.). New York: Arno Press.

Aspect, A., Dalibard, J., & Roger, G. (1982). Experimental test of Bell's inequalities using time-varying analyzers. *Physical Review Letters, 49*, 1804–1807.

Aspect, A., Grangier, P., & Roger, G. (1982). Experimental realization of Einstein-Podolsky-Rosen-Bohm *Gedankenexperiment*: A new violation of Bell's inequalities. *Physical Review Letters, 49*, 91–94.

Baars, B. J. (1996). *In the theater of consciousness: The workspace of the mind*. Oxford, England: Oxford University Press.

Baars, B. J. (2001). There are no known differences in fundamental brain mechanisms of sensory consciousness between humans and other mammals. *Animal Welfare, 10*, S31–S40.

Badash, L. (1972). The completeness of nineteenth-century science. *Isis, 63*, 48–58.

Barlow, H. B. (1953). Summation and inhibition in the frog's retina. *Journal of Physiology, 119*, 69–88.

Barlow, H. B. (1961). Possible principles underlying the transformations of sensory messages. In W. A. Rosenblith (Ed.), *Sensory communication* (pp. 217–234). Cambridge, MA and New York City: MIT Press and Wiley (Joint Publishers).

Barlow, H. B. (1972). Single units and sensation: A neuron doctrine for perceptual psychology. *Perception, 1*, 371–394.

Barlow, H. B. (1978). The efficiency of detecting changes in random dot patterns. *Vision Research, 18*, 637–650.

Barlow, H. B. (1995). The neuron doctrine in perception. In M. S. Gazzaniga (Ed.), *The cognitive neurosciences* (pp. 415–435). Cambridge, MA: MIT Press.

Barlow, H. B. (2001). The exploitations of regularities in the environment by the brain. *Behavioral and Brain Sciences, 24*, 602–607.

Barlow, H. B., Hill, R. M., & Levick, W. R. (1964). Retinal ganglion cells responding selectively to direction and speed of image in the rabbit. *Journal of Physiology, 173*, 377–407.

Basar, E. (1998). *Brain functions and oscillations: Volume II: Integrative brain function, neurophysiology and cognitive functions*. Berlin: Springer.

Basar, E., Gonder, A., Ozesmi, C., & Ungan, P. (1975). Dynamics of brain rhythmic and evoked potentials. II. Studies in the auditory pathway, reticular formation, and hippocampus during the waking stage. *Biological Cybernetics, 20*, 145–160.

Beckermann, A. (2000). The perennial problem of the reductive explainability of phenomenal consciousness: C. D. Broad on the explanatory gap. In T. Metzinger (Ed.), *Neural correlates of consciousness*. Cambridge, MA: MIT Press.

Bell, J. S. (1964). On the Einstein-Podolsky-Rosen paradox. *Quantum Theory, 1*, 195–200.

Berkeley, G. (1710/1998). In J. Dancy (Ed.), *A treatise concerning the principles of human knowledge*. Oxford, England: Oxford University Press.

Berkley, M. A., Kitterlee, F., & Watkins, D. W. (1975). Grating visibility as a function of orientation and retinal eccentricity. *Vision Research, 15*, 239–244.

Binet, A. (1907). *The mind and the brain*. London: Kegan Paul, Trench, Trubner and Co.

Blake, R., & Bellhorn, R. (1978). Visual acuity in cats with central retinal lesions. *Vision Research, 18*, 15–18.

Blakemore, C. (1973). The language of vision. *New Scientist, 56*, 674–677.

Blakeslee, S. (November 11, 2003). *(4) How does the brain work*. nytimes.com. Retrieved, from the World Wide Web: http://www.nytimes.com/2003/11/11/science/11BRAI.htl

Bland, R. G., & Jaques, H. E. (1978). *How to know the insects*. New York: McGraw-Hill.

Block, H. D. (1962). The perceptron: A model for brain functioning. I. *Reviews of Modern Physics, 34*, 123–135.

Block, N., & Stalnaker, R. (1999). Conceptual analysis, dualism, and the explanatory gap. *Philosophical Review, 108*, 1–46.

Bogen, J. E. (1995). On the neurophysiology of consciousness: 1. An overview. *Consciousness and Cognition, 4*, 52–62.

Bohm, D. (1952a). A suggested interpretation of the quantum theory in terms of "hidden" variables. I. *Physical Review, 85*, 166–179.

Bohm, D. (1952b). A suggested interpretation of the quantum theory in terms of "hidden" variables. II. *Physical Review, 85*, 180–193.

Bohm, D. (1980). *Wholeness and the implicate order*. London: Routledge.

Boring, E. G. (1950). *A history of experimental psychology*. New York: Appleton-Century-Crofts.

Brazier, M. A. B. (1961). *A history of the electrical activity of the brain*. London: Pitman Medical Publishing.

Bremer, F. (1935). Cerveau "isole" et physiologie du sommeil. *Comptes Rendus. Societe de Biologie, 118*, 1235–1241.

Bremermann, H. J. (1977). What mathematics can and cannot do for pattern recognition. In O.-J. Grusser & R. Klinke (Eds.), *Pattern recognition in biological and technical systems*. Heidelberg, Germany: Springer-Verlag.

Brindley, G. S. (1960). *Physiology of the retina and the visual pathway*. London: Edward Arnold.

Britten, H. T., & Newsome, W. T. (1998). Tuning bandwidths for near-threshold stimuli in area MT. *Journal of Neurophysiology, 80*, 762–770.

Brown, P. K., & Wald, G. (1964). Visual pigments in single rods and cones of the human retina. *Science, 144*, 145–151.

Bruce, C., Desimone, R., & Gross, C. G. (1981). Visual properties of neurons in a polysensory area in superior temporal sulcus of the Macaque. *Journal of Neurophysiology, 46*, 369–384.

Burrell, B. (2005). *Postcards from The Brain Museum: The improbable search for meaning in the matter of famous minds.* New York: Doubleday.

Byrne, A., & Hilbert, D. R. (1999). Two radical neuron doctrines. *Behavioral and Brain Sciences, 22*, 833.

Cabeza, R., & Nyberg, L. (2000). Imaging cognition II: An empirical review of 275 PET and fMRI studies. *Journal of Cognitive Neuroscience, 12*, 1–47.

Cagle, J. A. (2003). *Science and theories.* Retrieved, from the World Wide Web: http://zimmer.csufresno.edu/~johnca/spch100/science.htm

Cahill, T. (1996). *How the Irish saved civilization: The untold story of Ireland's heroic role from the fall of Rome to the rise of medieval Europe.* New York: Anchor Books.

Cajal, S. R. y. (1900). *Die Sehrinde.* Leipzig: Barth.

Cajal, S. R. y. (1906, December 12). *The structure and functions of neurons.* Paper presented at the Nobel Foundation Award Ceremony.

Cajal, S. R. y. (1911). *Histologie du systeme nerveux.* Paris: Maloine.

Casti, J. L. (1996). Confronting science's logical limits. *Scientific American* (October), 102–105.

Chaitin, G. J. (1982). Gödel's theorem and information. *International Journal of Theoretical Physics, 22*, 941–954.

Chalmers, D. J. (1995). Facing up to the problem of consciousness. *Journal of Consciousness Studies, 2*, 200–219.

Chalmers, D. J. (2000). What is a neural correlate of consciousness? In T. Metzinger (Ed.), *Neural correlates of consciousness.* Cambridge, MA: MIT Press.

Churchland, P. M. (1981). Eliminative materialism and it propositional attitudes. *Journal of Philosophy, 78*, 67–90.

Churchland, P. M., & Churchland, P. S. (1994). Intertheoretic reduction: A neuroscientist's field guide. In R. Warner & T. Szubka (Eds.), *The mind–body problem.* Oxford, England: Blackwell.

Coterill, R. (1994). On the unity of conscious experience. *Journal of Consciousness Studies, 2*, 290–311.

Cox, D. R., & Smith, W. L. (1954). On the superimposition of renewal processes. *Biometrika, 41*, 91–99.

Crick, F., & Koch, C. (1990). Towards a neurobiological theory of consciousness. *Seminars in the Neurosciences, 2*, 263–275.

Crick, F., & Koch, C. (1995). Are we aware of neural activity in primary visual cortex? *Nature, 375*, 121–123.

Crick, F., & Koch, C. (2000). The unconscious homunculus. In T. Metzinger (Ed.), *Neural correlates of consciousness* (pp. 103–110). Cambridge, MA: MIT Press.

Culbertson, J. T. (1950). *Consciousness and behavior: A neural analysis.* Dubuque, IA: William C. Brown.

Cummins, R. (1983). *The nature of psychological explanation.* Cambridge, MA: MIT Press.

Curtis, H. J., & Cole, K. S. (1942). Membrane resting and action potentials from the squid giant axon. *Journal of Cellular and Comparative Physiology, 19*, 135–144.

Dawes, R. M. (1994). *House of cards: Psychology and psychotherapy built on myth.* New York: Free Press.

Dayanand, S. (1999). Surface reconstruction. In W. R. Uttal (Ed.), *Computational modeling of vision: The role of combination.* New York: Marcel Dekker.

de Robertis, E., & Bennett, H. S. (1954). Submicroscopic vesicular component in the synapse. *Federation Proceedings, 13*, 35.

Dehaene, S., & Naccache, L. (2001). Towards a cognitive neuroscience of consciousness: Basic evidence and a workspace framework. *Cognition, 79*, 1–37.

Descartes, R. (1649). *A discourse of a method for the well guiding of reason, and the discovery of truth in the sciences* (English ed.). London: Thomas Newcombe.

DeValois, R. L., & DeValois, K. K. (1988). *Spatial vision*. New York: Oxford University Press.

DeValois, R. L., Smith, C. J., Kitai, S. T., & Karoly, A. J. (1958). Responses of single cells in different layers of the primate lateral geniculate nucleus to monochromatic light. *Science, 127*, 238–239.

Diels, H., & Kranz, W. (1966/1967). *Die Fragmente der Vorsokratiker*. Dublin: Weidmann.

Duhem, P. M. M. (1914/1954). *The aim and structure of physical theory* (P. P. Wiener, Trans.). Princeton, NJ: Princeton University Press.

Eccles, J. C. (1994). *How the self controls the brain*. Berlin: Springer-Verlag.

Edelstein, L. (1943). *The Hippocratic oath: Text, translation, and interpretation*. Baltimore: Johns Hopkins University Press.

Ehrenstein, W., Spillmann, L., & Sarris, V. (2003). Gestalt issues in modern neuroscience. *Axiomathes, 13*, 433–458.

Einstein, A. (1934). *Essays in science*. New York: Philosophical Library.

Einstein, A., Podolsky, B., & Rosen, N. (1935). Can quantum-mechanical description of physical reality be complete? *Physical Review, 41*, 777.

Elliot, M. A., & Muller, H. J. (2000). Evidence for a 40-Hz oscillatory short-term visual memory revealed by human reaction time measurements. *Journal of Experimental Psychology: Learning, Memory, and Cognition, 26*, 1–16.

Erwin, T. L. (1997). Biodiversity at its utmost: Tropical forest beetles. In M. L. Reaka-Kudla, D. E. Wilson, & E. O. Wilson (Eds.), *Biodiversity II*. Washington, DC: Joseph Henry Press.

Feisler, E., & Beale, R. (1997). *Handbook of neural computation*. New York: Oxford University Press.

Feldman, J. A., & Ballard, D. H. (1982). Connectionist models and their properties. *Cognitive Science, 6*, 205–254.

Ferrier, D. (1886). *The functions of the brain* (2nd ed.). New York: G. Putnam's Sons.

Fiorentini, A. (1972). Mach band phenomena. In D. Jameson & L. M. Hurvich (Eds.), *Handbook of sensory physiology: Volume VII/4*. Berlin: Springer-Verlag.

Fiorentini, A., & Radici, T. (1957). Binocular measurements of brightness on a field presenting a luminance grating. *Att Fond. G. Ronchi, 12*, 453–461.

Fodor, J. A., & Pylyshyn, Z. W. (1988). Connectionism and cognitive architecture: A critical analysis. In S. Pinker & J. Mehler (Eds.), *Connections and symbols* (pp. 3–71). Cambridge, MA: MIT Press.

Freeman, W. J. (1975). *Mass action in the nervous system*. New York: Academic Press.

Freeman, W. J. (1991). The physiology of perception. *Scientific American, 264*(2), 78–85.

Freeman, W. J. (2000). *Neurodynamics: An exploration in mesoscopic brain dynamics*. London: Springer-Verlag.

Freeman, W. J., & Skarda, C. (1985). Nonlinear dynamics, perception, and the EEG; the neo-Sherrington view. *Brain Research Reviews, 10*, 147–175.

Fukushima, K., & Miyake, S. (1978). A self-organizing neural network with a function of associative memory. Feedback-type cognitron. *Biological Cybernetics, 21*, 201–208.

Gabor, D. (1948). A new microscopic principle. *Nature, 161*, 777.

Gabor, D. (1949). Microscopy by reconstructed wave fronts. *Proceedings of the Royal Society of London (A), 197*, 454–487.

Galambos, R., & Davis, H. (1943). The response of single auditory-nerve fibers to acoustic stimulation. *Journal of Neurophysiology, 6*, 39–57.

Galambos, R., Makeig, S., & Talmachoff, P. (1981). A 40 Hz auditory potential recorded from the human scalp. *Proceedings of the National Academy of Sciences, USA, 78*, 2643–2647.

Galen. (177/1956). *On anatomical procedures* (C. Singer, Trans.). London: Oxford University Press.

Gall, F. J., & Spurzheim, J. C. (1808). *Recherches sur le system nerveux en general, et sur celui cerveau en particulier*. Paris: Academie de Sciences, Memoirs.

Galvani, L. (1791/1953). *Commentary on the effect of electricity on muscular motion* (R. M. Green, Trans.). Cambridge, MA: Licht.

Giese, M., & Xie, X. (2002). Exact solution of the nonlinear dynamics of recurrent neural mechanisms for direction selectivity. *Neurocomputing, 44–46*, 417–422.

Gödel, K. (1931). Uber formal unentscheidbare Satz der Principia Mathematica undverwandter Systeme I [On formally undecidable propositions in Principia Mathematica and Related Systems]. *Monatshefte fur Mathematik und Physik, 38*, 173–198.

Gold, I., & Stoljar, D. (1999). A neuron doctrine in the philosophy of neuroscience. *Behavioral and Brain Sciences, 22*, 809–830.

Goldscheider, A. (1906). Uber die materiellen Veranderungen be der Azzoziationsbildung. *Neurologisches Centralblatt, 25*, 146.

Golgi, C. (December 11, 1906). *The neuron doctrine—theory and facts.* Paper presented at the Nobel Foundation Awards Ceremony.

Graham, J., & Gerard, R. W. (1946). Membrane potentials and excitation of impaled single muscle fibers. *Journal of Cellular and Comparative Physiology, 28*, 99–117.

Granit, R. (1977). *The purposive brain.* Cambridge, MA: MIT Press.

Gray, J. A. (1995). The contents of consciousness: A neuropsychological conjecture. *Behavioral and Brain Sciences, 18*, 659–722.

Gross, C. G. (2002). Genealogy of the "grandmother cell." *The Neuroscientist, 8*, 512–518.

Gross, C. G., Rocha-Miranda, C. E., & Bender, D. B. (1972). Visual properties of neurons in the inferotemporal cortex of the macaque. *Journal of Neurophysiology, 35*, 96–111.

Grush, R., & Churchland, P. S. (1995). Gaps in Penrose's toilings. *Journal of Consciousness Studies, 2*, 10–29.

Guthrie, E. R. (1946). Psychological facts and psychological theory. *Psychological Bulletin, 43*, 1–20.

Haig, A. R., Gordon, E., Wright, J. J., Meares, R. A., & Bahramali, H. (2000). Synchronous cortical gamma-band activity in task-relevant cognition. *Computational Neuroscience, Neuroreport, 11*, 669–675.

Hameroff, S. R. (1999). The neuron doctrine is an insult to neurons. *Behavioral and Brain Sciences, 22*, 838–839.

Hameroff, S. R., & Penrose, R. (1996). Orchestrated reduction of quantum coherence in brain microtubules: A model for consciousness. In S. R. Hameroff, A. Kaszniak, & A. C. Scott (Eds.), *Toward a science of consciousness: The first Tucson discussions and debates.* Cambridge, MA: MIT Press.

Harris, C. S. (1980). Insight or out of sight?: Two examples of perceptual plasticity in the human adult. In C. S. Harris (Ed.), *Visual coding and adaptability* (pp. 95–149). Hillsdale, NJ: Lawrence Erlbaum Associates.

Hartline, H. K. (1935). Impulses in single optic nerve fibers of the vertebrate retina. *Journal of Physiology, 113*, 59P.

Hartline, H. K. (1938). The response of single optic nerve fibers of the vertebrate eye to illumination of the retina. *American Journal of Physiology, 121*, 400–415.

Hartline, H. K. (1940a). The receptive field of optic nerve fibers. *American Journal of Physiology, 130*, 690–699.

Hartline, H. K. (1940b). The effects of spatial summation in the retina on the excitation of fibers in the optic nerve. *American Journal of Physiology, 130*, 700–711.

Hartline, H. K., & Ratliff, F. (1957). Inhibitory interaction in the eye of the Limulus. *Journal of General Physiology, 40*, 357–376.

Hartline, H. K., Wagner, H., & Ratliff, F. (1956). Inhibition in the eye of Limulus. *Journal of General Physiology, 39*, 651–673.

Hebb, D. O. (1949). *The organization of behavior: A neuropsychological theory.* New York: Wiley.

Helmholtz, H. v. (1850). Vorlaufige Bericht uber die Fortpflanzung-Geschwindigkeit der Nervenreizung. *Arch. Anat. u. Physiol.*, 71.

Hempel, C. G. (1965). *Aspects of scientific explanation and other essays in the philosophy of science.* New York: Free Press.

Hempel, C. G., & Oppenheim, P. (1948). Studies in the logic of explanation. *Philosophy of Science, 15*, 135–175.

Henkin, L. (1967). Systems, formal, and models of formal systems. In P. Edwards (Ed.), *The encyclopedia of philosophy*. New York: Macmillan and the Free Press.

Hennig, W. (1966). *Phylogenetic systematics* (D. D. Davis & R. Zangerl, Trans.). Urbana: University of Illinois Press.

Hilgetag, C. C., O'Neil, M. A., & Young, M. P. (1996). Indeterminate organization of the visual system. *Science, 271*, 776–777.

Hilgetag, C. C., O'Neil, M. A., & Young, M. P. (2000). Hierarchical organization of macaque and cat cortical sensory mechanisms explored with a novel network processor. *Philosophical Transactions of the Royal Society of London. B., 355*, 71–89.

Hinton, G. E., & Sejnowski, T. J. (1988). Learning and relearning in Boltzmann machines. In D. E. Rumelhart, J. L. McClelland, & The PDP Research Group (Eds.), *Parallel distributed processing: Explorations in the microstructure of cognition. Vol. 1: Foundations* (pp. 282–317). Cambridge, MA: MIT Press.

Hodgkin, A. L. (1948). The local electrical charge associated with repetitive action in a non-medullated axon. *Journal of Physiology (London), 107*, 165–181.

Hodgkin, A. L., & Huxley, A. F. (1939). Action potentials recorded from inside a nerve fibre. *Nature, 144*, 710.

Hodgkin, A. L., & Katz, B. (1949). The effect of sodium ions on the electrical activity of the giant axon of the squid. *Journal of Physiology (London), 108*, 424–448.

Hon, G. (2001). Introduction: The how and why of explanation. In G. Hon & S. S. Rakover (Eds.), *Explanation: Theoretical approaches and applications*. Dordrecht: Kluwer.

Hooker, C. A. (1987). *A realistic theory of science*. Albany: State University of New York Press.

Hopfield, J. J. (1982). Neural networks and physical systems with emergent collective computational abilities. *Proceedings of the National Academy of Sciences, USA, 79*, 2554–2558.

Hopfield, J. J. (1984). Neurons with graded responses have collective computational properties like those of two-state neurons. *Proceedings of the National Academy of Sciences, USA, 81*, 3088–3092.

Horgan, J. (1999). *The undiscovered mind*. New York: The Free Press.

Hubel, D. H. (1957). Tungsten microelectrode for recording from single units. *Science, 125*, 549–550.

Hubel, D. H., & Wiesel, T. N. (1959). Receptive fields of single neurones in the cat's striate cortex. *Journal of Physiology, 148*, 574–591.

Hubel, D. H., & Wiesel, T. N. (1965). Receptive fields and functional architecture in two nonstriate visual areas (18 and 19) of the cat. *Journal of Neurophysiology, 28*, 229–289.

Hull, C. L. (1943). *Principles of behavior*. New York: Appleton Century Crofts.

Hurvich, L. M., & Jameson, D. (1957). An opponent–process theory of color vision. *Psychological Review, 64*, 384–404.

Igel, C., Erlhagen, W., & Jancke, D. (2001). Optimization of dynamic neural fields. *Neurocomputing, 36*, 225–233.

Ingber, L. (1985). Statistical mechanics of neocortical interaction: Stability and duration of the 7+/−2 rule of short term memory capacity. *Physical Review (A), 31*, 1183–1186.

Ingber, L., & Nunez, P. L. (1995). Statistical mechanics or neocortical interactions: High resolution path-calculation of short-term memory. *Physical Review (E), 51*, 5074–5083.

James, W. (1890). *Principles of psychology*. New York: Henry Holt.

John, E. R. (1990). Representation of information in the brain. In E. R. John (Ed.), *Machinery of the mind: Data, theory, and speculations about higher brain function*. Boston: Birkhauser.

John, E. R. (1972). Switchboard versus statistical theories of learning and memory. *Science, 177*, 850–864.

Joliot, M., Ribary, U., & Llinas, R. (1994). Human oscillatory brain activity near 40 Hz coexists with cognitive temporal binding. *Proceedings of the National Academy of Sciences, USA, 91,* 11748–11751.

Judd, J. S. (1991). *Neural network design and the complexity of learning.* Cambridge, MA: MIT Press.

Jung, R., & Spillmann, L. (1970). Receptive-field estimation and perceptual integration in human vision. In F. A. Young & D. B. Lindsley (Eds.), *Early experience and visual information processing in perceptual and reading disorders* (pp. 181–197). Washington, DC.: National Academy of Sciences.

Kaplan, A. (1964). *The conduct of inquiry: Methodology for behavioral science.* San Francisco: Chandler.

Karp, R. M. (1986). Combinatorics, complexity, and randomness. *Communications of the Association for Computer Machinery, 29,* 98–108.

Kennedy, D. (2004). Neuroscience and ethics. *Science, 306,* 373.

Kennedy, J. L. (1959). A possible artifact in electroencephalography. *Psychological Review, 66,* 347–352.

Kerlinger, F. N. (1986). *Foundations of behavioral research.* New York: Holt, Rinehart & Winston.

Kingsley, C. (1893). Vesalius, the anatomist. In C. Kingsley (Ed.), *Health and education.* New York: D. Appleton and Company.

Kinsbourne, M. (2003). *The multimodal mind: How the senses combine in the brain.* Retrieved from the World Wide Web: http://www.semioticon.com/virtuals/multimodality2/talks/kinsbourne.pdf

Kirkpatrick, S., Gellatt, Jr., C. D., & Vecchi, M. P. (1983). Optimization by simulated annealing. *Science, 220,* 671–680.

Kissler, J., Muller, M. M., Fehr, T., Rockstroh, B., & Elbert, T. (2000). MEG gamma band activity in schizophrenic patients and healthy subjects in a mental arithmetic task and at rest. *Clinical Neurophysiology, 111*(2079–2087).

Klee, R. (1997). *Introduction to the philosophy of science: Cutting nature to its seams.* New York: Oxford University Press.

Kockelmans, J. J. (1968). *Philosophy of science: The historical background.* New York: The Free Press.

Kohler, W. (1920). *Die physisichen Gestalten in Ruhe und im stationaren Zustrand.* Braunschweig: Vieweg.

Kohler, W. (1938). *The place of value in a world of facts.* New York: Liveright.

Kohler, W., & Held, R. (1949). The cortical correlate of pattern vision. *Science, 110,* 414–419.

Kohonen, T. (1977). *Associative memory: A system-theoretical approach.* Berlin: Springer-Verlag.

Konorski, J. (1967). *Integrative activity of the brain.* Chicago: University of Chicago Press.

Korzybski, A. (1933/1995). *Science and sanity: An introduction to non-Aristotelian systems and general semantics* (5th ed.). Ft. Worth, TX: Institute of General Semantics.

Krausz, E. (2000). *The limits of science.* New York: Peter Lang.

Kretschmer, E. (1925). *Physique and character.* London: Kegan Paul, Trench, Trubner.

Kuffler, S. W. (1953). Discharge patterns and functional organization of the mammalian retina. *Journal of Neurophysiology, 16,* 37–68.

Kuhn, T. S. (1970). *The structure of scientific revolutions* (2nd ed.). Chicago: University of Chicago Press.

Kuhn, T. S. (1977). *The essential tension: Selected studies in scientific tradition and change.* Chicago: University of Chicago Press.

Land, E. H. (1977). The retinex theory of color vision. *Scientific American, 237,* 108–128.

Landredth, A., & Richardson, R. C. (2004). Essay review of William R. Uttal's The new phrenology: The limits of localizing cognitive processes in the brain. *Philosophical Psychology, 17,* 107–123.

Lashley, K. S., Chow, K. L., & Semmes, J. (1951). An examination of the electrical field theory of cerebral integration. *Psychological Review, 58,* 123–136.

Lehar, S. (2003a). *Cartoon epistemology*. Retrieved October 1, 2003, from the World Wide Web: http://cns-alumni.bu.edu/~slehar/cartoonepist/cartoonepist.html

Lehar, S. (2003b). *Harmonic resonance theory: An alternative to the "neuron doctrine" paradigm of neurocomputation to address Gestalt properties of perception* [Internet]. Retrieved October 1, 2003, from the World Wide Web: http://cns-alumni.bu.edu/~slehar/webstuff/hr1.html

Lennie, P. (2003). The cost of cortical computation. *Current Biology, 13*, 493–497.

Lettvin, J. Y., Maturana, H. R., McCulloch, W. S., & Pitts, W. H. (1959). What the frog's eye tells the frog's brain. *Proceedings of the Institute of Radio Engineers, 47*, 1940–1951.

Levine, D. S. (2000). *Introduction to neural and cognitive modeling*. Mahwah, NJ: Lawrence Erlbaum Associates.

Levine, J. (1983). Materialism and qualia: The explanatory gap. *Pacific Philosophical Quarterly, 64*, 354–361.

Lindberg, D. C. (1976). *Theories of vision from Al-Kindi to Kepler*. Chicago: University of Chicago Press.

Ling, G., & Gerard, R. W. (1949). The normal membrane potential of frog sartorius fibers. *Journal of Cellular and Comparative and Physiology, 34*, 383–385.

Lloyd, G., & Sivin, N. (2002). *The way and the word*. New Haven, CT: Yale University Press.

Loftus, E. F. (1996). *Eyewitness testimony*. Cambridge, MA: Harvard University Press.

Loftus, E. F., & Ketcham, K. (1994). *The myth of repressed memory: False memories and allegations of sexual abuse*. New York: St. Martin's Press.

Lorente de Nó, R. (1934). Studies on the structure of the cerebral cortex. II. Continuation of the study of the ammonic system. *Journal of Psychiatry and Neurology of Leipzig, 46*, 113–177.

Lorente de Nó, R. (1938a). Analysis of the activity of the chains of internunical neurons. *Journal of Neurophysiology, 1*, 207–244.

Lorente de Nó, R. (1938b). Synaptic stimulation of motorneurons as a local process. *Journal of Neurophysiology, 1*, 195–206.

Luchins, A. S., & Luchins, E. H. (1999). Isomorphism in Gestalt theory: Comparison of Wertheimer's and Kohler's concepts. *Gestalt Theory, 21*, 208–234.

Lykken, D. T. (1998). *A tremor in the blood: Uses and abuses of the lie detector*. New York: Plenum Trade.

MacCorquodale, K., & Meehl, P. E. (1948). On a distinction between hypothetical constructs and intervening variables. *Psychological Review, 55*, 95–107.

Magoun, H. W. (1958). Early development of ideas relating the mind with the brain. In G. E. W. Wolstenholme & C. M. O'Connor (Eds.), *Ciba Foundation Symposium on the Neurological Basis of Behavior*. London: J & A Churchill Ltd.

Mandelbrot, B. B. (1983). *The fractal geometry of nature*. New York: Freeman.

Marks, W. B., Dobelle, W. H., & MacNichol, E. F. (1964). Visual pigments of single primate cones. *Science, 143*, 1181–1183.

Marr, D. (1982). *Vision: A computational investigation into the human representation and processing of visual information*. San Francisco: Freeman.

Martin, J. H. (1991). The collective electrical behavior of cortical neurons: The electroencephalogram and the mechanisms of epilepsy. In E. R. Kandel, J. H. Schwartz, & T. M. Jessell (Eds.), *Principles of neural science*. New York: Elsevier.

Matthews, G. (2000). Internalist reasoning in Augustine for mind–body dualism. In J. P. Wright & P. Potter (Eds.), *Psyche and soma: Physicians and metaphysicians on the mind–body problem from antiquity to enlightenment* (pp. 133–145). Oxford: Clarendon Press.

McClelland, J. L., Rumelhart, D. E., & The PDP Research Group. (1988). *Parallel distributed processing: Explorations in the microstructure of cognition. Vol. 2: Psychological and biological models*. Cambridge, MA: MIT Press.

McCollough, C. (1965). Color adaptation of edge-detectors in the human visual system. *Science, 1965*, 1115–1116.

McCulloch, W. S., & Pitts, W. H. (1943). A logical calculus of the ideas immanent in nervous activity. *Bulletin of Mathematical Biophysics, 5*, 115–133.

McFadden, J. (2000). *Quantum evolution*. London: HarperCollins.

McFadden, J. (2002). Synchronous firing and its influence on the brain's electromagnetic field. *Journal of Consciousness Studies, 9*, 23–50.

McGinn, C. (1989). Can we solve the mind–body problem. *Mind, 98*, 349–366.

McKirahan, R. D., Jr. (1994). *Philosophy before Socrates*. Indianapolis: Hackett.

Meyer, A. R., & Stockmeyer, L. J. (1972). *The equivalence problem for regular expressions with squaring requires exponential space*. Paper presented at the Proceedings of the 13th Annual IEEE Symposium on Switching and Automata Theory, 125–129, Los Alamitos, CA.

Michell, J. (1999). *Measurement in psychology: Critical history of a methodological concept*. Cambridge, England: Cambridge University Press.

Miller, G. A. (1956). The magical number seven, plus or minus two: Some limits on our capacity for processing information. *Psychological Review, 63*, 81–97.

Minsky, M., & Papert, S. (1969). *Perceptrons: An introduction to computational geometry*. Cambridge, MA: MIT Press.

Minsky, M., & Papert, S. (1988). *Perceptrons: Expanded edition*. Cambridge, MA: MIT Press.

Moore, E. F. (1956). Gedanken-experiments on sequential machines. In C. E. Shannon & J. McCarthy (Eds.), *Automata studies* (pp. 129–153). Princeton, NJ: Princeton University Press.

Moruzzi, G., & Magoun, H. W. (1949). Brain stem reticular formation and activation of the EEG. *Electroencephalography and Clinical Neurophysiology, 1*, 455–473.

Mountcastle, V. B., & Powell, P. S. (1959). Neural mechanisms subserving cutaneous sensibility with special reference to the role of afferent inhibition in sensory perception and discrimination. *Journal of Neurophysiology, 105*, 201–232.

Nunez, P. L. (1995). *Neocortical dynamics and human EEG rhythms*. New York: Oxford University Press.

O'Grady, P. F. (2002). *Thales of Miletus*. Burlington, VT: Ashgate.

O'Malley, C. D. (1965). *Andreas Vesalius of Brussels 1514–1564*. Berkeley: University of California Press.

Orponen, P. (1994). *Computational complexity of neural networks: A survey* (NC-TR-94-010). Egham, England: Espirit Working Group in Neural and Operation Learning.

Pachella, R. G. (1974). The interpretation of reaction time in information processing research. In B. H. Kantowitz (Ed.), *Human information processing: Tutorials in performance and cognition*. Hillsdale, NJ: Lawrence Erlbaum Associates.

Palade, G. E., & Palay, S. L. (1954). Electron microscope observations of interneuronal and neuromuscular synapses. *Anatomical Record, 118*, 335–336.

Parberry, I. (1994). *Circuit complexity and neural networks*. Cambridge, MA: MIT Press.

Parnell, J. A. (2002). A business strategy typology for the new economy: Reconceptualization and synthesis. *The Journal of Behavioral and Applied Management, 3*, 206–230.

Penrose, R. (1989). *The emperor's new mind: Concerning computers, minds, and the laws of physics*. Oxford, England: Oxford University Press.

Penrose, R. (1994). *Shadows of the mind: A search for the missing science of consciousness*. Oxford, England: Oxford University Press.

Penrose, R., & Hameroff, S. R. (1995). What gaps? Reply to Grush and Churchland. *Journal of Consciousness Studies, 2*, 99–112.

Pevsner, J. (2002). Leonardo da Vinci's contributions to neuroscience. *Trends in Neurosciences, 25*, 217–220.

Pieron, H. (1952). *The sensations: Their functions, processes and mechanisms* (M. H. Pirenne & B. C. Abbott, Trans.). New Haven, CT: Yale University Press.

Pitts, W. H., & McCulloch, W. S. (1947). How we know universals: The perception of auditory and visual forms. *Bulletin of Mathematical Biophysics, 9*, 127–147.

Poole, S. (2000). Mind games: Review of consciousness: How matter becomes imagination. Authors: G. Edelman & G. Tonono, *The Guardian*, June 24. Available at http://books.guardian.co.uk/print/0,3858,4032881-99945,00.html

Popper, K. R. (1959). *The logic of scientific discovery* (K. R. Popper, J. Freed, & L. Freed, Trans.). New York: Basic Books.

Pratt, W. K. (1991). *Digital image processing*. New York: Wiley.

Pribram, K. H. (1969). The neurophysiology of remembering. *Scientific American, 220*, 73–86.

Pribram, K. H. (1971). *Languages of the brain: Experimental paradoxes and principles in neuropsychology*. Englewood Cliffs, NJ: Prentice-Hall.

Pribram, K. H. (1991). *Brain and perception*. Mahwah, NJ: Lawrence Erlbaum Associates.

Pribram, K. H., Nuwer, M., & Baron, R. J. (1974). The holographic hypothesis of memory structure in brain function and perception. In R. C. Atkinson, D. H. Krantz, R. C. Luce, & P. Suppes (Eds.), *Contemporary developments in mathematical psychology*. San Francisco: W. H. Freeman.

Pulvermuller, F., Eulitz, C., Pantev, C., Mohr, B., Feige, B., Lutzenberger, W., Elbert, T., & Birbaumer, N. (1996). High-frequency cortical responses reflect lexical processing: An MEG study. *Electroencephalography and Clinical Neurophysiology, 98*, 76–85.

Pulvermuller, F., Kujala, T., Shtyrov, Y., Simola, J., Tiitinen, H., Alku, P., Alho, K., Martinkauppi, S., Ilmoniemi, R. J., & Naatanen, R. (2001). Memory traces for words as revealed by mismatch negativity. *Neuroimage, 14*, 607–616.

Quine, W. V. O. (1960). *Word and object*. Cambridge, MA: MIT Press.

Rakover, S. S. (2003). Experimental psychology and Duhem's problem. *Journal for the Theory of Social Behaviour, 33*, 45–66.

Rashevsky, N. (1948). *Mathematical biophysics*. Chicago: University of Chicago Press.

Ratliff, F. (1965). *Mach bands: Quantitative studies on neural networks in the retina*. San Francisco: Holden-Day.

Ratliff, F., & Hartline, H. K. (1959). The response of Limulus optic nerve fibers to patterns of illumination on the retinal mosaic. *Journal of General Physiology, 42*, 1241–1255.

Rescher, N. (1984). *The limits of science*. Pittsburgh: University of Pittsburgh Press.

Rescher, N. (1998). *Complexity: A philosophical overview*. New Brunswick, NJ: Transaction.

Ridley, H. (1695). *The anatomy of the brain*. London: Smith and Walford, Printers to the Royal Society.

Riesenhuber, M., & Poggio, T. (1999). Hierarchical models of object recognition in cortex. *Nature Neuroscience, 2*, 1019–1025.

Rispler-Chaim, V. (1993). The ethics of postmortem examination in contemporary Islam. *Journal of Medical Ethics, 19*, 164–168.

Rodieck, R. W., & Stone, J. (1965). Analysis of receptive fields of cat retinal ganglion cells. *Journal of Neurophysiology, 28*, 833–849.

Rolls, E. T., & Tovee, M. J. (1995). Sparseness of the neuronal representation of stimuli in the primate temporal visual cortex. *Journal of Neurophysiology, 73*, 713–726.

Rose, A. M. (1954). *Theory and method in the social sciences*. Minneapolis: The University of Minnesota Press.

Rosenblatt, F. (1958). The perceptron: A probabilistic model for information storage and organization in the brain. *Psychological Review, 65*, 386–408.

Rosenblatt, F. (1962). *Principles of neurodynamics*. Washington, DC: Spartan.

Rosenblith, W. A. (1961). *Sensory communication*. Cambridge, MA: MIT Press.

Rudner, R. S. (1966). *Philosophy of social science*. Englewood Cliffs, NJ: Prentice-Hall.

Rumelhart, D. E., McClelland, J. L., & The PDP Research Group. (1988). *Parallel distributed processing: Explorations in the microstructure of cognition. Vol. 1: Foundations*. Cambridge, MA: MIT Press.

Sagan, C. (1995). *The demon-haunted world: Science as a candle in the dark*. New York: Random House.

Salmon, W. C. (2001). Explanation and confirmation: A Bayesian critique of inference to the best explanations. In G. Hon & S. S. Rakover (Eds.), *Explanation: Theoretical approaches and applications*. Dordrecht: Kluwer.

Schiller, P. H. (1968). Single unit analysis of backward visual masking and metacontrast in the cat lateral; geniculate nucleus. *Vision Research, 8*, 855–866.

Searle, J. R. (1997). *The mystery of consciousness*. New York: New York Review.

Selfridge, O. G. (1958, November). *Pandemonium: A paradigm for learning*. Paper presented at the Mechanization of Thought Processes: Proceedings of a symposium held at the National Physical Laboratory, London.

Shams, S. (1997). Combinatorial optimization. In E. Fiesler & R. Beale (Eds.), *Handbook of neural computation*. Bristol, England: Institute of Physics Publishing.

Shannon, C. E. (1948). A mathematical theory of communication. *Bell System Technical Journal, 27*, 379–423.

Sheer, D. E. (1976). Focused arousal and 40-Hz EEG. In R. M. Knight & D. J. Bakker (Eds.), *The neuropsychology of learning disorders* (pp. 71–87). Baltimore: University Park Press.

Sheer, D. E. (1989). Sensory and cognitive 40 Hz event related potentials: Behavioral correlates, brain functions, and clinical application. In E. Basar & T. H. Bullock (Eds.), *Brain dynamics* (pp. 339–374). Berlin: Springer.

Sheinberg, D. L., & Logothetis, N. K. (1997). The role of temporal cortical areas in perceptual organization. *Proceedings of the National Academy of Sciences, USA, 94*, 3408–3413.

Sheldon, W. H., Harth, E. M., & McDermott, E. (1949). *Varieties of delinquent youth: An introduction to constitutional psychology*. New York: Harper & Row.

Sheldon, W. H., & Steven, S. S. (1942). *The varieties of temperament: A psychology of constitutional differences*. New York: Harper & Row.

Sheldon, W. H., Steven, S. S., & Tucker, W. B. (1940). *The varieties of human physique: An introduction to constitutional psychology*. New York: Harper & Row.

Shepherd, G. M. (1991). *Foundations of the neuron doctrine*. Oxford, England: Oxford University Press.

Sherrington, C. S. (1906). *The integrative action of the nervous system*. London: Constable.

Sherrington, C. S. (1940/1963). *Man on his nature*. Cambridge, England: Cambridge University Press.

Siegel, L. J. (2000). *Criminology* (7th ed.). Belmont, CA: Wadsworth/Thomson Learning.

Simpson, G. G. (1944). *Tempo and mode in evolution*. New York: Columbia University Press.

Singer, C. J. (1957). *A short history of anatomy from the Greeks to Harvey*. New York: Dover.

Singer, J. D. (1979). *The correlates of war I: Research origins and rationale*. New York: Free Press.

Singer, J. D. (1980). *The correlates of war II: Testing some realpolitik models*. New York: Free Press.

Souder, E., & Trojanowski, J. Q. (1992). Autopsy: Cutting away the myths. *Journal of Neuroscience Nursing, 24*, 134–139.

Sperry, R. W., Miner, R., & Myers, R. E. (1955). Visual pattern perception following subpial slicing and tantalum wire implantations in the visual cortex. *Journal of Comparative and Physiological Psychology, 48*, 50–58.

Spurzheim, J. C. (1832). *Outlines of phrenology*. Boston: Marsh, Capen, & Lyon.

Stevens, S. S. (1951). Mathematics, measurement, and psychophysics. In S. S. Stevens (Ed.), *Handbook of experimental psychology*. New York: Wiley.

Stewart, A. L., & Pinkham, R. S. (1991). A space-variant operator for visual sensitivity. *Biological Cybernetics, 64*, 373–379.

Stewart, A. L., & Pinkham, R. S. (1994). Space-variant models of visual acuity using self-adjoint integral operations. *Biological Cybernetics, 71*, 161–167.

Stigler, R. (1910). Chronophotische studien uber den Umgebungskontrast. *Pflugers Archive ges Physiologie, 134*, 365–435.

Stinchcombe, A. L. (1987). *Constructing social theories*. Chicago: University of Chicago Press.

Stockmeyer, L. J., & Chandra, A. K. (1979). Intrinsically difficult problems. *Scientific American, 240,* 140–159.

Stockmeyer, L. J., & Meyer, A. R. (2002). Cosmological lower bound on the circuit complexity of a small problem in logic. *Journal of the Association for Computing Machinery, 49,* 753–784.

Swofford, D. (2003). *Paup 4.0 for Macintosh: Phylogenetic analysis using parsimony.* Sunderland, MA: Sinauer Associates.

Tanaka, K. (1993). Neuronal mechanisms of object recognition. *Science, 262,* 685–688.

Tanaka, K. (2003). Columns for complex visual object features in the inferotemporal cortex: Clustering of cells for similar but slightly different stimulus selectivities. *Cerebral Cortex, 13,* 90–99.

Tanaka, K., Saito, H.-A., Fukada, Y., & Moriya, M. (1991). Coding visual images of objects in the inferotemporal cortex of the Macaque monkey. *Journal of Neurophysiology, 66,* 170–189.

Thorndike, E. L. (1913). *Educational psychology: The psychology of learning.* New York: Teachers College Press.

Thorndike, E. L. (1931). *Human learning.* New York: Century.

Tiitinen, H., Sinkkonen, J., Reinikainen, K., Alho, K., Lavikainen, J., & Naatanen, R. (1993). Selective attention enhances the auditory 40-Hz transient response in humans. *Nature, 364,* 59–60.

Timney, B. N., & MacDonald, C. (1978). Are curves detected by "curvature detectors"? *Perception, 7,* 51–64.

Turing, A. M. (1950). Computing machinery and intelligence. *Mind, 59,* 433–460.

Uttal, W. R. (1967). Evoked brain potentials: Signs or codes? *Perspectives in Biology and Medicine, 10,* 627–639.

Uttal, W. R. (1973). *The psychobiology of sensory coding.* New York: Harper & Row.

Uttal, W. R. (1975). *Cellular neurophysiology and integration: An interpretive introduction.* Hillsdale, NJ: Lawrence Erlbaum Associates.

Uttal, W. R. (1978). *The psychobiology of mind.* Hillsdale, NJ: Lawrence Erlbaum Associates.

Uttal, W. R. (1981). *A taxonomy of visual processes.* Hillsdale, NJ: Lawrence Erlbaum Associates.

Uttal, W. R. (1982). Neuroreductionistic dogma—A heretical counterview. In D. G. Albrecht (Ed.), *Recognition of pattern and form: Lecture notes in biomathematics* (Vol. 44, pp. 193–225). Berlin: Springer-Verlag.

Uttal, W. R. (1998). *Toward a new behaviorism: The case against perceptual reductionism.* Mahwah, NJ: Lawrence Erlbaum Associates.

Uttal, W. R. (2000). *The war between mentalism and behaviorism: On the accessibility of mental processes.* Mahwah, NJ: Lawrence Erlbaum Associates.

Uttal, W. R. (2001). *The new phrenology: The limits of localizing cognitive processes in the brain.* Cambridge, MA: MIT Press.

Uttal, W. R. (2002). *A behaviorist looks at form recognition.* Mahwah, NJ: Lawrence Erlbaum Associates.

Uttal, W. R. (2003). *Psychomythics.* Mahwah, NJ: Lawrence Erlbaum Associates.

Uttal, W. R. (2004). *100,000 years of dualism: From cave to cognitivism.* Mahwah, NJ: Lawrence Erlbaum Associates.

Uttal, W. R., & Cook, L. (1964). Systematics of the evoked somatosensory cortical potential. *Annals of the New York Academy of Sciences, 112,* 60–81.

Valenstein, E. S. (1986). *Great and desperate cures: The rise and decline of psychosurgery and other radical treatments for mental illness.* New York: Basic Books.

Valenstein, E. S. (1998). *Blaming the brain: The truth about drugs and mental health.* New York: The Free Press.

van der Eijk, P. (2000). Aristotle's psycho-physiological account of the soul–body relationship. In J. P. Wright & P. Potter (Eds.), *Psyche and soma: Physicians and metaphysicians on the mind–body problem from antiquity to enlightenment* (pp. 57–78). Oxford, England: Clarendon Press.

Van der Werf, Y. D. (2000). *The thalamus and memory: Contributions to medial temporal and prefrontal memory processes.* Unpublished doctoral dissertation, Vrije Universiteit, Amsterdam.

Velleman, P. F., & Wilkinson, L. (1993). Nominal, ordinal, interval, and ratio typologies are misleading. *The American Statistician, 47*, 65–72.

Vesalius, A. (1543/1949). *The epitome of Andreas Vesalius* (L. R. Lind, Trans.). New York: Macmillan.

Vesalius, A. (1543/1999). *On the fabric of the human body, Book II: The ligaments and muscles* (W. F. Richardson & G. B. Carman, Trans.). San Francisco: Norman Publishing.

Viana Di Prisco, G., & Freeman, W. J. (1985). Odor-related bulbar EEG spatial pattern analysis during appetitive conditioning in rabbits. *Behavioral Neuroscience, 99*, 962–978.

von der Malsburg, C. (1973). Self-organization of orientation sensitive cells in the striate cortex. *Kybernetik, 14*, 85–100.

von der Malsburg, C. (1981). *The correlation theory of brain function* (Internal Report 81-2, July). Goettingen: Max Planck-Institute for Biophysical Chemistry.

von Staden, H. (2000). Body, soul, and nerves: Epicurus, Herophilus, Erasistratus, the Stoics, and Galen. In J. P. Wright & P. Potter (Eds.), *Psyche and soma: Physicians and metaphysicians on the mind–body problem from antiquity to enlightenment* (pp. 79–132). Oxford, England: Clarendon Press.

Weisstein, N. (1972). Metacontrast. In D. Jameson & L. M. Hurvich (Eds.), *Handbook of sensory physiology: Visual psychophysics (Vol. VII/4).* New York: Springer-Verlag.

Wenger, M. J., & Townsend, J. T. (2000). Spatial frequencies in short-term memory for faces: A test of three frequency-dependent hypotheses. *Memory and Cognition, 28*, 125–142.

Werbos, P. J. (1974). *Beyond regression: New tools for prediction and analysis in the behavioral sciences.* Doctoral dissertation, Harvard University.

Werbos, P. J. (1988). *Backpropagation: Past, present, and future.* Paper presented at the IEEE International Conference on Neural Networks, San Diego.

Werner, H. (1935). Studies on contour: I. Qualitative analyses. *American Journal of Psychology, 47*, 40–64.

Westheimer, G. (2001). The Fourier theory of vision. *Perception, 30*, 531–541.

Widrow, B., & Hoff, M. E. (1960). *Adaptive switching circuits.* Paper presented at the IRE WESCON Convention, New York (pp. 96–104).

Wiener, N. (1948). *Cybernetics or control and communication in the animal and the machine.* New York: Wiley.

Wigner, E. P. (1961). Remarks on the mind–body question. In I. J. Good (Ed.), *The scientist speculates.* London: Heinemann.

Wiles, A. (1995). Modular elliptic curves and Fermat's last theorem. *Annals of Mathematics, 141 (Series 2)*, 443–551.

Wilson, H. R., & Cowan, J. D. (1973). A mathematical theory of the functional dynamics of cortical and thalamic neural tissue. *Kybernetik, 13*, 55–80.

Wolf, F. A. (1989). On the quantum physical theory of subjective antedating. *Journal of Theoretical Biology, 136*, 13–19.

Wright, J. P., & Potter, P. (Eds.). (2000). *Psyche and soma: Physicians and metaphysicians on the mind–body problem from antiquity to enlightenment.* Oxford: Clarendon Press.

Yang, Z. (1996). Phylogenetic analysis using parsimony and likelihood methods. *Journal of Molecular Evolution, 42*, 294–307.

Young, J. A. (1936). The giant nerve fibres and epistellar body of cephalopods. *Journal of Microscopic Science, 78*, 367.

Yule, G. U. (1926). Why do we sometimes get nonsense-correlations between time series? A study in sampling and the nature of time series. *Journal of the Royal Statistical Society, 89*, 1–64.

Zeki, S. (1993). *A vision of the brain.* London: Blackwell.

Author Index

A

B

C

D

E

F

G

H

I

J

K

L

M

T

U

V

W

X, Y, Z

Subject Index

D

E

F

G

H

I

J, L

M

N

O

P

Q

R

S

T

U

V

W

X, Y, Z